More praise for *The Mission*

"Ms. Priest's work is a powerful testi........ ... unparalleled breadth and depth of the mission facing American soldiers . . . extremely well researched . . . and should be read by all those interested in the central issues of the world today." —*New York Times*

"[One of the] five best books for understanding the Middle East."
—*Newsweek*

"Eye-opening descriptions of the armed forces in action in Washington and abroad." —*San Francisco Chronicle*

"A clear-eyed portrait of American military culture, and a subtle critique of the civilian leadership that governs the armed forces. . . . Rich instruction for policymakers, soldiers, and political junkies alike."
—*Kirkus Reviews*

"Priest does a marvelous job of conveying both the daily operating realities and the large-scale strategic tensions that go with America's new role." —*Washington Monthly*

"Priest's comprehensive reporting on what U.S. forces have already experienced in other parts of the world should be read by anyone interested in understanding the difficulties faced in Iraq today."
—*The Daily Yomiuri*, Tokyo

"A book that is consistently instructive and frequently disturbing."
—*National Review*

"Contains colorful anecdotal evidence to support two central truths about nation-building: It is an all-or-nothing endeavor, and the military cannot take the lead role." —*The Weekly Standard*

"*The Mission* will be cited and analyzed for years in the future for the understanding . . . of the thinking and mindset of our national leaders at a critical juncture in history."

—*Army Magazine*, Association of the United States Army

"Insightful reportage that integrates the small with the large scale."

—*Booklist*

"Priest provides numerous examples of officers and grunts performing nonmilitary tasks for which they aren't trained . . . a convincing argument why politicians must stop relying upon the military not only to implement foreign policy, but to shape it as well."

—*Seattle Post-Intelligencer*

"Instead of the Military being civilianized, the foreign policy of the United States has in effect become militarized. Priest is empathetic toward both the limited options open to high-level military and civilian policymakers and the difficulties faced by servicemen and women in the field in implementing those policy decisions, but argues that successive administrations have become excessively dependent on military forces to fulfill missions for which they are poorly suited. I highly recommend the book to students of current military affairs and foreign policy."

—*The Journal of Military History*

THE
MISSION

Waging War and Keeping

Peace with America's Military

THE
MISSION

DANA PRIEST

W. W. NORTON & COMPANY NEW YORK · LONDON

To Bill, Nick and Haley—

for their curiosity, patience and humor

"War Pigs": Words and music by Frank Iommi, John Osbourne, William Ward, and Terence Butler.
Copyright ©1970 (renewed) and 1974 (renewed) by Westminster Music Ltd., London, England.
TRO—Essex Music International, Inc., New York, controls all publication rights for the U.S.A. and
Canada. Used by permission.

For information about permission to reproduce selections from this book, write to Permissions,
W. W. Norton and Company, Inc., 500 Fifth Avenue, New York, NY 10110

Manufacturing by The Courier Companies, Inc.
Book design by Barbara M. Bachman
Production manager: Amanda Morrison

Library of Congress Cataloging-in-Publication Data

Priest, Dana.
  The mission: Waging war and keeping peace with America's military / Dana Priest.
    p. cm.
Includes bibliographical references and index.
  ISBN 0-393-01024-4 (hardcover)
    1. United States—Armed Forces. 2. United States—Armed Forces—Foreign service.
3. World politics—21st century. I. Title.
  UA23 .P68 2003
  355'.00973'0905—dc21   2002015986

0-393-32550-4 pbk.

W. W. Norton &Company, Inc., 500 Fifth Avenue, New York, N.Y. 10110
www.wwnorton.com

W. W. Norton & Company, Ltd., Castle House, 75/76 Wells Street, London, W1T 3Qt

1 2 3 4 5 6 7 8 9 0

Contents

THE
MISSION

Introduction

Pax Americana

A SWAT TEAM GUARDING ANTHONY ZINNI FACED OFF against Israeli snipers and tanks as the retired Marine Corps general climbed over the filthy barricades blocking Palestinian leader Yasir Arafat's encircled compound in Ramallah, the West Bank. In April 2002, as President George W. Bush's special envoy, Zinni had secured approval from the Israeli prime minister, Ariel Sharon, to meet with Arafat in the middle of an Israeli military offensive against the Palestinians. With water and electricity service cut off, the toilets inside the compound were overflowing and the stench was overwhelming. Arafat was spitting mad when Zinni arrived.

The Palestinians accused Zinni of conspiring with Israel to defeat Arafat. The Israelis accused him of cozying up to the Palestinians. In private, both sides admitted the same, sorry fact: "There can be no military solution to the problem." Zinni was certain of that, too. "You know," he groused later, as Palestinian suicide bombers and U.S. air strikes in Afghanistan competed for headlines, "there is no military solution to terrorism, either."

Yet U.S. leaders have been turning more and more to the military to solve problems that are often, at their root, political and economic. This has become the American military's mission and it has been going on for more than a decade without much public discussion or debate. Vanquishing terrorism is the latest example. U.S. diplomatic and economic efforts have lagged far behind the military's in the campaign against terrorism, as they did in 2001 and 2002 in dealing with the Israeli-Palestinian impasse.

In the spring of 2002, Israeli military attacks on the Palestinians were threatening to accomplish what Osama bin Laden had not: turning the entire Muslim world against the United States. Arab allies were reshuffling their coalitions and threatening embargoes. Violent anti-American demonstrations were spreading around the world. Yet the world's sole superpower was mustering only one retired general to pull the two sides toward the negotiating table. Zinni hoped he would be just a placeholder until someone with real clout in the administration, such as Secretary of State Colin Powell or President Bush himself, got involved.

But so far the president had paid only sporadic attention to the violence engulfing Israel and the Palestinian territories. From his ranch in Texas, Bush issued conflicting statements condemning terrorism, then Israeli aggression, then Arafat. He had hoped Israel and the Palestinians would sort this out on their own, without U.S. involvement. Bush rejected any suggestions that he pursue the style of personal diplomacy practiced by President Bill Clinton, just as he also rejected Clinton's policy of global "peacetime engagement." Too unfocused. Too open-ended.

At the Defense Department, the "new unilateralists," led by Defense Secretary Donald Rumsfeld, Deputy Secretary Paul Wolfowitz, and their chief policy guru, Richard Perle, chairman of the Defense Policy Board, had opposed sending Zinni to mediate. Tone deaf to the deep anti-American hatred welling up in the Muslim world, they opposed any action that would distract the administration from its ultimate goal: toppling Iraqi leader Saddam Hussein. Meanwhile, the Arab coalition so necessary to an anti-Iraq campaign withered.

Rumsfeld, Wolfowitz, and Perle, all civilian political appointees, faced off against a triumvirate of former military giants: Powell, a retired general and former chairman of the Joint Chiefs of Staff; Zinni, a former commander of U.S. Central Command; and Powell's deputy secretary of state, Richard Armitage, a former Navy SEAL whose short but intense military career had chiseled his rough-edged demeanor and ample physique. "They just aren't connected to the world," Zinni grunted dismissively of Rumsfeld et al. "Thank God for the State Department and Colin Powell—he's my hero. There are more military guys running things at the State Department than over at the Pentagon," he laughed. "Perle! Ha! A paper cut was his biggest scrape."

At Powell's urging, Bush had finally agreed to let Zinni step in and Zinni managed to convince the two sides to keep coming back to talk. When people become desperate, they need dispassionate leadership, he believed.

Zinni had pushed the same level of U.S. involvement throughout his time at Central Command, hammering Clinton's team to let him bring his resources to bear in crazy Yemen, forsaken Pakistan, and authoritarian Uzbekistan. He would have gone to Afghanistan and Iran, too, had his bosses allowed it—anything to keep these failed and nearly failed states from straying too far from the norms that kept the planet from self-destructing.

Zinni's interest in diplomacy struck him as part of an historical continuum. By doffing the uniform to become secretary of state and pushing his unpopular Marshall Plan through Washington, Gen. George Marshall had achieved the rebuilding of Europe after World War II. Gen. Douglas MacArthur had done much the same for postwar Japan. Marshall, reflecting on the conditions that gave rise to Nazism, warned more than once that the United States courted disaster if it again fell "into a state of disinterested weakness" and failed to lead Europe's postwar economic and political reconstruction.[1] Zinni saw Powell as a modern-day Marshall. Having championed the use of overwhelming military force at the outset of any war (in what came to be known as the "Powell Doctrine"), Powell was now arguing for overwhelming economic and political force to settle a rattled post–September 11 world.

But Bush was resisting. Both he and President Clinton before him seemed reluctant to leverage the unprecedented stature that the United States had acquired at the end of the Cold War as an empire without rival. As a consequence, both presidents, and the Congresses that governed with them, failed to capitalize on this historic pre-eminence to lead a messy world toward a more stable peace. It was easier to call up the military for a quick fix.

By 2002, America's military was unmatched by factors of ten. Its Special Operations Forces and the paramilitary teams of the Central

Intelligence Agency (CIA) had adapted fairly well to the asymmetric warfare of terrorists and their armies of supporters in Afghanistan. Their tactical offensives seemed likely to kill off Al Qaeda and maybe even capture Osama bin Laden. Yet despite their superiority, they could not stamp out terrorism; the seeds of that problem were planted in the soil of despair, isolation, and zealotry. Terrorism's ultimate defeat would not come on the battlefield at the hands of soldiers. Neither President Bush nor his armed forces had a strategy for that campaign.

Long before September 11, the U.S. government had grown increasingly dependent on its military to carry out its foreign affairs. The shift was incremental, little noticed, de facto. It did not even qualify as an "approach." The military simply filled a vacuum left by an indecisive White House, an atrophied State Department, and a distracted Congress. After September 11, however, the trend accelerated dramatically with the war in Afghanistan and the likelihood of U.S. military operations elsewhere. Without a doubt, U.S.-sponsored political reform abroad is being eclipsed by new military pacts focusing on anti-terrorism and intelligence-sharing.

All this comes at a time when decision-makers understand less and less about their military. Our elected leaders often treat men and women in uniform with either suspicion or excessive reverence, failing to ask probing questions or push hard enough for reform. Yet it is the responsibility of those civilians to set the military's direction, to use it as a tool when appropriate and otherwise to refrain from using it. At a minimum, Americans should understand the consequences of substituting generals and Green Berets for diplomats, and nineteen-year-old paratroopers for police and aid workers on nation-building missions.

I was reminded of these consequences often during my travels. One moment in particular lingers with me more than others. As I walked through the rundown town of Vitina, Kosovo, with a squad of infantry soldiers in November 2001, a woman in a tattered sweater beckoned me over to a small store. "Come inside please, we are a group of Serb women, and we have a declaration to give you." She probably figured I was with the U.S. government.

I borrowed the squad's interpreter, and accompanied by a young,

In early November 2001, Serb women from the villages surrounding Vitina,
Kosovo, risked their safety to meet and write a bill of rights. They also wanted
the local U.S. Army battalion to find them three sewing machines to start a
work cooperative. "We don't do sewing machines!" declared the Army battalion
commander in charge of Vitina, when presented with their request.   DANA PRIEST

well-armed infantry officer, I stepped inside. "I'm not with the military," I said, pointing to the soldier, "but he is."

Two dozen Serb women were in the room. They had come from half a dozen nearby villages, risking their lives to travel to Vitina, where Albanians were diligently trying to kill or scare off Serbs who remained after the 1999 war waged by the North Atlantic Treaty Organization (NATO) against Serb forces in Kosovo. The women handed me a four-page, handwritten declaration, asking that it be translated into English and delivered to the American lieutenant colonel in charge of the U.S. barracks in Vitina. This colonel, they understood, was the big boss. No matter how many times anyone told them the United Nations was in charge, they believed the real power lay behind the barbed wire of Camp Bondsteel nearby. The colonel assigned to Vitina, they hoped, would pass their request to the top.

The declaration was a sort of bill of rights. It said Serb women deserved to live in peace and with respect, that they should have the right to raise their children in safety. More concretely, the women wanted to work, and they were willing to leave their homes and husbands each day to support their destitute families. They wanted three sewing machines, with which they would set up a sewing cooperative. They would mend and make clothes and other items of fabric and leather.

Theirs was a spontaneous, entrepreneurial request that any development expert or aid worker would have seized upon. Not the military: "Sewing machines! We don't do sewing machines!" scoffed the battalion's bullet-headed lieutenant colonel when I inquired about the declaration his lieutenant had passed along to him.

* * * *

THE HEIGHTENED RELIANCE on generals, grunts, and Green Berets arose when the prospect of big, direct confrontations and smaller, unconventional wars between the superpowers ended. For a while, U.S. political and military leaders flailed about trying to redefine the country's national security interests. Military budgets and force sizes shrank, but even so, the Defense Department had more money and more people than any other foreign-focused government agency. With fewer threats, strategic-level commanders also had time and resources to worry about other things. More important, they had the inclination. Many officers, connoisseurs of history, viewed peacetime as an intermission between big wars. They wanted to use this intermission to prevent the next big conflict, which their think tanks predicted would be fought asymmetrically with low-tech weapons: suicide bombers, toxic chemicals, and deadly viruses wielded by worldwide terrorist cells funded by drugs, diamonds, and dirty money. The key to prevention, many came to believe, was to create multinational "neighborhood watch" groups—regional coalitions of nations—that would discourage the bad guys in the 'hood from straying too far and that would stop them if they tried something stupid.

No figures were more convinced of this approach than the generals who led the U.S. military's regionally focused unified commands. With discretionary money and time, these commanders-in-chief, or "CinCs" (pronounced "sinks"), set out on their own parallel course to "shape" the world, as instructed by the president and the secretary of defense. Fairly soon, the CinCs grew into a powerful force in U.S. foreign policy because of the disproportionate weight of their resources and organization in relation to the assets and influence of other parts of America's foreign policy structure—in particular, the State Department, which was shriveling in size, stature, and spirit even as the military's role expanded.

The four CinCs profiled here—Zinni, Gen. Wesley Clark, Adm. Dennis Blair, and Gen. Charles Wilhelm—anchored the CinCs' prominence in American history. Part of this prominence flowed from the force of their personalities. But much more important was their vision: the CinCs rightly saw the world as a connected whole. They pushed, not always successfully, to make their government understand this and live up to its responsibility to make the world a more peaceful place, as they defined it. All four men have since retired from military service, but their individual legacies and the importance of the regional CinC position remain strong. Their worldviews and their significance as players in American foreign relations also live on in each of their successors.

Besides vast resources, CinCs control powerful tools to further their aims. Their travels, mechanically elegant and ceremonial, are unmatched in grandeur by those of any other U.S. government official except the president and a few cabinet secretaries. But they also have a favorite secret weapon: the "quiet professionals," as the U.S. Special Operations Forces* call themselves. Long before Afghanistan made them famous, teams of special forces were discreetly operating in 125 countries. The end of Cold War political hostilities opened up the world to them, and the number of their overseas training assignments multiplied.

Special forces were often the tool of default when U.S. policymakers abandoned more difficult alternatives, such as long-term economic development or political reform won though creative diplomatic sticks and carrots. In Colombia, where a drug-fueled civil war has raged for decades, the only solution the United States has effectively promoted has been a military one, employing special forces troops to train the Colombian army in antinarcotics activities. This choice is partly under-

---

* I use the vernacular "special forces" to refer to Special Operations Forces generally. These include Army, Navy, and Air Force units under the U.S. Special Operations Command. The Army's special operators are called U.S. Army Special Forces and are just one unit—the most active—involved in foreign training.

standable: in places like Colombia, where there are no easy fixes, sending a group of gung-ho Green Berets is at least a tangible offering. But relying on them to stem the drug trade is a gamble at best. Yearly coca production has continued to rise, proof enough of the policy's failure.

In Indonesia, the Pentagon lobbied for a little-known loophole in the law so that special forces could maintain contact with the Indonesian military at a time when Congress had prohibited such contact in response to the Indonesian army's repeated human-rights violations. For at least ten years, CinCs have argued that military engagement can positively influence foreign military conduct. In the case of Indonesia, little evidence supports this view, and much suggests it was wrong. The most generous interpretation of this recent history is that the Pentagon and CinCs at the Pacific Command had a "tin ear" when it came to the Indonesian military's misconduct in East Timor and in rebellious provinces such as Aceh and West Papua. A more realistic view is that successive CinCs, and several U.S. ambassadors to Indonesia, chose to ignore those atrocities. But did these military-to-military relationships actually undermine Indonesia's march toward democracy and civilian rule? Certainly many Indonesians and human-rights activists believe they did. Proponents of continued military ties argue that the U.S. military example made the Indonesian armed forces more tolerant of the chaos accompanying their country's transition to civilian rule.

This critique of the special forces work in Indonesia may sound like a criticism of the men who carried it out. It is not. It is meant as a criticism of civilian leaders in Congress, the White House, and the State Department who failed to find more appropriate or nuanced engagement programs, and of Pentagon leaders who did not fully consider the context in which American troops operated, and continue to operate, abroad.

* * * *

MUCH OF THE AMBIVALENCE in foreign relations afflicting Clinton's presidency reflected a larger angst among civilian and military leaders over the proper role of the military in peacetime. On the surface, it might appear as if this question has been settled. September 11 provided a sudden clarity of purpose for the U.S. military and its leaders. President Bush defined it as "good versus evil." I beg to differ.

Although the war against Al Qaeda in Afghanistan was clear in purpose, we are now seeing that the hardest, longest, and most important
work comes after the bombing stops, when rebuilding replaces destroying and consensus-building replaces precision strikes. As the U.S.
Army's experience in Kosovo shows, the mind-set, decision-making, and
training of infantry soldiers rarely mixes well with the disorder inherent
in civil society. The mismatch of culture and mission can distort the
goal of rebuilding a country. In the hands of poorly-formed, misguided
troops, it can create disaster.

Such a mismatch was evident even to Pfc. Ian Smith, a nineteen-
year-old from Ventura, California, who sat at the computer stall next
to mine one evening in Vitina. Downloading music to his laptop,
he leaned back in his yellow plastic chair and offered an unsolicited
assessment of his Kosovo mission: "If you want to put a country back
on its feet, you can't send the military. You have to send reformers," he
said, meaning the civilians he imagined do these sorts of repairs.

Smith, however, had already lowered his expectations about the
"reformers." "This year all the NGOs [humanitarian organizations] are
gone. So we take firewood from the people who need it," meaning the
majority Albanians, "and give it to people who need it," meaning the
minority Serbs. He rolled his eyes. "The only way to make a difference
is when there's a TV in every house, a phone in every house. Make it
a first-world country and they'll feel advanced. If they see a difference,
that's the key."

Smith's infantry brethren are now in Afghanistan. They, too, believe
they are on an unnamed, open-ended mission on behalf of the United
States—even if the rest of America hasn't yet figured it out.

A NOTE ON METHODOLOGY

OFFICERS AND SOLDIERS OF VARIOUS RANKS AND IN DIVERSE
geographic locations tell this story. Most of the anecdotes, dialogues,
and impressions related here were gathered between 1998 and 2002.
During part of this time I wrote about the military for the *Washington
Post*. For the final eighteen months, I was on leave from that job. In my

research, I tried to achieve "fly on the wall" status, to be unobtrusive and to write down what unfolded before me. But I also relied on hundreds of interviews, many of them tape recorded.

For the view at the top, I traveled to thirteen countries with the three generals and one admiral who were regional CinCs in 1999. I interviewed each one of them many times afterward. For my research on the Army Special Forces, I visited with special forces teams in Colombia, Nigeria, Kosovo, and Afghanistan. I also spent time at the U.S. Army Special Forces Command at Fort Bragg, N.C., and at the special operations command at each CinC's headquarters. Much of the information about the twelve-man teams that helped topple the Taliban was gathered at Fort Campbell, Ky., home of the 5th Special Forces Group.

For the sections on the 82nd Airborne Division in Kosovo, I spent time with the 3rd Battalion of the 504th Parachute Infantry Regiment in Kosovo in 1999. I also interviewed key officers and others at Fort Bragg and elsewhere after the unit returned. In 2000, I returned to Vitina to walk the streets with soldiers of the new unit in town from the 101st Airborne Division. I also used 657 pages of sworn statements and other evidence from the Army's investigation into events surrounding the murder of eleven-year-old Merita Shabiu.

People are identified by the rank they held at the time of the episodes that appear here.

WASHINGTON, D.C., MAY 2002

Chapter One

A Different Kind
of World

★ ★ ★ ★

GEN. HENRY HUGH SHELTON, THE SIX-FOOT-FIVE
Chairman of the Joint Chiefs of Staff, looked even more imposing
than his job title. His starched posture and steel jawline squared with
his responsibility as the top military adviser to the president. His job
had been held by a series of legends, men whose careers each marked
an era: Gen. Omar Bradley of World War II, Gen. Maxwell Taylor of
Vietnam, Gen. Colin Powell of the Persian Gulf War.

Hugh, as Shelton is called, arrived at the top during an era no one
could name. The war plans he had carried to the White House included
cautious, high-altitude air strikes against Iraq, Afghanistan, Sudan, and
Kosovo. No fan of small wars or peacekeeping operations, Shelton was
cautious about risking American lives for uncertain foreign ends. He had
warned President Clinton in 1999 against sending low-flying Apache
helicopters into the Kosovo war, and had also advised against sending
even military police to keep order in East Timor. But he hung steady for
the troops and won them the most significant pay raise in years.

The chairman was chauffeured to Capitol Hill regularly during his
tenure to swat down volleys from senators complaining about broken
promises to pull U.S. troops out of Bosnia and the feckless dinging of
Iraq rather than embracing a more powerful response. Shelton would

absorb and rebut the criticism without even a flinch in his slow, baritone, Southern drawl.

In his three years serving as chairman, Shelton had grown into the ceremony of the job, but he still didn't like it much. He preferred working in the field with the soldiers. A dozen times he slipped out of his blue-carpeted office in the Pentagon's E-ring to parachute with troops. His aides loved these escapes because "the boss," as they called him, became giddy hours before the jump. The afterglow, they noted, lasted for days.

The chairman of the Joint Chiefs of Staff, Gen. Henry "Hugh" Shelton, formerly commander of the XVIII Airborne Corps, relaxed by skipping out of the office to parachute.   U.S. ARMY GOLDEN KNIGHTS

Shelton had grown up in a North Carolina farming family and met the Army through its ROTC program at North Carolina State University. He managed a cloth mill for a year after he graduated, then volunteered for active-duty. He went on to command troops twice in Vietnam, and years later to lead the 82nd Airborne Division, the XVIII Airborne Corps, and the secretive U.S. Special Operations Command.

After thirty-seven years in the Army, Shelton's reputation had survived all the pomp, circumstance, and twenty-four-hour scrutiny

Gen. Shelton stands behind Defense Secretary Donald Rumsfeld at a press conference on September 11, 2001. DEFENSE DEPARTMENT

of his final assignment. Generals and admirals inside the Pentagon's cutthroat circle of chiefs still saw Shelton as a team player. Ego under control. Heart with the soldiers. Not the most polished among them, but in the end he gave his allegiance where it belonged: to the commander-in-chief, the president of the United States.

Both the top brass and ordinary soldiers bestowed their highest accolade on him: the chief was a "warrior's warrior."

So it came as quite a shock to Shelton and officers around him when President George W. Bush's new defense secretary, Donald Rumsfeld, a product of the wealthy Chicago suburbs and the Republican Party, and the only person ever to have been appointed to serve a second tour as secretary of defense, relegated Shelton and his staff to the status of "second-rate citizens." Rumsfeld disinvited Shelton and his four-star service chiefs[*] from meetings. At press conferences early in Bush's presidency, where the secretary of defense traditionally shared the stage with the

---

[*] The service chiefs are the military leaders of each of the four services. Appointed by the president and confirmed by the Senate, they are the Army chief of staff, the Air Force chief of staff, the chief of naval operations, and the Marine Corps commandant. Each holds the rank of or equivalent to four-star general.

chairman of the Joint Chiefs, Rumsfeld hung on to the podium, refusing to step back even the polite footstep that would have allowed Shelton
space to respond comfortably to a question. "I want to reinstitute civilian control of the military!" the secretary bellowed during one meeting
shortly after he assumed the job. He was especially suspicious of those
who, like Shelton, had served in the Clinton administration.

Selected late as Bush's defense secretary, and with few political
appointees at his side when he took office, Rumsfeld relied heavily on
a handful of civilian aides who were even harsher in their treatment of
the men and women in uniform. Their attitude bordered on disdain,
many officers thought. Snide comments slipped out frequently: "You
all are screwed up here," or "You screwed up there." Never "we"—the
divide was always there.

The Defense Department's new leadership treated the Joint Staff
like shop stewards in a unionized corporation. Rumsfeld treated
Shelton and the senior military leadership as major impediments to his
plans for a twenty-first-century "transformation" of the military.* Secret
panels of external consultants were brought in to study fundamental
questions about the military's future. They often excluded military
representatives and ignored Joint Staff studies, such as a two-hundred-
page logistics-reorganization paper that had taken a year to prepare.
Everything the military had to say was "second-guessed at every turn;
[there was] always a demand for more information," Shelton would say
later. "They weren't willing to take anything for granted. If you said the
sun was up, they raised the blind and said, 'Let us see.'"

By May 2001, a rebellion had hatched in the ranks. After word of
the tension began to leak to the press, Shelton squelched it at a regular
8 A.M. meeting in the Operations Deputies Conference Room. There,
the Joint Staff directorate heads—of intelligence, operations, policy,
and plans—sat around a richly grained table in blue leather chairs.
Little blue speakers shaped like pyramids recorded their sessions.

---

* "Transformation" encompasses a long list of concepts, equipment, and practices
Rumsfeld advocated for moving the military out of the industrial age and into the
information age. The term includes streamlining the bureaucracy, modernizing
the structure of the armed forces (making them faster and smaller), and developing super-tech weapons that rely on bandwidth, not bombs.

Shelton addressed them from the center of the boomerang-shaped table. "Guys, get over it. Change is always traumatic for organizations," he told them. "This will all settle out, just do your jobs. Be the professionals that you all are and this will work itself out."

But it still hurt, he knew: "Looking around that room, looking at the quality of the guys sitting there, and the loyalty of those guys—these are guys who had spent 25 and 30 years of their lives trying to do the very best they could for whomever they worked for, and have worked for various presidents and organizations. The fact that they were now being treated as second-rate citizens, so to speak, was not good."

The men and women in uniform had expected great things from the new administration. Republican George W. Bush had won their votes with a promise to be the military's friend. He would be tough on enemies. He would pick his fights around the world more judiciously than Clinton's team. He pledged more money, fewer deployments, a renewed esprit de corps.

On Bush's defense team there would be no quirky poets like Clinton's last defense secretary, William Cohen, no Quaker pacifists like Cohen's deputy, John Hamre; neither of them had ever worn a military uniform. Bush's cabinet included two former defense secretaries and a former chairman of the Joint Chiefs of Staff, Colin Powell—"adults" when it came to national security, father figures with iron fists.

Rumsfeld fit the bill perfectly. Gruff, autocratic, impatient with public inquiry, and straight out of the 1950s—from his haircut to the often patronizing, father-knows-best way he spoke to subordinates. "Rummy," they called him behind his back, "the grandfather we never had." In the ranks of the military, he was a welcome change from Cohen, a former Republican senator from Maine, who had come across as wooden and hard to read. A pure politician, every hair on his head in place, Cohen carefully crafted every public statement. Rumsfeld was blunt, funny, and could sound genuine even when he was obfuscating. He answered charges that he had treated Shelton and others harshly as "flat false." He hadn't meant to circumvent anyone; he had set up so many study groups because he wanted answers to complex questions: "For some reason people think I know more than I know. And I know what I know, and I know what I don't know."[1]

Although Shelton felt snubbed by Rumsfeld, he also liked him. The new boss certainly was smart, hard-working, and in admirable physical shape for a sixty-eight-year-old and that counted for something at the Pentagon. He spoke confidently. The "building," as officers called the Pentagon, craved supervision even if it did come from the disingenuously modest Rumsfeld.

Born into the family of a Chicago executive, Rumsfeld had attended Princeton University on a scholarship, and became captain of the wrestling team. He spent three years in the Navy as a pilot and was an all-Navy wrestling champion. In 1962, at the age of thirty, this young Republican operative won election to the House of Representatives from Illinois. Seven years later he joined Richard Nixon's White House as director of the Office of Economic Opportunity, where he met and hired Dick Cheney as his special assistant.

A year later, Rumsfeld became a counselor to the president, and in 1972, he was appointed the U.S. ambassador to NATO. His European assignment nicely shielded him from the Watergate scandal. Resurfacing in Washington after Gerald Ford was elevated to the White House, Rumsfeld settled in as the new president's chief of staff, succeeding Gen. Alexander Haig. In 1975, his wrestling skills still intact, Rumsfeld came out on top when Ford shook up his top national security officials and anointed Rumsfeld, at age forty-three, the youngest defense secretary in history. He held the job for fourteen rough months just after the demoralizing withdrawal of American forces from Vietnam.

During his first tenure at the Pentagon, Rumsfeld outmaneuvered even Secretary of State Henry Kissinger. In 1976, Rumsfeld managed to reverse the National Security Council's backing for the landmark SALT II arms-limitation treaty being negotiated with the Soviet Union. At the time, Kissinger was flying to Moscow for a final round of talks on strategic arms. President Ford had indicated his support for the treaty, but Rumsfeld opposed it. "Rumsfeld afforded me a close-up look at the special Washington phenomenon," Kissinger wrote in his memoirs, "the skilled full-time politician-bureaucratic in whom ambition, ability and substance fuse seamlessly."[2]

During the Democratic administration of Jimmy Carter, Rumsfeld hibernated from national politics as chief executive officer of a pharmaceutical company, G. D. Searle & Co. in his home state of Illinois. During Ronald Reagan's presidency, he emerged briefly as the administration's special envoy to the Middle East. He later became chairman and chief executive at General Instrument Corp. In 1988, he considered a run for the presidency.

As the Clinton years were ending, Rumsfeld reappeared once again in elite Republican circles, where he became a forceful advocate for national missile defense (NMD). The successor to Reagan's so-called Star Wars program, NMD was meant to stop ballistic-missile attacks on the United States with a combination of space-, sea-, and land-based interceptor missiles.

In 1998, Republican congressional leaders named Rumsfeld to head a commission assessing the ballistic-missile threat to the United States. The commission concluded that the threat from North Korea and Iran was greater than the intelligence community had been warning. This assessment gave ammunition to hawkish Republicans, who had long believed that the Clinton White House downplayed such dangers because it opposed building missile defenses.

Space and high-tech intelligence were the centerpieces of Rumsfeld's ideas for transforming the U.S. military. Rumsfeld believed space represented the next battlefield and exploiting it not only could protect the United States but could give it tactical advantages as well. He tapped as advisers a whole group of space and missile-defense experts, including an Air Force general, Richard B. Myers, whom Rumsfeld would eventually pick to succeed Shelton as chairman of the Joint Chiefs of Staff. Myers, a strapping, Harley Davidson aficionado, led the U.S. Space Command and had briefed Rumsfeld's commission. Myers, too, championed this ultimate battlefield.

As partisan politics grew to dominate national security debates in the late Clinton years, many Republicans had come to see Shelton as part of the problem. Prior to the release of Rumsfeld's missile threat report, he had signed a letter to Senator James Inhofe (R-Okla.), a strong advocate of an anti-missile system. The letter had reaffirmed Shelton's support for a 1995 National Intelligence Estimate (NIE) that had predicted it would take fifteen years for any rogue nation to develop or acquire a ballistic missile capable of threatening the continental United States.

Rumsfeld's commission, in contrast, had suggested the threat could arrive within several years, and with little or no warning. The NIE undercut Republicans, who were urging that NMD be vigorously pursued.

One week after Shelton's letter reached Inhofe, North Korea test-launched a three-stage ballistic missile, the Taepodong I, taking the intelligence community completely by surprise. The test gave fodder to critics who believed the NIE findings were politicized.

To mute Republican criticism, Clinton had tossed $5 billion a year toward the development of a missile shield. But that money wasn't nearly enough to build it—everyone knew that. And Shelton had never challenged Clinton on the subject. In fact, none of the service chiefs supported development of missile defenses at the cost of conventional war-fighting programs. One more reason, Shelton figured, that Rumsfeld might mistakenly put him in Clinton's camp: "I think he felt like we were part of the old administration, that we were part of the problem, not looking for solutions. I don't know why he thought that. Like the press reported, most of the military was voting for Bush."

The other big reason, Shelton figured, that Rumsfeld had tagged him as a "Clinton man" was Shelton's support for something called "military engagement," the military's awkward post–Cold War term for interactions with foreign governments and militaries. By "engaging," U.S. commanders hoped to create personal connections that could be used in times of crisis and to build or hold together political partnerships to serve U.S. interests.

This strategy did not come naturally to Shelton. As a mid-level officer, he had viewed the armed forces as a combat tool to be employed to fight the nation's wars. But like other military leaders who pinned on their stars after the Cold War ended, he had grudgingly adapted to the nation's willingness to use the military in other ways: To stop genocide. For humanitarian relief. For military shows of strength to avert larger confrontations. Even for nation-building in places like Haiti and Bosnia.

This trend peaked under the Clinton administration during the 1999 Kosovo war. Then, the State Department and international-aid agencies in the U.S. government had taken a back seat to the only department left with any real muscle. More and more, the military represented the United States in the world. The last four defense secretaries had personally led the way.

Dick Cheney, who served as secretary of defense under Bush's father, then William Perry and Bill Cohen under Clinton, had each traveled incessantly. They courted foreign defense ministers and even presidents and prime ministers; in addition to discussing such mundane necessities as military bases, overflight rights, and arms sales, they kept doors open for political discussions as well. They flew around the world to close contentious bilateral "status of forces" agreements, assuring that countries with different legal systems would nonetheless honor U.S. laws when dealing with U.S. service members. Sometimes the secretaries even dealt with such details as the lengths and load-bearing capacities of runways used by U.S. cargo planes.

At least once a week Cohen feted a foreign leader at the Pentagon's river entrance with the royal treatment, red carpet and all. Most visitors received escorted tours of Washington and were charmed at elaborate soirees approaching the formality of state dinners. The Defense Department during those days was its own foreign ministry.

Rumsfeld reversed course completely, banning the word "engagement" altogether.* He assigned underlings to welcome and meet with foreign defense ministers. He announced that he wouldn't travel much. Whereas Perry and Cohen had each visited the Persian Gulf states twice within a year of being appointed, Rumsfeld wasn't going anywhere. "You couldn't blast him out of there with a jackhammer," Shelton laughed. Even Rumsfeld's staff was on him for it.

Part of Rumsfeld's hostility toward engagement, Shelton and other top military leaders believed, stemmed from the new administration's aversion to anything faintly Clintonian. Rumsfeld also believed, how-

---

* Rumsfeld has also tried to change the CinCs' name; "There is only one CinC under the Constitution and law, and that is POTUS," he told the Joint Chiefs of Staff's legal counsel, Col. Peter Carey, using the acronym for the president of the United States. Rumsfeld instructed Carey that all references to the "CinCs" to be changed to "combatant commanders." On October 24, 2002, Rumsfeld issued a memo officially changing the CinCs' title to "commander," as in "Commander, U.S. Pacific Command." "Effective immediately, the title 'commander-in-chief' shall be used to connote or indicate the president of the United States of America," Rumsfeld said. To avoid administrative costs, Rumsfeld decreed that existing stationery would be used until it ran out.

ever, Washington should not use the military for nation-building ventures just because it happened to be a lot easier and cheaper to use military personnel than to develop civilian agencies to do the job.

Others at the Pentagon suspected that part of Rumsfeld's dislike for international hand-holding had more to do with his vision of the United States as it entered the twenty-first century. For the first time in history, the United States was a superpower without military rival. Maybe it didn't need all these entanglements to remain on top. The word "empire" had begun cropping up. The secretary's office had sponsored a private study of the great empires—Macedonia under Alexander the Great, Republican Rome, the Mongols—asking how they maintained their dominance. What could the United States learn from the successes and failures of ancient powers?[3]

Most Pentagon leaders, and certainly the commanders in the field, thought retreating from the world would be disastrous. Plus, they had gotten used to the trappings, travels, and responsibilities of being regional CinCs. Nevertheless, an endless list of "engagement activities"—from multinational exercises to the hundreds of discreet forays by special forces—went on Rumsfeld's chopping block.

Rumsfeld wanted to pull all Americans out of Prince Sultan Air Base in Saudi Arabia, which had been the operational center for every U.S. military move against Iraq since the Gulf War. It was the command post for enforcing the no-fly zone in southern Iraq. Shelton and Gen. Tommy Franks, the commander of U.S. military operations in the Middle East, were dead set against the idea of withdrawing. Without the magnificent Saudi base or a suitable replacement, trying to send U.S. troops or planes to Iraq on short notice "would be a bridge too far," they told Rumsfeld. Besides, the Persian Gulf states take their cue from the Saudis. "You'll lose more than you'll gain," Shelton argued about the prospects of a withdrawal from the Saudi kingdom.

Rumsfeld's staff proposals also shook Frank's Tampa-based Central Command. Word came that the Office of the Secretary of Defense planned to reduce the numbers of U.S. troops quietly living on other isolated bases in the Persian Gulf, as well. They wanted to cut back on the thousands of trips to the region made by U.S. military personnel for joint exercises, military exchanges, and weapons deals.

Franks and Shelton, however, believed that close contact with government officials in the region was crucial to countering the major threats there: Iran's and Iraq's nuclear, biological, and chemical weapons ambitions and their support for anti-American extremists; Afghanistan's ruthless Taliban, who hosted Osama bin Laden. Indeed, Al Qaeda cells operated in most Persian Gulf states, sheltered by America's shaky allies—most notably Saudi Arabia, the United Arab Emirates, and Egypt. Despite the bomb attack on the USS *Cole* in the Yemeni port of Aden on October 12, 2000, which killed seventeen people, the generals thought it wrong to abandon Yemen, which recently had been favorably receiving them. Franks and Shelton argued that U.S. forces needed the web of support bases around the Persian Gulf should an emergency arise. It had taken the United States five months to fly and ship in the materiel needed to fight the Gulf War. The generals didn't want that kind of delay again. After some testy exchanges in the summer of 2001, Shelton and Franks believed they had prevailed.

But Rumsfeld's agenda was broader than the Persian Gulf. He wanted troops out of the Sinai Desert, where they had patrolled since April 1982 as symbolic guardians of the historic Camp David peace accord between Israel and Egypt. Withdrawal fit into the administration's plan to leave regional problems to the countries involved. Let the Israelis and Palestinians solve their own problems.

Rumsfeld had plans to yank troops from Kosovo and Bosnia, too. The Balkans, the administration believed, were a European problem. Bush had hinted at a pullout during his presidential campaign. Facing a chorus of European protests once he became president, however, he quickly retracted the idea. But Rumsfeld hadn't given up. He had ordered the Joint Staff to prepare a plan to remove all U.S. troops from Bosnia within a year, with withdrawal from Kosovo to follow.

Rumsfeld also rethought Clinton's foray into the drug-infested Andean region of South America, the Pentagon's most controversial mission. Rumsfeld had grave doubts about using the military to stop the drug trade; he had once called it "nonsense."[4] He thought drug abuse was best handled by families, schools, and churches. At the same time, the Bush administration wanted to scrap a congressionally mandated prohibition against helping Colombia's military fight its internal rebels—drug traffickers and those rebels were thoroughly intertwined, officers assigned to Latin American affairs argued.

Yet as Rumsfeld's team charged through lists of foreign operations, they underestimated the sea change in responsibility that had accrued to the regional CinCs in the last decade. The CinCs were in charge of military operations in four theaters around the world. The vestiges of World War II occupying forces in Europe and Asia, and with a new Middle East–focused U.S. Central Command created after the Soviet invasion of Afghanistan, the CinCs had become consumed by subterranean conflicts bubbling up under their feet: terrorist networks in Afghanistan, Pakistan, Sudan, Central Asia, and the Persian Gulf; organized crime and extremist political factions in Bosnia and Kosovo; the hegemony of corrupt, abusive militaries in Africa; ethnic factionalism in Asia; drugs and revolutions in Central and Latin America. While Pentagon-based majors and colonels toiled on Rumsfeld's grandiose transformation plans, the CinCs were sending as many people as they could muster to foreign countries to open or cement alliances with foreign militaries and their governments.

The staunchest advocate of this new "engagement" was a burly marine, Gen. Anthony Zinni. As CinC at the U.S. Central Command before Franks, he had launched cruise-missile strikes against Iraq, Afghanistan, and Sudan. Clinton sent him to defuse tensions between nuclear-armed India and Pakistan. He helped negotiate the handover of terrorists to the United States from Jordan. He had spent most of his time in a murky, hard-to-define netherworld that was neither war nor peace. There was no U.S. war on this invisible battlefield. No missiles were flying or bombs dropping, at least none the public could see. But from the inside, Zinni's world felt like a raging battle to shape the future.

While Bush's Pentagon embraced the technological possibilities of the dot-com boom, the Zinnis of the world turned to smaller and smaller units of soldiers. Elite Special Operations troops—the joint Delta Force, Army Green Berets, Navy SEALs, and Air Force Special Tactics and Combat Controllers—were operating discreetly around the world. The spectrum of missions supervised by the CinCs, both in geography and in the intensity of commitment, was enormous. First encounters were taking place in obscure places: in cities such as Tashkent, Astana, Ashgabat, and Bishkek; in African nations once off-limits for political reasons, such as Nigeria, Swaziland, and Rwanda. Since the end of the Gulf War, U.S. troops had tiptoed around the Persian Gulf on missions meant to make sure the region's inherited monarchies remained stable.

In Indonesia, whose army had tried to exterminate separatist movements in the archipelago and had stifled popular uprisings for democratic reform, the CinCs and the Pentagon leadership had become so mesmerized with engagement that they fought to win a secret legislative loophole to skirt congressional prohibitions on helping Indonesian troops. U.S.-Indonesian military relations went back to the mid-sixties; no CinC wanted to be the one to sever them.

In Europe, thousands of U.S. soldiers occupied Kosovo and Bosnia. They had fought Yugoslav leader Slobodan Milosevic's forces with precision-guided munitions launched from warplanes, but once on the ground, U.S. peacekeeping troops found that their task was anything but precise. Washington and European capitals, despite promises to the contrary, counted on the competence and plentiful supply of twenty-something soldiers to rebuild the Balkans.

This vast engagement was taking its toll on the U.S. armed forces, which were overstretched and overworked when Rumsfeld took his oath. Although the CinCs didn't always ask for these missions, once assigned to them, they applied every bit of money, resources, guile, and Washington savvy at their disposal to carry them out. These missions became their daily bread and butter.

Personalities played a large role. Their leadership skills, honed over years of competitive military service, ensured the CinCs dominated, particularly in the near absence of strong, countervailing civilian figures. That their overbearing influence might actually distort U.S. foreign policy goals was not a problem they thought much about.

Rumsfeld, a demanding and competitive person himself, seemed to sense some of this when he arrived. He called them "the kingly CinCs" and believed they needed to be taken down a notch. But first he focused inward, on the business of the Defense Department, the personnel, readiness, and procurement problems, and finally, "transformation."

On September 10, 2001, speaking before 23,000 Pentagon employees, Rumsfeld lashed out at the Pentagon's wasteful bureaucracy, calling it a threat to national security. Each dollar lost was a dollar less for new equipment, he railed. "Some might ask, 'How in the world could the secretary of defense attack the Pentagon in front of its people?' To them I reply, I have no desire to attack the Pentagon. I want to liberate it. We need to save it from itself."[5]

His railing grated on the upper echelons of the Pentagon. Tensions between the military and Rumsfeld had become so bad that for months Shelton had hoped for a crisis. Watching the military operate in a crisis would surely cure Rumsfeld of his distrust, Shelton thought. The secretary might then understand that the military's loyalty had switched to George Bush "two-seconds, no, a half-second after the president raised his right hand" to take the oath of office.

"I didn't pray for a war," Shelton admitted, "but I said several times, jokingly . . . 'when the chips are down and you call on them, they'll deliver.'"

★ ★ ★ ★

SHELTON'S CRISIS CAME the next day, September 11, but the chairman was nowhere near the Pentagon when it began. He was 35,000 feet above earth and thousands of miles away heading toward Hungary for a NATO meeting. U.S. officials quickly ordered all planes to land and closed the airspace over the United States. Shelton was literally trapped outside.

"Get clearance to turn around," he ordered his pilots, and told them to turn around anyway if they didn't get it. "We're not going to ask for permission, we're going to ask for forgiveness." Over the Atlantic, one of the world's busiest air corridors in the world, no chatter sounded on the pilot's radio.

As his plane approached New York City, Shelton moved up to the cockpit for a better look at where the World Trade Center towers had stood. Smoke boiled up 10,000 feet. "I just can't believe this is happening," he muttered to the pilots.

The CinC for the Middle East and Afghanistan was abroad, too, when the attacks began. In fact, Franks was asleep. On his way to

Pakistan, he had stopped to refuel near Chania, a magnificent ancient port city on the west side of Crete. Franks and his wife had gone trinket shopping and then returned to their hotel room to rest.

With the boss asleep, Frank's aide-de-camp, Lt. Col. Jeffrey Haynes, and his executive officer, Navy Capt. Van Mauney, were watching CNN with the CinC's communications technician, Sfc. Ken George. When the first plane hit the north tower at 8:46 A.M. in New York, Haynes made a mental note of how clear the weather was. Pilot heart attack? Mechanical problems?

"Was that a replay?" Haynes asked George as the second plane struck at 9:05 A.M.

"I'm going to wake up the CinC," Mauney said after he realized it was not.

"Roger that," answered Haynes.

Franks came immediately and settled his lanky six-foot-three frame into a chair in front of the television screen. Thick clouds of debris poured from the buildings as they collapsed. "UBL," Franks said blankly in his Texas drawl, using the military's shorthand for Osama bin Laden. "Thousands dead. This is bad."

Closer to home, but still far from ground zero, Zinni, Frank's predecessor, watched events unfold from the airy study of his new Williamsburg, Virginia, home. Glued to the television, Zinni fought back the temptation to say, "I told you so." But the feeling welled up inside him. He thought about the hammering he had taken in front of congressional committees of inquiry convened after the USS *Cole* was blown up by bin Laden's terrorists. Congress was always looking for someone to blame other than themselves, he thought.

Zinni had helped Yemen rebuild the Aden port. He had wanted to send military officers and Army Special Forces soldiers there to enhance Yemen's ability to stop terrorists from transiting though Aden to Saudi Arabia and elsewhere. But someone was always getting in his way with the argument that such involvement would be too risky, or politically incorrect. Zinni thought the best way to gather intelligence in the region was to send his people there. Begin simple contacts that might lead to more lucrative ones.

Congress and the State Department didn't buy the idea. They were constantly questioning and canceling his plans.

He realized right away that September 11 would change that.

* * * *

WHEN A THIRD AIRLINER hit the Pentagon at 9:39 A.M., Rumsfeld was in his office, where he liked to be. He had been meeting with a Capitol Hill delegation when he felt a tremendous shudder. He raced down the steps from his third-floor office and out of the building, running toward the smoke. He helped rescuers pulling bodies from the debris until a security agent convinced him to go back inside.

The secretary rushed into the National Military Command Center. His jacket was covered in dust when he entered the two-story room jammed with computers, wall maps, and wall-mounted television screens. In his matter-of-fact way he reported seeing thousands of pieces of metal and smelling jet fuel; he thought an airplane had hit the building.

Standing in front of Rumsfeld and a roomful of officers was Vice Adm. Scott Fry, the dry, all-business director of the Joint Staff. He ticked off a worldwide inventory of the things needed to protect the United States: Air National Guard fighters, Coast Guard ships, chemical and biological weapons response teams, Navy vessels, AWACS surveillance planes, Aegis radars. The nation's air-defense command launched combat air patrols over Washington, New York City, and the western coastline.

Fry's tone was detached, his tempo rapid-fire and controlled, thought Denny Klauer, the chairman's special assistant, who watched the orchestration of data and requests. Klauer had seen the chaos behind the curtain in other crises. On the outside, everything seemed to be clicking in; on the inside, he felt like throwing up.

The Pentagon's ventilation system carried smoke and cordite ash from the site of the crash across the nearly four-million square feet of office space and into the command center. People around Rumsfeld were coughing. Their eyes watered and noses ran. Everyone seemed calm, except the building maintenance people, who kept running in to take oxygen readings and deliver extra oxygen masks. After a while Rumsfeld moved to a vaulted, secure room near the Executive Support Center, his private bunker, which had a better air filter.

Videoconferences with Bush and Cheney had begun. The president directed fighter planes to shoot down civilian airliners in hostile hands—an unthinkable response, but one that had to be done. The passengers would die in either case. Unbeknownst to Bush's national security team, passengers on United Airlines flight 93 had come to the same conclusion: they launched their own assault on the hijackers, and their plane plowed into Stony Creek Township, eighty miles southeast of Pittsburgh, at 10:10 A.M.

As Fry and the Joint Staff reacted to the rapid fire of events, Rumsfeld calculated the next steps. He would help fashion the retaliation. His was a world of decisions. Thousands of them added up to how people around the globe treated each other. The world had turned deadly for Americans, and Rumsfeld's vision changed in the course of that hour.

Once he made it back to the Pentagon, Shelton remained huddled in his office with staff until well past midnight, preparing for the next day's meeting of the National Security Council. Rumsfeld's charge to him had been to "think broadly." Shelton pored over a dozen contingency plans for a military assault against several terrorist organizations. But after hours of review, he didn't see one good military option. No single strike, or series of strikes, would make a difference, he concluded. Terrorist organizations rarely had a central headquarters to bomb, or barracks to blow up. The targets just weren't there. As he walked down the faded brown limestone steps of the Pentagon's river entrance in the early morning, Shelton's larger concern was that the president would have unrealistic expectations. He might turn to the military for a quick fix, as Shelton believed Clinton had done too many times.

"The military understands very well that we are the hammer in the tool kit, but not every problem is a nail. There are other instruments," Shelton would say later, describing his concerns that night. During the Clinton years "it was always, 'What can you do militarily?'"

★ ★ ★ ★

OSAMA BIN LADEN abruptly ended Rumsfeld's campaign to rein in the armed forces. By mid-October, America's military had acquired even more authority, responsibility, and resources than it had quietly accumulated over the previous decade. Rumsfeld soon created another CinC post, that of the U.S. Northern Command. Its jurisdiction would be military operations in Canada, Mexico, and the United States. Not since World War II had a military officer been given that job.

Congress approved $375 billion in defense money after September 11, adding $66 billion to the previous year's appropriation. This was twice the increase that the Pentagon had requested. Not since the Reagan largesse in the mid-1980s had so much money been given to the military after so little debate. Plans were in the making to add $6 billion to military intelligence budgets.

Over the ensuing months, the U.S. armed forces would fight a new kind of war in Afghanistan. Operation Enduring Freedom combined the incredible human endurance of seventeenth-century-style Afghan warriors with the communications and air power technology of a twenty-first-century superpower. Twelve-man Army Special Forces teams rode horses with wooden saddles into battle with Pashtun tribesmen while their commanders tweaked war plans via videoconferences between colonels in Uzbekistan and Pakistan and generals in Florida. The Taliban regime in Afghanistan was quickly toppled, but Al Qaeda remained agile, with functioning communications links and better survival gear than some U.S. troops. CIA paramilitaries and covert Delta Force troops infiltrated Pakistan to find and destroy remaining pockets of Al Qaeda fighters.

A year later, however, the job remained unfinished, Bin Laden remained at large. Al Qaeda had scattered to corners unknown. Meanwhile, a secret campaign was unfolding globally against terrorism. It spanned four continents and involved a dozen countries. Rumsfeld put an Air Force general, Charles Holland, an unknown even in his own clubby service, in charge of tracking the worldwide effort as head of the U.S. Special Operations Command. Tall and taciturn, Holland's job was to link actions and devise offensives that crossed the CinCs' traditional geographical boundaries. This new approach made

sense in an era of transnational networks. But Holland's vast, expand-
ing world would operate clandestinely, behind a veil of secrecy. By law,
Holland's budget, programs, acquisitions, and operations were free
of the public scrutiny imposed on all other joint military commands.
Holland's ideas would not be publicly debated or examined. He gave
no interviews. He never appeared on television. His congressional
testimony in open session was meaningless. Most Air Force generals
did even know him, for he had long operated in the classified, subterranean world of Special Operations.

Even Rumsfeld began trotting the globe doling out praise and gifts
and seeking basing rights and intelligence-sharing arrangements with
foreign powers. Three weeks after the September 11 attacks, sweating
through his dark business suit, Rumsfeld met in a red tent in a remote
desert camp in Muscat, Oman, with the dagger-wearing, turbaned sultan, Qaboos bin Said. They snacked on dates and sealed a deal: Oman,
a low-key, steady ally, would purchase $1.2 billion in arms, including
12 F-16 fighters and 100-laser guided bombs, in exchange for grant-
ing the United States access to its huge air bases and numerous ports.
Previous American concerns about maintaining a balance of power
between Arab states and Israel were swept aside.

Rumsfeld went to other nations in the region with an endless list
of handouts. Secretly, the U.S. began to fortify an air base in Qatar to
replace its air operations center in Riyadh, Saudi Arabia. The Saudis
had refused even some U.S. requests to fly humanitarian supplies into
Afghanistan from the Riyadh facility after the war began. Relations
with the Saudis frayed badly.

Uzbekistan, an authoritarian state with an atrocious human-rights
record, became the regional hub for a new network of U.S. bases in
Central Asia. As a down payment, the Uzbek regime received $100
million in aid. "The interest of the United States is of a long-standing
relationship with this country, and not something that is focused on
the immediate problem alone,"[6] Rumsfeld declared as he stood next to
Uzbek president Islam Karimov, a Soviet-style autocrat previously near
the bottom of Rumsfeld's Christmas card list.

Dictators the United States had once sought to isolate now became *its*
dictators. Rebels and warlords it once cast off as lunatics were embraced.

What the United States couldn't negotiate, it tried to buy with cold cash, economic assistance, weaponry, and military training. The Pentagon's Defense Security Cooperation Agency, its bureaucracy for arms sales and training, set up an "Enduring Freedom Rapid Response Cell" to put weapons requests from new partners in the anti-terrorist coalition on a "fast track." Within a month, 30,000 M-16 rifles and a C-130 transport plane were transferred to the Philippines, where the most visible second front in the war against Al Qaeda had briefly developed.

The generals and admirals who watched these post–September 11 friendships bloom snickered to themselves. "Those who came into the administration with the idea that sheer U.S. power could accomplish things are realizing we must have coalitions lined up with us," Adm. Dennis Blair, head of the U.S. Pacific Command, told his associates.

"I have no axe to grind with Secretary Rumsfeld," Shelton concluded. "But he came in with certain preconceived ideas that I think he now sees—but I don't know whether he would admit it or not—were wrong."

Rumsfeld certainly didn't believe he had been wrong. The world had changed, not his view of it. "I would say that there [is] no question that the circumstances in the world have shifted," he told reporters traveling with him in October 2001. "In a year or two or three I suspect that we will see considerably different arrangements than existed prior to September 11, because the event is of that magnitude. And exactly how that will play out is unclear. The relationships have been refashioned after every significant world event. Therefore, I am confident that they will be in this case, even though we can't predict exactly what they will be."[7]

After the last seismic world event—the collapse of the Soviet Union—a Democratic administration, aided by a Republican-controlled Congress, had turned to the U.S. military to help manage world affairs. September 11 had forced the next realignment. This time a Republican administration, cheered on by both parties in Congress, was turning once again to the military for solutions. For America's military, though, it was almost business as usual. Taking the lead had become The Mission.

Chapter Two

THE RISE OF THE
AMERICAN MILITARY

* * * *

*L*ILTING MELODIES FROM THE U.S. AIR FORCE WOODWIND Quintet escorted guests up the marble White House staircase on the final February 15 of Bill Clinton's presidency. The nation's top military leaders, sixteen four-star generals and admirals in dark uniforms trimmed with gold, glided up gracefully, wives at their elbows in long gowns and light-catching jewels.

A quiet snow piled up on the window ledges outside. On the normally off-limits floor of the president's private residence, in the warm light of the Yellow Oval Room, butlers served cocktails as a dozen cooks scurried in the kitchens below. President and Mrs. Clinton appeared relaxed with their guests, rare as it was that such a somber crowd would gather in celebration. There were no campaign contributors. No political consultants. No movie stars. Only the country's most important military leaders—and the president treated them like intimates. Gen. Wesley Clark, in charge of operations in Europe, was "Wes." Adm. Dennis Blair, who managed the vast Pacific theater, had become simply "Dennis."

As dinner approached, the guests squeezed in around a thirty-foot-long crescent-shaped table that Hillary Clinton had commissioned in Chile. It was only the second time she had asked workers to haul it out so that everyone could sit within her husband's gaze and no one would feel left out. Waiters in white gloves slid Maine lobster, beluga caviar, and veal noisettes onto their plates as the U.S. Marine Band Strolling Strings breezed by. Bouquets of white flowers adorned the table. It looked like a wedding and felt like a family reunion.

Those in attendance had been through so much together: two massive troop deployments and bombing operations against Iraq; a near-divorce over gays in the military; the grief and guilt of lives lost in Somalia; an intervention in Haiti; half a million dead in Rwanda; air strikes against Bosnia; missile attacks on terrorist camps in Afghanistan; the president's impeachment; the bloody referendum in East Timor; the air campaign against Slobodan Milosevic's Yugoslav army. Thousands of U.S. soldiers were still in Bosnia and Kosovo. Twenty-five thousand more were hunkered down nervously around the Persian Gulf, guardians of America's incomplete victory from the last big, celebrated war.

Those events had caught the public's attention. But quietly, behind the scenes, the military had done so much more. It had stepped into a huge and growing gulf between America's unprecedented leadership role in the world and what the country's civilian leaders were willing to do to fill it.

"We had quite a year last year," Clinton told them, holding up a glass of white wine in tribute. "East Timor, our continuing missions in Iraq and North Korea, all the natural disasters that we've had to overcome from the Americas to Turkey. And I just want you to know that I am profoundly grateful. . . . I hope always, always, you will be as proud of what you have done for your country as I am tonight. I ask you to join me in a toast to all the people who serve under *our* command."

In the popular view, Clinton and the military never got along. For such a smart politician, Clinton had been so dumb in the beginning regarding his relations with people in uniform. But at the same time, on Clinton's watch the military slowly, without public scrutiny or debate, came to surpass its civilian leaders in resources and influence around the world.

Clinton knew that many men and women in uniform resented him for having sat out the Vietnam War and for his anti-military views in college. The first Vietnam-generation president, as a student he had

President Bill Clinton toasts the commanders-in-chief at a White House dinner, February 15, 2000. "Genetically we're all 99 percent the same," the president told his CinCs; if he couldn't fight them, which he tried to avoid, then he would try to join their formidable club. WHITE HOUSE PHOTO BY WILLIAM VASTA

written to a University of Arkansas ROTC commander in 1969 saying he sympathized with friends who found themselves "loving their country but loathing the military." Years later, the new president never even stood up for the views he had held back then. He never explained how he could have been against the war yet not unpatriotic, like thousands of other college students of his day. Thirty years later, when he became commander in chief, he seemed cowed by his past, afraid to really challenge the military on its shape or priorities for fear it would revolt publicly. He knew the glorious homecomings for soldiers from the Gulf War had been meant to make up for the public's lousy treatment of Vietnam veterans. Soldiers, sailors, airmen, and marines once again commanded an enormous intuitive respect from the public—probably trumping Clinton's own.

For many service members, the president's distasteful peccadilloes allowed them to personalize policy disagreements. Gen. John Shalikashvili, who as chairman of the Joint Chiefs of Staff worked closely with the president in his first term, believed that disliking the president became a kind of requirement for many Army officers. "It was very difficult for an Army officer to defend anything Clinton did," he later said. "You know—real men don't support Clinton."

Clinton did not help matters. He came into the White House without having learned to salute properly. He let his right arm dangle at his side when the national anthem played. Before he assumed office, the Joint Chiefs and its then-chairman, Gen. Colin Powell, threatened to resign if Clinton pursued his campaign promise to allow gays to serve openly in the armed forces.* Clinton team's had utterly misjudged the depth of military resistance on this issue. The episode symbolized the profound disconnect between the White House and the Pentagon.

Clinton's young staff, disdainful of the armed services, and unappreciative of their disciplined culture, created more problems. "I don't talk to the military," a female aide had scowled at the nation's most decorated active-duty officer, Lt. Gen. Barry McCaffrey, as he greeted her on the White House grounds four months into Clinton's first term.† Liberal young civilian staffers at the Pentagon, meanwhile, tried to move peacekeeping and disarmament to the center of the Pentagon's traditional agenda. At first ignored, they were eventually run out of the building.

To improve relations, Clinton and his White House made an unspoken pact with the military brass: Don't push us and we won't push you. There would be no substantial restructuring of the armed forces. No deeper cuts. No radical social changes. Over time, as the two camps confronted an unpredictable post–Cold War world together, their truce grew into a mutual respect at the top—and then into a troubling

---

* "The presence of homosexuals in the force would be detrimental to good order and discipline," Powell told students at the U.S. Naval Academy on January 11, 1993, nine days before Clinton took office. The only alternative to accepting the new policy, Powell said, is if "you still find it completely unacceptable and it strikes to the heart of your moral beliefs, then I think you have to resign."

† McCaffrey, the most decorated active duty Army officer, was twice awarded the Distinguished Service Cross for valor, had served as commander of the 24th Infantry Division (Mechanized) in the Gulf War, and was at the time of this insult Powell's senior envoy to the White House. The remark made the newspapers and reaffirmed every anti-military Clinton stereotype.

dependence. Military leaders learned that they would be consulted and their wishes given great weight. Clinton and his team learned that they could shove more and more duties onto the Defense Department, and the military would accept it and carry on.

Implicitly, the Pentagon leadership realized it was no longer enough "to fight and win the nation's wars," as the military wished its only job to be. The military would have to do more. There was no one else. Neither the president nor Congress was even making a strong case for a civilian substitute.

In fact, spending on diplomacy had marched steadily downward for decades. Congress had slashed the State Department's operations budget by 20 percent during the 1970s and 1980s. As the military expanded overseas, the State Department's squeeze forced the closure of more than thirty embassies and consulates, and 22 percent of the department's employees were cut from the payroll. "More money is not a substitute for an effective foreign policy," concluded Richard Gardner, a professor at Columbia University who served on the largest government-sponsored study of the State Department, "but an effective foreign policy will simply be impossible without more money."[1]

Instead of righting the imbalance, Washington came to rely ever more on the regional CinCs to fill a diplomatic void. They asked infantry and artillery officers and soldiers to help build pluralistic civil societies in countries that had never had them. They required secretive Special Forces to make friends with the nastiest elements in foreign militaries and turn them into professionals respectful of civilian authority.

In addition, Clinton and his team gave the Defense Department a slew of odd jobs that had formerly been spread out among civilian agencies. The military began to manage de-mining, anti-drug-trafficking, anti-terrorism, humanitarian disaster relief, and even disarmament programs. In his last days in office, Clinton tried to hand the military the AIDS crisis as well. They detested some of these new responsibilities, but once tasked, men and women in uniform did what they were assigned. A steady, self-propelling march was part of their training: it was hard to limit what generals and admirals did on their travels, or what jobs 82nd Airborne paratroopers ordered to rebuild Kosovo would take on.

Predictably, the military learned to operate in civilian realms, while their civilian counterparts in every agency grew more isolated, less knowledgeable, and less comfortable with the military world. Dozens of uniformed officers joined the staffs of the National Security Council, the State Department, and the CIA.[*]

Military officers grew deft at the art of politics. They offered free help to members of Congress serving on the committees that decide on Defense Department budgets, strategy and equipment. Each branch of the military also has a Capitol Hill staff of its own, the talents of which rival that of the renowned law and lobbying firms on Washington's K Street. If one of the services opposes an administration policy or direction, it has the networks and political savvy to thwart the White House in Congress—without fingerprints, of course, since lobbying by government agencies is forbidden by law.[†]

Some of Clinton's traditional liberal supporters—human-rights workers, church activists, and humanitarian organizations—were dumbfounded that their president would not confront the brass on two issues in particular: the international treaty banning anti-personnel land mines, a treaty that the Pentagon vehemently opposed; and the proposal to send commandos to apprehend war criminals in Bosnia, also rejected by military leaders. Even Clinton's most seasoned advisers agreed that the latter action was the key to bringing peace to the Balkans. But human snatches were a red line for the cautious Army leadership. "I made it clear that I would not support using the military to hunt down war criminals," said Shalikashvili. "We weren't going to take them unless we stumbled upon them. I felt the military had a horrible track record in chasing these kinds of criminals. Look at Mogadishu." Leave it to civilian SWAT teams, he argued.

* John M. Deutch, a former deputy defense secretary who served as director of central intelligence from May 1995 to December 1996, made CIA support to military commanders a top priority. He increased the number of CIA employees assigned to the CinCs' headquarters, stirring resentment among CIA officials who believed a heavy military focus distorted collection efforts.

† The State Department didn't even have an office on Capitol Hill until 2001, when Colin Powell put one there. Only a handful of State Department officials are assigned to the Pentagon. The position of political advisor to the CinC, known as the "Polad," is still considered off the fast track.

These new civilian responsibilities seemed to overtax the rigid military superstructure. Commanders complained that keeping 50,000 troops on deployments around the world was breaking the spirit of a force 1.5 million strong.[*] Yet the Army, the largest service and the one quickly becoming irrelevant, would not change on its own to make itself better suited to these relatively small, ever-changing tasks. The sacrifices would be too big for an institution built on big vehicles, heavy weapons, large troop formations, and redundant chains of command. Despite all the changes afoot in the world, neither the Clinton administration nor the Republican-led Congress that paid the bills insisted that the Army—which carried the bulk of these new responsibilities—reorganize in any meaningful way.

By the night of his White House dinner, a year had passed since Clinton's historic impeachment. Things had settled down. The Pentagon had come to a workable, even respectful, relationship with Clinton's team. And President Clinton liked and admired his generals and admirals. As he scanned the grand East Room of the White House, alit with an amber glow, the president seemed to want to join their circle. "If you take any set of people and ethnic group," he told them, "if you take 100 Hispanics and 100 people who are of Northern European descent and 100 Africans and 100 Asians, the genetic differences among individuals within the group would be greater than the genetic differences between any two groups. Genetically we're all 99 percent the same." That statement struck some at the table as a very Clintonesque way of glossing over differences. If he couldn't fight them, which he didn't dare, then he would try to join their formidable club.

To Clinton's right that night sat General Shelton. His mysterious 1,100-person Joint Staff occupied a warren of bland, low-ceilinged offices on the southwestern wedge of the Pentagon. Some of these

---

[*] Deploying 50,000 out of 1.5 million troops taxes the Army because of the so-called tooth-to-tail ratio the services maintain. In the Army, for example, it takes another 2–5 soldiers to support the deployment of one soldier overseas. These others, the Army argues, perform "stay-at-home" jobs such as logistics, medical care, training, recruiting, and office-work. One of the biggest criticisms of the Army in recent years has been its inability to shave this ratio.

offices were secured each night with combination locks and triple bolts.* The Joint Staff was the chairman's foreign policy think tank, rapid-reaction planning team, long-term strategy shop, and the keeper of the nation's thirty-three classified war plans. The members of the Joint Staff were nothing like the feuding civilian political appointees in the Office of the Secretary of Defense who were supposed to set policy. The Joint Staff had a "one team" esprit during a crisis and possessed unrivaled intelligence resources and the discipline to produce analyses and plans quicker than any other office of government.

Nearby sat Shelton's vice chairman, Gen. Joseph Ralston, an affable F-105 "Wild Weasel" Air Force combat pilot who excelled at politics and the art of compromise. Defense Secretary William S. Cohen, Clinton's third man in the post, relied on Ralston as the shadow chairman. Cohen had tried, and failed, to have Ralston named as chairman.† Cohen, though introverted, got along easily with Ralston, who was better then Shelton at working with the White House anyway. Ralston was the CinCs' "go-to" guy.

Scattered in between the officers and wives at the dinner table were the presidentially appointed leaders of the services—the civilian secretaries of the Army, Navy, and Air Force. Near them sat the uniformed service chiefs: the Army chief of staff, the chief of naval operations, the Air Force chief of staff, and the Marine Corps commandant, all

---

* Under Clinton, the importance of the Joint Staff rose with the increasing prominence of the CinCs. Although they work for the chairman, the Joint Staff, with the chairman's permission, also functions as the CinCs' Washington-based advocates.

† In June 1997, Ralston's nomination to become chairman of the Joint Chiefs of Staff fell victim to congressional uproar over the Air Force's decision to discharge its first female B-52 bomber pilot, 1st Lt. Kelly Flinn, the month before. Flinn was charged with adultery, lying, and insubordination involving an affair with a subordinate enlisted man. Ralston had had an adulterous affair with a CIA employee ten years earlier during separations from his first wife. They later divorced. Ralston had been confirmed by the Senate six times during his career and no one had ever made an issue of the relationship. But coming so close to the Flinn controversy, this time members of Congress perceived a double standard and let the administration know Ralston's nomination would face a challenge. Defense Secretary Cohen quickly backed off. Ralston's nomination as vice chairman sailed through months later without a hitch, and he was held in high esteem by the White House and his Pentagon peers.

four-star positions that used to be the pinnacle of military power. No longer. Over the past 15 years, fighting wars had become more of a joint effort shared by all the services. Thus the "service chiefs" have become unhappy administrators who no longer plan or fight wars. They make sure their services can recruit, train, and equip enough soldiers, sailors, airmen, and marines. They toil over training rotations and the structure of their forces. They hustle Congress to fork up enough money for the newest generation of weapons.

The service chiefs might complain the loudest about the military's adventures overseas, but by law they have to be prepared to carry out the president's National Military Strategy. Since 1995, this document called on the armed forces to be prepared to fight two major theater wars "nearly simultaneously."* Everyone understood those theaters to be North Korea and Iraq. But other new, real-world requirements, such as engagement and peacekeeping, were draining equipment and troops that the service chiefs wanted to husband for a real war.

As the service chiefs' power shrank, the CinCs' power rose. Four of those CinCs are "functional," charged with military transportation needs, space and nuclear issues, joint war-fighting experiments and homeland defense, and worldwide Special Operations Forces. The other five are the "regional CinCs," vastly more comfortable in the world of diplomacy than most of their contemporaries. Each had made the most of the political leeway they were given. They had pulled ambivalent civilian leaders into more decisive action abroad and worked to push them toward a regional approach to the world. Just as the concept of globalization had forced leaders to think of the world as one inter-connected biorhythm, the CinCs saw the same interwoven connections on security matters. Drug trafficking, criminal networks, and terrorism all transcended national borders. These blights developed in countries with enormous income disparities, where the

---

* In mid-2001 the Bush administration changed this requirement. The armed forces should be structured, equipped, and ready to secure a "decisive victory" in only one conflict, even as U.S. commanders were directed to continue planning for the possibility of operating "in two theaters in overlapping timeframes." By Sept. 2002, the continued war on terrorism and preparations for fighting in Iraq had begun to seriously tax the armed forces.

LINES OF AUTHORITY

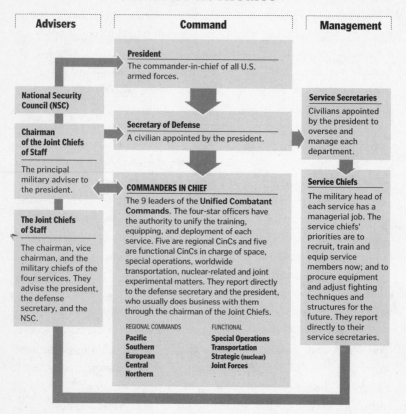

Advisers

Command

Management

President
The commander-in-chief of all U.S. armed forces.

National Security Council (NSC)

Chairman of the Joint Chiefs of Staff

The principal military adviser to the president.

Secretary of Defense
A civilian appointed by the president.

Service Secretaries
Civilians appointed by the president to oversee and manage each department.

COMMANDERS IN CHIEF
The 9 leaders of the **Unified Combatant Commands**. The four-star officers have the authority to unify the training, equipping, and deployment of each service. Five are regional CinCs and five are functional CinCs in charge of space, special operations, worldwide transportation, nuclear-related and joint experimental matters. They report directly to the defense secretary and the president, who usually does business with them through the chairman of the Joint Chiefs.

The Joint Chiefs of Staff

The chairman, vice chairman, and the military chiefs of the four services. They advise the president, the defense secretary, and the NSC.

Service Chiefs
The military head of each service has a managerial job. The service chiefs' priorities are to recruit, train and equip service members now; and to procure equipment and adjust fighting techniques and structures for the future. They report directly to their service secretaries.

REGIONAL COMMANDS

Pacific
Southern
European
Central
Northern

FUNCTIONAL

Special Operations
Transportation
Strategic (nuclear)
Joint Forces

© 2002, THE *WASHINGTON POST*. REPRINTED WITH PERMISSION.

The chain of command for the Defense Department and other national security agencies. In June 2002, Rumsfeld announced his intention to merge the space and strategic (nuclear) commands into one command. He also requested that the CinCs titles be changed to "unified combatant commanders."

prospect of a better future was dim. Problems that could threaten the United States—terrorism, unregulated migration, drug imports—all flourished in unstable, unjust political systems.

As Clinton held his glass up that February night, he toasted four men in particular: General Zinni, whose Central Command stretched from Egypt to Pakistan. An Italian-American from a blue-collar neighborhood of Philadelphia, Zinni had become obsessed with the endemic civil wars of Africa and the disenfranchised Islamic extremists in the withering hinterlands of Central Asia. Admiral Blair, a wiry, tight-jawed Mainer who headed the Pacific Command. Blair advocated the notion that U.S. military officers could reform their foreign counterparts. He pushed countries in his theater to send their officers to American schools and to open their hallways to U.S. planners and trainers. Blair didn't worry as much about a war between China and Taiwan as he would later about hostility between Beijing and President George Bush's new administration.

Directly across from Clinton sat the restless, forceful Army general Wesley Clark, U.S. commander in Europe and much of Africa. Clark was also the Supreme Allied Commander, Europe (SACEUR), the military leader of NATO's nineteen-nation political-military alliance. In Bosnia, he had pushed the U.S. military into responsibilities it had not held since World War II. He led NATO's first, real coalition war, the 1999 campaign against Yugoslavia that drove Serb forces from Kosovo. During both operations, he had fought a rear-guard battle against a reluctant Pentagon and Army leadership.

Rounding out the four was Gen. Charles E. Wilhelm, CinC for Latin America. Without a traditional foreign threat in his theater, this slender, gray-haired Marine Corps general widened the definition of humanitarian relief. Hurricanes and floods became a pretext to reintroduce American troops to former enemies, like the Marxist Sandinista army in Nicaragua. But his main preoccupation was chasing drug traffickers in the Andes, especially Colombia.

These CinCs had come of age under two precedent-setting, willful figures: Secretary of State Madeleine Albright and Shelton's predecessor as chairman of the Joint Chiefs of Staff, General Shalikashvili.

Both had been born and raised in Eastern Europe—Albright in Czechoslovakia, Shalikashvili in Poland—and both were "firsts" in the U.S. government. Albright was the first woman secretary of state. "Shali" was the first immigrant to become chairman. Both struggled at the pinnacle of their careers to define the military's role in the world.

Albright had first served the Clinton administration as its ambassador to the United Nations, from February 1993 until January 1997, while Shali was chairman. She became secretary of state in January 1997 and worked with Shali as chairman for ten months, until he retired and was replaced by Shelton. Albright's philosophy and manner had ticked off the brass. Many thought she behaved like "the world's mother-in-law" as she routinely scolded tyrannical regimes that were detaining and torturing their citizens, or slaughtering them in broad daylight, as Milosevic's troops had been doing in the Balkans throughout the 1990s. She had become a folkloric figure throughout the ranks of the military, whose officers endlessly repeated the question Albright, as ambassador to the United Nations, had had the chutzpah to ask Powell one day as they bickered over U.S. military intervention in Bosnia: "What's the point of having this superb military that you're always talking about if we can't use it?"

That thought had struck many Americans, too, as they watched grandparents shot on the street by Serb snipers in Sarajevo and children in Sierra Leone with bleeding stubs for arms. After all, $300 billion a year poured into the Defense Department to keep things humming. Perhaps America's military couldn't and shouldn't be everywhere, but shouldn't it be able to stop the most obscene affronts to basic human rights?

Powell's reaction to Albright's question had reaffirmed his hero status around the Pentagon's elite E-ring, where the service secretaries and service chiefs worked: "I thought I would have an aneurysm," Powell had said. "American GIs were not toy soldiers to be moved around on some sort of global game board."[2]

Although Albright accepted Powell's hero status, her true target was his doctrine that advocated overwhelming, decisive force against an enemy from the start, or nothing at all. That antidote to Vietnam had served the country well in the Gulf War. Albright, however, had a different model in mind. She wanted to perfect limited warfare for limited ends. "Coercive diplomacy," she called it. The administration had tried that with limited air strikes in Bosnia. But, in fact, that conflict ended only with the use of large ground offenses by the warring factions involved. The administration was trying it in Iraq, too, with the no-fly zones meant to box in Saddam Hussein's regime.

By 1999 the Clinton administration hoped coercive diplomacy would kneecap Milosevic's ethnic-cleansing campaign in Kosovo. But limited warfare was a concept with which the military, and the Army in particular, remained uncomfortable. Yet as Albright persisted, some military leaders, among them the regional CinCs, swung around to her point of view. The Pentagon leadership was still resistant, and Defense Secretary Cohen's office made it difficult for her to lobby the CinCs on the matter. But they couldn't stop her completely.

In early 1999, Albright's staff organized a small, off-the-record conference with retired ambassadors, generals, admirals, and scholars to assist the State Department in understanding the issue of "force and diplomacy." The night before the conference took place, on March 24, Albright invited an admiral and three generals to dinner in the State Department's elegant seventh-floor dining room.

The timing could not have been more ironic. Diplomatic efforts to stop Milosevic's rampage through Kosovo had recently collapsed. That very night, U.S. and European combat aircraft had taken to the skies over Yugoslavia. As General Shalikashvili drove to the Albright dinner, his protégé, General Clark, was feeling the crushing weight of failed statescraft. Clark had orders from NATO to initiate military action against Milosevic's forces in Kosovo.

Albright's guests stepped out of the elevators into the gilded James Monroe Reception Room. Attending were Zinni, retired Army general George Joulwan, who had preceded Clark as SACEUR, and Adm. T. J. Lopez, former commander of U.S. naval forces in Europe. Lopez had opened the first military contacts with Algeria in twenty years.

Albright was rushed and late. War hung in the air. But she was desperate for better answers than she had been getting.

Most of the guests were subdued. They had doubts about the Kosovo operation, which they realized was bound to be incremental and politician-driven. But Zinni acknowledged that the military could better adapt to new demands from people like Albright. "The military just has to do a better job of embracing them," he said. "They have to change the doctrine, and decide to do a better job on the ground."

A few guests stayed to watch Clinton's televised address to the nation. "I do not intend to put our troops in Kosovo to fight a war," Clinton pledged from the Oval Office. The generals groaned. Clinton had shown Milosevic his limits, a cardinal sin in military operations. The administration had a lot still to learn about blending diplomacy and force. As Gen. Klaus Naumann of Germany, then chairman of NATO's military committee, would later admit at a briefing during the war, "We need to find a way to reconcile the conditions of a coalition war with the principles of military operations such as surprise and overwhelming force. We did not apply either in Operation Allied Force [the name of the Kosovo air war], and this cost time, effort, and potentially additional casualties."

What principles would make limited military force—predictably restrained by politicians—more likely to succeed? The next morning in the green drawing room of the French-style Meridian House mansion on 16th Street N.W., Albright's conferees debated that question. Was it wise to employ military force to stop crimes against humanity and civil war? Historical references flew about the room, from the imperial policing habits of the nineteenth-century British Empire to the practices of the United Nations (UN), and the legitimacy of military action not approved by UN Security Council resolution.

When he rose to speak, Shali looked around the room through his rectangular gold glasses. His box-shaped jaw always set just so, he launched a couple of his own self-guided missives. The problem was not with the military, he said, but with civilians. "What we are doing to our diplomatic capabilities is criminal," he said in his clipped, Polish-accented English. "By slashing them, we are less able to avoid disasters such as Somalia or Kosovo, and therefore we will be obliged to use military force still more often."

If Albright was the nation's mother-in-law, Shalikashvili was its measured, self-effacing father, the first in a breed of new-thinking generals to make it to the top. As an eight-year-old in Warsaw in 1944, Shali had watched the Polish underground rise up against an occupying German army. Resisters took over his family's apartment, which was soon destroyed by German dive-bombers. Darting behind barricades of broken concrete and moving through underground sewer lines, for months Shali and his older brother went from cellar to cellar and to an occasional soup kitchen for food and lodging. Indiscriminate shelling and bombing killed tens of thousands of civilians in Warsaw. Shali, the grandson of a czarist general and son of a Georgian cavalry officer, left Poland for Germany in a train filled with the wounded. His family ended up with a distant relative in Peoria, Ill. He learned English watching John Wayne movies, graduated from college in 1958 with a degree in mechanical engineering, and was drafted into the Army as a buck private two months later.

He had been deputy commander of U.S. Army forces in Europe in 1991 when Gen. John Galvin, then the SACEUR, put him in charge of the 35,000-person Operation Provide Comfort, the first major U.S.-led multinational humanitarian effort since World War II. It turned into the largest military airdrop in history, even larger than the Berlin airlift. Using satellite photographs and Special Operations helicopters, officers found half a million refugees tucked into the rugged, snowcapped mountains of northern Iraq and southeastern Turkey, trying to escape Saddam Hussein's persecution after the Gulf War.

Gen. Shalikashvili was well trained for conventional war. He had practiced nuclear attacks against invading Soviets. But coaxing nervous Kurds out of the mountains was another matter altogether. Shali "had never even met an NGO," as he called the aid workers who risked their lives—without armor or weapons—to feed the hungry. He didn't understand their strange, non-hierarchical organizations. Looking back on ten years of similar emergencies, he said, it was hard to understand why Operation Provide Comfort was a big deal.

But it was. "[President George H.W.] Bush and [Defense Secretary Dick] Cheney sent me to Northern Iraq and that was my first introduction. I went when I was told," said Shali. "I really didn't know what a Kurd was—how stupid. I didn't know the Kurdish issue. I remember thinking to myself, how are you going to say something intelligent to the press? It was strange for the U.S. to be involved." Like the Kurds trying to find a foothold in the crumbling cliffs of northern Iraq, officers like Shalikashvili groped for a foothold in the new world.

In the Pentagon context, Shali so excelled at dealing with this new world that Gen. Powell gave him a fourth star and leapfrogged him in 1992 over several competitors into the top CinC's job in Europe. Working closely with Powell, Shali pushed the U.S. and former Soviet bloc countries into a far-reaching new set of military-to-military contacts. From Shali's European Command headquarters on Patch

Barracks in Stuttgart, Germany, colonels officed in the attic of building 2315 sent hundreds of small teams to the crumbling general-staff headquarters of thirteen countries across Central and Eastern Europe. Their mission was to help new governments restructure their armed forces and rethink the military's role in new democracies.

When Shali moved on to become chairman of the Joint Chiefs of Staff, he was faced with his boldest challenge yet: redefine America's role as the world's only remaining superpower. The task was not easy. Great angst pervaded his service and the Pentagon over operations that could not be defined as vital interests using old definitions. Military officers had long ago bought into the use of force to maintain free markets, to assure the flow of oil, and to destroy communist movements. The new operatives had vaguer objectives but were couched in grander terms: freedom from tyranny, the moral obligation to stop starvation and genocide. They sported a new name, as well, to distinguish them from real military missions: "Military Operations Other Than War"or MOOTW. Shali had counted them: there were never fewer than ten such missions afoot in the world each day.

"Real men don't do MOOTW," Shali often said, mocking the military's reluctance to plunge into peacekeeping and relief operations. He leaned on the services to be helpful, but he empathized with their distress. Unit commanders in the field fretted about their preparedness to go to war. These new missions interrupted training cycles—and they didn't like that.

Fret they might, his officers, but Shali had witnessed the effects of NATO and UN indecisiveness in Bosnia. Some 150,000 people died there before the United States directly intervened to stop the killing. He read that calamity as a lesson about America's leadership and "the price we pay when it isn't there."*

Shali became the first chairman to modify the cautious, black-and-white Powell Doctrine. He accepted Powell's view on overwhelming

---

* Even so, Shali argued against air strikes on Serbian artillery positions in Bosnia earlier that spring because he believed they would not achieve much. Stopping the war would require a "massive" infusion of ground troops, he said, which he realized was politically unrealistic. Privately, he was torn apart by NATO's passivity in confronting the worst bloodshed in Europe since World War II.

force. The United States had lost the war in Vietnam out of timidity, worried too much about a Chinese overreaction. The Vietnam bombing campaign had been too incremental and inconclusive, he believed. If troops were to go into Bosnia, he wanted twice the proposed 10,000. "We had to be the biggest dog on the block," he said. But Shali also believed the United States had an obligation to act to stop grave affronts to human dignity, like the wars in the Balkans. He came to believe that the United States owed a more aggressive response to the war in Bosnia, but overwhelming force would not be appropriate there. After the war ended, he mused privately, why not take an Army division from Europe and assign it to the Balkans? "If the people of the Balkans realized that America would be there, it would be great," he said. Big successes take time. The United States had been in Germany, Japan, and Korea for fifty years after World War II. "Why is it such a crime to suggest a similar longevity in Bosnia and Kosovo?" he asked.

Shali's worldview made no sense to those in uniform who linked failure in Vietnam to military incrementalism. Never again should they fight a war for peripheral interest. And never again should they consider a limited or incremental approach to anything. As these men pinned on stars and took over the military, they competed against leaders like Shali to determine the military's future.

THE
COMMANDERS

———

Chapter Three

THE CINCS:
PROCONSULS TO THE EMPIRE

★ ★ ★ ★

*L*IKE MOST YOUNG MARINES, LT. TONY ZINNI WANTED a taste of the action in Vietnam. In 1967, assigned to the 2nd Marine Division at Camp Lejeune, he watched anxiously as most in his company got orders to go to war. "Everyone will be a Vietnam vet but me," Zinni worried, "and I won't have any stories to tell at the bar."

The day he returned from his weekend wedding to his sweetheart, Debbie, his Vietnam orders were waiting: he was to report to the Marine Advisory Unit. Modeled after units in the French counterinsurgency campaign in Indochina, Marine advisers were assigned in pairs to a Vietnamese marine battalion. They wore Vietnamese uniforms and each had a "cowboy," a local enlisted man to look after him. "You're dead meat. You'll die out there," his friends taunted. But at the seemingly immortal age of twenty-three, with the war heating up, Zinni was thrilled to be joining such an elite unit.

Zinni went to Vietnam with the naivete that marked many Americans. He was there to do good, to fight the communists and make the country safe for democracy. But only a week into his tour, on liberty in Saigon, he and his buddies happened on a solemnly gathered crowd. They watched as a Buddhist monk set himself on fire, the only form of violent protest sanctioned by the pacifist religion. When the

Vietnamese saw the Americans, they chased after them. What an eye-opener. "I thought we were the good guys," Zinni remembered.

By 1967, the Vietnamese marines Zinni worked with had become the national strike force, headquartered in Saigon. They were a highly politicized military organization. One group Zinni had advised, the 4th Battalion of Vietnamese marines, had several years earlier helped the corrupt, CIA-supported South Vietnamese president Ngo Dinh Diem, and his brother, Ngo Dinh Nhu, both Catholics, put down a 1963 protest by Buddhist monks with a series of midnight raids on their temples. Later, the marines led a palace coup against Diem, then executed him along with Dihn Nhu.

Members of Zinni's Vietnamese company carried their own rice and live chickens into the jungle. When they ran out, they lived off the land, eating monkeys, duck blood soup, pythons, and lizards. Zinni had to adapt and the Vietnamese marines inculcated him in their ways. They particularly distrusted the German shepherd scout dog the U.S. Army had assigned to Zinni. They would not allow Zinni to take the animal on patrol, and one day, just to drive the point home, they killed it without his knowledge. When they showed the dog to Zinni, they explained it had died in "enemy contact." That night they treated their American marine to a special meal at a local restaurant. As a waiter brought out a large tray, they laughed, "Here's your dog. Eat up."

Vietnam's quartering act allowed marines to live with peasant families. Zinni often slept in their thatched huts, shared meals with the villagers, and listened to their dreams over tea at night. One mother asked to see pictures of his family, and she looked into his face to try to make sense of his presence. Why did you come here? she asked him. "We're here working for you, to fight communism, you know, democracy and freedom." he replied. But she wanted something else. "When are you going to change this?" she asked.

"When we defeat the North."

"No, no, no, not change things there, but there," she said, pointing toward Saigon. "If you want us to be free, change things there. You can't just defeat the communists."

Through his hosts, Zinni saw how narrowly focused the U.S. war effort really was. "They didn't support the communists, but there was nothing in Saigon worth fighting for, or dying for either. Their lot wasn't going to be better," he remembers thinking. "The more time passed, the more I became convinced that we weren't going to change anything in Saigon," he said. No matter how many Viet Cong or North Vietnamese were killed, Zinni thought, "it would not make things right." But the Pentagon and the White House hadn't yet faced that fact.

Zinni's first tour in Vietnam ended prematurely with the onset of chronic dysentery and a case of hepatitis. He lost fifty pounds and was shipped back stateside. After his recovery, he taught counterinsurgency and guerrilla operations at the Marine Corps' Basic School in Quantico, Virginia. He had also attended the Army Special Warfare School at Fort Bragg, where he learned guerrilla tactics, psychological operations, and the ideology of revolution. The toughest questions fascinated him, the ones he thought instructors couldn't answer: Why did a village become communist? Why had the Vietnamese national government failed to win the loyalty of its people?

By now a captain, Zinni returned to Vietnam in 1970 as company commander in the 1st Battalion of the 5th Marine Regiment, 1st Marine Division.[1] Many lieutenants he had trained at Quantico had been killed. Many of his Vietnamese colleagues were dead. By then, the Viet Cong's main forces had been destroyed and its units cut down to squad- and platoon-sized groups that spent much of their time hiding. The "Vietnamization" of combat units—turning more of the fighting over to South Vietnamese units—and social welfare schemes were priorities.

Most fighting on the American side was carried out by units like Zinni's, the so-called Pacifiers. Zinni's helicopter-borne infantry unit reacted to intelligence reports of enemy hideouts, to downed U.S. helicopters, and to enemy contact. Established in March 1970, the Pacifiers could go into action on ten minutes' notice.[2] Zinni's company, located on Hill 34 in the Da Nang Vital Zone, had 250 men and used weapons such as flamethrowers and automatic grenade launchers, which they hung on meat hooks in huts specially designed for quick loading onto the helicopters.

On November 3, 1970, Zinni's last day in the theater, his company escorted a captured North Vietnamese intelligence officer, a colonel named Loi, deep into the Que Son Mountains west of Da Nang to look for the North Vietnamese Army's Group 44 headquarters. With their deep gorges and hidden caves, the Que Son Mountains served as a major enemy supply system and hid extensive enemy base camps, storage caves, and secret trails. The colonel had agreed to lead them to the Group 44 headquarters, site of the field command for the North Vietnamese zone.

On that day, monsoon rains thrashed the thick jungle, thwarting the marines' first attempt to land. Later, as they picked their way slowly up an overgrown trail, Zinni's men spotted boot prints that bore no likeness to the tracks left by Ho Chi Minh sandals.* Hastily set booby traps lined the way, as did, occasionally, half-eaten food. "We've got Viet Cong in front of us," the scouts on Zinni's patrol reported as they crept up the gorge. Suddenly, the captured colonel stopped. "This is as far as they'll let you go," he told Zinni.

"What do you mean?" Zinni asked.

"Two companies are defending the ridgeline, one North Vietnamese army and one Viet Cong," he said. "They'll stop you now." They were 150 meters from the top of the hill.

All at once, the Vietnamese scout standing next to Zinni collapsed from a gunshot wound. The whole jungle exploded with gunfire. Bushes shook with bullets. Zinni was turning around to hand his radio handset back to the operator when three rifle rounds tore through his broad back, chewing up one-third of his muscle tissue. Zinni's blood soaked the jungle floor by the time a Marine medevac helicopter found a chunk of cliff dry enough to land on and evacuated the nine wounded and two killed. Forty-one enemy troops lay dead.[3]

The next day, Zinni's Marine company, led by his executive officer, found the enemy intelligence center in a cave carved into the bedrock and hauled off the central files of the Viet Cong's Quang Da Special Zone. The haul was the I Corps' most significant find of the war: the cave contained 500 U.S. Army-issued cots and rows of five-gallon coffee tins stuffed with the names, photos, and paychecks of double agents.[4]

Zinni was flown to Okinawa to recover and later received the Purple Heart. He became a company commander and guard officer with the

---

* Sandals made of old tires and worn by Vietnamese peasants.

3rd Force Service Regiment. His hundred-man Okinawa guard unit "was in hand-to-hand combat every third night" on post, sorting out race riots between marines, as well as murders, stabbings, and robberies. The job was hell, and the battles so petty compared to those in Vietnam.

As for Vietnam, Zinni's fellow marines wanted to put it behind them, recalled Zinni, and go back to real warfighting. Sweeping the entire war under the carpet, however, "just didn't strike me as quite right," he said. Too many unanswered questions haunted Zinni. The most profound weren't even being asked by his Marine Corps. How had the Americans misread the cultural context of the war? How did culture define politics? Why had the Vietnamese turned to the communists in the first place? And what made them so loyal in adversity? He believed his military's future would be determined by what the United States forgot, rather than what it understood, about the root causes of other nations' troubles.

Zinni's next "real" war was the Gulf War. He saw its backside in 1991 as chief of staff for General Shalikashvili's Operation Provide Comfort, the mission to feed and house Iraqi Kurds after the war. As postwar victory celebrations—"confetti parades," he called them—took place around the United States to welcome troops home, Zinni found himself in northern Iraq, where he watched the Kurds being starved to death, or killed, by Iraq's "defeated army" and squeezed by Turkey, a U.S. ally and member of NATO, no less.

"The first thing that struck me was, 'Hey, this war ain't over.'" Zinni watched as old people fought one another for food and mothers tossed their dehydrated babies into the backs of helicopters in the hope of getting them medical care. It didn't feel like a victory, he said.

Once on the ground Zinni had troubles. He had massive quantities of food and he couldn't get the Kurds to come down from their bleak mountain hideouts. They didn't trust the Americans or the odd, straight lines of tents the U.S. troops had put up for them. Zinni's single most important asset became a Kurdish-speaking Turkish-American intelligence officer, Nilgun Nesbett. "Nell, you gotta help me here," he pleaded. "I gotta understand this." The educated Kurdish exiles whom the U.S. military had brought along as translators didn't have any standing among the local tribes, she told him. Zinni couldn't figure out who the decision-makers were, and he couldn't decipher the tribal system. Vietnam had taught him to probe into a nation's culture for answers, to get on the ground to figure it out, and to realize the limits of what you can understand as an American. "We've got to understand what makes these people tick. I need a template to put against a culture and figure it out."

Nesbett made her way into tribal fortresses and returned with an answer. She introduced him to a Kurdish schoolteacher who sat down with him and explained the tribal power structure, who made decisions, and how decisions were passed down the line. "We need you to tell us what we're seeing," he told her. With her help, Zinni identified a different group of men to contact—the real leaders. He also ordered his troops to completely rebuild the villages. The neat rows of tents became circles of tents. Each circle had a tent for the male head of a family. The other tents were occupied by his wives and children. That did the trick. The Kurds came down from the mountains.

★ ★ ★ ★

ALMOST A DECADE LATER, in May 2000, the hatch of a glistening white converted Boeing 707 popped open and four security agents with concealed weapons and wireless earphones rushed down the stairway, fanning out onto the scorching tarmac. Snipers and an anti-terrorist SWAT team lurked nearby, positioned at the airport and along the route to the hotel to intercept trouble.

Maj. Jeffrey Haynes, the general's straight-backed Marine aide-de-camp, and a dozen other colonels, majors, and NCOs[*] poured down the plane's ramp, then stopped to glance back at the open hatch. Out stepped Gen. Anthony Zinni, commander-in-chief of the U.S. Central Command. The ribbons, medals, and stars on his size forty-six uniform jacket flashed like Morse code under the white-hot Bahraini sun.

As one shiny leather dress shoe reached the bottom step, his subordinates encased Zinni in a protective human bubble. As commander of all U.S. military forces and operations across a swath of twenty-five

[*] Noncommissioned officers.

Gen. Anthony Zinni, right, commander-in-chief, U.S. Central Command,
waiting in the Bahrain VIP reception area with U.S. Ambassador
Johnny Young.   MSGT. MARK CORMIER

countries, Zinni had acquired a power unheard of in the military in the course of America's history. His kingdom, or "CinCdom," as the staff called it, reached from the Horn of Africa across the Arabian Peninsula and into Central Asia. Iran, Iraq, and Afghanistan were his. From his heavily protected headquarters at MacDill Air Force Base in Tampa, Florida, Zinni was in charge of updating and executing eleven war plans, some of which included nuclear options, against countries in his theater.

But his mission was much more than planning for war. In fact, his real fights occurred behind closed doors, around quiet conference tables in foreign lands and in hushed, dimly lit military intelligence centers. Zinni scurried around his theater trying to win allies and coax reluctant states to close down terrorist networks poised to strike against the United States. He was at ground zero in a war to restore regional stability. That was the hardest part of his job, he confided—all these diplomatic missions. No one had given him a step-by-step plan or even a clear goal.

He couldn't even count on much help from the civilians supposedly in charge in Washington. The lack of direction drove him nuts.

On his travels, Zinni maintained the trappings of a war fighter in the heat of battle. This May 2000 journey would take him across ten time zones, including stops in Bahrain, Kyrgyzstan, Kazakhstan, and Uzbekistan. Throughout, his entourage would be within earshot of his quietest request and within sight of the flick of his finger, a movement that might mean "We've got to get going," or "Now what?" The protective bubble also allowed the "unified combatant commander," as the CinCs are known in military parlance, to concentrate fully on refining a war strategy, whether in a dusty desert tent in the Middle East or a bunker headquarters in Western Europe. Zinni, however, walked straight from his plane into the military airport's gold-trimmed VIP lounge for an obligatory tea, plopping onto a down-filled settee covered in bright pink satin. He wasn't yelling commands or convening with grubby subordinates in battle fatigues. Instead, he folded his cantaloupe-sized hands in his lap and waited for cardamom tea to be served by dark brown attendants, former slaves larger and hairier than he.

When he'd rattled his tea cup, it had been swiftly collected. Robe-clad servants ushered Zinni into an armor-plated black BMW, one of the dozen in his official motorcade that careened down the barren, blocked-off streets to a gigantic, glass-encased hotel, a place with two swimming pools, a sparkling beach, tennis courts, a first-class spa, and Dior and Chanel shops.

In these reaches, foreign leaders expected Zinni be more than just a marine, even more than a four-star general. It was an honor, Zinni believed, that they accorded him the standing of a political diplomat. But at the same time, at the twilight of his military career, as one of the most powerful generals in the world, he felt frustratingly helpless. Countries turned to him to stop chronic civil wars, uproot terrorism, cure starvation and arrest what they saw as the dangerous course of American isolationism.

Zinni did not look the diplomat. Short, burly, and camel-nosed, he still bench-pressed 300 pounds at the age of fifty-three. In some ways, he looked more like the debt collector he had been for a summer in

Philadelphia during college, when he had shown up on people's door-steps at 3 A.M. His staff fondly nicknamed him "the Godfather," and for kicks, they would bring cigars and cognac to an occasional Officers' Club film screening. As he watched more and more officers of his vintage take up golf, Zinni grunted: "If it doesn't draw blood, it ain't a sport."

Just about everything with him was a competition. Card-playing, exercise, eating, drinking. "Did you try the horse meat?" he would prod his staff after a meal in Uzbekistan or a Persian Gulf state. "Did you eat the camel's-milk yogurt? What about the goat's eyes and sheep's head?" Many nights on the road he was up late with his officers swapping stories that teemed with heroic violence, wild women, and barracks humor.

Zinni valued his rabble-rousing beginnings. He used a fictitious "Uncle Guido" to weave tales about courage, sacrifice, and stupidity: "These people come to me and the other CinCs and ask, 'What's more important to you—air power or ground power?' Incredible! Just think about it. "My Uncle Guido is a plumber. If I went to him and asked, 'What's more important to you—a wrench or a screwdriver?' he'd think I'd lost my marbles."[5]

Zinni's mother had worked as a seamstress in a clothing factory and his father had been an airplane mechanic in World War I, and later, the head caretaker for a wealthy Philadelphia family. The youngest of three children, Zinni worked his way through Villanova University as a salesman and stock boy, becoming the first in his family to earn a college degree. In college, he signed up for a summer Marine training program on a whim and, after graduation, was commissioned a second lieutenant. He liked to tell the story of how, during summer Marine Corps platoon-leader class, he was placed on probation for mouthing off, for his dirty rifles, and for other basic discipline problems.

A blunt speaker, he spared no institution, and especially not the military and its civilian overseers. "The only reason Desert Storm worked," he once said, "was because we managed to go up against the only jerk on the planet who actually was stupid enough to confront us symmetrically, with less of everything, including the moral right to do what he did to Kuwait." He deplored rivalries among the services and chastized military leaders for teaching ensigns and second lieutenants "to recognize their sister service as the enemy. . . . We could not produce a joint fire-support doctrine out of Washington or the doctrine centers to save our asses."

He still describes Vietnam as a fiasco in which platoon and company commanders "lost faith in our senior leadership." Defense Secretary Robert McNamara was a favorite target. McNamara, Zinni proffered, "decided that all services should have a common combat boot. Further, he decreed that to economize there would be no half sizes. So I had to wear size 10 instead of 9½, my regular size. My feet are still screwed up to this day, thanks to Robert Strange McNamara. And that just about symbolizes the leadership we had back then."[6]

Zinni's irreverence toward authority endeared him with troops. But he was also a closet intellectual who read books of poetry and Islamic history between briefings. In a conventional, tactical setting, he thought "outside the box" before the phrase was in vogue. Zinni was the first commander to employ non-lethal weapons—sticky foam and sponge-shooting guns—in the 1992–93 Somalia relief effort.

Washington had sent him three times to Mogadishu: once to oversee humanitarian relief, again to retrieve the remains of dead American pilots, and finally to supervise the retreat of peacekeepers. Somali warlords he had met there wrote him long afterwards, hoping, correctly, that he still cared about their country. "I'd like to go back to Somalia," he said wistfully, a sentiment not shared by many others in uniform. "I really would."

When traveling, he endured vodka-drenched toasts in Turkmenistan, tribal dancing in Kenya, falcon-hunting and nightlong town hall meetings in the Persian Gulf, and being led around palaces by the hand, "like a little boy," by the eldest male in more than one royal family. He met with African kings and princes, emirs, presidents and prime ministers, defense chiefs and military officers. Zinni chuckled that he had become a modern-day proconsul, descendant of the warrior-statesmen who ruled the Roman Empire's outlying territory, bringing order and ideals from a legalistic Rome. Julius Caesar, Caesar Augustus—they would have understood. His compatriots, he knew, did not.

★ ★ ★ ★

AMERICAN GENERALS AND admirals, emissaries for fifty years of the world's strongest military, had long exercised independent influence abroad and competed with U.S. diplomats, corporations, and intelligence agencies to shape foreign policy. But during the 1990s, the sheer weight of their budgets and the heft of political authority handed them by the White House and the Pentagon had tipped the balance of power in favor of the CinCs and their institutions. In a decade when Congress significantly slashed money for diplomacy, the CinCs' headquarters had grown to more than twice their Cold War sizes. With a combined budget of $380 million a year, their resources were lavish compared to the civilian agencies that by law and tradition were supposed to manage U.S. foreign relations.[*] It was not just a matter of money, though. The Pentagon gives each regional CinC a long-distance aircraft and a fleet of helicopters for short flights. In-flight refuelers are available for very long trips. Some CinCs travel with an entourage of up to thirty-five officers and senior noncommissioned officers. By contrast, the secretary of state is the only U.S. diplomat with a dedicated aircraft and security entourage. All other diplomats must fly scheduled commercial airlines or hitch rides on military planes.

When not traveling themselves, the CinCs continually dispatch admirals and generals who work for them, and colonels and majors by the dozen. These officers plan exercises, share technical assistance, promote the sale or donation of American military equipment, or resolve policy disputes before the CinC arrives.

Traffic also ran the other way. Many foreign defense leaders and top military officials trooped through Zinni's Tampa headquarters. Several times a week he entertained such visitors in his beautiful

---

[*] According to figures provided by the CinCs' budget offices, the budgets for each of the regional CinCs increased by at least 35 percent between 1990 and 2000. The budget of Southern Command, for example, in 1990 was $26.2 million; by 2000 it had grown to $112.8 million, adjusted for inflation. This big increase included $27 million in funds to combat drug-trafficking and $8.4 million for intelligence. Much of the increase came about when the command assumed administrative responsibilities that the Army once had. Pacific Command's budget, $57.2 million in 1990, had grown to $108.2 million by 2000. Central Command's budget, $36.7 million in 1990, grew to $55.2 million by 2000 (all 2000 figures are adjusted for inflation).

REGIONAL COMMANDS

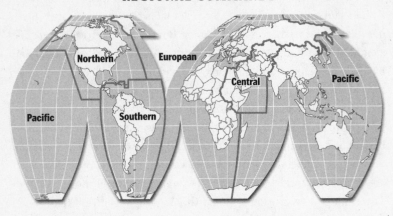

The Pentagon divides the world into five regional commands, each with its own regional commander-in-chief. ©2002, THE *WASHINGTON POST.*
REPRINTED WITH PERMISSION.

home. (Four-star regional CinCs earn about $135,000 a year, not counting perks, which include a palatial private residence, guarded twenty-four hours a day by electronic shields and small armies of security guards.) His wife befriended their wives. He sponsored working lunches and briefings in their honor collecting a table full of generals, admirals, and diplomats to hobnob with visitors. Several times a year Zinni hosted international conferences; costing hundreds of thousands of dollars, on subjects ranging from terrorism to water purification. He invited to these meetings all of the ambassadors and top generals from the twenty-five countries in his realm.

As busy as they were, with surprise U.S. missile launches against Iraq and Afghanistan, and the enforcement of the no-fly zone over Iraq, much of Zinni's staff spent its time preparing and executing peacekeeping deployments, humanitarian interventions, emergency relief for natural disasters, and hundreds of large and small training exchanges with newly independent nations and old allies. Officers once tasked to develop and update top secret war plans also have to figure out how to put strife-torn nations back together and transform inflated, unprofessional armies into professional, U.S.-equipped forces that will work in U.S.-sponsored multinational alliances.

While Zinni's successor, Gen. Tommy Franks, was running the war in Afghanistan, he also took time to enlarge his "engagement" branch. He gave the office jurisdiction over military arms sales and transfers—the most concrete inducement that bought many countries' cooperation. This move acknowledged that long-term efforts to restore peace would depend not on high-tech weaponry or American moral authority, but on food relief, economic assistance, on-the-ground intelligence, and even old-fashioned leverage in the form of weapons sales and training.

Like the European colonialists who divided up Asia and Africa, the Defense Department draws and redraws the CinCdoms every two years as part of its biannual review of the Unified Command Plan.[7] The chairman of the Joint Chiefs of Staff recommends to the president and the defense secretary changes guided by the size and geopolitical importance of individual countries. Which command a country ends up in determines the prism through which the United States views its relations.* When the states of Central Asia first won their independence from the Soviet Union, Zinni's predecessor, Gen. J. H. Binford "Binney" Peay III, former commander of the Army's 101st Airborne Division in the Gulf War, wanted to use alliances with those states to encircle and contain Iran. But the Central Asian countries fell within U.S. European Command, where the focus was on getting them to look toward Europe and away from Mother Russia for political and economic inspiration. When the biannual review gave the Islamic states of South and Central Asia to Central Command, it signified a recognition by the president and the secretary of defense that Islamic fundamentalists and the terrorist cells they bred posed a new threat throughout the region.

---

* To limit the possibility that the CinCs will get drawn into long-term regional disputes, the world's chronic hot spots are divided between two CinCs. Thus India sits within the Pacific Command, but Pakistan falls under the Central Command. Israel is within the European Command, but most of the rest of the Middle East is part of Central Command.

The joint commands' headquarters are huge, even by the standards of the U.S. government. Even the smallest of them, the command that deals with Latin America, has a staff of about 1,100. More people work there dealing with Latin American matters than at the departments of State, Commerce, Treasury, and Agriculture, the Pentagon's Joint Staff, and the office of the secretary of defense combined.

The largest CinC headquarters is that of the U.S. Pacific Command, situated on a hillside overlooking Pearl Harbor at Camp H. M. Smith in Hawaii. About 3,600 people work there and on the command's other posts. Of the 300,000 troops assigned to the Pacific Command, some 100,000 are forward deployed, mainly in South Korea and Japan. The rest are in Hawaii, Alaska, and the continental United States. By contrast, the U.S. Central Command has no combat troops permanently assigned to it. But in 2000, some 1,050 people worked at its headquarters in Tampa, and 450 others belonged to service components assigned to the command at various locations around the United States and in Saudi Arabia, Kuwait, and Bahrain.

Bountiful resources and an open-ended mandate allow the CinCs to engage with tiny countries that seem far outside the U.S. sphere of interest or concern. Admiral Blair, an admirer of the famed Gurkhas of Nepal, ordered his staff to help improve the medical program for the Gurkhas serving in the Nepalese army. Zinni worried about pirates in the Seychelles who were cutting fins off sharks to sell as delicacies and poisoning coral reefs with cyanide. He ordered his staff to look around for surplus patrol boats that might be given to that island nation to equip a coast guard.

The regional commands also sponsor intellectual centers for study and problem-solving. As executive agents for the Defense Department, the CinCs spend more than $50 million a year on five foreign-studies institutes for U.S. and foreign officials. Two of them, the George C. Marshall European Center for Security Studies at the foot of the Bavarian Alps and the Asia-Pacific Center for Security Studies in Honolulu, Hawaii, spend as much money as small colleges. Each institution oversees its own curriculum, faculty, and professional staff. High-ranking military officers from around the world attend these institutions. Another $20 million a year funds conferences that include nonmilitary topics, such as environmental degradation, medical care, police training, piracy, and drug trafficking.

The CinCs are also the main users of the training programs run by the U.S. Special Operations Command, many of which are classified. With the CinCs' blessing, and often at their initiative, special operations forces have forged ties with their counterparts around the world. Such personnel were the first members of the U.S. military seen by weary countries such as Kazakhstan and many of the war-torn countries of Africa.

Congress funds a special operations effort called the Joint Combined Exchange Training (JCET) program, at more than $20 million a year, excluding the costs of troops and transportation. The JCET program allows American troops to train in foreign tactics and terrain, particularly in unique jungle or mountain conditions. The program proved useful after September 11 when administration officials wanted to station troops in Uzbekistan and Pakistan as part of the anti-Taliban offensive. But the goals of the program, which gets very little oversight from Congress, reach far beyond just training. It assists armies fighting drug traffickers, teaches counterinsurgency techniques in countries with domestic stability problems, and trains troops in counterterrorism tactics, which usually include urban warfare and hostage rescue.

The CinCs' staffs also administer the State Department's main foreign-military training efforts, under the rubric of the International Military Education and Training (IMET) program. The United States pays the cost of training some 8,200 foreign military officers each year. The training of another 18,700 students is paid for by their own countries. From Central Command countries alone, 2,500 foreign military students participated in IMET in 2001.

An even larger share of a regional command's budget is spent on one of four huge, round-the-clock intelligence centers. Some 1,800 people, 1,000 of them reservists, work for the Pacific Command's Joint Intelligence Center, which has seven satellite offices in the continental United States. These centers track everything from massive movements of armies and war equipment to transnational terrorists. They even follow lone missionaries and humanitarian aid workers who show up in obscure, dangerous places. During the Gulf War, after intelligence failures on the battlefield became obvious, the CIA reluctantly made providing intelligence to the military a top priority. It sent a record number of analysts to help out at CinC headquarters.

★ ★ ★ ★

BUT A CINC'S ABILITY to move around in the world is his greatest intelligence weapon. Zinni's converted Boeing 707 came with three pilots, six mechanics, two navigators, and nearly a ton of spare parts, all there to avoid being stranded on some inhospitable plot of earth. When Zinni traveled by car, three "communicators" went with him, carrying cell phones, a secure satellite radio, and a ninety-pound encrypted satellite phone stashed in a backpack. Once, Zinni had to return an emergency call to the chairman of the Joint Chiefs while riding a camel in the Saudi Arabian desert. Only once during his tenure was Zinni incommunicado: he lost contact for several hours when he went fishing with a United Arab Emirates prince, motoring 55 miles out to sea on the prince's yacht to an oil platform in Iran's territorial waters.

Even in the most far-flung reaches, U.S. military decorum and promptness holds fast. Zinni's political adviser, Ambassador Laurence Pope, half-jokingly called Zinni's personal staff "Klingons"—majors and colonels obsessed with seating charts, itineraries broken down into five-minute intervals, and extreme punctuality. More than one ambassador has been left standing alone on the street after he arrived at the hotel curbside thirty seconds behind schedule.

Of all Zinni's retinue, his most important personal assistant was Maj. Haynes. Each CinC has an aide-de-camp, and some go on to become generals themselves. Most CinCs, and most service chiefs, were aides earlier in their careers. An enlisted aide irons and packs the CinC's clothes and, when the CinC is at home, cooks his meals too. But for Zinni, Haynes took care of all the rest. His job was to anticipate every need: messages from the answering machine, gifts for dignitaries, Zinni's favorite peppermint pick-me-ups. Haynes also wrote the scripts for uniform changes. (The Marine Corps has six uniforms, in addition to civilian casual and business dress.) One day, the schedule called for four garb changes, one accomplished in a room off a stairwell during a five-minute break between appointments. The next day, as Haynes was reading off the rigid schedule, Zinni grumbled: "We're not changing again today!"

Zinni's trek through Bahrain and across his region was the twelfth and last such marathon in his three-year tenure. In Bahrain, where he was to attend a regional conference, he was welcomed like a royal by hundreds of Persian Gulf officers and sheiks, and by the seventy U.S. and civilian defense officials in attendance. Security was tight at the conference, the topic of which was an attack early-warning system for the region; even the American ambassadors invited had trouble angling their way through the robed, armed guards positioned around Zinni's armored BMW.

Officially, Zinni was outranked at the meeting by the six American ambassadors to the Persian Gulf countries. But in any motorcade, the CinC rode in the lead car. Ambassadors wandered the hotel lobby, alone and unnoticed, and slept in regular-sized rooms. The CinC's team occupied an entire hotel wing. He stayed in a suite the size of a house, patrolled by half a dozen visible security agents and a dozen unnoticeable ones. Inside, his staff installed 1,200 pounds of gear, in duplicate: secure phones, fax machines, computers, printers, transformers, surge protectors, and an emergency backup energy supply so Zinni could be in touch no matter what the conditions. Every day, a hundred pages flowed in though the fax machine, about half of them classified.

The two-week trip for forty people to Bahrain and Central Asia cost the U.S. government $98,700, plus $1,500 for each hour of flying time. Zinni's Central Command would also pick up the $450,000 bill for the conference in Bahrain. But Zinni didn't pay much attention to these bills. His balance sheet wouldn't be measured in dollars and cents, but in accumulated confidences and influence. They were his mission.

Chapter Four

THE ROYAL CINCDOMS OF THE PERSIAN GULF

* * * *

WHEN GEN. ANTHONY ZINNI TOOK CENTRAL COMMAND in August of 1998, he had few doubts about the weakness of the Gulf Cooperation Council. On paper, the GCC looked like a functioning coalition, but this group of nations that had allied with the United States against Iraq for the Gulf War was nothing like NATO, an organization that could actually get things done. It was, instead, a gaggle of feuding, incestuous neighbors who had trouble even agreeing to meet, much less deciding what to discuss. Although the United States was not a member of the GCC, the Gulf states needed Zinni as a unifier just as Europe needed its supreme allied commander, also an American.

In Europe, defense treaties were drawn up by lawyers and diplomats. NATO's troop levels, its equipment purchases, and the compatibility of its varied systems were constantly scrutinized by the military commands of its nineteen members. Its ministers debated ethics, politics, and, in the case of the Kosovo war, even what types of facilities to bomb.

By contrast, military cooperation in the Persian Gulf depended largely on handshakes and personalities. Everything was bilateral, nation to nation, man to man. U.S. leaders had long accepted this as "the Arab way," despite the fact that U.S. taxpayers were paying billions of dollars each year to protect these countries from one another and from Iraq, Iran, Syria, and Libya. The United States hired out its military as a regional mercenary force for Arab rulers who could not raise their own armies.*

After the Gulf War, when U.S. prestige in the region stood high, Washington missed an opportunity to codify new arrangements and force the Gulf states to make more professional use of their U.S. weapons and training. Talk of organizing a regional force to relieve the U.S. military from having to repeat its Gulf War involvement barely registered. As for leaning on the Middle East's monarchs to allow democratic political change, no one ever talked about that. The Saudis paid the United States $60 billion for the Gulf War, which for the desert kingdom was nothing more than a pure money transaction. Relations would proceed as they always had.

The lack of a strong, cooperative alliance also meant that whenever the United States wanted to punish Iraq for infractions of the U.N. Security Council resolutions under which the Gulf War had been prosecuted, Zinni had to go hat-in-hand to each country in order to secure takeoff, landing, and overflight permission for U.S. planes. Ambassador Pope, Zinni's soft-spoken political adviser, described the art of securing these agreements as "allocating forces so you got everyone a little pregnant." Some countries would accept refueling planes only. Others allowed spy planes. Some banned bombers from their soil but would okay launching missiles.

Zinni was frustrated that no coherent strategy existed among the region's countries. A NATO-like organization, with the U.S. in the lead, would give any country the political cover needed to make difficult decisions. The Gulf states were becoming increasingly hostile to suggestions of another low-level bombing campaign against Iraq. But they didn't support sanctions, either. The "Gulfies," Zinni said, either wanted to kill Saddam Hussein or to live in peace with him. Zinni's Bahrain conference, however oblique its agenda, was an attempt to pursue what had long been abandoned by political leaders back home: building trust among countries in the region. Perhaps one day

* Thousands of U.S. troops had been stationed in Kuwait for ten years before Lt. Gen. Tommy Franks, who was at the time Zinni's Army commander, reorganized Kuwait's Army in 1998. Since then he hoped Kuwaiti soldiers might actually be able to defend their own country against another Iraqi offensive, at least until large numbers of U.S. troops could be ferried in.

they might act together; for now, he would settle for gathering them for talks about something nonthreatening. The Bahrain conference, focused on a shared computerized early-warning system for biological and chemical weapons attacks, was painfully slow and boring, made worse by rudimentary show-and-tell Power Point slides.

Zinni shrugged: "If we come walking in ordering everyone to do a certain thing, its much less effective than if they come to the same conclusion themselves," But, he added in a whisper, "it's like watching paint dry, isn't it?"

At the end of the conference, generals from Bahrain ushered Zinni into a gigantic, colorfully painted tent, the sort common at wedding feasts. But inside were gas masks and oxygen tanks, anti-contamination space suits and other survival gear. Zinni surveyed it all slowly, as if selecting from a delectable buffet. Then his handlers pointed him outside toward the reviewing seats, from which he watched solemnly as Bahraini soldiers, shielding their eyes against an untimely sandstorm, recovered bodies from a mock chemical-weapons attack and decontaminated the nearby sands.

Zinni had another unassigned but critical role in the region. Each time some top official in Washington spouted alarmist anti-Iraq rhetoric, Zinni rushed out to the Gulf to calm fears that Saddam Hussein was about to strike. One such trip took place after Defense Secretary William Cohen, who paid great attention to the region, held up a bag of sugar demonstrating roughly how much biological toxin it would take to wipe out a major city. Zinni's hosts would always ask him the same question: Are you serious this time? "Of course we're not serious," Zinni thought to himself. "We're just going to go up there and drop a few bombs and whack the Iraqis around a little bit. Saddam's still going to be standing at the end of it."

Another time, he had to calm nerves after Cohen scared a prince in Bahrain by lecturing him about Ricin, a protein from the castor-bean plant so deadly that a speck of it on the skin can kill an adult. Unable to come up with a good translation from English to Arabic, the translator told the sheik that Cohen was worried about "killer beans."

"One drop on your skin and it can kill you," said Cohen, who worried greatly about weapons of mass destruction.

"Get the tea! Get the coffee!" the prince cried out in alarm to the attendants, immediately ending the discussion.

Washington's rhetoric and posturing, much of it performed for domestic political gain, played entirely differently in the Arab capitals within striking distance of Baghdad. "If you suddenly walk in and say, 'We're not going to take him out and go to Baghdad, but we've got to poke a stick in the cage of that tiger,' well, they think that might get [Saddam] riled up. He's got bad stuff that can make your skin blister and your eyes fall out. . . . Well, this little guy [from a Gulf state], he's sitting here thinking, 'I don't want to screw with him. I don't want to get him mad. If we're not going to take care of him and kill him, why do I want to be poking sticks in his cage?'"

Zinni's reluctance to poke the tiger sometimes influenced policy decisions in Washington. In late 1997, the Clinton administration decided that U.S. pilots should be more aggressive in enforcing the no-fly zone in southern Iraq. "We're losing face," one top White House official told Zinni's staff. Iraqi pilots frequently stuck their noses just across the 33rd parallel, the boundary of the no-fly zone, then flew back deep into Iraq. The White House needed a confrontation to show Capitol Hill and the ever-critical United Nations that the remaining shred of their Iraq policy still mattered, now that Iraq had kicked out the UN weapons inspectors. Zinni received early word that the White House planned to ask him to order pilots to draw Iraqi fire. The U.S. pilots, of course, would have to respond.

"If they want me to start a war, I can do that," Zinni told his closest aides. But this game-playing, as he saw it, was militarily unsound. What if a pilot got shot down? Would it lead to a war? Was Washington politically prepared for that?

Gen. Joseph Ralston, vice chairman of the Joint Chiefs and the Pentagon's usual representative at high-powered meetings of the cabinet secretaries' deputies, conveyed the White House's formal request. "They want you to do this," Ralston told Zinni.

"Well, if someone wants me to do this," Zinni replied sternly, "you can send me an order." No one would push it that far, Zinni knew; the White House desire to be more provocative was dead.

★ ★ ★ ★

AMERICA'S MIDDLE EAST policy has long been determined by the White House and Congress. The Israeli-Palestinian peace process. Support for Israel, Egypt, and Saudi Arabia. The post–Desert Storm war of attrition against Iraq. The isolation of Iran. All originated in successive administrations and were debated at length by Congress.

But time and again, those political institutions turned to military solutions—either deploying American troops and warships, or increasing military assistance and training missions in the region. Policymakers wrongly assumed that the main highway to political stability ran through the Pentagon. In reality, nothing—certainly not a billion-dollars worth of new helicopters, missiles, and tanks—could replace political dialogue and the tough, hard work of diplomacy. Washington's short-sighted approach would begin to seriously unravel by the spring of 2002.

This dependence on military solutions in the Middle East dated back decades. And U.S. Central Command had been essential to it. After the 1967 British withdrawal from the Suez Canal, the United States relied on its two principal allies, Iran and Saudi Arabia, to maintain the appearance of stability in the Persian Gulf. But 1979 undid that strategy. That year brought the overthrow of the shah of Iran, followed by the seizing of hostages at the U.S. Embassy in Tehran and the Iranian Revolution led by Ayatollah Ruhollah Khomeini. The Soviets invaded Afghanistan. Long lines at U.S. gas stations made the American public feel economically vulnerable for the first time since World War II.

In January 1980, President Jimmy Carter declared that ensuring the flow of oil through the region was a vital national security interest. This so-called Carter Doctrine was to be implemented by the Rapid Deployment Joint Task Force, which the president created in Tampa three months later.* But with sparse forces, inadequate funding, and

---

* The Rapid Deployment Joint Task Force was first headed by Gen. P. X. Kelley, who later became commandant of the Marine Corps. The task force was subordinate to the U.S. Readiness Command, which no longer exists but which had been head-quartered at MacDill Air Force Base since 1972. The task force was plagued by problems, according to Jay Hines, historian at U.S. Central Command, including "long lines of communication, lack of regional bases and forward-based assets, and poor understanding of local conditions."

THE PERSIAN GULF

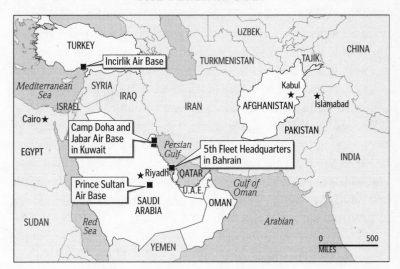

BY BECKEE MORRISON © 2002, THE *WASHINGTON POST*. REPRINTED WITH PERMISSION.

The four U.S. military bases shown are just part of the massive
U.S. infrastructure in the Persian Gulf region.

confusing chains of command, the task force never caught up with events. Civil war broke out in Lebanon; an attack on the Marine Corps barracks in Beirut followed, killing 241 Americans. Iran and Iraq went to war. President Anwar Sadat of Egypt was assassinated. And a new phenomenon arose: Middle East terrorism, complete with airplane hijackings and car bombs. President Ronald Reagan turned the task force into a full-fledged unified command—the Central Command—on the first day of 1983.*

---

* The U.S. Central Command's area of responsibility originally included Egypt and the Persian Gulf, the Horn of Africa, Pakistan, and Afghanistan. In October 1999 it acquired the five former Soviet republics of Central Asia: Kazakhstan, Kyrgyzstan, Tajikistan, Turkmenistan, and Uzbekistan. Unlike the Pacific and European Commands, Central Command has few combat forces permanently assigned to it. When operations occur, forces are temporarily assigned to it by the Joint Forces Command or the Special Operations Command.

U.S. diplomatic efforts to forge a peace in Israel went forward, without success, but otherwise U.S. foreign policy in the region was one-dimensional—and that dimension was the military. As a consequence, American peacetime military power in the region reached "historic levels" during Zinni's tenure.[1] Some 25,000 service personnel were in his theater at any one time. Another 5,000 ground troops were quietly dispatched to Kuwait after September 11. Thousands were sent to Afghanistan. Rarely did anyone get a glimpse of the new billion-dollar base at Al Udeid in Qatar, the largest pre-positioning facility in the region; its long runway provided an alternative to the air operations center in Saudi Arabia, use of which was limited by the Saudi monarchy, which feared it would appear too subservient to its American ally and military protector. Some 5,000 American airmen worked and lived at Prince Sultan as "tenants."

Indeed, none of the states involved wished to publicize these deployments. The presence of Americans on Islamic holy land in Saudi Arabia was highly controversial among Islamic states (and one reason Osama bin Laden called for a jihad against the Saudi monarchy and the United States). American troop deployments in Kosovo and Bosnia attracted a lot of media attention, but until Saudi Arabia refused the United States full cooperation after September 11, the Pentagon had kept its gulf deployments out of the news.

For years the Pentagon disguised its permanent presence in Kuwait by calling it an exercise, "Operation Desert Spring," a four-month rotation of troops that amounted to a continual deployment of 1,500 soldiers. For years, Saudi Arabia, Kuwait, Oman, Bahrain, Qatar, and the United Arab Emirates have hosted more than two dozen small posts for U.S. intelligence facilities, ammunition and vehicle storage, refueling equipment, and command and control facilities. Special Operations forces have been particularly active in the Persian Gulf, quietly training counterparts from nearly every nearby nation.[*]

---

[*] Special U.S. Navy and Army units operate the UN-sanctioned maritime interdiction program to stop unauthorized supplies from reaching Iraq and unrefined Iraqi oil from being shipped out. Each year, troops from the 5th Special Forces Group conduct infantry and coastal-craft training with the most elite units of nearly all the Persian Gulf states, including Bahrain, the United Arab Emirates,

Retired American military officers add to the U.S. presence. Since 1975, some 1,400 U.S. citizens work there each year as contract employees of the Vinnell Corp. of Fairfax, Va., to train the Saudi National Guard, which exists to preclude a coup by the Saudi army and to mollify rival clans.

The two-way flow of Saudi and American pilots and technicians is substantial. Most Saudi pilots train in the United States. Hundreds of U.S. service members travel to the region to sell U.S. weapons and train troops in the use and maintenance of the approximately $125 billion worth of weapons that the "Gulfies" have bought since 1973. More than half of that cache, about $83 billion, was purchased by the Saudi government, which hosts 77 U.S. personnel who live there to deal with arms transfers.[2]

* * * *

WITH SO MUCH OF the U.S.–Persian Gulf relationship anchored by his military activities, Gen. Zinni often found himself agreeing with the gulf states' perspectives and priorities. His empathy and attention to nuances endeared Zinni to the region's leaders. The Saudi princes might have serious quarrels with the White House, but they trusted Zinni, and for good reason: he knew and trusted them.

In May 1998, the Saudi defense minister, Prince Sultan bin Abdul Aziz, dressed head to toe in a white flowing robe, ushered a delegation of American senators into the sitting room at Al Salam Royal Palace in Jeddah. Zinni hung back toward the rear as the politicians he was escorting admired the one-of-a-kind silk carpets that lay atop the world's finest marble floors.

Zinni had wanted Senator Ted Stevens (R-Alaska), the powerful chairman of the Senate Appropriations Committee, to be the center of attention. Stevens had traveled halfway around the world with some of his colleagues to press the Saudis to pay more toward the costs of stationing 5,000 American soldiers and airmen in the kingdom. The

---

Kuwait, Saudi Arabia, Oman, and Qatar. A continual presence is maintained in the year-round exercise in Kuwait once known as Iris Gold and now renamed Desert Spring. Two command and control elements are housed in the region, one in Bahrain, one in Kuwait. Much more was added in fall 2002 as the United States prepared to go to war against Iraq.

troops were there, after all, to protect the flow of *their* oil to *his* gas pump. The amount of money was not trivial, and Zinni knew the Saudis were feeling the sting of slumping oil prices. He wanted to help the Saudis make their case.

Zinni was just about to sit down, near the end of a long row of chairs, when Prince Sultan spotted him. "My commander!" the prince called out, beckoning the burly general to sit at his right, on the satin couch—the place of honor and partnership. "Come! Come! Please. Sit with me. You are my shield!"

The prince reached out his soft hand, took Zinni's, and held it in his lap for the entire meeting. There would be no distance between them—the senators were bound to see that, as would their influential staffs. If the prince felt he was failing to make his case, he could expect Zinni to jump in for him; they were of one mind.

Zinni thought he might catch some ribbing later about the hand-holding. "I'll never live this down," he thought. Here he was, tough marine, holding hands with a pampered prince, trying to convince a bunch of grumpy American senators from the Appropriations Committee to see the world the Saudi way.

The senators, who in addition to Stevens included Pete Domenici (R-N.M.), Daniel Inouye (D-Hawaii), Kay Bailey Hutchison (R-Tex.), Conrad Burns (R-Mont.), Pat Roberts (R-Kans.), and Bill Frist (R-Tenn.), hadn't taken long to start complaining as they strolled around the opulent Red Sea compound of Saudi Arabia's ambassador to the United States, Prince Bandar bin Sultan. Two swimming pools, acres of marble, and sumptuous silver—why should Americans have to pay many millions to house troops in this country? How could the Saudis plead poverty yet live in such grandeur?

Zinni and the prince made their case to the senators. The Saudis were paying more than their fair share: $200 million to build a new base, $500 million to maintain it, $82 billion in arms purchases over sixteen years. They provided all sorts of assistance-in-kind at the base. They were America's staunchest regional ally and wanted us to stay. This was a long-term relationship, not one to be measured fiscal year by fiscal year.

Gradually, Zinni and the prince won the senators over. Upon returning to Washington the senatorial committee settled for an amendment to the 1998 emergency supplemental appropriations bill that simply urged the president "to encourage other nations who are allies and friends of the United States to contribute to the burden being borne by the United States in preventing the government of Iraq from using Weapons of Mass Destruction."

During his tenure as CinC, Zinni traveled to Saudi Arabia fifteen times. He often attended *majlis*, a sort of town hall where the kingdom's acting ruler, Crown Prince Abdullah, received common people asking for favors and advice, and listened to poetry readings in his honor. Once he had even brought Secretary Cohen along. They had watched as thousands of people gathered in a giant room, settling onto oriental carpets as had been done within Saudi tribes for hundreds of years.

Zinni liked the Arab culture; it reminded him of his Italian heritage. He went falcon hunting and rode a camel into the desert with the royal family. He filled his own home with handwoven rugs and handmade copper water jugs. He even designed a *majlis* sitting room for his house, where guests could lounge on cushions along the wall.

He had also developed a great respect for the Saudis and their monarchy as well as for the leaders of other Arab states in the region. He thought they were doing a good job balancing the demands of closed, traditionalist societies with the tugs and pulls of modernity. Even the monarchies, he judged, practiced a kind of democracy; the *majlis* was one form. "People weren't dissatisfied with the leaders," he said. People weren't leaving the kingdom in droves, they weren't seeking political asylum like they were in lots of other countries in his theater. "I don't know what's in a label if the people support the form of government," he said, defending critics who pushed for quick democratic change. He saw some changes, but they were coming slowly.

Critics in the United States charged that the U.S. military had sold out in supporting some of the world's most undemocratic regimes, the hereditary monarchies of the Middle East. "Democracy" is not listed as a goal on standard U.S. military briefing charts for the region, although it is a U.S. goal in every other part of the world. The treatment of women and the presence of imported slaves were taboo subjects. But Zinni sneered at those he called "non-proliferationists," who opposed

Marine Gen. Anthony Zinni, commander-in-chief, U.S. Central Command, atop
a camel in Saudi Arabian desert. Zinni once took a call from the chairman of the
Joint Chiefs of Staff while riding a camel, using a sixty-pound satellite phone his
aides carried wherever he went.   MSGT. MARK CORMIER

selling U.S. weapons to these states. He described human rights advocates who wanted to put conditions on U.S. military engagement as
people "who want to deliver health care only to people who are completely healthy." Engagement, he believed, would promote a slow crawl
toward democracy.

Zinni penetrated as far inside the monarchy as any foreigner could.
"It's a secret society, and they trusted him," commented Wyche Fowler,
the U.S. ambassador to Saudi Arabia during Zinni's tenure. Too far
inside, some thought.

Zinni's view of Saudi Arabia as a benevolent monarchy clashed
with other information the U.S. government had received, but never
acted on, concerning the royal family. Since 1994, the National Security
Agency had collected electronic intercepts of conversations between
royal family members. Investigative journalist Seymour Hersh had
written a devastating account of the monarchy for *The New Yorker*.[3] The
intercepts depicted a corrupt regime alienated from the country's reli-

gious rank and file and deaf to complaints about extremists operating within its borders.

Fifteen Saudis participated in the September 11 attacks. Young Saudis who had joined violent foreign-based Islamic groups had also led terrorist attacks against U.S. interests in Saudi Arabia, Kenya, Tanzania, and Yemen. Despite its vast oil income, the royal family was failing to create a nation that could sustain and better its population, half of which was under the age of eighteen. Unemployment, government cuts in education and housing, and a sizable national budget deficit plague the kingdom. "The solution is jobs," said Maj. Gen. John Marcello, who served as chief of the U.S.'s Saudi military training mission there. All the while, eavesdroppers quoted by Hersh caught the royals talking of bilking the state and arguing about acceptable graft from government contracts.

Prince Bandar brushed aside talk of corruption in a 2001 interview with PBS's *Frontline*.[4] The royal family spent nearly $400 billion developing the country, he noted. "If you tell me that [in] building this whole country . . . we misused or got corrupted with fifty billion, I'll tell you, 'Yes.' . . . So what? We did not invent corruption."

Zinni himself noticed a rising anti-Americanism all over the Middle East during his trips to the region. "The Arab street," meaning popular opinion, had grown increasingly hostile to the U.S. military presence. Much of this he blamed directly on Washington's unwillingness to craft a durable peace between Israel and the Palestinians. He complained time and again that the United States wasn't doing enough to solve the problem. After all, it had considerable leverage that it had never even threatened to use: an annual aid payment of nearly $3 billion a year to Israel and millions spent on development projects in the West Bank and the Gaza Strip.

By the time Zinni made his final trip to Bahrain, his priorities were aligned more with those of the Arab regimes than with those of his bosses in Washington. The White House and Congress had fixated on Iraq and its quest to make weapons of mass destruction. Gulf potentates, however, fretted more about political change in Iran. They wanted help in sealing their borders from extremist organizations that might destabilize their monarchies. Zinni could feel the tremors of economic change brought about by falling oil revenues, but he didn't see much pressure from Washington to push Gulf states to diversify their economies.

His inability to get Washington to refocus its priorities was a constant source of frustration that left him feeling isolated and estranged. "Washington reacts to Beltway issues," he said one day. "It doesn't mean anything out here." Washington had given him the resources to travel and the instructions to befriend allies in his area of operation. Those allies expected him to help solve their problems.

The blurring of military and political lines vexed some military officers. They weren't merely being asked to implement policy; they were shaping it, too. A growing gap had opened between what the military was being asked to do and the diplomatic tools and coordination it was given to work with. Zinni had a political adviser from the State Department, but little other diplomatic support. He met with the U.S. ambassadors in the region when he traveled, but hardly ever with the Washington-based State Department officials who were charged with managing the larger picture. By law, the State Department had all the responsibility, but Congress had given it few resources lately. State wasn't in a position to implement anything.

Oddly, Zinni saw the Office of the Secretary of Defense as the biggest stumbling block to coordination between the military, the White House, and the Departments of State, Justice, and the Treasury. Those executive-branch kingdoms saw interaction as a threat to their sovereignty. All the CinCs felt the same.

"We are just not set up right for engagement in the world," lamented Admiral Blair. "It's a tangled mess of people trying to do the right thing, but we'd never resolved the lines of authority" between the Pentagon, the State Department, the CIA, and half a dozen other agencies involved in U.S. foreign policy. "There was no unified team when it counted." Good people worked in all of the agencies, Blair believed, but they were limited by their own stovepiped organizations and turf battles.

The CinCs, too, were straitjacketed by bureaucratic politics. The great respect and authority Zinni enjoyed in the Middle East diminished once he stepped on American soil, where civilians maintained the pretense of being in charge. Four-star generals may have been courted by foreign kings, princes, and presidents overseas, but if they hobnobbed with too many elected officials on Capitol Hill, or staffers at the White House and the State Department, off to the woodshed they went. The Pentagon leadership wanted no competing bureau-cratic alliances that might expose policy disagreements within the department.

When the CinCs were in Washington, Chairman Shelton required them to submit an hour-by-hour schedule. This micromanagement was imposed in July 1998, after Shelton heard that General Clark had discussed a limited air strike against Yugoslavia with Deputy National Security Adviser James Steinberg. Both Clark and Steinberg pled inno-cent, but the schedule control became a rule nonetheless.

* * * *

INTERESTINGLY, THE DISPARITIES in treatment that Zinni and his fellow CinCs experienced—nearly complete independence and regal standing abroad, but near powerlessness in the halls of the nation's capital—were the unintended consequence of the Congressional deci-sion to bestow—without even realizing it—increasing power on the CinCs over the last half-century. Congress's original aim had been to curb interservice rivalry and competition, not create a separate foreign-policy track.

As far back as the Spanish-American War in 1898, bickering between Army and Navy commanders had led to paralysis, in this case, over which force would capture the critical Cuban port of Santiago. The Army commander, who finally captured Santiago's mine-infested harbor and port with little Navy assistance, was so angry at his naval counterpart that he then refused to allow the Navy to participate in the signing of surren-der documents.

The Japanese attack on Pearl Harbor gave ultimate testimony to the pettiness of service parochialism. No one below the president had been given authority or responsibility to combine and analyze intelligence collected separately by the Army and the Navy. Had someone been given this responsibility, the U.S. might have noticed the major Japanese mili-tary movement that preceded the devastating attack. In 1941, the Army's commander in Hawaii, Lt. Gen. Walter Short, mistakenly thought the

Navy was conducting long-range air reconnaissance, while the Pacific Fleet commander, Adm. Husband E. Kimmel, wrongfully assumed the Army's radar was operating correctly. There was "a complete failure in Hawaii of effective Army-Navy liaison during the critical period" in the days before the attack, a subsequent Senate investigation found. "Neither commander knew what the other was doing with respect to essential military activities," nor did they bother to ask.[5]

But Pearl Harbor reflected a larger problem: nowhere were the different branches of the military cooperating enough. In the Pacific, service competition led to two separate theaters altogether: Gen. Douglas MacArthur in the Southwest Pacific Area reported to the Army chief of staff, Gen. George Marshall, but Adm. Chester Nimitz in the Pacific Ocean Area reported to the chief of naval operations, Adm. Ernest J. King. Until the National Security Act of 1947 was adopted, the War Department and the Navy Department existed as entirely separate entities. In that year, Congress created the Department of Defense and established three of the five joint regional commands that exist today.*

In 1953, the president and the defense secretary agreed to make the services the administrator for the regional commands. Five years later, Congress passed the Department of Defense Reorganization Act, which strengthened the authority of the secretary of defense and gave increased power over the regional commands to the Joint Chiefs of Staff.† The latter, though, was still a loose collection of service chiefs,

---

* The original commands were the same as the ones in place at the end of the war. The U.S. Forces, European Theater, was created when Gen. Eisenhower's Supreme Headquarters Allied Expeditionary Force was dissolved in July 1945. It became the U.S. European Command on March 15, 1947. The Pacific Command and the Caribbean Command (which eventually became the Southern Command), were formed in 1947 too. An Atlantic Command incorporated parts of South America until October 1993. An Alaska Command existed between 1947 and July 1975, and a commander-in-chief, Far East, lasted from Gen. MacArthur's assumption of that position on January 1, 1947, until July 1, 1957. The Central Command came into being on January 1, 1983. And the newest regional command, the Northern Command, was created on October 1, 2002.

† The act also legally established the Marine Corps and the Naval Air Force. In the president's message to Congress of April 3, 1958, President Dwight Eisenhower set out the reform's major objectives: "Strategic and tactical planning must be completely unified, combat forces organized into unified commands, each equipped

each angling to better his particular branch. The CinCs of the three regional commands spent most of their time on military tasks, with the exception of the dual-hatted European CinC, who was also SACEUR, NATO's top military commander. From the start his hand contained politics and policy along with military matters.

Despite the 1958 reorganization, service rivalries flourished. Many blamed the failure in Vietnam on civilian micromanagement, but the services were culpable, too. They had carved out large missions for their own people, fought their own air wars, and agreed to only limited coordination. Even the evacuation of U.S. troops and citizens from Saigon was split between two commands, one on land and one at sea. Each had a different "H-hour" for the pullout. Colin Powell blamed such service parochialism as one reason why "the Joint Chiefs had never spoken out with a clear voice to prevent the deepening morass in Vietnam."[6]

The breaking point came in 1980 with Operation Eagle Claw, the botched attempt to rescue fifty-three American embassy personnel held hostage in Tehran since November 1979. That operation failed, in part, because each service wanted a part of the action, but none would submit to coordinated training. The Marine Corps, for instance, insisted that its pilots fly the helicopters into Iran from the aircraft carrier USS *Nimitz*, even though Air Force special-warfare helicopter pilots, who had more experience flying long distances would have been better suited to the task. But Gen. David Jones, the chairman of the Joint Chiefs, had had no authority to order Navy admirals to accept the more logical choice, which would have been to use Air Force pilots and special operations helicopters. At dawn on April 24, 1980, in the Iranian desert, the rescue attempt was aborted after three of the mission's eight helicopters became disabled—furious sandstorm had jammed their machinery. As the evacuation got underway, a helicopter flying too close to the ground sliced into a transport plane full of fuel and ammunition. The transport plane burst into flame, killing eight men.

The invasion of Grenada proved that troubles remained. The

---

with the most efficient weapons systems that science can develop, singly led and prepared to fight as one, regardless of Service."

October 25, 1983 assault on that tiny Caribbean island was meant to restore order, protect American medical students, expel armed Cuban construction workers, and restore the democratically elected government. Service rivalries, however, nearly did the mission in. The Army was tasked with taking the southern half of the island, site of the medical schools, the airfield, the capital, and Cuban and Grenadan forces. The Marine Corps was assigned the northern half. But the Army could not communicate with the Navy admiral who commanded the operation from offshore; their radio systems were incompatible. One enterprising Army sergeant simply found a Grenadan pay phone and used his AT&T calling card to reach his office at Fort Bragg, in an attempt to coordinate fire support with naval forces. Another Army soldier from the 82nd Airborne borrowed a UHF radio from Marine Corps headquarters on the USS *Guam* to request fire support and the repositioning of Navy destroyers, but he did not know the secret Navy codes to authenticate his request. Naval aviators flew into combat on the first day "with absolutely no knowledge or coordination" with the unit of Army Rangers that had gone ashore. Paratroopers from the 82nd Airborne Division, on the other hand, moved so rapidly that they arrived only with the packs on their backs—no vehicles and no long-range communications gear.[7]

As a Senate Armed Services Committee report noted in 1985, the organization of the nation's military produced "a heightening of civilian-military disagreement, an isolation of [the office of the Secretary of Defense], a loss of information critical to effective decision-making, and, most importantly, a political weakening of the Secretary of Defense and his staff. The overall result of interservice logrolling [was] a highly undesirable lessening of civilian control of the military."[8]

Chairman Jones sought broad cooperation from the Defense Department to change the system. He created a study group of retired generals, hoping their evaluation would yield the support he needed. He got nowhere. President Reagan's new secretary of defense, Caspar Weinberger, wouldn't go along, for too many questions about the Pentagon's structure and management might undermine congressional appropriations, Jones recalled him arguing. Jones became known as "the hangover" chairman; everyone just waited for him to fade away.

Instead, Jones decided to take his ideas for a reorganization of the military to Capitol Hill. He did so quietly at first, during a closed-to-the-public session of the House Armed Services Committee. But Jones's low-key approach flew right over some members' heads, and little came of his private pleadings. So Jones went public.

All of the service chiefs publicly opposed the Goldwater-Nichols Defense Department Reorganization Bill. With their foot-dragging, it took five years, dozens of hearings, and a 628-page report before it finally became law in 1986—passed by overwhelming margins.*

The Goldwater-Nichols Act gave CinCs the power they have today. That law elevated the chairman of the Joint Chiefs to the role of principal military adviser to the president. It gave CinCs the power to direct and "unify" all weapons use, training, and tactics in their theaters. The "unified combatant commands" it established would be the military's "war-fighting" headquarters. Each CinC had oversight of a geographic region of the world. Each had generals and admirals from all four services reporting directly to him. Interservice rivalry lingers, however.†

In this war-fighting capacity, Gen. Wesley Clark, as CinC in Europe and NATO's military commander, directed the Kosovo air war against Yugoslavia. Zinni launched strikes against Iraq. Adm. Dennis Blair would have led the response had there been any conflict between Taiwan and China, or North and South Korea. Gen. Charles Wilhelm was without an active war plan for possible conflict in his theater, the Southern Command. But he directed, with heavy State Department input, U.S. military action in the anti-drug war in Colombia. He also would manage the response to any implosion in Cuba.

---

* The vote was 383 to 27 in the House and 95 to 0 in the Senate.

† For example, during the 1991 U.S. Air Force–managed air campaign against Iraq the daily "air tasking order," which assigned targets and orchestrated flight paths to the operation's 1,200 strike aircraft, grew to 300 pages, according to former vice chairman of the Joint Chiefs William Owens in his account of the Gulf War (see endnotes to this chapter). But the Navy's secure electronic communication systems were incompatible with the Air Force's, requiring daily shuttle flights to carry paper copies of the orders from headquarters in Riyadh to six aircraft carriers in the Red Sea and the Persian Gulf, from which Navy combat planes took off and landed. This cumbersome process cut the number of attacks the Navy could launch and hampered coordination with Air Force planes.

Goldwater-Nichols also simplified the chain of command. The four-star service chiefs who headed the Army, Navy, Air Force, and Marine Corps now must answer to presidentially appointed civilian service secretaries. But a CinC's line of authority runs directly to the defense secretary and the president—even the chairman of the Joint Chiefs was explicitly removed from the CinC's chain of command. In practice, though, a CinC's relationship with the defense secretary depends greatly on the secretary's personality and on the CinC's relationship with the chairman, for the chairman is in daily contact with the secretary and does not want to compete with the CinCs for attention.

As defense secretary, Dick Cheney met regularly, and often alone, with the CinCs when they were in Washington. He was not shy about giving strong direction, often without consulting the chairman. He abruptly replaced Gen. Frederick Woerner Jr., head of the Southern Command, with Gen. Maxwell Thurman when the administration decided to get more aggressive toward Panamanian dictator Manuel Noriega. "Mad Max" Thurman was the first CinC to use the new war-fighting authority, creating a joint task force that invaded Panama in 1989. Next came Gen. Norman Schwarzkopf, who as head of U.S. Central Command, led forces in the Gulf War from a forward-deployed headquarters in Riyadh, Saudi Arabia.

Les Aspin, the cantankerous former chairman of the House Armed Services Committee, became President Clinton's first defense secretary. No schmoozer, Aspin had barely engaged with the CinCs before he resigned in January 1994. William Perry, who succeeded Aspin, was a graceful but granite-like figure who became a de facto secretary of state, dominating the lackluster Warren Christopher and the rest of the disorganized foreign policy crowd in Clinton's first term. "I need to visit every CinC," Perry told his military assistant, Maj. Gen. Paul Kern, when he first came on board—and he did, at least twice a year. Perry had many gifts: he was a mathematician and the father of Stealth technology, and he often discussed the tiniest operational details with the CinCs. He once sent the commander of U.S. Central Command, Gen. J. H. Binford Peay III, back to the drawing board after he had briefed Perry on his war plan against Iraq. The plan had been in preparation for two years, but Perry found it wholly inadequate. "I intend to make my own mistakes, not other people's," Perry told one close aide.

Perry's reign as defense secretary proved historic. He was the first to see that the military could be used to "shape" the world in peacetime, by using military-to-military relations to seduce countries into the U.S. sphere of ideas and geopolitical interests. This vision became part of the Clinton administration's National Security Strategy, which guides the military's overall operations. The strategy directed the CinCs to "shape, prepare, respond" all over the globe. But the CinCs had no standing orders and little guidance about how to carry out this new mission. They translated those vague instructions into a frenetic travel schedule for themselves and hundreds of deployments dubbed "peacetime engagement activities."

Some CinCs had grown comfortable with their new responsiblities by the time Perry resigned in 1997. His successor, William Cohen, was aloof with the CinCs whom he had hired. Cohen had written several books of fiction and poetry, and he enjoyed surprising audiences with obscure literary references. But most of the CinCs found him uncommunicative, a mystery. He delegated nearly all contact with them to Shalikashvili's successor, Gen. Hugh Shelton. Shelton seemed much less at ease with the CinCs' political-military role than he was with taking care of the troops.

Cohen liked their forward-leaning personalities, but he regarded the CinCs' growing independence and worldview as problematic. He once forbade Zinni to hold on-the-record media interviews. In congressional testimony, Zinni had publicly criticized administration support of a small band of Iraqi exiles who claimed they could bring down Saddam Hussein. "There are congressmen today who want to fund the Iraqi Liberation Act and let some silk-suited, Rolex-wearing guys in London gin up an expedition," Zinni believed. "We'll equip a thousand fighters and arm them with $97 million worth of AK-47s and insert them into Iraq. And what will we have? A Bay of Goats, most likely."

Walter Slocombe, the undersecretary of defense for policy, was testifying with Zinni that day. Afterward Slocombe counseled Zinni privately to be more nuanced when speaking to the Senate.

"Nuanced?" Zinni replied. "I'm a marine!"

Clinton's national security adviser, Samuel Berger, wanted Zinni fired for his comments to the committee. Shelton conveyed Berger's message: "What gives you the right to say that?"

"Well," Zinni chuckled, "for starters, the First Amendment."

As they grew in importance, the CinCs often clashed with the military services too, mainly over personnel. In the Army War Plans Division, room 3E543 of the Pentagon, action officers toil long into the night behind grungy, dark brown doors thick with paint. Those working inside once held glamorous jobs shuffling men and women around the world and making preparations for war; prior to Goldwater-Nichols, an assignment in that office was the most sought after on the Army staff. A host of Army superstars, going back to Dwight Eisenhower, had run the War Plans Division. But no longer. These days the division works, unofficially, for the CinCs. When a CinC requests Army troops and equipment for exercises or operations, the officers in room 3E543 must find them within the worldwide Army inventory. One day, besieged by requests from the field, the officers there renamed themselves, tongue-in-cheek, "The CinCs Requirement Task Force."

Chapter Five

THE INVISIBLE FRONT LINE
OF CENTRAL ASIA

* * * *

MAY 2000. TWO DOZEN MOTORCYCLE POLICE ROARED down the four-lane thoroughfare parting traffic for Gen. Anthony Zinni's motorcade as it zoomed through Tashkent, Uzbekistan's dingy capital. "Get your asses off the road!" screeched a voice from a loudspeaker, warning vehicles and pedestrians.

When the convoy reached Tashkent's tallest hotel, Zinni and his entourage were whisked up its glass elevator to a suite where the CIA station chief was waiting. A portly man wearing a laminated U.S. embassy security badge, the station chief leaned forward on the sofa. He and the U.S. ambassador, Joseph Presel, had a lot to report.

The Afghanistan-based militant Islamic Movement of Uzbekistan (IMU) was gaining momentum. Since 1993 it had sought to install an Islamic regime in Uzbekistan. Thousands of Muslim fighters from Afghanistan and Chechnya had joined the IMU. They were hiding in the Fergana Valley, a pitifully poor but fertile region straddling the border with neighboring Kyrgyzstan.

Uzbekistan's president, Islam Karimov, a former Communist Party boss, was only making matters worse. His KGB-trained security forces had jailed thousands of Muslim believers.[*] Many languished for years

---

[*] The KGB was the state security service of the Soviet Union. Its sphere of operations encompassed both domestic security and international espionage.

without trial in a new prison where electric shocks, burnings, beatings, rape, and tuberculosis were rampant.

"Karimov's tactics, which are to arrest everyone with a beard, are providing additional converts to the IMU," reported Presel, a career diplomat. The Uzbek president had banned opposition political parties. "Far more insidious is the downturn in the economy. Half the population is under 18, and Islam is seductive to them. They can go to Pakistan for training." Karimov wasn't doing a thing to reform the economy, to give people hope.[1]

Kidnappings, the CIA chief warned, were the IMUs major source of funds. They got $5 million to release some Japanese geologists, and $500,000 for a Kyrgyz general. "If you're a guy looking for a jihad, the IMU is the best jihad going," he continued. "This thing will wash to the Caucasus, the Balkans, Eastern Europe and will come home to the United States to roost."

The three Americans contemplated how they could make their offices back home pay attention. "We in the West aren't thinking very hard about this," Presel lamented. The other two nodded.

To muddy things even further, U.S. policy toward the region was completely fragmented. A gaggle of entities—the Pentagon, Central Command, the U.S. embassy, economic aid agencies, Justice Department units, the Customs Bureau, the Drug Enforcement Agency, the Federal Bureau of Investigation, and CIA—squabbled over money, turf, and authority. "The system is badly broken," Zinni complained. "We use chewing gum and bailing wire to keep it together."

Zinni wanted something Washington was resisting—more contact with Pakistan, Uzbekistan, and the other "stans" of Central Asia.[*] The White House and the State Department, however, publicly insisted on a near freeze in relations. Pakistan was being punished for pursuing its nuclear-weapons program and because its self-appointed president, Gen. Pervez Musharraf, had taken power in a coup in October 1999. Yet by most measures, Pakistan's people had more freedom of speech, press, and religion than did their counterparts in any of the Persian Gulf countries coddled by the United States.

* Afghanistan, Kazakhstan, Kyrgyzstan, Tajikistan, and Turkmenistan.

The chill imposed on U.S. relations with Uzbekistan had to do with its government, a Soviet-style dictatorship that badly mistreated its own citizens. The United States wanted to prod Uzbekistan in the right direction with its words. But its deeds contradicted those words. For behind the scenes, the CIA's paramilitary teams were training and equipping nearly a dozen anti-Taliban warlords and their fighters, some of them Uzbeks, hoping they might someday move against Afghanistan and Osama bin Laden. The CIA used Uzbekistan to launch surveillance equipment that helped them keep track of bin Laden.[2]

Of all these warlords, none was more ferocious then Gen. Abdurrashid Dostum, an ethnic Uzbek factional leader renowned for his ruthlessness and Machiavellian alliance shifts while running an anti-Taliban fiefdom in northern Afghanistan. The CIA knew Dostum well. He had fought in the communist-backed Afghan army during the Soviet occupation from 1979 to 1989. He had then become an enforcer for President Mohammed Najibullah, the Soviet-installed communist ruler. In 1992, as the anti-communist, U.S.-backed, Islamic mujahideen were on the verge of toppling Najibullah's government, Dostum switched sides and helped them capture Kabul. Soon after, he switched sides again and fought the mujahideen in factional warfare that reduced Kabul to rubble.

In his stronghold, the northern city of Mazar-e-Sharif, the reputed hard-drinking atheist set up an independent municipality. He started an airline to smuggle goods in from the United Arab Emirates; he collected taxes from local truck drivers and set up health care and education systems. When the Taliban captured Mazar-e-Sharif in 1997, Dostum fled to Turkey.[3] He would return to Afghanistan in April 2001 to partner again with former rivals in the Northern Alliance. By October, with the help of CIA equipment and a game plan crafted at CIA headquarters in Langley, Va., and the Central Command's in Tampa, Dostum began his final rout of Taliban forces.

The CIA and its covert paramilitary operators were also helping Karimov's National Security Service (NSS) track down and apprehend bin Laden's supporters in the IMU.*

---

* All of this changed after September 11. Uzbekistan quickly emerged as a willing partner in Washington's fight against terrorism, and the Bush administration

Relations between the CIA's clandestine service and the Uzbek NSS went back to February 1999, when six bombs had detonated nearly simultaneously in Tashkent. Investigators believed one of bin Laden's top lieutenants, Uzbek-born Juma Namangani, the IMU's founder, was trying to kill Karimov. To help the Uzbeks find Namangani, the CIA had given the NSS satellite radios and listening devices. But the Uzbeks were still having trouble intercepting the IMU's calls. When they did, the defense forces and the NSS couldn't coordinate fast enough to catch anyone.

To counter IMU attacks, the Central Command—with Ambassador Presel's support—had given Uzbek special forces night-vision goggles, 150 radios, 16 old Humvee vehicles, and $20,000 worth of cold-weather gear.

In 1997, Army Special Forces had landed in Central Asia to provide training. The Americans climbed mountains with elite units from Kyrgyzstan, Kazakhstan, and Uzbekistan. They worked on field tactics, airborne assault operations, and counterinsurgency training in Uzbekistan. They had come back every year since, but neither Presel nor Zinni thought it was really enough to enable the Uzbek soldiers to effectively counter the insurgents.

All this activity cost money, of course, and Zinni's team was running out of it. To fund exercises, they drew on a pot of Cooperative Threat Reduction program funds intended for use in reducing the nuclear weapons arsenals bequeathed to Central Asian states by the Soviet Union. Central Command bought some equipment with its own

---

began treating it like the region's big dog. More than 1,000 troops from the Army's 10th Mountain Division set up camp in the California-sized nation of 25 million people. Special Operations Forces from the Army, the Navy and the Air Force joined them. Congress and President Bush quickly ponied up, first with a $25 million weapons grant then with a $100 million payoff, about $47 million of which went toward military training, equipment, and education, initiatives Zinni had been pushing for years.

"America will have a continuing interest and presence in Central Asia of a kind that we could not have dreamed of before," Secretary of State Colin Powell told the House International Relations Committee in early February 2002. Soon came a base in Kyrgyzstan for 3,000 American airmen, other bases in Uzbekistan, Pakistan, and Tajikistan, and two aircraft carriers afloat in the northern Arabian Sea. These initiatives placed an American boot print in Russia's and China's backyard.

operations and maintenance funds. Zinni was continually looking for other ways to pay for exercises.

The huge imbalance between the diplomatic civilian resources being offered by the United States and the largesse of the U.S. military and CIA worried every U.S. ambassador in the region. Adding covert military and security programs would only tip the balance further, the ambassadors believed. How could the leaders of these countries take U.S. pressure toward democracy seriously if most of Washington's handouts were for surveillance, weapons, and counter-terrorism training?

It was the same story all across Central Asia. Pakistan, Kyrgyzstan, Kazakhstan, Turkmenistan—these were Zinni's invisible battlefields, encircling the pariah Afghanistan. His soldiers moved around in the region attracting little notice. Washington thought of this region as the periphery of U.S. interests; Zinni considered it the front line.

Zinni had come to Central Asia five times during his CinC tenure. "I wish I could get someone from the State Department to pay this much attention," quipped Presel. The general's staff made dozens of trips here during his tenure as CinC. So did the one-star generals under Zinni's command. His persistence convinced the directors of the CIA and the FBI, and Secretary of State Madeleine Albright, to visit Central Asia in 2000. The agencies had put together a working group on the Central Asian-problem of border security; monitoring the porous, disputed border was key to stopping radical Islamic fighters and teachers who easily slipped across it. But Zinni couldn't get his civilian boss to come out. "Too busy," Cohen's people told him. Zinni always felt like he was outside, tapping on the window, waving his arms, trying to get Washington's attention.

Diplomats and humanitarian organizations for years have wrestled with popular and political indifference to their priorities. They have always confronted the limits of America's attention span and its willingness to engage overseas. Now the CinCs felt those limits too. Part of the reason might have been Central Asia's alphabet soup problem. As with the Balkans, Americans couldn't follow the crisis, the jumble of foreign names, much less see its connection to their problems.

"We are the sole remaining superpower; everybody is turning to us," Zinni said one afternoon in his aircraft high over the Middle East. "Everybody thinks we're going to help in the reordering of the world. But it's all self-ordering now, and when you self-order, it's like a roll of the dice. We are not doing enough to direct or structure the new order." He and the other CinCs did see a temporary opening—a sort of "interwar" period between the Cold War's end and whatever was next, possibly World War III. This notion propelled them on their lengthy journeys around the world. They wanted to shape the new world order, to avert the chaos and subversion that might well follow if they did not. "I'm a big believer in chaos theory," Zinni proclaimed. "Everything's either self-ordered, or you can help order it. After World War I no one was paying attention. No one listened to Woodrow Wilson and the League of Nations. We withdrew and went home and we ended up with a disaster: we had to fight World War II. We helped order the post–World War II environment, especially in Western Europe and the Far East. Then, when the communists did fall, we weren't ready. We have not been prepared for the last ten years."

His failure to gain attention for Central Asia and to bring Washington around to his world-view was an alien problem for Zinni. His military career had always allowed him to feel strong and powerful. But now, at the pinnacle of the Pentagon's hierarchy, he sometimes felt weak and inconsequential. And so he searched for an easy concept to get Washington's attention, a gimmick to crystallize the seriousness of the problem. "We should call these the front-line states," he told Presel and the CIA station chief as they ended their conversation in the Tashkent hotel suite. The original "front-line states" had been those surrounding South Africa; they were both harassed by South Africa and united in upholding trade sanctions to pressure Pretoria to change its apartheid system of government. In the same way, Zinni hoped to encircle and cut off support for Afghanistan's Taliban regime. Presel and the CIA thought it was as good an idea as any.

"Okay," Zinni said, wrapping up the meeting, "what's the message for this trip?"

"We're here. We care. There are limits to what we can do," Presel replied, ticking off talking points that wouldn't raise expectations too high. "The military is one factor in it. We only nag people we care about."

"Got it," Zinni said.

* * * *

THE LANDS OF Central Asia have long been in thrall to their geography, lying as they do along the great Silk Road linking China to the Mediterranean. Conquered and reconquered by Islam, the Mongols, imperial Russia, and Great Britain, in the 19th century Central Asia was the backdrop for the "Great Game" competition for political domination between Britain and Russia. As colonies of the Soviet Union, the states framed by the Alai Mountains and the Aral Sea were forced to adopt atheism and accept the KGB and large militaries.

But these interlopers lost, over time, to ethnicity and culture, which trumped political borders and military power. Central Asia's patchwork of tribal, religious, and ethnic loyalties survived even Soviet domination and extends today into China, Turkey, Iran, and Afghanistan.[*]

The end of the Cold War left Central Asia with the poorest lands of the former Soviet Union. Without Moscow's subsidies, economic production plummeted. Infant mortality and rural illiteracy rose. The newly independent governments clung to old-style, centralized security controls, which made economic innovation and political reform nearly impossible. Moscow, meanwhile, narrowed its interests in the region to stanching the rise of militant Islam on Russia's southern borders.

Early on, Zinni realized that Central Asia, relegated to the periphery, was descending into chaos. He approached it gingerly, not wanting to be seen by either Central Asians or Russia as a promoter of a second Great Game, one in which the United States dueled with Russia or China. "There's an apprehension about what the United States might want out of this," he confessed. "Each of these countries is just now starting to get its own identity. . . . These are all authoritarian one-man shows."

In Samarqand, the old capital of Uzbekistan, Zinni had stood at the grave of Tamerlane, the bloodthirsty Turkmen Mongol who had

---

[*] The authors of the Trilateral Commission report described the new Central Asia succinctly: "There are large numbers of Uzbeks and Tajiks and Kyrgyz in China. There are more Azeris in Iran than in Azerbaijan. The Kazakhs, Kyrgyz, Turkmen, and Uzbeks (and Azeris) are Turkic peoples; the Tajiks speak an Indo-European language related to [the] Farsi spoken in Iran."

CENTRAL ASIA

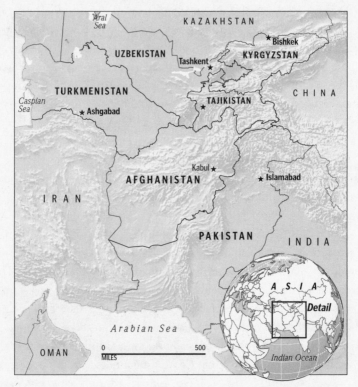

BY RICHARD FURNO– © 2002, THE *WASHINGTON POST.* REPRINTED WITH PERMISSION.

conquered and plundered in the 1300s, building an empire that stretched from India to the Mediterranean Sea. Addressing a group of Central Asian officers, Zinni was asked straight out, Was the United States trying to replace Russia as the region's hegemon? What, exactly, were his intentions?

"I am not a Tamerlane," Zinni replied. "I didn't come here to conquer you."

After the Central Asian nations became independent in 1991, Washington had debated what its policy toward the region should be. Should it leave Central Asia in the Russian sphere of influence or pull it toward the West with painful economic and political reforms? An activist approach would require economic assistance and a strategy.

Zinni and other military officers took the long view: there was too much at stake to leave the region alone. Kazakhstan's oil reserves rival those of the North Sea. Turkmenistan sits on the world's fifth-largest natural-gas deposits. Azerbaijan had just signed the "deal of the century"—an extraordinary extraction agreement with an Anglo-American oil consortium. The pipeline routes for the export of oil were not yet set, but Zinni figured that the U.S. military might someday be asked to ensure an uninterrupted flow of Central Asian oil to the world market, just as it had done in the Persian Gulf.

The other pipeline that worried Zinni was the one that exported terrorism. Zinni wanted to pull agencies of the U.S. government together to develop a coordinated approach to the terrorism problem. But that job belonged to the State Department, which hadn't done nearly enough. As a result, when Zinni flew out to the region, he found himself making excuses for the superpower he represented.

During his visit in 2000 with the Uzbek minister of defense, Gen. Lt. Yuri Agzamov, Zinni had nothing more to offer him as a present than a single sleeping bag, hastily borrowed from the U.S. defense attaché. It was a symbolic placeholder for $20,000 worth of used and surplus military equipment he had assigned a two-star general to wrest out of the Defense Department's paperwork maze.

"Thank you for paying attention to our country," Agzamov told Zinni across a table set with a tea service, and piles of pistachios, apricots, and walnuts.

"We're not getting the other agencies of our government interested in supporting some of the programs in the region . . ." Zinni began.

"Yes, but we have good friends at the special forces," Agzamov continued. "We want more radios, some command and control equipment, computer simulation for combat affairs . . ."

"I ask for your patience," Zinni replied. "The special forces can respond quickly but not everyone can. It's our job to push our own bureaucracy."

"The heads of these terrorist organizations are like Kamikazes," the

Uzbek general pressed. "It's not hard for the leaders to cross borders. Afghanistan is still the center of terrorism. They are coming from Saudi Arabia, Chechnya. Everything is connected."

"What I tell people in the U.S. is that you are on the front-line of this war," Zinni assured him, trying out his new marketing concept. "But this is a war we must all fight. We are beginning to see in the U.S. that this is everybody's problem. We must help solve the problems in Pakistan, Afghanistan, and elsewhere. . . . This is an immediate problem. You can't take your time. . . . One of the Central Command's obligations is to tell this story as many times as we can."

The competing story in Washington was that the United States had no business cuddling up with regimes that could not distinguish between violent Islamic groups and simple political opponents. Each of the countries Zinni visited on this trip—Kyrgyzstan, Kazakhstan, Uzbekistan, and Turkmenistan—featured repressive security forces that engaged in torture, illegal imprisonment, and sham justice to eliminate opposition parties. The State Department's human rights reports singled out Uzbekistan as "an authoritarian state with limited civil rights." Kyrgyzstan's elections, it reported, were "marred by serious irregularities" and its "human rights record [had] worsened." In Kazakhstan, "the deteriorating human rights situation mirrored the country's deepening economic and demographic crisis," the 2000 report stated. That country's former president, Nursultan Nazarbayev, acknowledged widespread police torture of detainees, with methods that would "surprise the most out-and-out sadist," he admitted. Police seared suspects' bodies with hot irons or froze them with streams of icy water. [4]

Human Rights Watch had investigators in each country. They declared that Turkmenistan's campaign to "suppress even the most benign political expression" amounted to "unrelenting repression against its own citizens . . . a campaign to control or stop the activities of all civil and religious associations as well as individual dissidents." [5] "Rubbing shoulders with people in Turkmenistan is an absurd excuse to maintain military contact," said Kenneth Roth, executive director of Human Rights Watch. "We should increase the cost to Turkmenistan's ruler for not adhering to a basic rule of law. We should not reward [him] with military contact." Economic assistance, help in transforming the political system, offering inducements to modernize—those are the areas on which to concentrate first, Roth asserted. Many foreign policy experts agreed.*

Zinni believed that the worst policy would be to let failing states fail. Rogue states such as Afghanistan, Iraq, and Libya were the hardest to control and predict. Rather than shun them, he thought, the United States should somehow help them rejoin the community of nations. "We shouldn't isolate these countries, they're too important. There are too many problems in that region with Afghanistan and Iran and we don't need Pakistan becoming a fundamentalist state or a rogue state or being taken over by a bunch of hard-liners."

Ditto for Yemen. Zinni had sent special operations teams there to figure out that Wild West country. Yemen, a "sort of" democracy, had held the first open parliamentary elections in a region dominated by tribal monarchies. "Yemen, Somalia, and Sudan were problems for us because they were sanctuaries for terrorists," Zinni said. "They had terrorists who transited through the area, and they had trouble internally handling tribes that don't respond to central government." But after a couple of special operations training missions, the U.S. ambassador to Yemen, Barbara Boudine, had cut off Zinni's outreach programs, allowing only a de-mining school near the port of Aden. Zinni and his successor, Gen. Tommy Franks, had been working on "intelligence exchange," regular visits by his "J2" (his intelligence chief), when the USS *Cole* was attacked. After the attack, relations were frozen—a bad idea in Zinni's opinion. After September 11, Washington's attitude toward Yemen, as elsewhere, flip-flopped. Bush eagerly offered Yemen $400 million in U.S. aid, special operations training, and intelligence support.

Pakistan presented a parallel case of isolating a country near the brink of failure. Pakistan's military and its intelligence service, the

---

* For example: "The threat of violence by militant Islamic movements in Central Asia is real, but has been greatly exaggerated by regional governments and by other countries including Russia, China and the United States," wrote Gareth Evans, president of the International Crisis Group, a moderately liberal nongovernmental organization, in a March 1, 2001, letter accompanying his report on Central Asia. "The risk is that government crackdowns will worsen the situation: the answer is not more repression but more freedom and democracy."

Inter-Services Intelligence Agency (ISI), had supported the Taliban, helping it defeat the Northern Alliance.[*] In the CIA's opinion the ISI had been completely compromised and worked closely with the Taliban and bin Laden. But Zinni saw Pakistan's leader, Gen. Musharraf, as a force pressuring the Taliban toward moderation. Acting on that opinion, the Pentagon, led by Zinni and the vice chairman of the Joint Chiefs, Gen. Joseph Ralston, had single-handedly kept the door open to Pakistan.

Pakistan had been the single most important ally in the U.S. proxy war against the ten-year Soviet occupation of Afghanistan in the 1980s. Only a year after the Soviet withdrawal, however, Congress and the White House had imposed sanctions required by the Pressler Amendment. Passed in 1985 but waived by the president every year until 1990, this amendment punished Pakistan for continuing to develop nuclear weapons and for selling missile components to China. The law also froze the delivery of fighter jets already purchased by Pakistan and, eventually, cut off nearly all other U.S. military contact.

Such sudden hostility did not sit well with some U.S. military officers. They had come to know, admire, and depend on Pakistan during the Soviet occupation of Afghanistan. Some bonds just couldn't be blown away by the changing winds of Washington politics. So the Pentagon found a quiet way to maintain relations. At the behest of the Special Operations Command, a 1991 law had sailed through Congress almost unnoticed. The law, Section 2011 of Title 10, allowed special

[*] Much good reporting has been done on this subject. Jane's Sentinel Security Assessment of Afghanistan, posted on the web on September 25, 2001, (at www.janes.com) says Pakistan provided training, weapons, ammunition, and logistical and financial support to the Taliban in the mid-1990s. Pakistani officers reportedly became combat advisers for the Taliban and Pakistani youth were recruited by the ISI to join the Taliban ranks. Pakistan recognized the Taliban government in May 1997. Pakistani military personnel maintained and operated Taliban aircraft and tanks. Countries in the region assert that 1,500 Pakistani troops aided in the Taliban's victories against the Northern Alliance in 1998. The Northern Alliance alleged that between 5,000 and 10,000 Pakistanis fought with the Taliban in the July–August 1999 offensive. When Gen. Musharraf took power in Pakistan, he pressured the Taliban to moderate their policies. He tried to close the border, restricted trade, and brought Iran into a political dialogue to help resolve the Afghan problem.

operations troops to train in most foreign countries if the Pentagon certified that the training mainly benefited U.S. forces. This loophole offered a way to evade Congressional sanctions on Pakistan, Indonesia, and Colombia. By 1993, Special Operations Command had essentially created its own, separate foreign-policy track. In fact, on the very day in late May 1998 when President Clinton urgently warned Pakistani leaders that their proposed nuclear-weapons test would bring world condemnation, U.S. officers at the Pakistani army general headquarters in Rawalpindi were polishing plans to mingle 60 American and 200 Pakistani special operations soldiers during exercises outside Peshawar, near the border with Afghanistan.

Zinni's respect for the Pakistani military dated back to his 1992 stint in Mogadishu as commander of the humanitarian relief mission in Somalia. The Pakistanis, ill equipped and poorly trained for peacekeeping, were to secure the Mogadishu airport and seaport. But from the time of their arrival, they were pushed around by marauding Somali gangs. Snipers shot at their tents. They lost control of the port. Twenty-four Pakistani peacekeepers died in a single ambush on June 4, 1993, after which clansmen disemboweled and skinned some of the Pakistani dead in an attempt to terrorize the entire operation.[6] Though reluctant to continue the mission, the Pakistani government stayed the course. Pakistani troops roamed the worst Mogadishu streets, using their American-made M-48 tanks to protect American soldiers riding in lighter vehicles through close-quarters gun battles more intense than anything in the Gulf War.

Zinni had returned to Somalia several times to troubleshoot after the humanitarian relief mission ended. In October 1993, he was there again after Somali fighters shot down two U.S. Black Hawk helicopters and killed eighteen Americans. Zinni went there to negotiate the release of a captured chief warrant officer, Michael Durant, and to put a cease-fire in place.

In March 1995, Pakistani soldiers were the rear guard for departing Americans. Zinni orchestrated the tricky withdrawal of forces beforehand, at Pakistani army headquarters in Rawalpindi with the then-chief of army staff, Gen. Adbul Waheed. Waheed's position was the most powerful in all of Pakistan—even more powerful than the prime minister. The two generals amicably worked out the most minute details for the pullout, including plotting tides for the exit of the last brigade. Zinni remembers it as the most complicated tactical operation of his career. Relieving and replacing troops under fire was bad enough; doing it with different nations' armies, each with unique tactics and procedures, was nearly impossible. The Pakistani troops performed excellently, and his respect for them grew.

Three years later, when the Pakistanis threatened to test a nuclear device, President Clinton sent Zinni with Deputy Secretary of State Strobe Talbott to Islamabad to talk Gen. Waheed out of the idea. They didn't succeed. Pakistan tested anyway. When Musharraf became Pakistan's chief of army staff, Zinni pressed Washington and reluctant U.S. diplomats in Islamabad for permission to get to know him. After their first meeting, "they just clicked," Zinni said. He found Musharraf "very pro-Western in his outlook": He had a dog. He wore Western-style clothes. He spoke eloquently about democracy. They both agreed that whatever happened between their two countries, they would try to maintain their relationship "even on the thin thread of our personal friendship," Zinni recalled. Zinni and his staff often branded some counterpart a "good guy," code for acceptance into the brotherhood. To him, Musharraf was a "good guy."

When the Pakistani army staged a coup in October 1999, the Clinton administration sent a stern protest to Musharraf, who had appointed himself head of state, or "chief executive." A nuclear-capable, unstable nation had plunged into fresh turmoil and Washington waited anxiously: How would Musharraf react? When the general finally responded to the U.S. message, he placed his call not to President Clinton, Secretary of State Madeleine Albright, Defense Secretary Cohen, or the U.S. ambassador in Islamabad. Instead Musharraf telephoned Zinni, who happened at the time to be sitting with Cohen at an airfield ceremony in Egypt.

"Can I answer it?" Zinni asked the defense secretary as his communicator held out the phone.

"Yes," Cohen replied, "just don't commit to anything."

"Tony," Musharraf began, "I want to tell you what I'm doing. . . ."

Zinni believed the Pakistani general when he told him he had no other choice, that democracy had become a sham. "I want democracy in substance and not just labels. . . . I don't want you to think I did something that wasn't motivated by the best intentions for Pakistan," Musharraf said.

Zinni told Musharraf he was "sorry to hear it had to come to this. . . . I have all the respect for you in the world. I'm sure you'll do the right thing."

Musharraf broke many of his promises. He banned political parties from meeting and increased the army's role in government, well beyond the normal purview of national defense. Eighteen months after he installed himself as chief executive, Musharraf got rid of the figurehead president and gave himself that title, too.

Such connections as Zinni had with Musharraf were valuable, even unique in the region, but they played poorly in Washington, which viewed them not as opportunities but as threats. Zinni and the other CinCs got cold-shouldered when their relationships with foreign leaders grew deeper than the diplomatic ties. The Clinton administration avoided using Zinni to deepen relations with Pakistan, to push for more control over the terrorist cells that Musharraf allowed to train and organize within Pakistan's borders. They left those efforts largely to the CIA.[*]

Right up until his retirement in the summer of 2000, Zinni pushed the administration to open a public, diplomatic door to Musharraf. He thought it unwise to have a covert relationship and nothing else. Besides, he believed, Musharraf was ready for more. "The center

---

[*] Bin Laden became a major focus of U.S. military and intelligence efforts in 1998 after he issued a *fatwa*, or Islamic religious decree, urging believers to kill Americans. In August of that year two truck bombs killed 220 people and injured more than 4,000 at the U.S. embassies in Kenya and Tanzania. Bin Laden emerged as the orchestrator of these attacks. Shortly afterward, President Clinton signed a highly secret presidential "finding" authorizing the CIA to use covert means to disrupt and preempt bin Laden's operations, according to the *Washington Post*'s investigative journalist Bob Woodward. In an October 3, 2001, story Woodward reported that in 1999 the CIA had secretly trained and equipped some sixty Pakistani commandos to enter Afghanistan to capture or kill bin Laden. That operation, arranged with the help of Pakistani's then-prime minister, Nawaz Sharif, was aborted in October 1999 when Sharif was overthrown in Musharraf's coup.

of gravity for terrorist activity is Afghanistan," Zinni told President Clinton at a CinCs' conference in February 2000. "Pakistan is the key to this. We've got to keep Pakistan a democratic state, and right now Musharraf is all they have and you can't let him fail, in my view." He had urged Clinton to visit Pakistan during his scheduled trip to India later that year, and Clinton took his advice.

"I know I make them nervous," Zinni said in 2000 of his civilian colleagues. "But I think U.S. policy toward Pakistan is wrong. . . . If Musharraf fails, hard-liners could take over, or fundamentalists, or chaos. . . . We can't let Musharraf fail. . . . We ought to stay engaged."

He felt the same way about all of Central Asia and mused about it often. "No one ever asked them what they wanted," he said of the U.S. approach to the Central Asians. "They are unsure what to make of the relationship with the United States. . . . What I regret is, I should have been more vocal and forced the issue some. I tried to pick my fights; I thought the system would take care of it. I didn't realize how difficult this was."

Zinni never could find a way to provoke a serious policy discussion without getting himself in hot water with the defense secretary, who was, after all, his boss. Going behind Cohen's back to Capitol Hill was not an option. He and General Wilhelm had tried to get Shelton to allow Congress and the State Department more influence over the CinCs' overseas "engagement programs." Zinni and Wilhelm wanted to share their classified Theater Engagement Plans, the blueprints for these programs, with Congress. No, Vice Chairman Ralston had told him at an annual CinCs meeting in 2000. If Congress can identify the money, then they can take it away; the most sensitive programs would become vulnerable to politics. "You don't want to do that, guys," Ralston argued at the CinCs meeting. "Just leave it in a big pot here at [the Defense Department] so it doesn't get scrutinized as it goes through Congress." The officials at Defense would work it out among themselves each year.

The CinCs entire budget for new missions would remain classified. Likewise, the four-inch-thick Theater Engagement Plans were stamped "secret" too. The Joint Staff intentionally kept it out of Congress's hand.

At a minimum, CinCs "ought not be off on our own," Zinni would say later. "You have to be radical, give the CinCs more authority. You have a lot of "suits" running around who wouldn't want to give CinCs political authority. But we already have it."

★ ★ ★ ★

THE MOTORCADE INTO dusty Bishkek, Kyrgyzstan, a dozen used sedans and vans, bounced over the potholed roads at eighty miles per hour, past green mountain ranges, grazing goats, and barefoot shepherds. The city looked like a throwback to the 1950s.

Central Asia's poorest country, Kyrgyzstan kept its ties to Russia strong in 2000. And although some Soviet-era factories still produced conventional missiles, Kyrgyzstan was also willing to expand its relations with the United States—if the Pentagon came through with enough military equipment and training.

Zinni's first chore on this visit was to listen patiently as the defense minister, Lt. Gen. Esen Topoyez, asked for U.S. equipment and joint exercises and then complimented Zinni on the fact that the relationship with the United States "had acquired a continual and steady nature." Zinni had worked hard to establish that steadiness. His staff had visited the country more than twenty times.

At Kyrgyzstan's request, which was backed by the Army Special Forces commanders who loved to work in such rugged terrain, Special Forces teams were sent to train 300 Kyrgyz soldiers in counterterrorism in 2000. A year earlier, some 1,000 armed IMU militants from neighboring Tajikistan swept into Kyrgyzstan on their way to mounting attacks in Uzbekistan. The Kyrgyz military was unable to apprehend them as Uzbekistan and other countries in the region demanded. Kyrgyzstan's military had suffered casualties in the attempt.

To demonstrate the extent of U.S.-Kyrgyz cooperation, Zinni was escorted to the Koi-Tash Army Base, where a team of U.S. Army Special Forces troops had spent four months training their Kyrgyz counterparts in "peacekeeping" methods, a euphemism for lethal tactics. As rain poured down, Zinni watched a "peacekeeping" exercise from under a dripping umbrella. The scenario called for foreign soldiers to be checking identification at a mock refugee checkpoint when a riot breaks out. Suddenly, mock "terrorists" popped up from foxholes. The "peacekeepers" promptly shot them dead, searched them for identification, and left the bodies out in the open.

Seizing a foothold in this remote corner of the world required unusual patience. During a day of tours and formal meetings on his next stop, in Kazakhstan, Zinni was ushered into a military-school auditorium and seated before a television screen. For fifteen minutes a video showed a female singer, clad in a leopard-skin bikini, singing the Kazakh national epic poem in sacred tribute to Kazakh soldiers. The music so thrilled the ranking Kazakh officer, he leapt up from his seat, closely followed by the U.S. defense attaché, a female colonel. Both of them grabbed the microphone and sang along, then offered it to Zinni, who politely declined.

Finally, Zinni moved on to Turkmenistan. Ashgabat, the capital, looked like the land of Oz. Its streets were lined with oversized, skyscraping monuments to President (for Life) Saparmurat Niyazov. Giant portraits of Niyazov hung from dozens of white marble office buildings. Not a soul could be seen on the long streets and walkways leading up to the Emerald City–like presidential abode. All locals were kept at a distance by guards ringing the perimeter streets. Turkmenistan has a simple form of government: no legal system, no unhindered press, no political parties. Only "Turkmenbashi, father of all Turkmen," as Niyazov likes to be called.

And oil. Rich from the country's huge natural gas and oil reserves, Niyazov's government was throwing up dozens of gigantic stone museums and starkly modern hotels amid the plains and mountains within view of Ashgabat.

Niyazov called his foreign policy "positive neutrality," otherwise known as playing hard to get.

Zinni tried to warm up his hosts, but they were too dour and too uncommitted. He talked about friendship, about military professionalism, about his desire for military exchanges. "Are there any other areas you'd like to discuss?" he asked the defense minister five minutes into their meeting. No one spoke up.

"We hope you will come back after you retire," the minister finally responded.

"What about pipeline security?" Zinni tried.

"Well, this will be addressed as soon as the pipeline is arranged," the defense minister answered dismissively.

* * * *

AFTER FOURTEEN DAYS away from Central Command headquarters, Zinni and his team headed home. It had been exhausting for the aides, communicators, security guards, and executive officers. They nodded off on the airplane. But the general was anything but relaxed. Unsolved diplomatic problems weighed on his mind. As he lay back on a red headrest embroidered with four white stars, his thoughts turned to the region's strategic importance—and to his own legacy as he faced retirement.

"There's a fundamental question that goes beyond the military," he began. "It's, What is our obligation to the world? We preach about values, democracy, human rights, but we haven't convinced the American people to pony up. If the American people say our economy is good, our lives are good, then they would accept, I believe, that that's the right thing to do. But there's no leadership that steps up and says, 'This is the right thing to do.' In fact, support for this kind of thing becomes fodder for your political opponents in Congress.

"That's the basic problem. It's not whether the Washington bureaucracy can be adjusted. There's got to be political will and support for these things. We should believe that a stable world is a better place for us. If you had a policy and a forward-leaning engagement strategy, the U.S. would make a much greater difference in the world. It would intervene earlier and pick its fights better."

Several hours later, after his crew had refreshed itself with a couple of games of spades, dinner, and more spades, Zinni returned to the unanswered questions that would dog him forever: "I now realize I should have done more to pull together a program on Central Asia. I've been thinking about asking Cohen for a meeting." And still later, he looked down at his forearms, balled up his fists, and tightened his arm muscles. "I should have pushed harder."

MacDill Air Force Base was humid, almost steaming, when Zinni's plane touched down on May 18, 2000. What once felt like a luxury—a private plane with private flight attendants and an entertaining view of

Gen. Anthony Zinni's entourage departing Astana, Kazakhstan.
In the foreground is an aide, Lt. Col. Neil McElhannon.
Zinni is approaching the stairs. DANA PRIEST

midair refueling—had become cramped, stuffy, and noisy after forty-four hours in the air.

Zinni popped out first and hopped into his chauffeured sedan. Maj. Jeffrey Haynes, his aide, was close behind, carrying the boss's uniform bag. They sped off. Ninety-odd pieces of luggage were passed hand over hand down the airplane ramp. Not even off the tarmac, the staff began planning Zinni's next trip. In a few days, he would be off to Kenya, Yemen, and the Seychelles. For that trip, he would be in the air longer than he would be awake on the ground. But he wanted to fit it in: the trip would be his last before he passed his CinCdom to Tommy Franks.

Lt. Col. Manuel Chaves, the trip coordinator, and one of Zinni's security aides were already refining the daily trip schedule as they bounced along in a van full of luggage. "Sir, on the trip to Kenya, do you know if the CinC is going straight to his room after we land?" the security aide wanted to know.

"Oh, I doubt it," said Chaves, grinning.

THE
SPECIAL FORCES

Chapter Six

INSIDE THE WIRE WITH
SPECIAL FORCES

★ ★ ★ ★

IN ADDITION TO USING THEIR OWN DIPLOMATIC HEFT, over the past decade the CinCs have sent Army Special Forces to buddy up with foreigners of every ilk. Hulking mountainmen in Kyrgyzstan. Skinny tribesmen in Yemen. Israeli commandos. Jordanian skydivers. Russian paratroopers. But except for the people they were assigned to befriend, special forces soldiers have maintained a closed society. The men like it that way; it has worked well for them for fifty years. The less anyone outside "the family" knows about them, the better—and that includes the "conventional" Army. On big Army missions they strive to maintain their separateness, even on slow-burn peacekeeping missions, like the one in Kosovo.

No one was permitted to enter Camp Bondsteel, the 755-acre fortress for American soldiers in Kosovo, without a U.S. military identification or escort. Inside, the camp was further segregated by a twenty-foot-high perimeter fence wrapped in thick black burlap delineating the territory of a 10th Special Forces Group headquarters unit. In case anybody from the "regular Army" still didn't get it, a warning sign on the gate out front offered one more chance: "You Are Entering a Secure Area. Turn Away Now. Deadly Force May Be Used if You Proceed Any Further." To soldiers inside the wire, within the highly secure special forces area, the Army was the other side of the family, the side they happened to marry into, but are not related to by blood.

Behind the gate to the segregated area, a black armored Cadillac SUV and a heliport sit on choice real estate—the high ground—first claimed by Maj. Mark Marchant, the unassuming Bravo Company commander in the 2nd Battalion. Part of the advance party that had visited the post when it was still rolling wheat fields, Marchant had quickly staked his claim. He'd designed barracks for his A-teams, an operations center, and a gym. The gym has nearly as much equipment as the regular Army gym outside the wire, where ten times the number of troops work out. The operations center, a computer powerhouse, can talk to U.S. headquarters in Stuttgart, or Washington, or even to an airborne command center circling miles above.

Two years into the Kosovo peacekeeping mission, in November 2001, there were few big secrets to keep and few classified missions to undertake. The compound, known as the SOCCE—the Special Operations Command and Control Element—was more a state of mind than a military necessity. One of its chief accomplishments was to underline the special forces' elite status and their need to remain free of "Mother Army."

Mother Army was still a slow, smothering organization, all but irrelevant in a world of small wars and invisible battlefields. Searching for a new psychology, its leaders had adopted peppy Madison Avenue slogans like "An Army of One" and snappy attire, like the beret formerly worn only by special forces. The Army's chief of staff, Gen. Eric Shinseki, had traded track treads for wheels on the Army's armored vehicles and that was supposed to make a big difference, too. But not much of substance had really changed.

While the Army clung to its battalions, brigades, and divisions, the special forces cling to their Operational Detachment Alpha (ODA), the fabled A-team of a dozen men that has existed since the unit's official beginning in 1952. The team still re-creates, after all those years, the family, the tribe, the brotherhood.*

---

* There are no women on Special Forces A-teams. Women are found at the battalion level, though, in the signal, logistics, psychological operations, and military intelligence units that accompany A-teams into the field on large deployments.

Until the war in Afghanistan, though, the Army treated the special forces like a fifth, bothersome service branch that it would rarely figure into its grand schemes, big wars, or fast-track leadership promotions. The separation was mental and complete. Brig. Gen. Leslie Fuller, head of the Special Operations Command, Europe, had "U.S. Army" embroidered on his pocket, but when he talked about his career, he used phrases like "When I left the Army . . . ," referring to 1989 when he left the infantry to become a special forces commander.

Special forces, trained as elite saboteurs and counterinsurgency experts, were nonetheless assigned delicate feats of local diplomacy from Afghanistan to Zimbabwe. This touchy-feely "diplomatic crap," as some of them called it, clashed with the warrior side of a special forces soldier. In the new days of long-range, standoff weapons and casualty-free air wars, their combat is still the personal and up-front kind. They train to infiltrate enemy lines on horseback, in scuba gear, on dune buggies, on skis, by parachute, helicopter, submarine, or plane. Strapped to their legs and backs are knives, machine guns, lasers, and night-vision goggles.

Some speak longingly of the fights they haven't yet seen. "It takes something special to be in SF, you know," one pale, dark-eyed staff sergeant whispered at a restaurant in Kosovo one evening. "Not everyone wants to kill somebody. Not everyone could, you know. Not everyone has it in them. I do. What keeps me going is that thought. . . . If you're lucky, you'll get one war in your life. Everyone here," he said, nodding to his teammates, "should be waiting for and wanting that moment."

A typical Special Forces mission these days, even in Afghanistan, requires more patience and improvisation than weapons and assassinations. No amount of antiterrorist tactics and laser weaponry can assure success in cooling off local political disputes, coordinating the delivery of foreign assistance, or repairing phone lines or water systems. Welding these two traits—Rambo and the Peace Corps volunteer—you come up with a man like Rick Turcotte, team sergeant for Team 055, operating in Urosevac, Kosovo, a twenty-minute drive outside Camp Bondsteel. Turcotte's Herculean build stretched the limits of the light brown Army t-shirt he wore in his team's freezing-cold dining room one autumn night. With thick salt-and-pepper hair, styled in a crew cut, he could have been cast in *Special Forces: The Movie*.

Turcotte had enlisted directly from civilian life into special forces in 1979, an entry path dropped and not reinstituted until the war in Afghanistan ignited a fierce demand for special forces soldiers. Raised on a horse farm in Maine, the eighteen-year-old Turcotte had wanted to jump out of airplanes, work far from hovering bosses, and see the world. He's lived his wish for twenty-three years, so far.

On his first mission, in 1981, Turcotte trained the Fijian military for its debut peacekeeping mission to the Sinai Desert to enforce the 1978 Camp David Accords. He later worked on communications in the Honduran jungle supporting U.S.-backed "contra" guerrillas working to overthrow the leftist Sandinista government in Nicaragua. Then he shipped out to Asia, where he trained elite soldiers from Thailand, the Philippines, Malaysia, Indonesia, and Singapore.

Turcotte followed the turmoil in Eastern Europe and the Soviet Union on his next assignment as a member of the Delta Force's hostage-rescue team in West Berlin. He was in a bowling alley when the Berlin Wall fell, unaware of events that would soon shake his world. Then he returned to Asia, this time working in Korea and China and becoming part of the first American military team to explore Siberia—in a kayak with Russian Eskimos. After a stint in language school, he returned to the 10th Special Forces Group and began a series of trips to the Balkans: first in Bosnia working as a liaison with French, Ukrainian, and Russian peacekeeping units, then as one of a team verifying Serb demilitarization in Republika Srpska in eastern Bosnia. In between, he trained foreign troops in Turkey, Austria, Lithuania, Slovakia, Estonia, and Germany.

Turcotte, like most members of the 10th Special Forces Group, spent most of 2001 away from home—285 days either abroad or on training exercises in U.S. mountains, lakes, or oceans. He wore the pace as a badge of honor. His team burst out laughing when he answered a question about whether the nonstop deployments affect morale: "Being gone so much doesn't affect their morale," he said, looking around the dinner table at the Urosevac house. "It may affect their marriages and their family life, but it doesn't affect their morale."

When the Kosovo air war ended, special forces teams acted as the Army's early eyes and ears on the ground trying to understand the subterranean forces that would dominate postwar society. When Albanian rebels tried to gain control of territory within Serbia, in the Presevo Valley, Army Special Forces troops and Navy SEALs were sent to discourage them. When Macedonian Albanians rose up against the government in Skopje, Macedonia, two years later, special forces were sent in to quiet the rebels. Now, Special Forces troops in Kosovo mainly gathered information on the Serb and Albanian communities to detect threats to American KFOR forces.[*]

The A-teams treated the symptoms of the problems that plagued Kosovo—grenade attacks, bombings, isolated killings—not the root causes that would cripple the society for years to come. Turcotte understood the limits of his efforts much better than the civilian leaders who so often sent him abroad and expected great advances. "I've been to sixty-three countries in twenty-three years. It's tough to look back and say, I made a difference. You just don't know."

More than any other team member, the team sergeant molds an A-team's collective personality. He's the NCO who has worked the longest and knows the team best. In Urosevac, Capt. Kelly Smith was team leader, in charge of the mission, but Turcotte ran the men.

Sfc. Steve Gernet, no wallflower himself, said the biggest fear of any team member was the possibility he might let down "dad," the team sergeant. Gernet did it once with Turcotte, he admitted sheepishly, looking over at him. A weapons specialist, the first time Gernet lectured on the 81-mm mortar to a group of foreign troops, someone asked him a question he couldn't answer. "If I ever ask you another question and you don't know the answer to it, you're fired!" Turcotte blasted him. Gernet hit the books, studying everything he could get his hands on. Turcotte smirked and shrugged at the incident. "Yeah, he won't do that again!"

Turcotte's cohesion-building style, explained Captain Smith, was "Choke, hug. Choke, hug."

"The power you have, some of it's addicting, but you're guiding an incredible collection of men," Turcotte confessed. "There's an amazing kinship and brotherhood."

---

[*] KFOR (Kosovo-Force) is the NATO peacekeeping force in Kosovo. It comprises soldiers from a number of NATO member countries, including Americans.

Although filled with large personalities and egos, Army Special Forces functions on the concept of being nearly invisible and almost always discreet. Every man on the team, like every piece of equipment they carry in their rucksacks, has a unique purpose.

Its basic unit is the A-team, commanded by a captain. An A-team has ten to twelve men, each with a speciality. Five A-teams and a headquarters make a company-sized Operational Detachment Bravo, commanded by a major. Three Bravos and a headquarters make a battalion-sized Operational Detachment Charlie, commanded by a lieutenant colonel. Three battalions plus a support group company and a headquarters make a Special Forces Group (SFG), commanded by a colonel. An SFG group, at roughly 1,380 men, is the largest Special Forces (SF) unit. (Each Operational Detachment Delta is a covert Delta Force unit commanded by a colonel. Operating under the Joint Special Operations Command, the entire Delta Force of about 2,000 men is led by a brigadier general and works separately from the rest of SF.)

Special Forces groups are assigned to regions of the world, although all are headquartered in the United States. The 1st SFG works in the U.S. Pacific Command's theater. The 3rd SFG works with the U.S. European Command in all of Africa except the Eastern Horn. The 5th SFG, historically the busiest, has the U.S. Central Command's theater, which takes in the Middle East, the Persian Gulf, the Horn of Africa, and Central Asia. The 7th SFG is assigned to Central and Latin America and the Caribbean. The 10th SFG has most of the U.S. European Command's theater, mainly Central and Eastern Europe, the Balkans, Turkey, Israel, and Lebanon. There are also two reserve groups, the 19th and 20th SFGs.[*]

When in its care-and-feeding mode—being staffed and trained— an SFG falls under the U.S. Army Special Forces Command at Fort Bragg. But when its teams deploy overseas, it becomes an asset of the regional CinC.

---

[*] The 1st Battalion of the 1st SFG is based on Okinawa; the 2nd and 3rd battalions are based at Fort Lewis, Wash.; all three 3rd SFG battalions are based at Fort Bragg; all three 5th SFG battalions are based at Fort Campbell; the 7th SFG's battalions are at Fort Bragg; the 10th SFG's 1st Battalion is based in Panzer Kasern near Stuttgart, Germany, and its other two reside at Fort Carson, Colo.

U.S. Army Special Forces, also known as the Green Berets, is one type of specialized unit within a larger set of specialized Army, Navy, and Air Force forces that together are called Special Operations Forces, or SOF.*

The Army's special operations units include the SF, the 75th Ranger Regiment, the short- and medium-range infiltration and extraction aircraft units of the 160th Special Operations Aviation Regiment, and civil affairs and psychological operations (PSYOPS) specialists. The covert Army units include the Delta Force, operating under the Joint Special Operations Command, and the CIF, (CinC's In Extremis Force), usually detailed from other units and used primarily for hostage rescues and as a CinC's bodyguards.

All SF teams must be proficient in a set of common skills: close-quarters combat, scuba diving, driving a small boat. They can assemble, drive, and maintain modified Humvees or dune buggies dropped by aircraft and assembled on the ground. They must be competent at parachuting, dropped from either military planes or disguised commercial aircraft flying above 12,000 feet, so high that an oxygen tank is needed to sustain the soldiers in the thin air. They also must know how to survive a quick insertion "HALO" (high altitude-low opening) that requires soldiers to drop thousands of feet in free-fall without opening their parachutes until the hard ground is just 3,500 feet away. Some teams specialize in scuba operations and cold-weather mountaineering. Advanced equestrian skills, once a rare specialty, have been revived in the wake of September 11.

The Army Special Forces have five main missions. "Special reconnaissance" includes activities such as hunting Iraq's Scud ballistic missiles during the Gulf War or sneaking around the mountains of Afghanistan to set up remote cameras that can monitor Al Qaeda caves from positions a mile away. "Direct action" covers raids and

---

* The Navy units include the SEAL (sea, air, land) teams, patrol coastal ships, and special boat units. The Navy's clandestine unit is SEAL Team 6, an anti-terrorist force. The Air Force special operations units provide medium- to long-range air-infiltration teams, specially equipped gunships, and aerial refuelers. The Marine Corps, which is exempt from the 1986 legislation that created the U.S. Special Operations Command, maintains forward-deployed Special Operations Capable Marine Expeditionary Units.

ambushes such as those carried out against Panamanian dictator Manuel Noriega's savage "dignity battalions" after the 1989 invasion of Panama. "Unconventional warfare" encompasses the range of activities undertaken in Afghanistan, including training and equipping foreign fighters, organizing alliance troops into a cohesive force, coordinating with other units via radio and phones, and calling in close air support.

The "counterterrrorism" mission is carried out by covert Delta Force and SEAL Team 6, supported by specialized Air Force units. Their activities include hostage rescues and assaults on terrorist organizations. In some cases, such as the 1993 assassination of Colombian drug lord Pablo Escobar, the covert American units trained or other-

A 1st Special Forces Group (Airborne) soldier supervises as a Thai rifle company advances on a target during Exercise Cobra Gold 2001. SSGT. AMANDA GLENN

wise assisted specialized foreign units who actually carried out the rescues and assaults.

Finally, the bread-and-butter mission of Army Special Forces is "foreign internal defense," a concept refined in successive campaigns against communism but yet to be fully adapted for the post–Cold War period. This task calls for special forces to "organize, train, advise, and assist" a foreign military so that it can "free and protect its society from subversion, lawlessness, and insurgency," according to Field Manual 31-20, "Doctrine for Special Forces Operations," issued in April 1990.

Being in high demand, the SOF community escaped the downsizing that the George H. W. Bush and Clinton administrations imposed on conventional forces after the Soviet Union dissolved. Instead, SOF became a larger force—now comprising some 46,000 troops—than ever before. SOF also avoided some of the budget restrictions that have shackled the conventional services. For example, Congress gave the U.S. Special Operations Command $4 billion for 2001, and contemplated another 20 percent for the next year.

SF soldiers live in a private, intense world. Shielded from public view by tall fences and security systems, they also live cloaked in official, go-to-jail government secrecy. They rarely seek attention or publicity. Stripes, oak clusters, and stars define the standing of regular Army soldiers to a colleague, but some SF soldiers strip the coveted rank patches and unit insignia from their uniforms altogether.

Still, in Kosovo, an SF soldier was easy to spot. Strict regulations required regular Army soldiers to wear full body armor, helmets, and assault rifles whenever they left Camp Bondsteel. SF troops, by contrast, wore camouflage fatigues without armor or helmets and sported longer hair and even mustaches. While the conventional Army built trenches and guard posts to distance itself from the Kosovars, SF soldiers moved into smaller accomodations in town to be closer to their new communities.

Turcotte ran the house in Urosevac, twenty minutes from Camp Bondsteel. Just off a main road into town, inconspicuously located behind a used-tire lot, the house itself might have looked like every other house in the American peacekeeping sector of the province, except that, inside and out, it had been turned into a fortress. The Army had hauled in two-story-tall cement security walls, erected sand-filled cardboard-and-wire baskets, and strung concertina wire around the perimeter. Floodlights and surveillance cameras monitored the full 360 degree surroundings. Another set of cameras captured every movement inside. Ballistic curtains blast-proofed the windows and thick iron bars kept everybody else out.

A six-foot-long satellite antenna resembling a giant laser sat on the second-story front porch bouncing encrypted messages up to a satellite and down to Patch Barracks outside of Stuttgart.

Each SF house in Kosovo had a living room with a giant television set. Equipment webbing, uniforms, radios, family photos, and books lay about each bedroom. Specially designed black survival gear, machine guns, pistols and knives, night-vision goggles, all in sets of eight, hung from hooks around the "ready room." Four communications systems gave each house instant access to the mother ship—the SOCCE at Camp Bondsteel.

There were no women anywhere. But sex, or at least the talk of it, was a constant—in wall art, in conversation, and in jokes. Even in otherwise boring Central Command's Special Operations Command briefings: "Special forces!" barked one briefer, his voice rising with enthusiasm. "We penetrate deeper, stay longer, and deliver a bigger payload!"

The Alpha-male den in Kosovo is a relentlessly competitive place, with unforgiving physical standards and unspoken psychological codes of conduct. Most team members are conservative in outlook and disdainful of rank and hierarchy for its own sake. The job attracts risk-takers and daredevils, but commanders try hard to weed out "cowboys" who could endanger the team. It's similar to the esprit de corps found in the American firehouse. As team members themselves point out repeatedly, they have each volunteered three times to be wherever they are: first for the regular Army, then for airborne training, then for the grueling Special Forces Qualifying Course.

The Army is under pressure to enlarge special forces but faces steep hurdles in doing so. Only 25 percent of the initial candidates make it. Reenlistment rates ran only about 50 percent in 2002. By 2004, roughly 50 percent of all SF will be eligible to retire.

New members have an arduous role to fill on the team that can last many months, until a another new man comes in. "They come in with an inflated idea of who they are," said Turcotte. "It's a ritual to run them hard." At a minimum the new guy has to clean the house. But usually he is subject to much tougher treatment aimed at humbling him, making him dependent on the group, and imposing the team leader's particular standards of discipline.

When Josh Twitty, affectionately dubbed "Dog Nips," was sent to a team in the 10th SFG's 2nd battalion, deployed in Kosovo, the team sergeant and the sergeant major of the headquarters company cooked up a plot designed to zap his ego down a couple of notches. They arranged to have Twitty overhear the team sergeant, Tony Foor, arguing with Sgt. Maj. Beau Todd, the company's senior NCO. Foor told Todd he wanted Twitty off the team: "I don't want *her*," Foor yelled. "I want her out." Within the team, whenever Foor addressed Twitty, he used the female pronoun and spoke to him through a third party: "Tell her. . . ."

Twitty took it. He sat on the couch at the team house in Kamenica, in northern Kosovo, for a month, not saying a word unless he had to. "When you're new, you just have to sit back," he said. His life improved when "Skippy," Jake Marschall, showed up and took the FNG (fucking

MSgt. Tony Foor's Special Forces Team 051 practices cold-weather training in Fox Park, Wy., in February 2001. Every year the team spends weeks in the mountains practicing survival and tactical operations in high altitudes, including infiltration, navigation, and travelling by helicopter, snowshoes, skis, and snowmobiles. Here the team is fast-roping from a special operations MH-47E Chinook helicopter. MAJ. MARK MARCHANT

new guy) spot. Skippy made the mistake of being late to physical training (PT) his first day. So the team put him on a stretcher and did PT on
top of him.

"My team doesn't even know my name," a new sergeant in another
group moaned at the dinner table one night. "They don't know whether
I have kids or where I live." The others rolled their eyes, smiled, and
kept eating.

Foor and his team leader, Capt. Sid Crews, used humor to keep
peace among the "ten angry men," as they called themselves, who
lived, ate, worked, played, and slept in the same house in Kamenica for
six months.

"Everyone feeds on everyone else's mistakes," said Foor. "You're
not allowed to have bad days," he explained, "because then you'll show
weakness."

"If someone gets angry, everyone gangs on up on them," explained
Crews, nicknamed "Jowls," a reference to his round face. "You open the
garage door, everyone drives in. You better shut it quickly or watch out.
And if you hear bitching, the game's on."

Crews had gotten caught bitching the night before, and his "Oh, my
leg" quote was scribbled on the drawing board in the ready room for all
to ridicule. "You can't harbor the tension," said team member Henry
Hollis. "You have to just get it out."

Crews purged bad feelings every night when he named the BAR
HUB (Bitch Award Recipient for Head Up Butt). It was once awarded to
the medic who washed his hands with alcohol-based soap, then tried to
stub out a candle with his fingers, setting himself on fire. Another award
went to the team member who cut up a hot pepper for stew and then went
to the bathroom before washing the spice off his hands. Foor, the team
sergeant, got the award for "lying to the family" about a jar of premier-
quality peanut butter his team found in his room, American comfort
food they longed for in Kosovo. "I should have lit the damn peanut butter
on fire," he said, after having had to defend himself repeatedly.

Other groups have come up with their own steam-blowing techniques. One former team leader carries boxing gloves on deployments.
Another preferred bare hands. "If two guys on a team have a problem, I

say, let them fight it out," said Sgt. Maj. Joe Callahan, who had been the team sergeant for several 7th SFG teams. "Not until they roll around, stick each other in the eye, and become so tired they look ridiculous fighting, can they become friends."

SF members are addicted to competition and challenge. Just about everything they do boils down to a race, a duel, a challenge. If Foor shoots at the bottle on the firing range in the mountains near the Kamenica house, everyone shoots at the bottle. Crews shoots the rock, everyone shoots the rock. No more rock.

Once a year, Crews takes his team "Chinese skiing" for fun. It might be mistaken for normal downhill skiing, but the goal is to hurt anyone who falls. Run over his leg. Break his finger. Whatever. "We can't wait 'til this year's," he said, laughing along with the rest of the pack.

A Halloween party on an SF base in Nigeria in 2002 turned into a competition to see just how bad Osama bin Laden could look as a costume. And just how much beer someone could ingest without taking a breath. The daily morning jog turned into a road race. Five miles got stretched to ten, then fifteen. Seven-minute miles became six-minute miles.

Turcotte had everyone out of the house by 6 A.M. on a run with pistol and radio. No one ever knew how long the run would last, or how fast they would go. When it was over, they gather for "the Ring of Steel," usually twenty sets of flare kicks (performed from a squatting position). Then they took turns leading further exercises—"hate crimes," they called them. They left the weights for the evening. "I tell the captain, an A-team is a sword," said Turcotte. "If you let me sharpen it, you can do anything you want with it. You can cut something with it. You can kill something with it, whatever."

At home, in Fort Bragg, standards are set in endurance competitions. The last one Lt. Col. Tim Sherwood, a 3rd SFG battalion commander, competed in included a twenty-mile road march with a fifty-five-pound rucksack. At mile eight his command staff donned bulky, hot biological- and chemical-warfare suits. At mile ten they had to work their way through a weapons of mass destruction obstacle course. Then two of the men carried two five-gallon jugs of water.

There followed a half-mile paddle across a lake in a rubber boat, before a final, six-mile dash to the finish line.[*]

Mock hostage rescues and endurance competitions keep the troops primed for the excruciating training exercises, fondly dubbed "suck fests." They take place every couple of months in the snow, the mountains, the jungle, sometimes in the black water of night.

Smith's team in Urosevac had hiked and skied into Dead Horse Canyon in Colorado, whose sheer horizontal cliffs would be a challenge even to expert climbers. But Smith's men carried 110-pound rucksacks and made some of the climb on skis. The team spent ten days in the heavy snow and subzero weather practicing infiltration, rescue, and survival tactics. To stay together and survive the blinding weather, they slept in one big snow cave they dug, which included a ten-foot-deep fire pit inside. But falling snow from the trees snuffed out the fire. Cold, wet, tired, and hungry, the exercise became a test of whether the soldiers could get out alive. Even the helicopter that brought company commander Marchant to check on everybody belly flopped on landing. When Marchant climbed out, he nearly disappeared in neck-deep powder.

Training also includes techniques for repressing fear. "Fear is like the worm at the bottom of the Tequila bottle," said Sfc. Joe Back, a blond, Irish-looking former instructor at the special warfare school. "I see it like this: There's a level somewhere in the back of the brain. You try to keep the worm from coming out of it. No don't come out, don't come out. . . ."

The scuba course was excellent preparation, thought Shane, a team member at the Urosevac house. With a blacked-out mask and no partner, the final test in the scuba course includes trying to figure out why your air supply is gone, and fixing it before it's too late. The test begins

---

[*] Sherwood's men carried the concept to Nigeria, where they concluded an eighteen-mile march after midnight one night while waiting for their regular training mission to begin. Outfitted in helmets that looked like diving helmets, and with night-vision goggles, they surprised more than one shepherd sleeping with his cows. His men also rehearsed hostage-rescue techniques in their hotel. Using the top two floors, they threw the lights off, put on their night-vision goggles, and pulled out their red laser target-designator guns. They rescued the hostage, played by their visiting commander, without tripping over the furniture, or hurting each other or the hostage—an accomplishment that sounds easier than it actually is.

only after team members are pushed to the point of exhaustion with other swimming and bobbing drills. "Most of it is mental," Shane said, closing his eyes, reaching around his head to the imaginary air tanks and air line. Routine exercises include infiltrating a harbor on a moonless night. Team members tie themselves together with a nylon cord so they won't get lost with the eighty pounds they carry on their backs. The scuba badge is such an insider's award that few regular Army soldiers even recognize it. "We tell them we're Army astronauts," said Back. "But it's not about *them*."

★ ★ ★ ★

THE 10TH SFG, which has the Kosovo mission, was the first group to be formed in 1952 at Fort Bragg.* Its mission was mainly to operate behind the lines in case the Soviet Union or, later, the Warsaw Pact, invaded Western Europe. Known as "Sneaky Petes," the group was viewed by the regular Army with suspicion; it was regarded as a fifth service branch.

In the mid-1960s, as President John Kennedy watched the popular challenges to postcolonialism from Third World rebels and leftist political parties, he came to believe they were all interconnected. He saw a worldwide insurgency sponsored by communist China and the Soviet Union, and he turned to the special forces to stop it. According to SF historians, JFK's appreciation for the independent mindset and skills of the special forces dated back to his wartime experience as a PT boat commander. He liked their style, too, and lifted the Army's ban on the SF signature, the green beret, modeled on the headgear, worn by the British Royal Marine Commandos, so they could be easily distinguished from the regular army crowd.

Kennedy's support, though, was much more concrete than endorsing a beret. In 1961, he dramatically expanded special operations, including Navy and Air Force units, into a worldwide counterinsurgency force. They would rely on the doctrine and tactics of uncon-

---

* Navy SEALs and Air Force "Air Commando" units were created at this time too. Their progenitor was the U.S.-Canadian 1st Special Service Force of World War II, led by Lt. Col. Robert Tryon Frederick.

ventional war—jungle combat, PSYOPS, long-range reconnaissance, sabotage—to defeat guerrilla forces on their own territory. "We need a greater ability to deal with guerrilla forces, insurrection, and subversion," he said in his address to Congress that year. "We must be ready now to deal with any size force, including small externally supported bands of men; and we must help train local forces to be equally effective." The Green Berets, Kennedy declared in 1962, must "be able to help those who have the will to help themselves."

Special Forces had a jump on him, though. By 1957, one SF team from the newly activated 1st SFG, based on Okinawa, trained fifty-eight Vietnamese army soldiers at the Commando Training Center in Nha Trang.[1] They would become the first Vietnamese special forces unit. Two years later, in July 1959, SF A-teams from the Fort Bragg–based 77th Group (which no longer exists) had been secretly working in Laos, in a clandestine operation code-named White Star. The 1954 Geneva Accords on Indochina, which gave Laos independence, forbade an American military presence, so the soldiers at first disguised themselves as civilian contractors.[2] Their job was to teach basic infantry skills to the ineffective, nonchalant Laotian military to counter the more disciplined pro–North Vietnamese Pathet Lao. In 1961, when the French withdrew from Laos, the SF teams became combat advisers in a CIA-led effort to train "shock" companies to carry out raids and ambushes against the Pathet Lao.

The SF mission in Southeast Asia expanded quickly as the war in Indochina intensified. In 1960, twenty SF trainers from Fort Bragg shipped off to South Vietnam; by 1964 the entire 5th Group, some 1,300 men, had been sent over. In late 1969, a total of 3,741 special forces were in the country, marking the height of their involvement.[3]

The SF teams set up 285 Vietnamese Civilian Irregular Defense Group companies to try to turn civilian minority groups in Vietnam—mainly the isolated Montagnards—into paramilitary strike forces and hamlet-based "self-defense" militias. The SF trained 6,000 strike-force troops and 42,000 village militiamen.[4] But the camps were vulnerable to attack, and the troops' integration with the regular Vietnamese army was nearly impossible. "The value of some of these bases was questionable, and a few were more of a liability than an asset," wrote Gen. Bruce Palmer Jr. in his seminal The 25-Year War.[5]

In 1963, the special forces in Vietnam were given the dangerous job of guarding the porous borders against infiltration and resupply efforts. By 1965, as the conventional Army showed up en masse, the SF and their paramilitaries went on the offensive, becoming a more central source of intelligence for finding enemy forces. They participated in special strike missions, including parachute assaults and helicopter insertions, and were paired with conventional Army units. They also began "civic action" projects ranging from dental hygiene to flood control. They conducted long-range reconnaissance patrols inside Viet Cong and North Vietnamese army havens. The "mobile guerrilla force" or "Mike" units were cleverly self-sustaining in the deepest enemy territory. One resupply technique used warplanes to drop 500-pound napalm containers modified to hold food and water.[6]

In January 1964, the covert Military Assistance Command Vietnam-Studies and Observation Group (MACV-SOG) was formed with the help of 5th SFG soldiers and Navy SEALs. It had ample funding squirreled away in the Navy's annual budget.[7] Its exact mission was shrouded in secrecy, but the bottom-line mission was to stop North Vietnamese infiltration into the country from Laos. To do this, MACV-SOG soldiers mined trails, captured and interrogated prisoners, raided camps, and risked daring night-time low-altitude parachute landings and close-quarters combat in the hot, sweaty jungle. The super-secret unit worked directly for the Joint Staff through the Military Assistance Command-Vietnam, which took over many of the CIA's covert and clandestine operations after that agency lost credibility following the unsuccessful Bay of Pigs effort to overthrow Cuba's communist leader, Fidel Castro.

To the American public, Vietnam was a war tragically lost. To many SF soldiers, however, the war stands as an example of courage and success. For instance, history's most celebrated SF mission is one in Vietnam that missed its intended target, but which Special Forces commemorate as an unmistakable signal to the communist north about American capability and resolve. The Son Tay prison, which held American prisoners of war (POWs), stood twenty-three miles outside Hanoi, the North Vietnamese capital. On November 20, 1970, two HH-53 helicopters and one HH-3 helicopter loaded with fifty-six SF soldiers, and three spare HH-53s for the prisoners, flew out of Udorn, Thailand, and passed unnoticed in the quarter-moon sky over Laos and into Vietnam. The helicopters were protected by an umbrella of aircraft: A-1Es, F-4s, F-105s, MC-130Es, and two C-130 tankers for refueling. Unfortunately, all the POWs had been transferred to another camp before the raid began. But military historians believe the undetected raid so deep inside the enemy's territory shook North Vietnamese confidence and convinced the Chinese to reduce their support of the North in the war. Immediately thereafter, the North Vietnamese herded the American POWs into the "Hanoi Hilton." This was the first time all had been together. In Hanoi they received better treatment and the U.S. government was given its first list naming those being held.

When the war ended, the 1st and 3rd groups were disbanded. The 5th SFG, which had starred in Vietnam, found itself with little to do. The one exception was a new unit, Operational Detachment Delta, a covert, specialized anti-terrorist force authorized by President Carter to counter the new, unconventional tactics of the 1970s: airplane hijacking and kidnapping. The Delta Force's chief architect was Col. Charlie Beckwith, commandant of the Special Forces School at Fort Bragg. "Chargin' Charlie" had once been an exchange officer with the British Special Air Service, after which he modeled the unit. Forty troops made up the first unit, an antiterrorist group code named Blue Light. The 1st Delta Force was activated shortly thereafter, in October 1977. It had fewer than 100 men (A and B squadrons, plus support), and grew only to approximately 300 by the early 1980s. By the millennium, 2,000 men made up Delta Force.

Delta has had a mixed record of achievement and disaster. More than once, its shortcomings have led to major organizational changes, not only in the SOF commands, but throughout the entire armed forces. Operation Eagle Claw, the botched attempt in 1980 to rescue the fifty-three Americans being held hostage in Tehran, Iran, led to the adoption of the most significant national security reform in fifty years, the 1986 Goldwater-Nichols legislation. While that bill was being debated, special operations units suffered other embarrassments such as Operation Urgent Fury, the 1983 invasion of the tiny Caribbean island of Grenada, where four members parachuted into rough seas and drowned. Half the members of the unit sent to rescue the British ambassador were wounded by Grenadan troops. In 1984, members of SEAL Team 6 got into a standoff with Italian carabinieri as they attempted to take custody of the hijackers of the cruise ship *Achille Lauro*.

The Reagan administration, a blessing to the rest of the military, viewed SOF with skepticism. Senior leaders at the Pentagon, who had been leery mid-level officers during Vietnam, tried to starve the program to death. But some in the civilian leadership favored secretive operations and used the Panama-based 7th SFG for clandestine operations in the administration's war on communism in Central America. The 7th SFG played a major role in strengthening the Salvadoran armed forces during that country's 12-year civil war, and in helping the contra rebels weaken the leftist Sandinista government in Nicaragua.

To fix special operations' continuing problems, though, Senators Sam Nunn (D-Ga.) and William Cohen (R-Maine) added an amendment to the 1986 Goldwater-Nichols Act. The amendment elevated special operations to its own joint command, thereby unifying the special operators of all services. The U.S. Special Operations Command was set up across the street from the U.S. Central Command on MacDill Air Force Base in Tampa.

The Nunn-Cohen amendment also gave the command a golden goose, creating a separate funding source for special operations and a unique, nearly autonomous administration unrivaled by any other in the Defense Department even today. The Air Force, Army, and Navy are each headed by a presidentially appointed, Senate-confirmed civilian secretary (the secretary of the Navy also heads the Marine Corps) and are subject to as much budget and operational scrutiny as Congress and the public dish out. But not so for the unofficial fifth service. Most of the Special Operations Command's budget is classified. Civilian oversight is conducted by an assistant secretary of defense. The Special Operations Command is also the only unified command to determine its own force structure, set its own funding requirements, procure its own equipment, and determine—by itself—how best to train and deploy its units.

The 1989 invasion of Panama was the first military action to test this new "joint" authority. The regional CinC, Gen. Maxwell Thurman, relied heavily on SOF. By contrast, the CinC for Central Command,

Gen. Norman Schwarzkopf, a skeptic of special operations from his Vietnam days, when some units had run amok, wrote special operations out of his original plan for the Gulf War. But his neighbor at Special Operations Command, Gen. Carl Stiner, had other ideas. Stiner devised plans to use SOF in several ways: for deep reconnaissance, as advisers to Kuwaiti resistance fighters, and as "coalition liaisons" coordinating the foreign military involved on the ground.

Schwarzkopf learned, as did Gen. Tommy Franks, who held his post ten years later, that he couldn't do the job without SOF. The opening night of the Gulf War starred Air Force and Army special operations helicopters flown by Delta Force pilots who blew up Iraq's air-defense radar facilities. Special forces also trained and traveled with Kuwaiti resistance fighters and scoured the landscape for elusive Iraqi Scud ballistic-missile launchers.

Three years after the Gulf War, Delta Force's public glory would be overshadowed by tragedy in Somalia. There, eighteen Rangers and Delta Force operators died in Mogadishu after Somali fighters shot down two Black Hawk helicopters ferrying soldiers on a mission to capture lieutenants of Somali warlord Mohamed Farah Aidid. As Mark Bowden concluded in his book *Black Hawk Down*, "the policy that led Task Force Ranger to Somalia in the summer of 1993 was the result of America's new and uncomfortable role in the world. . . . The lesson our retreat taught the world's terrorists and despots is that killing a few American soldiers, even at a cost of more than five hundred of our own fighters, is enough to spook Uncle Sam."[8]

Somalia left a mark on the American military psyche that has dominated mission planning. Force protection became a top priority. Risk aversion handcuffed Special Forces, too. The Pentagon would not allow them to get involved in apprehending war criminals in Bosnia during the 1990s, so small CIA paramilitary units were sent instead and achieved little. Nor were SF teams allowed even to set foot inside Kosovo during the air war. Too risky, Washington concluded; one casualty might diminish the political resolve back home and undermine the larger mission. Afghanistan would change all of that.

Chapter Seven

A-TEAMS IN AFGHANISTAN

★ ★ ★ ★

SGT. MARTIN STEWART, OF THE 528TH SPECIAL OPERA-
tions Support Battalion, was outside under Uzbekistan's black night
sky, setting up the U.S. headquarters base, when the war against
Afghanistan began on October 7, 2001. A flash of white light to the
south at first startled him, but then brought relief. Finally, Stewart
thought, his president and his armed forces were taking charge. "I knew
it had begun, that our commander-in-chief had decided to get it done,"
he would say later. "Play time was over." He knew that the restraints on
warfare of the last decade would be lifted. After all, the Taliban would
not be removed by cruise missile strikes alone. In the drab olive tent
of his fellow soldier, Sfc. William Bruce, cheers and high fives erupted.
"It's on!" shouted Bruce. America had opened the first front in its war
on terrorism. They were witnesses.

Over the following ten days, as bombs and missiles from U.S. warplanes pitted the drought-parched earth of Afghanistan's plains and
mountains, a handful of special operation forces soldiers waited in
complete isolation at the former Soviet Khanabad Air Base in Karshi,
Uzbekistan. Team 555 had twice tried to make it into Afghanistan, to
join the war against the Taliban and Osama bin Laden's Al Qaeda network. But high winds and dense clouds had foiled them both times,
forcing the Air Force's largest and most powerful all-weather helicopters, the MH-53J Pave Lows, back to base.

Then, finally, on October 19, two blacked-out helicopters made it in, rocking violently through a night storm that wrapped the Panjshir Valley in a milky gray burkha. The Pave Lows felt like tin to the soldiers being jolted from side to side in the back. One chopper was flying blind, its electronic sensors knocked out by the bad weather.

"Pull up! Pull up!" one pilot shouted to his co-pilot from the cockpit of the helicopter as he headed into the shrouded mountainside. The upward jolt startled CWO David Diaz, who was hanging on in the back. He and the eleven other soldiers split between the two helicopters made up Team 555 of the U.S. Army Special Forces, the first A-team infiltrated into Afghanistan during the war. Diaz's team was the vanguard of a small, nearly invisible U.S. ground presence that would help topple the Taliban with stunning speed and test a new template for warfare.

The helicopter landed with a thud after midnight—and well off script, like many war scenarios. Both choppers had put down in the wrong place. On that moonless night, the two halves of Team 555 were separated by several miles and one small mountain. With 300 pounds of gear for each man to lug, and uneven rocks underfoot, exploration was out of the question.

Moments after disembarking, as the choppers sped away, Diaz saw little dancing lights approaching. Flashlights, he thought. Their illumination rendered his night vision goggles useless. This couldn't be the reception party he was expecting; they certainly wouldn't be shining a blinding light his way.

"I'm going to try to talk to these guys," Diaz told his men. "If I hit the ground, I expect you guys to start shooting."

He began walking, a Beretta strapped to his thigh and a stubby machine gun in his hands. Suddenly, a huge silhouette appeared. "A monster of a man," in Diaz's words, walked toward him. His clothes seemed soaking wet. The man reached out his hand.

"Hi. I'm Hal!" the monster roared in thoroughly American English, explaining that he had had to swim a river to get there. "Damn glad to meet you!" Thus did the CIA, for Hal was a CIA paramilitary operative, welcome the first special forces into Afghanistan, setting in motion a war plan that would mix a cocktail of air attacks, intelligence, and tiny ground units to undo the Taliban with lightning speed.

★ ★ ★ ★

SPECIAL FORCES HAD been quietly carrying the military's banner for unconventional warfare for five decades. At the height of their involvement in Vietnam, 3,750 Special Forces soldiers—known then as Green Berets—trained paramilitary and South Vietnamese strike forces, conducted raids, and led a campaign they thought would win the hearts and minds of the Vietnamese people. In the 1980s, they advised Central American militaries fighting leftist guerrillas. In the 1991 Gulf War, they hunted Iraqi Scud missile launchers, conducted long-range reconnaissance, and accompanied Kuwaiti resistance fighters back into Kuwait City.

But not until the war in Afghanistan did special forces play such a central role in a conflict—and with such small numbers. Just over 300 men were pivotal in undoing the Taliban. They executed three missions: synchronizing the unorganized forces of ethnic Uzbek and Tajik Afghan opposition groups in the north; building small armies out of Pashtun tribesmen in the south; and relaying targeting information that enabled Navy and Air Force pilots to drop bombs onto Al Qaeda and Taliban positions with devastating precision.

These missions depended on a new relationship between U.S. military and intelligence personnel, as well as an improvised partnership with Afghan tribes. Under the pressures of war, these relationships were forged quickly.

Before the war began, top-ranking U.S. military officials cautioned the political leadership in Washington that it would take until summer 2002 to break the Taliban's five-year hold on power. Instead, it took just 49 days, from Team 555's debut on October 19 until the Taliban fell to the Northern Alliance in the southern city of Kandahar on December 6. The special forces inserted into Afghanistan totaled 316 men: eight A-teams, four company-level units, and three battalion-level commands. All reported to a Joint Special Operations Task Force at Khanabad, 100 miles north of the Afghan border. Nearly every team included one or two CIA operatives and an Air Force Special Operations combat controller, expert at guiding high-flying aircraft to minuscule targets.

Team 555—the "Triple Nickel"—is part of the U.S. Army's 5th

Special Forces Group, based at Fort Campbell, Ky. One of five active-duty Special Forces Groups, the 5th was given the Afghanistan mission because it traditionally worked operations in the U.S. Central Command's theater.

By the start of the war, Zinni had been succeeded as CinC by the Army's Gen. Tommy Franks. A lanky artillery officer from Texas, Franks was quite unlike the man he replaced. Whereas Zinni was unusual in every way, Franks struck many as thoroughly conventional. Steeped in the use of large, conventional forces in battle, Franks found himself leading America's most important unconventional war since Vietnam.

Zinni had believed part of his job was to keep the public informed about the military's actions. Every day he had welcomed the press into his operations center in Somalia to make that point. Gen. Norman Schwarzkopf, the CinC at Central Command who led U.S. forces during the Gulf War, had shared that view. Schwarzkopf became the bellowing, camera-friendly commander of daily press briefings in the Gulf. Schwarzkopf was comfortable with Middle Eastern cultures from visiting his father, who had headed the U.S. military mission in Iran. Franks, by contrast, had spent his childhood and much of his career in Texas, playing the "good old boy," as he liked to described himself. Rising before dawn, he would sing along to country-and-western music while jogging on his treadmill.

Franks had little time for the media. A year before the Afghanistan war began, Franks summed up his approach to the CinC's job this way: "My business is a secret business." He believed that no one outside his circle needed to understand what he was doing. "My job is not to educate the ignorant," he once told his staff. So Franks had the phones at his headquarters monitored and refused interviews and press conferences in the first months of the war, until he was ordered by Rumsfeld's public-affairs staff to be more forthcoming.

Franks grew up an orphan and enlisted in the Army in 1965. He liked to cultivate the image of a Southern simpleton. That style remains a caricature in vogue among the Army leadership. Franks spent fourteen months in Vietnam. He was wounded three times, and received three Purple Hearts. After spending four years in two armored cavalry regiments, he is said to have developed a keen sense of the complex orchestration that infantry, armor, and artillery units perform on the battlefield. He was an assistant division commander in the 1st Cavalry Division during the Gulf War. Later, he would command the Army's 2nd Infantry Division in Korea and the 3rd Army from Fort McPherson, Ga.

Zinni backed Franks to succeed him at Central Command precisely because the country's focus in 2000, when Zinni stepped down, was on a possible ground war against Iraq. Under Zinni, Franks had been the three-star commander of Central Command's Army forces, dubbed ARCENT, and he "was grounded in the war plan," Zinni believed.*

Franks drove his staff hard. But even those who cringed in his company found him sharp, quick, and highly entertaining. His deadpan comic delivery and timing sometimes rivaled Rodney Dangerfield's. Informed that the Defense Department was hyperventilating over some insignificant problem in Afghanistan, Franks quipped with impeccable timing, "Just tell them to breathe through their noses." To the young officer who began his briefing with the customary "How are you, sir?" Franks shot back, "I'm the best you'll ever meet." In the first weeks after September 11, when tension at his headquarters grew palpable, Franks told his staff, "I've been thinking about slitting my wrists or going bowling."

With the punishing Soviet occupation of Afghanistan still fresh in everyone's mind, a conventional Army invasion was out of the question. Too many American casualties. Too much risk of getting bogged down as an occupying force. Too likely that bin Laden would remain at large. The mission begged for an unconventional approach.

Afghanistan had been at war for twenty-three years. Its sole experiment with democracy had lasted just eight years, ending in a coup in 1973 that deposed the king, Zahir Shah. A long battle between communist, liberal, royalist, and Islamic factions ensued. In 1979 the Soviet Union, fearing the emergence of a radical Islamic state on its southern

---

* In the ARCENT job, Franks had reshaped the Kuwaiti armed forces, giving them the capability to defend their tiny country against an Iraqi invasion long enough for the American forces to arrive. Franks put in place a joint Army-Marine headquarters in Kuwait and brought in additional war equipment for his "lily pad," as he liked to call it, from which he could quickly move large numbers of ground forces.

border, invaded the country. Several thousand battle-hardened mujahideen fighters, inspired by radical Islamic fundamentalism, took up
arms and wore the Soviets down over ten years. Among the mujahideen leadership was a man named Osama bin Laden, a son in one of
the wealthiest families of Saudi Arabia. Bin Laden portrayed his convic-
tions as religious.

The mujahideen resistance got help from Pakistan's ISI and the
CIA, which provided money, equipment, and training. The mujahideen killed 15,000 Soviet soldiers during the fighting. More than one
million Afghan fighters and civilians died.

After the Soviet pullout, Afghanistan fell into an equally harsh ethnic war waged by competing warlords. The cruelty and hardship they
wrought drove many Afghans to support an ethnically Pashtun group
of religious students, the Taliban, who popped onto the scene in 1994.
Trained in Pakistan's religious schools, by 1996 their brand of rigid,
religious governance had swept across 90 percent of the country.

Roughly one-quarter of the Taliban's estimated 40,000 fighters were
foreigners: Pakistanis, Arabs, Chechens, and Central Asians, together
with a smattering of Europeans. From these volunteers, bin Laden also
built a more exclusive network, Al Qaeda, which in Arabic means "the
Base." It operated a dozen camps in Afghanistan and trained as many
as 15,000 militants. These disciples, in turn, spawned smaller terrorist
cells in fifty other countries, including Egypt, Indonesia, Pakistan, and
Somalia.

Bin Laden's first publicly announced goal was the overthrow of the
corrupt monarchy in Saudi Arabia and the expulsion of Americans
from Saudi holy land. In 1998, his jihad became more focused. That
February, he issued an Islamic ruling, or *fatwa*, calling on Muslims "to
kill the Americans and their allies—civilians and military."

The U.S. government suspected bin Laden and Al Qaeda of links
to at least six major terrorist attacks against U.S. interests: the 2000
attack on the USS *Cole* in the Yemeni port of Aden, bin Laden's ances-
tral home; the 1998 bombings of the U.S. embassies in Kenya and
Tanzania; the 1996 bombing of Khobar Towers, a U.S. military dormi-
tory in Dhahran, Saudi Arabia; and the 1993 bomb attack on the World

Trade Center. Some 266 people were killed and 5,500 injured in these six attacks.

Inside Afghanistan, the Taliban enforced a radical, authoritarian interpretation of Sunni Islam. They massacred adherents of Shi'a Islam. Their edicts forbade girls from attending school and women from working or appearing in public without being veiled from head to toe. Hindus and Sikhs were required to wear yellow clothes. The regime banned laughing in public, music, pictures, movies, and oddly, chess and bird-watching. Soon, Taliban intolerance and cruelty spawned another civil war, this time between the Taliban and the Northern Alliance, a loose army of anti-Taliban forces that ruled the northeastern Panjshir Valley even during the Soviet occupation.

The war plan President Bush accepted considered the unconventional nature of the country the United States was about to invade. The CIA's paramilitary units and the Army's covert Delta Force would search for Osama bin Laden and Al Qaeda's leadership. Meanwhile, Army Special Forces—working with CIA operatives and Navy and Air Force pilots—would team up with the Northern Alliance, the very people whose violent, uncompromising ways had driven the Afghan people to seek refuge in the Taliban to begin with.

Northern Alliance commanders—who had killed 25,000 people during an attempt to govern after the Soviets left—had agreed to a marriage of convenience. They could muster some 15,000 troops from their three ethnic groups—the Tajiks, Uzbeks and Hazaris—to defend the country's northern territories from the Pashtun-dominated Taliban. But they were a backward group of fighters, long supplied by Iran and Russia, financed by opium and weapons trafficking, and led by commanders of varying Islamic persuasions.[1] Their guerrilla tactics included shelling civilians and "engaging in rape, summary executions, arbitrary arrests, torture and 'disappearances.'"[2] After a decade of fighting the Taliban, the Northern Alliance had wound up controlling only 5 percent of the country.

Now the special forces would be asked to turn American airpower, with its high-tech machinery and capabilities, into a partner for a rickety cavalry force comprising bearded Afghan warriors, some of whom went into battle barefoot. The matchup stretched the experience and imagination of generals at the Central Command and the Pentagon. But it did not faze Chief Warrant Officer Diaz.

Diaz's "Triple Nickel" had won the right to be the first special forces A-team to enter Afghanistan in a competitive vetting process. Diaz, a slight, youthful thirty-eight-year-old, had spent seven months on a CIA-led mission along the Afghan-Pakistan border in 1987. Team 555 also included men who, along with Diaz, had survived combat in Iraq, anarchy in Somalia, and a decade of training lackadaisical Arab armies. Finally, the 555 was a scuba team, the most physically demanding specialty within the 8,800-strong Army Special Forces community.

The 555's CIA partners on the ground—they called themselves "Phil" and "Hal"—were part of a larger CIA effort dating back to the winter of 1999 when the IMU had tried to assassinate the Uzbek president. The IMU had close links to Osama bin Laden: its founder's sister was one of bin Laden's wives. After the assassination attempt, Uzbek prime minister Islam Karimov allowed the CIA to launch picture-snapping Predator unmanned aircraft and other elements of a bin Laden surveillance program from his country. The agency also cultivated contacts with close to a dozen anti-Taliban warlords, some living in Uzbekistan, whom they hoped would one day go after the Taliban just across the border.

Phil, fluent in Russian, led the meetings with the Afghan commanders, most of whom were Soviet trained and Russian speaking. Hal, a former Navy SEAL, was part of the CIA's growing paramilitary unit from the highly secretive Special Activities Division. Like other CIA teams infiltrated into Afghanistan shortly after September 11, Phil and Hal had worked with covert Army and Air Force units to designate landing zones, establish safe houses, and vet anti-Taliban commanders before the Special Forces arrived. They also distributed to the Northern Alliance thousands of AK-47s, mortars, and rocket-launched grenades, most of them from former Soviet bloc countries. A river of basic communications gear, medical supplies, shoes, and jackets flowed into the war. Some critical items were ferried over steep, forbidding mountain ranges in MH-47 Chinook helicopters from the 160th Special Operations Aviation Regiment. Others were air-dropped from Air Force MC-130 Talons.

After the midnight rendezvous with Diaz's men, Hal brought the team to a safe house in Astana, a village in the lush Panjshir Valley. This ethnically Tajik slice of north-central Afghanistan had been home to Northern Alliance leader Ahmed Shah Massoud. Massoud, nicknamed the "Lion of Panjshir" because he never allowed the Soviets to control the valley in the 1980s, had been assassinated by Al Qaeda operatives two days before the September 11 attacks.

Astana stood on the steep western slope of the valley. It had several crude landing strips that would be used to drop off special forces teams and tons of supplies. At the safe house, the team met Phil, a tall blond operative from the CIA's analytical branch who wore a beige canvas sports coat. Phil briefed Diaz's team on the details of their mission: At daybreak, the team would link up with forces under the command of Gen. Mohammed Fahim, Massoud's soft-spoken, handpicked successor. Fahim held the title of Northern Alliance defense minister (he is now defense minister for the Afghan interim government). They would work mainly with Gen. Bismullah Khan and his two subcommanders, generals named Sharif and Babajan, who had commanded troops in a three-year standoff with the Taliban at the Bagram airfield, 30 miles north of Kabul.

Team 555 would first help U.S. warplanes destroy the Taliban front line near that airfield, which hugged the Northern Alliance's southern front line. The opposing fronts were sometimes only a thousand meters away from one another. After clearing the Bagram area, the team was to search for and vanquish Taliban and Al Qaeda strongholds in the 35-mile stretch of barren land, the Shomali Plain, leading south to Kabul. Finally, they would help the Northern Alliance seize Kabul. A defeat at Kabul would deal a great psychological blow to Taliban troops concentrated in the south. It also would be a particularly sweet turn of events for Fahim, who had led Massoud's triumphant forces into Kabul in 1992 on the heels of the Soviet retreat.

Phil and Hal had been promising Afghan commanders that U.S. airpower would take down the Taliban. But after two weeks of weather delays and other hang ups, the Northern Alliance commanders had begun to grouse publicly about the bombing; none of it seemed connected to their ground campaign plans. "This weak work is not enough

AFGHANISTAN

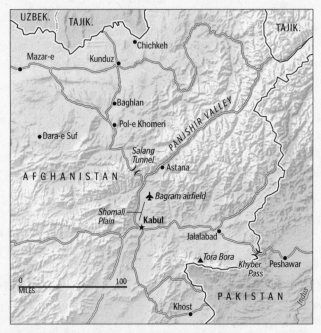

to destroy the enemy forces," Yonus Aanoni, a Massoud associate, complained to American reporters. "If the Americans think they can destroy terrorist bases in Afghanistan this way, it's not true." Finally, on October 20th, Phil had something more concrete to offer. "Here's the special forces team I've been promising you," he said, introducing Diaz's team to General Bismullah at a second safe house nicknamed the "Eagle's Nest," in a speck of a village named Taqhma.

Bismullah was friendly but reserved. "Okay, show us what you can do," he said.

"All you have to do is show me where to start," said Diaz.

At 7 A.M. the next morning, a four-man Special Forces survey team sneaked as close as they could to the Taliban front line to assess their position and search for targets. The view startled them. The Taliban had added 2,000 troops to the force of 5,000 it had stationed there at the time of Massoud's assassination. With the naked eye the team could see Taliban tanks, artillery, troops, command posts, vehicles, and ammunition bunkers. They counted more than fifty targets.

The scouting team called back to Diaz, who had gone to the Bagram control tower, which overlooked the corroded carcasses of several Soviet MiG fighters. The control tower offered a perfect view of the front line. Diaz radioed Sfc. J.T. back at the safehouse in Taqhma.* "Bring the CAS equipment, fast!" he ordered, referring to the binoculars, laser target designator, global positioning system (GPS), and other equipment used to identify targets and plot their coordinates for aircraft. He quizzed Technical Sergeant Calvin, the Air Force special operations combat controller who had joined the team in Uzbekistan: Could Calvin redirect aircraft already in the air and begin bombing right away?

J.T. lugged the ninety-pound equipment backpack up to the control tower at just about the time the aircraft started showing up. General Babajan, a stout, jovial commander, had arrived by then too, along with an entourage that filled the windowless, 20-by-20-foot control tower overlooking the airfield. "Look over there," Diaz told Babajan, handing

---

* Some, but not all, special forces soldiers requested that only their first names or initials be used in this book, citing concern for their own safety. Others asked not to be named at all, and so will be identified here only by their rank.

him the binoculars. "That's the target." He pointed toward a buried antiaircraft artillery gun sticking up from what looked like a mound of mud and at a command-and-control shack identified by a protruding antenna. The first aircraft, an F/A-18 Hornet off the USS *Theodore Roosevelt*, demolished the shack and the artillery gun with a bomb blast that flung dirt and fiery shards of metal three stories into the air.

Team 555 members survey the Taliban front line from the control tower at Bagram airfield, 30 miles north of Kabul. The team, with the help of Northern Alliance commanders, forced the Taliban out of the Shomali Plain and then moved onto Kabul. TEAM 555

The fireworks were immediately upstaged by cheers and laughter from the alliance commanders. Babajan shook the team members' hands and hugged Diaz. His larger security force standing at the base of the tower erupted in cheers and applause. "We're making history!" Calvin shouted. Babajan scribbled in his notebooks, listing targets struck and those he wanted struck. "Can we shoot too?" he asked. Sure, they told him. Babajan ordered his troops to fire some artillery rounds.

Hal, meanwhile, was throwing up the rotten egg he had eaten that morning for breakfast. The team had warned him against eating it, but he had shrugged them off, like he did with most everything else. "Hal-heave-a-stan," they nicknamed him.

An hour later, the Taliban struck back: artillery shells whizzed in, exploding in front of and behind the tower. The team was pinned down. Calvin crouched. Phil hit the floor. Two special forces soldiers scrambled down the rickety metal staircase. "Everybody stop where you're at and get back up here!" Diaz yelled at the two soldiers. Clearly their predeployment chest-beating had given way to fear. "Here's the deal: We will not be effective" if we bug out. "Don't even bother to duck," he said, explaining that the Taliban were bad shots. "It would be just luck if they hit us."

The team stayed at Bagram seven hours, until dusk, directing a continuous flow of aircraft to the Taliban front lines until there were no more aircraft available. Back at the safe house that evening, the Afghans feted the Americans with a huge feast—and a long list of targets for the next day.

* * * *

FOR NEARLY A WEEK, the 555 was one of only two special forces teams inside Afghanistan, and the only one doing much. It had the entire range of Air Force and Navy planes at its call: F/A-18, F-14, and F-15 fighters; B-52 and B-1 bombers; and AC-130 gunships. To identify the many targets, the team split in half and used two observation posts that lay two miles apart.

From his hidden observation posts around the Bagram airfield, J.T.'s binoculars teemed with enemy targets: Mud and straw huts where the Taliban slept. Rusted jeeps he had watched them drive in. A village they had turned into a headquarters with barracks. A shack that he believed to be a command post because of its rooftop antenna. Small columns of men walking ridgelines, cooking fires burning near trenches, artillery and mortar pieces, and tanks that glistened in the sun after the morning haze had burned off. Sometimes they saw black-shrouded figures, whom U.S. intelligence had identified as Al Qaeda operatives.

Those villages, shacks, and shadowy figures were also being observed by Sfc. Tom Rosenbarger, a fourteen-year veteran of the 5th

J.T., a member of Team 555, in the team's safe house, surrounded by communications gear he used to keep in touch with commanders in Uzbekistan and other parts of Afghanistan. TEAM 555

Special Forces Group, who sat 1,500 miles away in the space-age Combined Air Operations Center (known as the CAOC, pronounced "Kay-ock") at the Prince Sultan Air Base outside Riyadh, Saudi Arabia. He and others in the special operations liaison cell there monitored radios and gun-camera video and helped analyze imagery and intelligence on targets requested by the team. To verify targets, pilots and targeteers had unprecedented information: CIA intelligence from the ground, pictures from satellites, and real-time images from P-3 spy planes and Predator drones.

Rosenbarger held another equally critical job. He was the link between two parallel worlds: the Air Force's high-tech, precision aviation and the Army Special Forces' seat-of-the-pants, in-the-dirt unconventional warfare. Surrounded by dust-free computers, real-time imagery, and digital equations of weather, time, and space, most Air Force officers in the CAOC had little idea what special forces teams did. At first they doubted the teams could be effective. "Understand, this is UW," Rosenbarger remembers telling one skeptical Air Force officer, using the abbreviation for "unconventional warfare," the raison d'être for Army Special Forces. "What's UW?" the Air Force officer asked. Still, Rosenbarger's Air Force colleagues adapted quickly, especially after he sneaked them copies of bomb damage assessment reports. The reports showed a lot of military equipment had been destroyed in "villages."

The Air Force leadership had resisted hitting small targets like troops and vehicles during the Kosovo air war, which were hidden under the trees and hard to find. They preferred to destroy large or politically sensitive sites with major "strategic" value, like top ministries or command centers. But these targets didn't exist in Afghanistan. So pilots and planners adapted, learning to strike one jeep, a pair of mud mounds, a small cluster of Taliban fighters.[*]

Team 555 had their Air Force liaison, too. Technical Sergeant Calvin, the special operations combat controller from the 720th Special Tactics Group who accompanied Team 555 in Afghanistan, taught them to call in CAS (close air support) and to talk in a language that pilots understood: smooth, calm, peppered with Air Force slang. To Navy and Air Force pilots flying thousands of feet above, few of the things that Team 555 identified looked like military targets. And sometimes the minumum 15,000-foot altitude imposed by Washington for the pilots' safety rendered it impossible for pilots to see what the teams saw. So in the initial days of the war, J.T. and the others had learned they would have to give pilots more than just target coordinates to convince them to drop their ordnance. "We started to play this terminology game," said Diaz. He told the nine soldiers[†] and Calvin, "Yes, it is a civilian village, mud hut, like everything else in this country. But don't say that. Say it's a 'military compound.' It's a built-up area, barracks, command and control. Just like with the convoys—if it really was a convoy with civil-

---

[*] Significantly, in the Afghan campaign, the Air Force all but abandoned its standard seventy-two-hour "air tasking order" (ATO) cycle previously required to orchestrate a day's worth of aircraft but which could be tweaked on a moment's notice. In Afghanistan, air planners vetted targets and sent aircraft to strike many of them within twelve hours or less. Often, they sent up planes in anticipation, redirecting them to strike targets after they were already in the air. For still greater flexibility, air planners divided the country into thirty "kill boxes" in which pilots could loiter, waiting to be directed to "emerging" targets.

[†] One of the twelve initial A-team members had since left the country.

ian vehicles they were using for transport, we would just say, 'Military convoy, troop transport.'"

In the beginning at least, the 555 pled its case often to pilots. The pilots would say, "'I see a city. I see a town,'" J.T. explained. "I would say, well no, you see a cluster of five buildings. Near one of these buildings you'll see a cluster of vehicles. While they may look like Toyota Land Cruisers, they are used to move troops and ammunition. . . . Yes, it's a mud hut. We live in mud huts. They live in mud huts. We fight out of mud huts. They fight out of mud huts. There are no good guys there anymore." Similar discussions ensued over Taliban convoys that would rumble out of a mountain pass every night moving from Kabul to Bagram, mistakenly assuming they would be safe from air strikes if they

Team 555 members in a hideout in the mountains surrounding the Shomali Plain, with satellite phones and GPS equipment they used to direct Navy and Air Force planes to Taliban targets. TEAM 555

hugged the Northern Alliance front line. Some of the convoys included women and children, whom the team concluded must be Taliban family members. "We knew the only people who were going to travel from here to Kabul were combatants, and in some cases, their family members," said Diaz. In those cases, he added, "the guidance I gave my team, and the guidance from [headquarters], is that they are combatants."

Pilots quickly came to trust the Triple Nickel's judgment. But the complexities of identifying targets and avoiding civilians remained a strong concern throughout the war's first phase. Pentagon targeting practices came under scrutiny each time Afghan villagers and journalists reported civilian casualties. The Pentagon, always defensive about the allegations, often outright denied mistakes that otherwise appeared obvious. It claimed, too, that it kept no record of civilian or enemy deaths, although each team filed detailed daily reports that included such information. Still, Air Force planners were taking more care than in any previous war to minimize the chance of killing innocent civilians.

In the strictest sense, unarmed civilians can never be considered combatants. Under international law, military forces must take "all feasible precautions" to avoid civilian casualties, attack only military objects, and weigh the value of striking when civilian casualties are likely to occur. Where targets often look like or are interspersed among civilian entities, the military has an obligation to ask, "Is that a trade-off that can be justified?" This is what Diaz and his soldiers believe they did.

The rules of engagement allowed extraordinary measures when soldiers came under fire. One afternoon in early November 2001 as J.T. and a local Afghan commander hunted for targets from the turret of a building southeast of Bagram, the sandbags in front of them suddenly began popping with the impact of machine gun rounds. J.T.'s laser designator was knocked to the ground.

J.T. radioed for help. "Is there anything out there?" he asked, seeking an answer from a pilot, any pilot. "Please . . . anything." No response. J.T. and the Afghan began to climb down a ladder propped against the building. The Afghan commander was handing the radio to J.T. when it squawked with a familiar call sign: "Poison one-one." They scurried back up and a comforting, if frantic, dialogue ensued, during which J. T. directed the pilot to the targets.

"Poison one-one," the pilot said in a monotone. "Advise and ready for fighter check in."

"Tiger zero-one," J.T. answered. "Advise and ready for target talk-on."

Over the next hour, forty-five bombs rained down on a 300-by-100-meter area. "Shack on target!" J.T. yelled to indicate a direct hit. "Shack on target!"

"It was beautiful," J.T. later recalled. "The whole area was loaded with machine guns and mortars. . . . We completely smoked everything."

The Taliban sometimes unwittingly helped U.S. troops with their targeting. Many Afghan Taliban and Northern Alliance soldiers were friends who found themselves drafted into opposite sides of the war. They would communicate over their amateur radios, even taunting each other in the heat of battle. "Your bomb missed us," one would say. "Where did it land?" the Northern Alliance officer would respond, after some coaching from the Americans. The Taliban would respond: "Five hundred meters to the north," or "A thousand meters to the south." The combat controller had only to recalculate the coordinates and pass them to the nearest aircraft, which could restrike the target within minutes. Team 555 calculated that a week of this banter wiped out many of the Taliban commanders and destroyed much of their communications network.

The Taliban weren't the only people soldiers learned to trick. News reporters frequently flocked to the Bagram tower to interview the effervescent General Babajan. Once, as planes streaked toward their targets, Babajan stood surrounded by fifty journalists crowded around the tower. They wouldn't leave, but while they remained the team could not guide warplanes to new targets. Babajan knew that the aircraft had limited loitering times, so he ordered his troops on the perimeter to fire their AK-47s toward the tower. "You've got to go!" Babajan shouted to the reporters above the sound of the firing. "The tower is under attack!" That did it. Reporters screeched away in their vehicles, passing within feet of the special forces soldiers disguised in beards and Afghan clothing and riding in Soviet-made jeeps.

For twenty-five straight days, often around-the-clock, Team 555 directed 175 aircraft sorties over a 60-by-30-kilometer area. Their targets were sometimes as close as 1,000 meters from their observation posts at the Bagram airfield, sometimes as distant as 18 kilometers away.

★ ★ ★ ★

THE SPECIAL FORCES owed part of their success in Afghanistan to others. Just two weeks after September 11, tiny advance teams of CIA, Delta Force, and Air Force covert operatives had been quitely spirited into Afghanistan and Uzbekistan. One of the first things to roll off the

C-17 cargo plane at Khanabad Air Base in Uzbekistan was a container of body bags and a refrigerator van for preserving bodies. The Graves Registration specialists quickly moved to the perimeter; in deference to morale, they kept the body bags out of sight.

A portable machine shop soon followed, equipped with welding torches, grinders, air compressors, and every tool imaginable. This shop could fix or rebuild any piece of metal the military brought in. Swimming pool–sized rubber bladders held enough fuel for hundreds of planes, helicopters, all-terrain vehicles, motorcycles, and generators. Special operations pilots, touching down at night in top-secret landing zones, ferried in tons of ammunition, potable water, food rations, underwear, sunscreen, and "Class 6" personal items—cigarettes, chewing tobacco, toothpaste.

Close behind these combat support units came the 112th Signal Battalion, charged with linking the Soviet-era Khanabad outpost to twenty-first-century America. The 112th possessed a magnificient machine, a camouflaged TSC-93 satellite terminal—a truck with a giant satellite dish on its back and 12,000 pounds of ancillary equipment. With the TSC-93, technicians opened up secure telephone, fax, and Internet service into Europe and the United States. They established communications lines down into the field, too, where Special Forces with book-sized notebook computers could download highly classified operational updates complete with maps, satellite photos, and the locations of enemy troops.[*] The TSC-93 brought commanders in the United States right to the battlefield.

As early as October 13, the commander of the Air Force's 16th Special Operations Group, a colonel, sat behind a folding table inside the command center. Behind him, soldiers had hung a banner with the code name for the Afghanistan mission: Task Force Dagger.

The colonel stared into a little camera set up ten feet away, and his voice and image were instantly beamed to a series of satellites and ground stations across Europe and the United States. His tented

---

[*] The dust from the dozens of landing aircraft collected immediately on the TSC-93's wiring and transmitter. To keep them clean, signal technicians wrapped the equipment in Saran Wrap and covered the terminal's dust filters with t-shirts that they changed every six hours.

operational center reached the Pentagon, the White House situation room, and the CIA. It linked him to the CAOC and to General Franks at Central Command and the Special Operations Command, both in Tampa. Within a week, the signal unit was running eight videoconferences a day between the mission's commanders. Power Point slides illustrated battlefield plans. What began as 250 encrypted telephone calls a day between U.S.-based commanders and the theater of operations ballooned to 550 in the twelve-hour period known as "the pitch of battle."

1st Sgt. Mike Murray had helped set up the first videoconference and he marveled at the capability. But he also knew the war wouldn't be won by gadgets, no matter how sophisticated. "The technology *supporting* warfare is incredible," he said. "The technology *of* warfare is still nuts and bolts." In this case, "it still came down to that poor, dumb bastard on horseback."

Those would be Team 555's Afghan partners. The team's work with General Fahim north of Kabul echoed that of three more A-teams that infiltrated Afghanistan beginning in the second half of October: Team 553 in the central Bamian province, Team 585 around Kunduz and Chichkeh, and Team 595 in Dara-e-Suf, a remote mountain valley and headquarters of that team's new partner, Gen. Abdurrashid Dostum, the ruthless, alliance-shifting warlord.

For eighteen days after Diaz's Team 555 first arrived, those four teams, plus two fifteen-person battalion-level headquarters—some seventy-eight soldiers in all—accounted for the entire Special Forces presence in Afghanistan. Yet they set the stage for the fall of the northern two-thirds of the country.

With such small numbers, most A-teams split into three-man detachments. Some went for weeks without seeing other Americans, maintaining contact via satellite radio. One team was ferried into place in a rattletrap, Soviet-made MI-8 HIP helicopter that "barely cleared some of the highest peaks" of the 25,000-foot peaks of the Hindu Kush, according to that team's official report. One three-man detachment from Team 595 worked out of an observation post dug into a hilltop, an eighteen-hour horseback ride from the closest U.S. soldier.

Horses, in fact, were a brief but uncomfortable fact of life for the Americans. Only two of the 595's soldiers had ever ridden a horse.

During their first hours on the ground in Afghanistan, the burly special forces soldiers suddenly found themselves on wiry mountain ponies, astride stiff wooden saddles with stirrups so short their knees jammed into their armpits. Even some Northern Alliance fighters were injured or killed when their horses fell off the sheer mountainsides. Some senior officers considered the horseback rides as dangerous as any part of the mission.

The team assigned to Dostum consisted of fresh-faced twenty- to thirty-year-olds. They had little in common with the grizzled warlord whose officers were accused of throwing disloyal soldiers down wells and tossing grenades in after them. Dostum's men rode ponies into battle against Taliban armor and artillery, at times carrying fewer than 20 rounds. Most of the 595 had never seen combat.

Dostum worried that the death of even one U.S. soldier might weaken American commitment to the war, he told Mark, the young captain assigned to him. The Special Forces soldiers convinced him otherwise, though they were unsure on this point themselves, being products of the risk-averse military of the 1990s. "The problem we have as soldiers," said the 595's team sergeant, Paul, "is we don't make policy. We can say, 'We're committed,' and the next day, Congress can say, 'No we're not.' We end up being very vague on those statements."

During the first weeks of November, six more Special Forces A-teams and one company-sized headquarters flew into Afghanistan. Three went north, two south, and one headed to the eastern province of Herat. So did the lieutenant colonel in charge of the 5th Special Forces Group's 3rd battalion. He and seven others arrived at Dara-e Suf, joining Team 595. The lieutenant colonel's job was to coordinate the battles of three major Northern Alliance commanders, including Dostum, and to take Mazar-e-Sharif, the northwestern city that Dostum had once controlled. Mazar-e-Sharif held strategic value because it could open a supply pipeline to allied forces elsewhere in the north.

By the time the lieutenant colonel arrived, Dostum had allied himself with former enemies Attah Mohammed and Mohammed Mohaqiq to take the city. All were eager to have communications capability, to keep track of each other. Each Afghan commander was given an Inmarsat satellite phone to speak to the others and to the lieutenant colonel. The American also had his own line of communication with the A-teams attached to each commander.

To design their offensive, the lieutenant colonel rolled out a 4-by-6-foot laminated map that the alliance chiefs marked with X's and O's and arrows. Dostum and the officer planned to encircle Mazar-e-Sharif, but all harbored great concern that Taliban forces would resist and turn the battle into a house-by-house fight, "absolutely the worst kind of fight you can be in," the U.S. officer said. But as they approached Mazar-e-Sharif, the lieutenant colonel found that his toughest job was merely getting the forces of all three commanders into the city without fratricide. When they started squabbling, he would pull from his chest pocket a piece of the World Trade Center he had been given and remind himself, "This is why we're here."

The night before the battle, Dostum and the other commanders' troops arrayed themselves on the ridges overlooking Mazar-e-Sharif and watched convoys of Taliban troops flee. The American called in fierce air strikes. "We saturated the battlefield with small close-air-support cells and we hit the Taliban if they were engaging us, if they were trying to maneuver into a favorable position," he said. "We engaged them while they were moving and if they tried to retreat. They simply could not move."

The Taliban front line collapsed right away on the night of November 9. Taliban soldiers fled, abandoning trenches, leaping from tanks, and scrambling into trucks and jeeps for a getaway. Hundreds fled south and east to Samangan and Kunduz provinces. U.S. aircraft flew in to attack some fleeing fighters, but they did not ask the Afghans to intercept them on the ground. Northern Alliance troops on the hilltops, reported the lieutenant colonel, "were simply ecstatic."

Dostum immediately set his sights on Kabul and Kunduz. But so did Fahim and the other commanders. For weeks Washington had been urging the Northern Alliance leadership not to move on the capital. The United States needed time to negotiate a power-sharing agreement among Afghanistan's ethnic blocs, but fighting was about to overtake diplomacy.

★ ★ ★ ★

COMPETITION FOR KABUL was not an impulse unique to Afghan commanders. Diaz did not want another team's general to beat his—Fahim—into Kabul. The capital's liberation represented a major symbolic victory, both nationally and internationally. "I tried to play him against Dostum by saying, 'Hey, we don't want to be last. Why aren't we starting?'" Diaz revealed.

So they struck a deal. Fahim agreed to ready his troops if Diaz would hit a list of targets Fahim drew up. The list included key villages and other targets to make the ground offensive easier. For two days beginning November 10, Diaz's team called in 25 strikes and, by its estimates, killed 2,200 enemy combatants and destroyed 29 tanks and 6 command posts. Yet reporters who visited the area soon afterward saw no evidence of such heavy destruction.

Fahim's troops donned brand-new Chinese-made uniforms, readied their weapons for the offensive, and stayed in their garrison. Fahim had agreed to give Diaz twenty-four hours' notice before his troops began their move south. Diaz estimated it would take Fahim's foot soldiers ten days to advance the thirty miles to Kabul. His superiors, even more cautious, were predicting a long spring offensive beginning in four months.

On November 12, his team sergeant, Greg McCormick, radioed Diaz with news from the Afghan subcommander he was working with. "They're moving out in two hours," he reported. "We tried to stay ahead of them with the bombings," said McCormick, "but at some point we did have to stop because they were moving faster than we could calculate where they were at—so we wouldn't blow them up. . . . We knew their objective was Kabul and they weren't going to be slowed down by our bombing."

As they moved south, the Northern Alliance allowed thousands of Afghan Taliban fighters to switch sides. Nothing was ever simple in Afghanistan, however. Several suicide bombers mingled among the defectors and blew themselves up in an effort to kill those switching sides. Conversely, "There was a lot of hand-shaking involved, especially between Afghani and Afghani," said McCormick. But this surrender deal did not hold for non-Afghan fighters—the Arabs, Pakistanis, Chechens, and others. "The Pakis and other foreigners [that the Northern Alliance] couldn't care less about, they were going to kill them," said McCormick.

"We absorbed the native Afghanis. The Arabs and Pakistanis were all killed trying to escape—supposedly." Many other Taliban fled south.[*]

By dawn on November 13, the Northern Alliance troops approached Kabul. Fahim held the lead. As it turned out, Fahim had resorted to a

Sporting the beards and Afghan clothes that provided their disguises, Team 555 posed in front of the U.S. embassy in Afghanistan, which had been closed since 1989. The team found the embassy frozen in time, and checked for bombs before the Marines arrived to officially raise the flag. CWO David Diaz is in the middle row, third from the right.   TEAM 555

time-honored Afghan practice: he simply bribed several subcommanders to slow down so that he could take the city. "He paid them off to stop," said Diaz. Team 555's jeeps were surrounded by a crush of cheering Afghans.

Once in the capital, the team made its way to the American embassy,

[*] Stories of war atrocities were difficult to prove. An article in *Newsweek* magazine cited a confidential UN report quoting a witness as saying 960 Taliban were killed under the control of warlord Gen. Abdurrashid Dostum. Dostum acknowledged that 200 prisoners had died while being transported in shipping containers, but claimed they had suffocated unintentionally. Physicians for Human Rights, meanwhile, said hundreds died en route to a prison in Sherbergan and ended up at a mass gravesite in nearby Dasht-t-Leili.

which had been closed since 1989. Marines, who guard American embassies around the world, were to be allowed to open the embassy doors and raise the American flag in front of an international media corps. But the 555 entered first, to check the building for booby traps.

Inside, the embassy stood frozen in time. The ambassador's desk still brimmed with papers. The team looked around the compound, opening drawers and peering in closets. In the refrigerator, the 555 found four soda cans wrapped in brown paper and, curiously, labeled "bomb." A map of Kabul clung to the wall. Open bottles sat, covered in dust, behind the Marine Corps bar, a standard recreation room in many embassy compounds.

* * * *

AFTER THE NORTHERN ALLIANCE reopened the Bagram airfield, the commander in charge of the super-secret Joint Special Operations Command arrived with a covert Delta Force team. They set up an operations and intelligence center from which actions against bin Laden and Al Qaeda would be directed.

The JSOC operation was off-limits even to the special forces and certainly to the larger, conventional troops, such as the Army's 10th Mountain Division, which would later join the big fight at Tora Bora. The CIA set up its own operations too. Its most highly sensitive operations in Afghanistan were assigned the code name Focal Point. Files labeled Focal Point required extra-special clearance in order to be read. Few regular Army, Special Forces, or other covert military operations got Focal Point clearance. These separate operations created a confusing chain of command and sometimes overlapping operations, but more importantly, they disproved the long-held doctrine of "unity of command" on the battlefield. With so many ultra-sensitive operations, no one commander, no matter what his rank, could be certain he knew of and directed all the players on his battlefield.

* * * *

IMMEDIATELY AFTER KABUL FELL, signs of trouble with the Afghan allies appeared. Diaz's team was twice visited by the Afghan commanders who had worked alongside them. The Afghans came bearing coordinates; they wanted Diaz's team to call his bombers and fighters to an area just south of Kabul. Enemy territory, they insisted. Calvin sent the Afghan requests to the base at Karshi, which passed it up to the CAOC in Saudi Arabia. The request, Calvin recalled, bounced right back: the target requested was not Taliban, it was a rival alliance faction. "It is a problem between them," the response noted.

The fall of Kabul on November 13 provided a moral boost to the Afghan political leadership as it struggled to organize and equip a fighting force in the south territory it had not controlled in years. But in selected areas, the Taliban's resolve seemed only to strengthen.

On the night of November 13, Special Forces Team 586, paired with Gen. Daoud Khan, came under heavy fire at a power plant in the northern city of Taloqan, near the Tajikistan border. It began when one of Daoud's subcommanders advanced toward Kunduz before the agreed-upon offensive was to begin. The original plan had been "to blitz through the Taliban all the way to Kunduz," the team reported to head-quarters, but Kunduz was the last northern stronghold of the radical Islamic militias and every warlord in the north wanted to be there first.

Instead, struggling against a fierce enemy counterattack, Daoud's commanders got stuck at Taloqan, 35 miles to the east, and asked the special forces to save them. This they did. The team's initial bomb damage assessment report offers a rare glimpse at the intensity of destruction wrought by U.S. warplanes late in this rapid-fire war. On the first day of the attack around Taloqan, U.S. planes destroyed three Taliban command-and-control buildings and four cargo trucks. They killed or injured 85 Taliban, a number that grew each day. On November 15, they reported 386 casualties. Then 120, then 300, then 253. On November 23, with enemy forces on three sides and taking sniper and machine-gun fire, the Taloqan special forces team guided aircraft to 12 vehicles, bunkers, and 450 troops. In all, the team filed reports claiming 2,139 Taliban dead.

All the while, some thirty miles away, Kunduz had been under siege. Now Daoud headed west, only to be turned back by his chief rival, General Dostum, just ten miles shy of the city. By then, the lieutenant colonel of Team 595, who had been assisting Dostrum, had worked out a plan to seize Kunduz. Dostum, Daoud, and four other

regional warlords—"every Northern Alliance warlord who had a formation of any size"—wanted in on the action.

The operation was complex. The battalion commander had no battalion but rather 8,000 fractious Afghan troops to keep track of, plus
six special forces teams (some eighty men in all). "Deconflicting" the
forces—making sure neither the warplanes above nor the troops on the
ground fired on a friendly force—was like simultaneously orchestrating six disorderly marching bands. All target requests by individual
special forces teams were first submitted to the battalion commander
and plotted and rechecked by his Air Force special operations combat
controller. Then the targets were sent up his chain of command and
back down again, to the pilots.

The siege of Kunduz dragged on for two weeks, in part because
many of the Taliban fighters were Pakistanis, Chechens, and Arabs
who refused to surrender (knowing they would most likely be killed
if they did). Although the Afghan Taliban were encouraged to switch
sides and join the alliance, Dostum promised the foreigners only that
they would be held for trial rather than executed right away. Daoud,
whose army included many former hard-line mujahideen, was said to
favor immediate execution.

By the first evening of the offensive against Kunduz, November 25,
some 600 of the Taliban's foreign fighters, most of them Pakistani, had
surrendered. They were arrested and driven overnight to a jail in Mazar-e-
Sharif. Meanwhile, another 1,500 Taliban had slipped out of Kunduz and
were heading back towards Mazar-e-Sharif. Among those who wanted
to surrender in Kunduz were some senior Taliban leaders who claimed
to have been wounded and were seeking medical care. But just as they
were to be met by Dostum, he learned from informants that they were
part of an assassination plot. "We knew they were trying to kill General
Dostum," said the captain. "The Taliban had hired a band of assassins to
find General Dostum. We knew it was their tactic to defect in an effort to
get closer to him." Special forces saw the plot as part of a larger scheme
to recapture Mazar-e-Sharif. All the Northern Alliance commanders, and
all the top Americans ones as well, had come to Kunduz and were now
distracted by the fight there; meanwhile prisoners at the Qala-i-Jangi fort-
turned-prison outside Mazar-e-Sharif had begun blowing themselves up

with grenades. The 450 inmates then overpowered their guards, killed CIA operative Johnny "Mike" Spann, and stormed the armory.

When the revolt ended three days later, burned and bloated bodies lay everywhere. Five Americans had been injured when a U.S. bomb, launched in an attempt to put down the uprising, struck the wrong side of the building.

But Mazar-e-Sharif remained under alliance control.

★ ★ ★ ★

IN THE NORTH, the military campaign had preceded the political one. In the south, military might followed politics.

In the north, Afghan warlords conceived and executed their own war plans. In the south, however, there were no warlords and no standing armies. Pashtun leader Hamid Karzai knew where he wanted to be: Kandahar, the Taliban's spiritual capital and the base of its power. But he wasn't sure how to get there, nor how to wrest the city from the Taliban once he arrived.

During the second half of November and the first week of December, another five A-teams, three Special Forces company staffs, and another battalion commander made it into Afghanistan. They had come to build armies that could solidify Karzai's political strength among tribal lands in the southern provinces of Uruzgan, Kandahar, and Helmand. Capt. Jason Amerine's Team 574 had been ferried into Taliban territory to work with Karzai. With an initial force of only one hundred fighters, Karzai and Amerine's forces—later joined by the 2nd Battalion commander, Lt. Col. David Fox, and his staff—swept through the south, fighting the Taliban but also building tribal allegiances that would support Karzai's drive into the final goal, the city of Kandahar.

Their first victory came on November 17 when they captured Tarin Kot, a city some sixty miles north of the city of Kandahar. From there they moved southwest, skirting Kandahar to De Maymand, then onto the town of Seyyed Mohammed Kalay, thirty miles from the ultimate goal. Each day they waited at their safe house for tribal elders to decide whether to support Karzai. Karzai's satellite-phone diplomacy was coupled with verbal messages brought by courier on horseback to surrounding villages. Volunteer fighters were promised food, clothing, and shelter, which special operations aircraft ferried in. Each day Karzai's force grew by dozens. Each night, before they moved forward, the team and Karzai would wait for a local report on the location of Taliban forces. "The tribal elders would say, 'Right here in these orchards, there are a lot of Taliban vehicles,'" remembered Maj. Don Bolduc. An AC-130 gunship would be dispatched to check it out. Sure enough, said Bolduc, "there they were."

At Seyyed Mohammed Kalay, the team was pinned down for two days by a Taliban counterattack aimed at preventing the alliance from taking the town's bridge, the last between the alliance and Kandahar. The fighting became intense, nearly enveloping the Americans at one point. M. Sgt. Jefferson D. Davis, nicknamed "J.D.," sensed the worry rise within his team. "Ah, we have an AC-130 with us," he told them calmly. "We're good." One U.S. soldier was shot in the shoulder and evacuated. But they soon moved on. Karzai's makeshift force was now up to 600 men.

The Taliban, sensing their final days were near, fought constantly. "They kept on you, day and night" with small arms and sniper fire, said Bolduc. Radio transmissions picked up by their Afghan partners, he said, revealed that the Taliban "wanted to get Hamid Karzai." The Taliban must have known it was their last chance. So the U.S. troops kept Karzai far from the firefights and put helicopters on alert status in case his immediate evacuation were needed.

Most of Team 574 had never been in combat before and the constant whiz of bullets and not-so-distance mortar fire unnerved some. Many turned to J.D. to get their bearings. "When we would get nervous he would just tell us, 'We're going to stick together. We're going to be okay,'" said Sfc. Vaugh Berntson. J.D. knew them better than they knew themselves. "Hey Bad Brad," he joked with SSgt. Brad Fowers to buck up his courage, "you ready for this?"

Amerine's team and Lieutenant Colonel Fox's staff were joined at Seyyed Mohammed Kalay by another dozen special forces soldiers who arrived at 3 A.M. on December 5. By then, makeshift Afghan forces from all over the south were converging on Kandahar. Bolduc told the newly arrived troops to bunk down for a few hours and be up on a nearby hill at 8 A.M. for an orientation briefing.

When the sun came up, Bolduc and other team members noticed a complex of Taliban caves "2,264 meters away," as Bolduc recalled, on the next ridgeline. SSgt. Hamid Fathi was up top too on an adjacent ridgeline, seated on the rocky ground, with Karzai's chief organizer, a former anti-Soviet fighter. The Americans had nicknamed Karzai's man "sergeant major," because the old Afghan was so well organized. Fathi handed the sergeant major a set of binoculars and pointed to the caves where Fathi said the sergeant major should watch as warplanes blasted them apart. "Come to the right a little bit," Fathi motioned to him.

As the sergeant major raised his binoculars, a devastating explosion—an errant 2,200-pound satellite-guided American bomb—blackened the consciousness of the soldiers who lived to talk about it. Three U.S. soldiers and five Afghans were killed instantly. Among them was J.D., who had been handing out Rice Krispie treats he had received in a package from his wife. Forty other Americans and Afghans were wounded. Two of the dead Afghans landed on Bolduc, who was walking up the hill after retrieving a package his wife had sent him. Bolduc and Fox both suffered shattered eardrums. Bolduc's hip was badly damaged. Only four men in their unit were unharmed—with only one day to go before they were to enter Kandahar. Bolduc and Fox refused evacuation.

The accident occurred when an Air Force combat air controller changed a battery on a GPS device he was using to determine coordinates for targets to be struck. The controller did not realize that after the battery was changed, the machine would revert to displaying the coordinates for the GPS's location, instead of those for the intended target.

Replacement special forces soldiers flew in that night. The next day they retook the bridge at Sayyed Mohammed Kalay and moved on to Kandahar without incident on December 6. The Taliban had fled Afghanistan. The first phase of the war was over.

But Bolduc's job was hardly over. "Okay, Don," Fox told him the next morning. "I need you to come up with a plan on how to make Kandahar city stable, safe, and secure . . . and you need to brief me on it in a couple of hours."

"Is that all you want, sir?" Bolduc said, laughing. "Nooooo problem."

His first thought was of Gen. George Patton, who had divided

Berlin into four sectors after World War II. So Bolduc drew four sectors onto his map of Kandahar and then subdivided the city's outskirts into another five. He assigned each one a special forces unit and a small Afghan force to set up roadblocks, disarm civilians, and enforce a curfew. He also drew up a chart with the civilian authorities needed in each sector: chief of police, fire department, "a financial guy," schools, customs. By sunset, after a daylong meeting with Afghan political leaders, the first draft of Kandahar's future as a civil society was fixed.

That was hopeful news for a country that had spent the last twenty-three years at war. But bad news appeared quickly. The Taliban were not the only enemy of peace. Northern Alliance factions, unknowingly abetted by American troops, had begun competing for the spoils of war.

★ ★ ★ ★

WHILE BOLDUC'S AND other teams moved throughout the southwest securing surrenders, in the north, Team 532 was becoming entangled in a political minefield they did not detect until it was too late. Their partner was Jeff Naderi, an Americanized Afghan who had attended elementary school in Allentown, Pa., in the 1970s. His father had once been governor of Baghlan province, whose capital was Pol-e-Khomri, just south of Kunduz. Naderi had returned to his native Afghanistan to help unseat the Taliban. Now known as Sayyed Jaffar, he quickly earned the admiration of the twelve-man special forces team assigned to help him. Friendly and fluent in American culture, he claimed to have big plans for Pol-e-Khomri and Afghanistan's Ismaili Muslim community, a Shia offshoot that resided in the Kayan Valley.

Jaffar had no real army after infiltrating back into the country through Tajikistan a few weeks before the U.S. bombing started. So the Special Forces built him one. From the first 150 volunteers, they built a force of 1,000. All had shown up at Team 532's doorstep in the valley soon after hearing that the Americans had arrived. Jaffar demanded a disciplined force. He made his men shave their beards and march in orderly columns. This impressed the Americans, too.

Pol-e-Khomri, however, was in the hands of Gen. Khalil Anderabi, a non-Ismaili ethnic Tajik who was part of the Northern Alliance and allied with General Daoud. Jaffar, an ally of Daoud's fiercest rival, General Dostum, convinced his special forces team that if they just showed up in town with his troops, Anderabi would give up. Anderabi and the townspeople were supposedly just protecting the town until Jaffar and his men could return. "What we envisioned," said Sfc. Jay, "is that we would do our movement up to the city and once the people saw that we were on the hills, this [Anderabi] guy would capitulate . . . [and] our guy would come in and reestablish his [family's] governorship."

On December 12, Jaffar's troops positioned themselves on a steep ridgeline above Pol-e-Khomri and sent a couple of men surreptitiously down to a cement factory in town, to keep watch. The men counted sixteen tanks in the immediate area, none of them Jaffar's.

Clouds covered the city below. From the ridgeline, there was only one way out, a narrow trail, "the most treacherous route I've ever been on," said Sfc. Jay. Jaffar told the U.S. troops that he had convinced the city elders to meet among themselves and persuade Anderabi to retreat. Jaffar negotiated with Anderabi by cell phone as one of Anderabi's tanks rumbled toward Jaffar's troops. Spotting the tank, the team called in a warplane to circle overhead, "just to let him know the capability was there if we needed it."

The team had been waiting on the ridgeline for two hours when suddenly tanks, artillery, and antiaircraft rockets blasted Jaffar's front line, which was not far from the Americans. Half the team scrambled into a trench on high ground; the other half slinked down to guard the exit trail and were pinned down.

Anderabi's mechanized vehicles chugged up the ridgeline. Mortars thudded nearby, spewing fire and dirt into the air. The Americans, convinced that their man Jaffar was a man of peace caught in a web of war, stepped in with the best they had: warplanes. Pilots raced to the team's aid as soon as the emergency call for help went out. The team knew this decision would be controversial, for they were sending U.S. warplanes to attack an allied force. Good guys against good guys, green on green. "When they zeroed in on us and we were pinned down on the hill," said Jay, "we had to make a decision and the decision was, bomb."

One ferocious bomb splashed its red-hot shrapnel near the menacing tank. Everything went silent. No more lumbering vehicle. No foot-steps. No more single shots. Dead silence for about twenty minutes. Then, all at once, Anderabi's forces opened up again. Bullets, rockets, war whoops, all flung in their direction.

The team's top commander in the theater, Col. John Mulholland, back at Khanabad in Uzbekistan, had been working the phones him-self trying to get General Daoud to stop his subordinate. Anderabi's and Jaffar's differences had to be worked out peacefully, he argued; Special Forces couldn't be put in this position, defending both sides of a battle with U.S. firepower. But the shooting continued.

The U.S. troops, meanwhile, continued to help aircraft strike Anderabi's heavy weapons. In the middle of a barrage of bombs and missiles, Jay saw women and children playing just 200 yards away from a 122-millimeter howitzer firing round after round. "That just blew my mind," he said. "The kids are outside playing and they don't even bat an eyelash. A guy's out there plowing his field."

Stifled in his effort at a peaceful resolution, Mulholland pulled the plug. He dispatched an emergency force to extract Team 532 from the area immediately. The team members protested. They liked Jaffar. They believed in his vision for a peaceful, prosperous community. Mulholland ordered them out anyway. The 532 said a hasty goodbye to Jaffar and left him with some rock 'n' roll CDs. Jaffar's soldiers escorted the Americans to a nearby landing zone, where an MC-130 Combat Talon transport plane and two Black Hawk helicopters lifted them out of Afghanistan. For extra protection, an AC-130 gunship hung nearby.

Reporters on the scene counted four air strikes that day, as did a member of the humanitarian group Swedish Committee for Afghanistan. By midafternoon, two hospitals began receiving the wounded. Reports in the *New York Times* and the *Boston Globe* cited local officials who said fifteen civilians had died, along with thirty of Anderabi's soldiers and fourteen of Jaffar's.

But at U.S. Central Command, a spokesman denied that U.S. war-planes had dropped bombs on Pol-e-Khomri or that U.S. soldiers were anywhere nearby. Months later, Central Command confirmed that one precision-guided bomb had struck near its target, enough to stop the menacing tank.*

Two days after the A-team left, Jaffar's men tried and failed to take the Pol-e-Khomri by force. Tajik soldiers and Pashtun former Taliban fighters teamed up against him, and although Jaffar promised to surrender, he then fled. "We took a large amount of time trying to avoid bombing these people," said Team 532's senior officer. "But when the fire started coming too close to the men, it was either them or us. I wasn't going to let my guys get killed for some stupid reason." He didn't have a clue what the two Afghan commanders were fighting about and, he said, he didn't care.

---

* Rear Adm. Craig Quigley had told the *New York Times* at the time, "The only place we've bombed since the fall of Kandahar has been the Tora Bora area." He also denied that a special forces team had been there, even after confronted with evidence—clothing and equipment—found by *Times* reporter Carlotta Gall on the scene that day. When questioned about it again months later for this book, Quigley's staff rechecked bomb damage assessment reports from December 12. They confirmed that one team had been there and that precision-guided munitions had been launched as a result of the team's call for help. They could not explain Quigley's initial statement or the discrepancy in the numbers of air strikes.

Chapter Eight

BELOW THE RADAR
IN NIGERIA

★ ★ ★ ★

JUST FOUR DAYS AFTER SEPTEMBER 11, AS COMMANDERS prepared the war plan for Afghanistan, a weathered blue Russian MI-8 utility helicopter packed with U.S. Army Special Forces troops swooped down onto a grassy field in remote northwestern Nigeria. Cattle herders and their skinny animals scattered as the thump of blades grew louder. Children of the nomadic Fulani tribe, dressed in colorful scarves and dresses, grabbed their baskets and dashed into the dirt alleyways of their mud-walled village.

A knot of broad-shouldered, tight-jawed special forces troops piled out of the helicopter with characteristic flair, carrying big black guns and wearing Darth Vader sunglasses. They had reached Birnin Kebbi, a Muslim city under *sharia* (strict Islamic law) rule. In the dusty marketplace, posters of Osama bin Laden aiming a Stinger anti-aircraft missile launcher sold briskly. An ancient Hausa city, Birnin Kebbi had formed part of the Sokoto Caliphate, the vast centralized Islamic state created in the early 1800s by jihad, a holy war led by the Fulanis.

Before sunrise the next day, news of the soldiers' arrival had spread throughout Kebbi state, where electricity and potable water exist for only a handful of well-connected politicians, military officers, and foreign entrepreneurs. Birnin Kebbi's people believed the American soldiers had come to dig a long trench to the border of Niger, thirty miles

NIGERIA

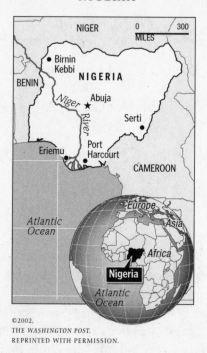

away. From there, explained the state's governor, Americans would launch an attack against Sudan, a country long on Washington's list of states sponsoring terrorism.

It was said on the streets of Birnin Kebbi that Nigeria, Africa's most populous Muslim country, was being pulled into the war on terrorism against its will. And   certainly not with the agreement of blue-black Muslims like the one operating a poster-and-Koran stand in town. For him, bin Laden was a hero, and to him and many others in rural Nigeria, America had launched a war against Islam itself. People like this vendor saw bin Laden not as an evildoer or a terrorist, but rather as the four-star commander of a modern-day jihad against the technological world. Many Nigerians doubted bin Laden had anything to do with the attacks on the United States. No, the World Trade Center towers were destroyed by the Jews "because they want to force America to war," Alhaji Lateef Farouk, leader of the radical Saudi-funded Izala Islamic Movement in Nigeria told the *News*, a weekly magazine. "They want America to fight Islam under the guise of fighting terrorism."[1]

Nigerians believed bin Laden was standing up for them, the destitute, hungry Muslims who couldn't afford to send their children to school, didn't own a computer, and rarely rode in a car. Nurudeen Adam

SSgt Bruce Fitton, the intelligence officer for the 3rd Battalion of the 3rd Special Forces Group, with a Muslim vendor in Birnin Kebbi, a city in northern Nigeria. The poster at right shows Osama bin Laden, who is considered a hero by many local residents, holding a missile launcher on his shoulder. DANA PRIEST

Galadanci, leader of the militant Atajdid movement in the Muslim-dominated state of Kano in the north, called the attack "retributive justice . . . a way of telling America that you cannot destroy Islam." Atajdid claimed more than 200,000 adherents across northwestern Nigeria. Its leaders taught that jihad was a necessary condition for practicing Islam.[2]

Many Muslims in Nigeria, as elsewhere around the world, believed bin Laden was punishing America for its economic embargo against Iraq. Those sanctions had killed thousands of innocents—more than the number of combatants killed in America's much-heralded Gulf War.

Bin Laden was also scolding the United States, they believed, for denying the Palestinians a homeland and for supporting an Israel whose snipers assassinated Palestinian leaders and whose warplanes pounded refugee camps. He was killing Americans for sending soldiers to oil-rich Saudi Arabia to prop up a monarchy that had long maintained its rule through corruption, repression, and isolation. He was getting back at America for having used cruise missiles to destroy a pharmaceutical plant in Sudan; poor Muslims in Sudan would have to go without their medications because of that attack. And in the months that followed the air strikes in Afghanistan, Nigeria's Muslims watched as innocent Afghan women and children were maimed and killed by bombs and missiles that the United States rained down on an another underdeveloped Muslim population—people very much like themselves.

Never mind the rest of the story. They didn't know, or want to know, about any of that.

Muslims in the nearby city of Kano, also under *sharia*, began to rally in support of bin Laden just days after September 11. On October 12, just after services at the Kano City Central Mosque, leaders of the Movement for the Revival of Islam filled the air with fiery anti-American speeches. They burned an effigy of President Bush and an American flag. "Sai, Osama" (It is Osama or nobody else) they chanted, whipping the crowd into a frenzy and dispensing them into this Hausa-dominated city. Before long, non-Hausa minorities were being hacked to death in their homes. Hundreds were killed by Hausa gangs. The Nigerian national news dubbed it an anti-American rally, but much more than that, it was a tribal clash as well. The next day marauding young Hausa thugs burned churches as well as mosques and torched stores and cars. They were reacting to their own poverty, not to anyone else's religious affiliation.

By mid-October 2001, more Nigerians had died in anti-American violence than in any other of the Muslim countries that erupted in protest against the U.S. war on bin Laden and his Al Qaeda network. Thousands of Nigerian soldiers had been deployed to quell the riots, battering and killing still more of their people. The military had perfected that skill in sixteen years of military rule that had ended only with the peaceful election of a civilian government in May 1999.

Nigeria gained independence from Great Britain in 1960 and immediately fell under the fist of wanton military dictators. Civilian rule sprouted from 1979 to 1983, only to wither again until President Olusegun Obasanjo became president in 1999. Operation Focus Relief was Washington's reward to Nigeria for taking another stab at democracy. The program sent hundreds of special forces soldiers to train five Nigerian battalions of 800 soldiers each. The U.S. soldiers would also train one Ghanaian and one Senegalese battalion, which would then go into nearby Sierra Leone to keep the peace in that godforsaken pit of violence.

U.S. policymakers hoped that the training would also change the Nigerian military's view of itself. Civilians at the State and Defense Departments, who thought up the program, counted on a "rub-off effect" from American special forces. They hoped Nigerian soldiers would see the benefits of professional standards and training and want to adopt them for their own. Maybe special forces could pull it off, but the odds were not good.

Operation Focus Relief said a lot about the times. For decades, the federal government and Washington's inside-the-Beltway brain trust had poured money into studying the Third World and Africa. Even so, no one had gotten very good at mapping out, and then executing, long-term strategies to solve Africa's massive problems. Funds and programs came and went with each new administration and each new majority in Congress. As a result, sixty U.S. soldiers might walk through hip-deep bushy fields with a battalion of underfed Nigerian soldiers, showing them how to conduct an ambush, but no cadre of U.S. economists flew there to train officials in the country's economic ministry. No legion of agronomists camped out in the middle of nowhere to help improve farming techniques. Battalions of teachers did not deploy to repair the educational system. The Peace Corps was marginalized and outdated.

Using the American military to address global problems had become almost a reflex in Washington. But even the best U.S. troops could deal only with the symptoms, not the causes, of incipient problems. Military programs did little to help political systems move from dictatorship to democracy, or economies from government control to the free market.

This overemphasis on the military concerned many Nigerian intellectuals, too. They looked to the United States for greater inspiration and practical help than an infantry tactics course could provide. "When you have a military entrenched in politics in such a fundamental way, you must see military engagement as just a step in the transformation, not an end in itself," said J. Kayode Fayemi, director of the Centre for Democracy and Development in Lagos. U.S. training programs, he believed, were designed in a way that proved Washington's interest "in stability rather than the development of democracy," a much harder, long-term process.

U.S. embassy officials in Abuja nonetheless crowed that Nigeria had become the largest African recipient of bilateral U.S. assistance after it adopted a democratic path. To be sure, one-third of the money, $55 million a year, went for military training and equipment.[*] The American military, having spent years on such intense "engagement" missions, was prepared and ready to go. The same was not true of other, atrophied agencies of the U.S. government, such as the Justice Department and its minuscule police-training bureau; that side of the U.S.-funded initiatives had not gotten off the ground in the two years since the funding was allocated. Yet police reform was badly needed in Nigeria, given the dominant role police ought to play in quelling domestic unrest. Nonetheless, only military-to-military relations seemed able to flourish.[†]

That American troops could make a difference in Africa, given their other commitments, was a controversial idea within the U.S. military. Competing viewpoints still exist today, as they did in a cold November in 1998, when the two CinCs who divided Africa met in a secure room at the Ritz-Carlton hotel in the Pentagon City mall, across the street from the real Pentagon. They held views as dissimilar as the civilian clothes they showed up in. Gen. Anthony Zinni wore khakis and a short-sleeved, colorful madras shirt. Gen. Wesley Clark sported a navy blue Burberry blazer. Playing referee was Franklin Kramer, assistant

---

[*] For comparison, about $100 million a year was spent on food and development programs administered by the U.S. Agency for International Development.

[†] After September 11, U.S. ambassador Howard Jeter recommended that Nigeria receive the counterterrorism training they have been asking for, and that the two countries begin more serious intelligence exchanges.

secretary of defense for international affairs. After the waiters, wearing security earphones, were pushed out of the room, only the generals and a gaggle of aides remained.

Zinni had come to convince Clark to spend more time and money on Africa. Hold more conferences. Do more training. Offer more assistance. Africa had preoccupied Zinni for years. "Did you know millions of people will die between now and next week in Africa, and no one cares?" he once asked abruptly in the middle of a conversation on a plane trip far from Africa. "When you go out there and see these people, you're their only hope sometimes. You feel bad because you're delivering peanuts." U.S. efforts to train a peacekeeping force in Africa to intervene in the nastiest civil wars were "too small," he complained. "It doesn't prepare anyone to be a peacekeeper. They need sophisticated training programs, intelligence support, strategic lift. We throw them half-baked programs." The government in Washington gave "lip service" to Africa, he thought. "Nobody cares about it. We dehumanize it. But if you see it happen, it's hard to feel you can't do something. You can say, 'I can at least distribute food.'" He had once convinced Gen. Hugh Shelton, chairman of the Joint Chiefs of Staff, to give him $800,000 to pay the Air Force to distribute food brought in by aid workers during the 1997–98 Kenyan floods.

Walking into the meeting, Zinni's political adviser, Ambassador Laurence Pope, had lightheartedly warned his boss about taking on impossible missions, especially in Africa. "Let's not light a candle, let's just curse the darkness," Pope had joked.

"No," Zinni shrugged, "I want to light a candle." He was, Pope decided, a Wilsonian democrat at heart.

Clark had brought charts and graphs to refute Zinni's position. Look at the corruption here, he said. Look at the human-rights violations there. Beware of unintended consequences. He didn't want to waste the money. Africa was a civilian problem, not a military one. Nor was Clark alone in his skepticism. His successor at the Eurpoean Command, Gen. Joseph Ralston, felt the same: "We don't want to train these guys; they are as corrupt as hell," he said once after Nigerian soldiers manning a checkpoint had shot at U.S. troops in a case of miscommunication. "Unbelievable things happen."

The United States couldn't just walk away from Nigeria, however. The largest Muslim country in Africa was also what the experts called "a regional anchor state." Stability and prosperity there might anchor the continent. Instability, by contrast, would suck in surrounding countries and infect all of sub-Saharan Africa. Foreigners had invested $7 billion in Nigeria; its land held 25 billion barrels of proven oil reserves, much of it a light, environmentally attractive crude that supplied 8 percent of U.S. oil imports.

Unfortunately the Nigerian anchor was rotting. Its rulers had ransacked national oil revenues. Lawyers believe Gen. Sani Abacha, the last military dictator, had siphoned billions into anonymous overseas accounts.* Incredibly, Nigeria found itself having to import refined fuel. Electrical outages were as certain as the sunset. Once an exporter of food, Nigeria became a net importer. The income of a typical Nigerian plunged from $1,250 a year in 1986 to $250 in 2000. Public safety was nearly nonexistent. Soldiers, police, and the feared internal police routinely beat, kidnapped, and killed protesters and jailed detainees and journalists. Female genital mutilation remained widespread, along with child prostitution and slavery.

By the time Nigeria elected Obasanjo, the country had become "a criminally mismanaged corporation where the bosses are armed and have barricaded themselves inside the company safe," according to journalist Karl Maier. "Nigeria's leaders, like the colonialists before them, have sucked out billions of dollars and stashed them in Western banks."[3]

The United States was gambling that its soldiers could inspire Nigerian troops to become more professional at home and on peacekeeping missions abroad. But they were up against much more than language and culture. The problems that beset Nigeria as a whole also infected the Nigerian military. The country's string of military dictatorships had been a disaster for the armed forces. To protect themselves

* On June 8, 1998, Abacha died at age fifty-three, during "a Viagra-fueled orgy with three Indian prostitutes," according to *Newsweek International*. President Obasanjo disclosed in February 2000 that Abacha had stolen more than $4 billion in less than five years as president. Abacha took $2.3 billion straight from the treasury, awarded $1 billion to front companies he controlled, and took $1 billion in foreign bribes, he said.

from possible coups, military dictators had bled the military bone white of resources and good judgment. Just as top generals felt entitled to steal from the national defense budget, mid-level officials thought it the privilege of their rank to steal the food and paychecks of their enlisted subordinates.

Of the $300 million Nigeria spent in 2001 on defense, most went for unaccountable "overhead" and little for capital expenditures. By 2000, Nigeria's navy had 19 admirals, 34 commodores, and 10,000 sailors but no operational vessels. The air force of 10,000 men had fewer than 20 flyable jets. Its MiG-21 fleet had been grounded since 1989. The army of 68,000 had three tanks, a couple of light-infantry vehicles, and few working troop-transport trucks.[4] In Serti, where special forces trained the Nigerian 20th Infantry Battalion (Mechanized), all sixteen trucks belonging to the "mech" unit rested on cement blocks, every single tire gone.

* * * *

DURING THE GLOBAL standoff between the United States and the Soviet Union, the two superpowers had carved up Africa. During a the thirty-year period between the independence of most of Africa and the end of the Cold War, the United States had shipped $1.5 billion in arms and other military equipment to armed forces in Africa,[5] but with the breakup of the Soviet Union, most military channels to Africa were severed. No longer did U.S. policymakers feel obligated to match their Soviet opponent country by country. No longer, in fact, did many of them feel obligated to do much in Africa at all. The 1993 Somalia debacle, where eighteen service members were killed, soured what goodwill remained in Washington. Six months after Somalia, half a million people in Rwanda were slaughtered in just thirteen weeks. The United States had barely done a thing to stop the massacre.[6]

Bernd "Bear" McConnell, the deputy assistant secretary of defense for African affairs in the Clinton administration, had devised the Nigerian training program. He saw right away, and firsthand, how tough the job would be. In September 2000, four-car convoys were necessary to protect U.S. dignitaries from the bandits lurking on every streetcorner in Lagos, home of the Nigerian Ministry of Defense. McConnell was riding in such a convoy on his way from the airport to a conference when a van packed with laborers cut in front of his car. The next thing McConnell knew, the lead vehicle in his convoy had screeched to a halt. A Nigerian policeman ran toward the van, waving his pistol wildly, which he then fired at the van. Bang! Bang! Bang! Bang! The van's four tires exploded. People bounded from the vehicle. "Oh this is great," grimaced McConnell, a gravelly voiced bear of a man, to the embassy's chargé d'affaires. "An international incident and I just got here." But it was not an international incident, it turned out—just daily life in Lagos.

In fact, the "Nigerian context" had shoved itself in McConnell's face even before he got to Nigeria. The Nigerian armed forces had given the Pentagon a wish list. The generals wanted F-16 airplanes and tanks. The Pentagon staff sent its reply: no way. No armor. No air power. No heavy weapons. Individual soldier equipment and logistical supplies. That's it.

McConnell's Lagos meeting underlined Nigeria's deep morass. As he sat in the cavernous Ministry of Defense talking to the leaders of Nigeria's army, navy, and air force, the room's lights flickered on and off—the daily brownout. Hardly anything fazed this former Air Force AC-130 gunship pilot, who had toughed it out in Balkan politics, but McConnell couldn't believe what he was hearing in that room. The chiefs reiterated their requests for big guns, fighter jets, and tanks. After a while, McConnell called a break and stepped into the corridor to stretch his legs. The Nigerian air force chief of staff, Air Marshal Isaac Mohammed Alfa, followed him.

"We want to talk about when the F-16s are going to arrive," Alfa whispered.

"Excuse me?" McConnell replied.

"The F-16s."

"I'm sorry, you must have misunderstood my presentation. We're here to offer training. We tried to emphasize this is not a military sales program."

When the meeting resumed, so did the issue. Gen. Victor Malu, Nigeria's army chief of staff, lashed out at McConnell for including topics such as the international rule of law and human rights in the training package. "We don't need this!" Malu insisted. "Where are the guns?" McConnell turned to his assistant, Charles Ikins, a Marine Corps reservist, and said quietly, "We need people out of the room. I'm about to get blunt here." Everyone but Malu was invited to take another break. "Look," McConnell told Malu, "This is easy: we have a C-5 cargo plane ready to arrive in three weeks. I'll stop the airplane if we can't agree. But you can't have the equipment without the training. Do you want this plane or don't you?" Malu agreed, but his acquiescence was incomplete.

An admired general with rising political aspirations, Malu publicly criticized the U.S. program when it finally began in October 2000. "It's an infringement on Nigerian sovereignty," he told the press, for the package required that Nigeria abide by the Leahy Amendment, which stipulated that the record of any foreign soldier applying for a training program had to be vetted. If the U.S. embassy judged that a person or his unit had been involved or implicated in human-rights abuses, that person would be disqualified.*

The law's application was spotty; few embassies dedicated a full-time staff member to the vetting process. Also, the information on foreign soldiers was only as good as the embassy's information-gathering, which relied heavily on local, nongovernmental human rights groups. But U.S. soldiers tried hard to comply with the law, knowing they would be held accountable for mistakes. Still, the fact that the process could delay the training infuriated Malu. In defiance, when the first 770 Nigerian soldiers had finally been vetted and training was set to begin, Malu added 80 more at the last minute whose names were not on the vetted U.S. list. The U.S. refused to start the program. They needed the names of the 80 new students to vet them. The Nigerians refused. It was a standoff. The $90 million program was in jeopardy, as

---

* The language of the amendment, sponsored by Senator Patrick Leahy (D-Vt.), Congress's leading human-rights advocate, reads: "None of the funds made available by this Act may be provided to any unit of the security forces of a foreign country if the Secretary of State has credible evidence that such unit has committed gross violations of human rights, unless the Secretary determines and reports to the Committees of Appropriations that the government of such country is taking effective measures to bring the responsible members of the security forces units to justice." The amendment was first enacted as part of the fiscal year 1997 Foreign Operations Appropriations Act and was broadened in 1998.

was all the political will Congress, the White House, and the Defense Department had mustered to start it.

Col. Victor Nelson, the portly, affable, U.S. defense attaché in Nigeria, was frantic. He knew Malu was the problem. Lower-ranking officers had told him they wanted to cooperate but were simply not authorized to give Nelson the names. A few days later, Nelson found himself in a one-on-one meeting with a Nigerian division staff officer. The officer was holding the list. He wanted to be helpful, he repeated, but he just couldn't be. Nelson understood the opportunity: he jerked the list out of the officer's hands and walked briskly away. "I owe him a uniform," Nelson thought later.

Malu disapproved of Nelson's chutzpah. He wanted him transferred, he said in a cable to the U.S. ambassador, for his "pushy and aggressive attitude." When that didn't work, Malu lobbied through the Nigerian embassy in Washington to get Nelson fired, but the Defense Department would have none of it. To make a point, the next Pentagon general to visit Nigeria publicly presented Nelson with the Defense Meritorious Service Medal.

But Malu hung on. His public rhetoric became more heated. Finally, in May 2000 President Obasanjo demanded Malu's resignation and the resignation of the other service chiefs. "This is a watershed for Nigeria," Ambassador Jeter said later, after the peaceful dismissals. "It is a clear assertion of civilian control over the military. And they resigned gracefully, without a lot of grumbling."

A perennial line of questions ran through such operations in the developing world: Should the United States, as General Zinni put it, wait until the patient was cured before administering health care? Could American training inspire an African military to become more professional? Or would improving its tactical skills only make its soldiers more effectively ruthless and ultimately undermine democracy? Would an American military presence validate the everyday arrogance of Nigerian officers, who, from colonel on up rode around in chauffeured sedans, stopping traffic and ordering their goons to assault pedestrians who didn't move out of the way fast enough. All of these questions and debates were embedded in Operation Focus Relief.

The special forces had had more than a decade to get used to being the tool of choice when everything else seemed too hard to pull off. When the Soviet Union collapsed, small special forces teams quickly set up in Russia, Poland, and Hungary to develop new military relationships there. A dozen years later, members of an A-team trained to teach de-mining became the first American troops in nearly sixty years to resume military relations with the Vietnamese army. In Africa alone, the 3rd Special Forces Group has taught light-infantry and other military tactics to troops in Benin, Botswana, Cameroon, Equatorial Guinea, Ghana, Guinea-Bissau, Ivory Coast, Kenya, Malawi, Mali, Mauritania, Mozambique, Namibia, Nigeria, Rwanda, Senegal, Sierra Leone, Swaziland, Togo, Uganda, Zambia, and Zimbabwe.

In responding to such high demand, the special forces adapted as best they could. At first it seemed odd that a staff sergeant might be asked to brief a minister of defense or even a president. Soldiers routinely swapped stories about dining with the country's top general or scrambling for a coat and tie for the ambassador's reception. Capt. James Spivey, one of the U.S. company commanders in Nigeria, met with the king of Swaziland. He felt honored, he said, but also a little out of his depth. The king told him, "I'd really like to meet your ambassador," Spivey recalled.

In Nigeria, U.S. soldiers were particularly proud of winning over local religious leaders and tribal chiefs, even the Muslim ones. In Serti, a town in the southeast where another company of special forces was training a Nigerian battalion, the local religious leader had brought his horses into camp for the soldiers to ride. In Birnin Kebbi, the blue-robed chieftain of the Fulani village had come to relax at the officers' club with the company's major. They chatted about their families and raising cattle and about how Nigeria's weather reminded the major of his home in Texas. The soldiers pocketed these encounters as gold; "It builds trust," they believed.

Even so, meetings could be uncomfortable and forced—not so much because the soldiers were American, but because they were soldiers. The language of diplomacy and politics was like a second language for them—learned, not natural. But they accepted it and tried their best to become fluent. "This is what we do. We spend most of our time accomplishing foreign policy objectives," said Maj. Mike Bownas as he sat at the hot, sticky U.S. logistics base outside the Nigerian capital, Abuja. "We really are the CinC's foreign policy tool."

* * * *

IN LATE 2001, news from Afghanistan reached the 3rd Special Forces Group soldiers who lived in tents equipped with Internet service at the headquarters operations center outside Abuja. The war in Afghanistan was a flashback for Sfc. Frank Antenori, a talkative, opinionated medic. Antenori had just completed the special forces "Qualifying" course and been assigned to the 5th Special Forces Group in 1989 when his team was sent to the U.S. embassy in Pakistan on Operation Brass Hat, part of a CIA-led mission to train Afghans resisting the occupying Russians. His team of medics shuttled back and forth near the Pakistan-Afghan border teaching the mujahideen combat medicine.

Before he had joined the special forces, Antenori had worked as an Army nuclear-weapons specialist. He was familiar with high stakes. He thought his mission to train the mujahideen, who did not share his worldview, was a high-risk kind of deal. "Every country I go to, I think in the back of my mind, 'What side of the fence will these guys be on in ten years?'" he said. Now, sitting in his medic's tent in this hot and dusty corner of Nigeria in late October 2001, Antenori asked himself that question again as he taught combat medicine to the Nigerian military. That very week the Nigerian army had made its own international headlines when its soldiers began slaughtering hundreds of innocent tribal people in the state of Benue.

The mixed crew of Russian and American helicopter pilots who flew the special forces into the Nigerian heartland in the winter of 2001 had recorded the aftermath in Benue. The U.S. State Department paid a joint U.S.-Russian company, International Charter Inc. (ICI), to pay Sergei and his fellow pilots to fly American military personnel and diplomats around Nigeria. The helicopters were owned by the Russian government. The American crew members were former 3rd SFG soldiers. The world had certainly changed.

Half an hour out of Abuja, a helicopter ferrying a visiting U.S. general descended from 750 feet to just above the treetops and zoomed into combat mode, "nap of the earth" flying, at 150 mph. Following the earth's contour, it hugged the steep mountainsides and curvaceous muddy rivers for miles, like a hand running over the curves of a human body. But the response to this biggest of birds was anything but sooth-ing. Trees splayed. Tribesmen and cattle galloped away, and children cowered and shielded their bodies from the backwash. Some men lay down flat; perhaps they hoped to fade into the soil and go unnoticed. But from fifteen feet above the treetops, roofs, and rivers, nothing went unnoticed.

Days earlier, the Nigerian army had swept into Benue, southeast of Abuja, and begun burning the villages of the Tiv tribe. A week earlier, ethnic Tiv militiamen had hacked to death and beheaded nineteen sol-diers. The soldiers had been in Benue to keep the peace between the Tivs and Jukuns, long-feuding tribes. The army swiftly took revenge. In one village alone, Gbeji, the soldiers had herded men into the main market square, executed them, poured gasoline on the bodies, and set them afire.

An ICI crew member had filmed part of the violence the week before. Now, buffeted by the wind rushing in the helicopter's open door, he popped open his computer, scrolled through his digital images, and stopped at the one with the flames roaring up from a pillbox-shaped grass hut. A soldier's figure, obscured by the day's shadow, was point-ing a rifle at a woman in a pink dress. The woman was running away.

Similarly burnt-out villages now passed below the helicopter. Dotted with black circles, where huts used to be, the villages had been aban-doned. For miles in between the scorched villages, Nigeria seemed peaceful. Giant flocks of white birds flew over a herd of cattle. Mounds of cassava grew in neat rows. Out of nowhere a railroad car appeared, half-submerged in a muddy river, having fallen off a bridge years before. "All this land, miles and miles of it, and one day some tribe decides to wipe out their neighbors because they've hated them for a long time," a special forces major yelled above the roar of the helicopter engine. "The reason I like Africa so much," he added later, "is because it's human nature in its rawest form. No emotions are suppressed." It all just hangs out, man's evil soul. The desire to kill other men, to steal from them. Everything was up for grabs nearly all the time. The major carried a concealed Beretta pistol.

From the air, the tents at the special forces' Serti camp, to the east near the border of Cameroon, looked as orderly as those rows of cassava mounds. Green lizards scurried across the tents, pausing to trap crunchy grasshoppers. One rested on the mosquito netting covering a cot. Outside the camp, dilapidated barracks housed Nigerian soldiers and their families. Wives in ragged dresses sat under the leafless trees minding their dusty, half-naked children. "O-ebo, o-ebo, o-ebo" (white man, white man, white man), the children chanted as the American soldiers drove by in their spiffy white jeeps.

Maj. Dave Duffy, a company commander in charge of training 700 Nigerian soldiers of the 20th Infantry Battalion (Mechanized), had served in Haiti, another ungovernable country, where he had acted as police chief and town mayor. He then moved on to train soldiers in Uganda, Zimbabwe, Mali, and Kenya. He had learned the limits of American military largesse in Africa: "I'm not here to change the Nigerian army," he said, his strawberry blond crew cut standing at attention. "I'm here to say, 'Here are some basics.'"

Those basics included learning how to carry an AK-47 so you don't shoot someone by accident. Learning how to shoot so you hit the target. Learning how to shoot in the semiautomatic position to really do some damage.

The Serti camp's firing range was surrounded by guinea corn, bean fields, and brown termite mounds. Locust bean trees swayed at the perimeter. Behind a row of paper human torsos, Jamtel Hill reared up, covered with bright green scrubs. Yellow and white butterflies fluttered about. Tribal marks creased the skinny dark-chocolate-brown faces staring at the paper torsos. Slashes on cheeks. Lines on foreheads. Notches on ear tips. The first in a long row of camouflage-clad soldiers leaned forward, raised his rifle, and braced his foot on grain bags marked "Shop No. 29 Monday Market. Borno State."

"At this time I want you to lock one magazine and load," the trainer called out through a microphone. "Adjust your sandbag. Make sure the safety is on. Shooters, take your safety off. Commence firing!" The steely rat-tat-tat, rat-tat-tat of the guns echoed off Jamtel Hill and bounced across the sky.

Once the Nigerians got better at individual combat skills, their trainers organized them into squads of ten men each. They spent the day walking through bushy fields practicing how to move together without detection. They learned hand and arm signals and wedge-shaped formations. They learned to hit the dirt rather than spring up when they heard gunfire. At night the Americans shot off flares while the troops practiced "react to the enemy drills." Drop to the ground. Stay close to your team. Move together.

The U.S. Army delegates authority. But in the Nigerian army, a senior Nigerian noncommissioned officer (NCO) was never given independent authority over his troops. Changing this attitude was a top priority for the Americans, who knew the value of decentralized decision-making on the battlefield. The special forces trainers watched as the enlisted squad leaders struggled to get their assault lines into position. Where was the flank security? Where was the compass man?

As they squatted in the bush, setting up an ambush, one trainer whispered to a squad leader: "What happens if you make contact here?" They could see a dirt trail at the bottom of the small hill. Soldiers role-playing the enemy were about to cross it. Before they did, though, an unexpected Fulani tribeswoman appeared in the distance, her dress billowing in the breeze. She carried a basket on her head.

"Sir, they are confused," the squad leader confided to a trainer with a long-haired Madonna tattoo on his forearm.

"Well, unconfuse them," the trainer commanded. Take charge. "How are we going to enter that assault line? It's going to be quick, right? Maintain your space, right?" After the attack, count your soldiers immediately. "Know where your men are."

Nigerian enlisted soldiers liked the training, but their officers seemed too proud—or too lazy—to go into the field with their troops. Some resented the fact that American NCOs, not officers, were there to train them, too. It didn't sit well that their soldiers might actually learn something from the Americans.

"As a matter of fact, nothing is new," a young Nigerian officer, Captain Martins, sniffed dismissively as he stood off the training range in the sparse shade of a tree. His arms folded across his chest, Martins represented the great pride of a Nigerian generation that had finally made peace with their former colonizer, the British. But he and his peers resented the dominance of this new American empire that attached so many conditions to its assistance. He and others wondered why the Americans just didn't leave the training to the British. Why confuse the Nigerians with two doctrines, two sets of nomenclature, two attitudes? "It's just a chance to keep training," he shrugged.

Higher-ranking officers weighed the program's value differently. "To me this doesn't look like peacekeeping," said Maj. Yusuf Hasan, the 2-IC (second in command) of the battalion in Serti. "The training is very comprehensive. It trains you to operate anywhere. It teaches you how to maneuver on the ground. It's a shell you can use anywhere." Hasan particularly liked the hands-on training with explosives. Hand grenades. Flares. Claymore mines. He had never used them before. "If you want to practice, you need to blow the real thing," said Hasan excitedly. "You have to blow a lot of dollars. The simulation is almost as real as the real thing. These are things the soldiers like."

The Claymores, used to defend soldiers from attack as they retreated, were particularly useful in such an unsafe world, Hasan insisted. He had fought in Liberia and Sierra Leone. Even battles won can be reversed at any moment, he emphasized. "Experience reveals that the world cannot be trusted; when the rebels decide to disarm, they can change their mind. On the battlefield, the Claymore will be a last-minute resort."

Before the special forces left Nigeria, they supplied their new brethren with equipment for their deployment into Sierra Leone—the tangible lure that seduced them onto uncomfortable, thistle-strewn training fields. The supplies were significant for a battalion that had no running cars, let alone a weapon for each soldier: 6 trucks, 776 AK-47s, 24 M-60 machine guns, 100 armor jackets, 15 tents, 60 Motorola radios, 775 mess kits, boots, buckles, and uniforms. Plus 1,555 water canteens, 775 shovels, 170 compasses, and medical supplies. These were all things the Nigerian government could afford to buy, but refused.

Oddly, maintenance was not part of the training program. Few spare parts were warehoused and no gunsmithing kits were included in the supplies. U.S. soldiers guessed that the Nigerians would simply drive their new vehicles until they broke down. In this regard, the program had the smell of an American-style quick fix. Bear McConnell believed, simply, that Congress would support nothing more at the time. "If we don't fund sustainment training, we should all be arrested because this is a $90 million program," McConnell said. "My fear is, we'll do this in a typical American way and say, 'Well, we're done with that.'"

Such skills and equipment were supposed to make the Nigerians better fighters in Sierra Leone, where they had considerable experience. Nigeria had first participated in the ECOMOG West African regional peacekeeping force in Liberia in 1990 and had spent more than $5 billion of its own money on peacekeeping since then. Some 2,000 Nigerian soldiers had died trying to stop regional civil wars. Nigeria had captured the capital of Sierra Leone from the Revolutionary United Force (RUF) in early 1999. Later that year, Washington helped engineer a settlement, known as the Lomé Accords, to end Sierra Leone's civil war. It included a place in the government for RUF leader Foday Sankoh, whose forces had made a habit of hacking off children's arms and killing whole villages. In the months that followed, the UN assembled a peacekeeping force (UNAMSIL) to replace the Nigerians. But as soon as Nigeria withdrew its last troops in early May 1999, the RUF overran several UN positions and took 500 UN peacekeepers hostage. It was a colossal embarrassment. Since no American president would consider sending U.S. troops into Sierra Leone, the alternative was to make the Nigerian peacekeepers better at the job when they went back in as the core of UNAMSIL.

But the Nigerian troops had only jabbed half-heartedly at the RUF when they returned. They rarely sought the RUF out or engaged them in any significant way. Meanwhile, other problems surfaced. In September 2000, Nigerian soldiers were accused by the UN ground commander of collaborating with the RUF to mine and trade diamonds.[7] But their performance improved. By January 2001, most U.S.-trained troops had "for the most part, not behaved improperly," concluded investigators with Refugees International.[8] Initial UN reports were largely positive.

The Nigerian battalions that had been trained by the special forces in fact had achieved a measurable improvement, according to Amb. Michael Sheehan, a former special forces officer himself, who visited the Nigerians in Sierra Leone in his role as an assistant secretary-general at the UN. At full strength with 17,500 troops, the UN force had disarmed 46,000 combatants in Sierra Leone, occupied the entire country, and provided security for the government of Sierra Leone to expand its geographical authority, which it had been reluctant to do. With new Nigerian military leaders and troops trained together, the mission was "in much better shape," Sheehan said. He and others hoped the experience would help Nigerian soldiers and officers get used to working under a civilian authority. In this case, the Nigerians, as UN peacekeepers in Sierra Leone, he believed, were being compelled to adopt higher human-rights standards than they were used to at home.

It was a beginning, the best anyone could expect.

Chapter Nine

GAMBLING WITH
GREEN BERETS IN COLOMBIA

★ ★ ★ ★

THE SIGHT OF U.S. TROOPS MIGHT HAVE MADE A SPLASH in Nigeria, but halfway around the world, swaggering Green Berets in floppy "boonie" hats seemed a mere flashback to three decades of U.S.-led counterinsurgency campaigns in America's backyard.

At 8 A.M. on November 20, 2001, the restaurant Hooters opened for business in the al fresco officers club on Larandia Army Base. The base lay in the middle of Colombia's Caqueta province, which was under guerrilla controlled until April 2002. A waitress wearing tight black pants and a bustier, stiletto-heeled shoes, and bright blue eye shadow stopped at a table full of U.S. soldiers. She stood inches away from a strapping gringo staff sergeant sporting a dark mustache and chewing on a ten-inch cigar. He had the bearing of a man in charge.

Outside, skinny young Colombian soldiers whacked at the grass and scrubs with machetes. Fuzzy orange Chiapara tree flowers brightened the former ranch's deep green fields. Colombian soldiers from the "counterguerrilla" battalions ran footraces against soldiers from the counternarcotics battalion undergoing U.S. special forces training.

The staff sergeant and four tables filled with his jovial teammates belonged to the 7th Special Forces Group, which had been training and advising militaries in Central and Latin America on how to defeat rebel armies and drug cartels for more than five decades. Their standard tool

COLOMBIA

LARIS KARKLIS—©2002, THE *WASHINGTON POST*. REPRINTED WITH PERMISSION.

kits included hands-on lessons in urban raids, jungle warfare, patrolling rivers, and counterterrorism. Just that week they had taught Colombian police and military troops how to rescue hostages from terrorists. The repertoire included how to file into darkened rooms, gouge out people's eyes, and break the fingers of suspects who won't cooperate.

Civil war has ensnared Colombia for forty years. In the last twenty years, cocaine has transformed the equation for the worse. Corrupt government officials, impoverished peasants, and lush jungles have conspired to make Colombia a hospitable place for coca farmers and drug traffickers. The United States grew greatly concerned. By 2002, nearly all the cocaine on America's streets came from Colombia. Cocaine fuels crime and crime has robbed a generation of poor Americans of their future. Drugs had become an American tragedy with an unending ripple effect.

And yet, in ten years, the only solution Washington had effectively funded, staffed, and promoted to end Colombia's drug plague—and the rebel guerrilla movement it had taken over—was a military one. Efforts at police reform had been half-hearted and half-funded. A U.S. crop substitution program was a failure. The U.S. ambassador to Colombia, Anne Patterson, admitted as much privately in early 2002. The U.S. government never backed the peace talks actively supported by Colombia's first honest broker, President Andres Pastrana. U.S. presidents Clinton and Bush had allowed a few Republican members of Congress to dominate the policy-making process—and those members crafted an approach consisting mainly of equipping and training the Colombian military.

Relying primarily on Colombia's military to solve America's drug problem was a huge gamble. It also meant sending special forces back to a neighborhood where, in the past century, Green Berets had repeatedly invaded and occupied many nations.

Relations between Latin American militaries and their citizenry were supposed to be different now, in the new millennium. The continent had liberated itself from a slew of military regimes. The generals were out of power, their military solutions shelved. Economic and political evolution had taken their place. So when the U.S. military arrived on counterdrug training missions—which it did increasingly in the 1990s—the troops were ordered to keep a low profile. Top political and military officials in Latin America did not want their people to think they needed Washington's help, or that the gringos were in charge again.

In fact, Gen. Charles Wilhelm, the commander in chief of the U.S. Southern Command from 1997 to September 2000, had trouble getting his boot in the door anywhere he traveled in Central and Latin America. U.S ambassadors and other diplomats liked having him visit from his headquarters in Miami. He always brought a goody bag of engineers to repair roads and dentists to fix peasants' teeth. But the political leaders in the countries of his theater were wary of the man whose chest of ribbons reached up to his shoulders. He reminded them of their traumatic pasts.

* * * *

THE HISTORY OF U.S. military intervention in Central and Latin America dated back 175 years, to the Monroe Doctrine, the policy that

Gen. Charles Wilhelm, head of U.S. Southern
Command from 1997 to September 2000.

U.S. SOUTHERN COMMAND

anything happening in Latin America would be considered of vital interest to the United States. William Walker, a renegade American Marine, had invaded Nicaragua in 1855, declared himself president, and ruled for two years until Costa Rica went to war against him and forced him to surrender. Similar, if less bizarre, U.S. interventions went on virtually nonstop until the late 1980s.*

From 1947 to the late 1980s, the Southern Command's CinC was rather like a viceroy. He had 11,000 troops stationed mainly in Panama (where the United States owned and operated the Panama Canal) and could call up a small army when he needed it.† During that time,

---

* The list of American interventions is long, and includes the Dominican Republic (1905, 1965); Nicaragua (1912, and President Reagan's 1980s "contra" war); Mexico (1914); Cuba (1961); El Salvador (the entire 1980s); Grenada (1983); and Panama (1989); as well as CIA-assisted coups in Guatemala (1954) and Chile (1973).

† Today about 2,500 U.S. airmen and troops are stationed in the theater, most of them on drug-hunting missions based out of Puerto Rico. Another 500 or so are stationed in Honduras, and dozens more reside at three aerial logistics bases used to maintain and support drug-interdiction flights.

"Southcom" was a hot place to be for action-seeking special forces members. A-teams were constantly in the field. Knowledge of one foreign language—Spanish—could get them by in just about the entire theater. Soldiers in the 7th rotated into other groups less frequently and many of them were the sons of Green Berets who had themselves made the 7th their home. They called themselves "the family."

Green Berets from the 7th saw themselves quite differently than did many of the people in whose countries they fought. They were "liberators of the oppressed," according to their group slogan, "de oppresso liber," and as such took credit for ending the twelve-year civil war in El Salvador. "What people don't realize is we actually helped El Salvador," said a staff sergeant named Joe, dressed in a black "jungle warfare" T-shirt. "It was a secret war and, in reality, it was a great success." They believed they had helped swing Latin America from military dictatorships to democracy during the late 1980s and 1990s too.

Those people whom Joe referred to saw a different reality, however. Critics in the United States, including many in Congress, believe the American military prolonged and intensified the violence in El Salvador, which claimed 75,000 lives, including those of Jesuit priests and Catholic archbishop Oscar Romero. Thousands died at the hands of right-wing paramilitary units that operated in collaboration with the Salvadoran army. That army, in turn, operated under the watchful eye of its American military advisers.

By the mid-1990s, Argentina, Brazil, Chile, Guatemala, Paraguay, and Uruguay had all adopted elected, civilian-led governments. Peace and democracy turned Southern Command into the only regional CinCdom without even one war plan on the shelf. Washington and the Pentagon had concluded that no war anywhere in the region would threaten U.S. national security—good news in any other part of government, but for the CinC it meant struggling to stay relevant. Wilhelm no longer had any combat troops permanently assigned to him. His peers derided his post as "the sister CinC." Still, he fought to stay in the game. "Every military in the region is rethinking its role," Wilhelm said on a plane ride to the region in June 2000. "There is no external threat to this region right now. Most internal threats are laid to rest. They are refocusing on internal security, on regional peacekeeping and counterdrug operations. I'd like to play a larger role in the actual restructuring of the militaries."

Few civilians back home thought that was a good idea. For starters, Congress had enacted a body of laws in the mid-1970s and 1980s restricting U.S. military and police training operations around the world. The Leahy Amendment (discussed in the preceding chapter) and other legislation aimed to ensure that America's military never again associated with abusive armies who murdered their own citizens. When Colombia's civil war became increasingly intertwined with the cocaine trade, Congress worried that if the U.S. stepped in, it would become embroiled in another bloody El Salvador–style counterinsurgency. So Congress drew a line: U.S. military assistance and equipment could be used to defeat drug trafficking, but not political insurgents.

This farcical distinction ignored the fact that guerrillas protected the traffickers and received millions of dollars a year in return. The mythical line was a necessary one, however, in order for proponents of U.S. military involvement in the drug war to gain U.S. political support. Cocaine was far too big a problem for the administration to ignore, and opponents of military intervention were unable to win sufficient congressional support for an alternative.

Congress was not the only place where U.S. military involvement in Latin America was unpopular. Many politicians in Central and Latin America who desperately wanted help in dealing with the drug scourge were nonetheless reluctant to have the U.S. military on their soil. Nowhere was this more evident than in Panama. After thirty years of allowing the Southern Command to be headquartered on Quarry Heights in Panama City, in 1997 the Panamanian government voted to kick the U.S. military out altogether when control of the Panama Canal reverted to Panama.

This unceremonious boot out Panama's door shocked the Pentagon. Wilhelm certainly was stunned: "I fought so hard to keep forces in the region [during the negotiations on the canal turnover]," he said, shaking his head as he walked through the gates of the U.S. embassy in Panama. "I thought there was a 99 percent chance we'd still have troops here." Some Panamanians didn't stop there. They wanted to dig up the bodies of U.S. service members buried at the Corozal cemetery and send them home. The U.S. embassy's political officer had described the lingering acrimony starkly at a meeting with Wilhelm during his visit. "The relationship with the U.S. military is like a fish flopping around on a deck," the political officer said. "Is [the relationship] a keeper? I'm not sure at high political levels it's clear yet."

"The Panamanians, they abhor uniforms," said U.S. Ambassador Simon Ferro. "We have to get around the concept that General Wilhelm doesn't fit in. He's used to dealing with other generals. Here, since Panama has no armed forces, he's dealing with a complicated civilian force, with the minister of justice and so on."

At the dawn of a new century, Wilhelm stood out as the most traditional of the regional CinCs. With broad shoulders and twinkling blue eyes, he was concise, literal, uninterested in Washington politics. He brimmed with slogans about duty, honor, and country—and with endless clichés. "I'm as serious as a heart attack," he was fond of saying, dead seriously.

Born in Edenton, N.C., Wilhelm had been raised in Washington's suburbs of Arlington and Alexandria, where his father worked as a lawyer for the American Red Cross. Wilhelm attended Florida Southern College, majored in journalism, and was an unremarkable student by his own account. After graduation, he joined the Marine Corps because that is what his friends did. Besides, he said, he had no better plans at the time. "I'm the most unlikely person to have ended up where I ended up."

Wilhelm served two tours in Vietnam, and many of his friends died there. He was awarded a Silver Star and a Bronze Star for acts of bravery during extended heavy fighting. He believed in the war when he went there, and he still believes in it. "I felt we did a lot of good things there," he said. The political realities that struck his fellow Marine, Capt. Anthony Zinni, did not concern Wilhelm. "I wasn't concerned about Saigon. I was concerned about what was over the next hill." His conclusion after years of reflection: "I don't lay Vietnam solely at the feet of the civilians. It fell down in the execution. We had no unifying strategy—or not one that ever made sense to me."

The next time Wilhelm faced another gigantic morass, he had been tasked to organize food relief for starving Somalis. Somalia reminded him of Vietnam: counterinsurgency operations in each place hadn't been adapted to the country's culture, he thought. The point was so basic, but it escaped the American military time and again. Perhaps that was because the U.S. military itself had grown increasingly isolated from its own country's culture, as study after study showed.

In December 1992, when Wilhelm went to Somalia, he saw Marine Corps and Army soldiers under his command lose their discipline and, he thought, their humanity. The anarchy of the place was like a relentless sun beating down on their sunburned foreheads day after day. Somali crowds pushed the troops to their limits. The Americans reacted harshly, shouting back and brandishing their weapons. They hated everything about Somalia.

Finally, Wilhelm called his troops together to confront the issue. "Ninety percent of the people here are like you and me," he told them. "They are trying to make a living. They want their sons and daughters to do better than they did. It's been rough out there. . . . It begs for a benevolent approach." Wilhelm sent out a bulletin to be posted at every headquarters. He called it "30-day Attitude Adjustment." It read, "If we're not careful we will start thinking that we're at war and we may forget that our mission here is one of peace and humanitarian assistance." The memorandum instructed them to wave and smile at Somali children, to be patient in traffic jams. "The people of Somalia need a friend—not just another oppressor in desert camouflage utilities."[1]

Ten years later, Wilhelm remained dogged by the lack of acceptance of the U.S. military. He could not bear the fact that segments of the Latin American population saw him as "another oppressor." Using the means available to him—a stream of devastating natural disasters—he strove to change Latin American attitudes.

In 1998, former president Jimmy Carter had called Wilhelm on his cell phone from Managua, Nicaragua. Carter was there helping Nicaragua dig out after Hurricane Mitch devastated the country. He asked Wilhelm to send his troops to pitch in. Wilhelm turned the request into a way to restart relations with the region's only country, besides Cuba, that remained on the U.S. blacklist. Within twenty-four hours, Wilhelm flew 70 percent of the U.S. inventory of iodine into Managua. A day after that, hundreds of tons of superchlorinated bleach were on their way.

Next, Wilhelm wrangled Congress and the Pentagon into letting him visit Nicaragua. The country had been off-limits to high-level U.S. military officials ever since the 1979 Marxist Sandinista revolution, which the Reagan administration had tried for years to reverse. Wilhelm became the first CinC to step on Nicaraguan soil in twenty years, and he went on to lead a $30 million U.S. relief effort in Central America after the hurricane. He even squeezed $800,000 out of the Pentagon for engineering to help rebuild Central America's infrastructure. Wilhelm returned to Nicaragua five times and brought in hundreds of troops on construction, humanitarian, and civic action operations.

Gradually, Nicaragua's army grew to appreciate him as a fence-mender. On February 2, 1999, Wilhelm was invited to address the high command of the Nicaraguan army at its Managua headquarters. He led off with a tribute to Augusto Sandino, the revolutionary who fought a bloody battle against the U.S. Marines in 1927, forcing them to abandon their twenty-year occupation.[2] Sandino's assassination five years later by Nicaragua's national guard was reportedly approved beforehand by a U.S. diplomat in the country.

During his speech, Wilhelm called the Nicaraguan army a "first-class organization" and concluded with words pierced by historical irony: "One of the characteristics of the American people, and especially of its military, is our capability to pay tribute and honor to the abilities of those who had been our adversaries, once the battle is over," he said. "It has taken us too long to recognize Augusto Sandino in this way, but on this occasion, I want to do so. . . . You have demonstrated your love of country, and as Sandino said, 'As long as Nicaragua has sons that love her, Nicaragua will be free.'" The Nicaraguan officers cheered wildly. Later, their leadership agreed to begin discussing how the two countries might hold joint exercises and cooperate on counter-drug efforts. "We got into Nicaragua on a tailwind supplied by a hurricane," Wilhelm would later chuckle.

The fight to stop drug trafficking, however, overwhelmed all other problems Wilhelm faced. Like the four Southern Command CinCs before him—Army generals Maxwell Thurman, George Joulwan, Wesley Clark, and Barry McCaffrey—he used Washington's declared "war on drugs" to open the door ever wider for broader military relations.

President Reagan's 1986 National Security Decision Directive 221 had declared drug trafficking to be a threat to national security. The military leadership disliked that decision; they wanted no role in what was ultimately a social problem ill-suited to military solutions. They complained repeatedly to Congress that the true solution—stopping the demand for drugs—was a mission that rightfully belonged to police and local drug-rehabilitation programs.

But in August 1989, facing an unprecedented surge of drug-related violence in America's cities, President George H. W. Bush insisted that the Defense Department become the "single lead agency" for detecting and montoring drugs coming into the United States.[3] He issued National Security Decision Directive 18 directing the military to assist law-enforcement agencies with drug interdiction. The military thus became part of an interagency effort focused on stopping drugs at their source, along the Andean ridge of Latin America.

If the military was to be part of the government's anti-drug war, General Joulwan, the CinC from 1993 to 1997, wanted it to help lead the charge. "King George," as his staff called him, was a Lebanese American who understood the hurly-burly of Washington's many competing circles of power. The drug business was like a balloon, Joulwan argued. Squeeze it in one place and it pops up somewhere else. Reduce it in Colombia, and the traffickers would move across the border to Bolivia. Clamp down there, it moves back to Colombia or into Peru. The only answer, Joulwan believed, lay in a regional strategy, which would be much harder to execute.

For his briefings to Congress he carried around a drawing of a beehive being visited by dozens of bees. The hive represented the Andean ridge, where the drugs were produced. The bees were the processing labs and the airplanes, and ships that hauled the drugs from the hive to the United States. The Caribbean provided the bees' transit routes. Wouldn't it make more sense to destroy the hive than to chase after all the little bees? Joulwan would ask members.

In his campaign to give the military a new "drug war," Joulwan easily won over the U.S. ambassadors in Latin America, but his highest aim was to pull the CIA, Drug Enforcement Agency (DEA), FBI, Customs Service, and the military into one room and make them work together. "One Team, One Fight," he called it. A great idea, but nearly impossible to execute in Washington. The competition between turf-conscious federal agencies, which saw the drug war as the only "hot" war that could justify larger budget requests, trumped the effort to work together.

Joulwan envisioned the solution as more than just a military attack on the hive. His top-notch commandos and fast planes, working with DEA agents, could break up the cartels, but then what? Where was the crop-substitution program? Where were the new roads to bring the crops to market? Where was the political dialogue to allow guerrillas to disarm and the wars to end, as in El Salvador? "We just don't know how to close the deal," Joulwan would say years later, as he watched Colombia implode. "We know how to begin something. We don't know how to end it."

Support in the region for a U.S. military role in fighting drugs varied greatly. Colombia's military and political elites were eager to have the United States rescue them from themselves. In Panama, however, political leaders wished to give the U.S. military no new reason to return to their front yard. When Howard Air Force Base in Panama closed in May 1999, the United States was forced to find new locations for the 2,000 antidrug aircraft sorties a year that were being flown out of Howard. Wilhelm moved his planes to new air bases—euphemistically called "forward operating locations"—in Manta, Ecuador, and on two Dutch islands, Aruba and Curacao. But Wilhelm needed another site. He had asked Peru and Costa Rica, but both had declined. So he went back to his friends in El Salvador. In March 2000, the U.S. and Salvadoran governments signed an agreement to house U.S. aircraft and personnel at Comalapa International Airport outside San Salvador, the capital. In July 2000, the legislature, dominated by a coalition of pro-American, right-wing parties, ratified the treaty.

Wilhelm hoped the new agreement, and deeper Salvadoran commitment to the U.S.-led war on drugs, would provide a reason to increase U.S. assistance to the Salvadoran military. During that country's civil war, which lasted from 1980 to 1992, the Salvadoran military had consumed 20 percent of its nation's budget. In 2000 that figure had dropped to 5 percent. The generals of both countries wanted to find a way to get Salvador's military more resources.

On his last trip to El Salvador before he retired, Wilhelm set plans in motion for bigger and better interaction between the two armed forces. At the Joint Staff headquarters in San Salvador, surrounded by maps marked "secret," Wilhelm laid out his strategy for giving the Salvadoran armed forces a larger role in the regional drug fight. Opening the new U.S. air base would "make El Salvador the focal point of the counterdrug activities in Central America," he told Antonio Rafael Calderon Hurtado, El Salvador's top general. "We realize, in a diplomatic sense, this plan is for counterdrug only. As a practical matter, all of us know this agreement will give us a superb opportunity to increase the contact with all our armed forces in a variety of ways." He continued: "I hope to further exploit this opportunity to provide modest support to you and your modernization efforts."

Calderon believed his country had more than just a drug-trafficking problem to worry about. "We suspect another guerrilla movement: communists," he told Wilhelm. He thought the Americans should go after them too. He asked Wilhelm for "strategic intelligence, legal advice, equipment, and training." A cautious Wilhelm offered to arrange a meeting at his Miami headquarters for the police chiefs and military heads of Colombia, Peru and Bolivia to discuss joint police-military operations. But he didn't buy into Calderon's theory that the guerrillas were making a comeback. "It's street crime," he said to his staff as he rode off from the meeting.

In any case, Wilhelm had a bigger problem to the south. The civil war in Colombia reminded him of Vietnam. But, as he liked to say, "this ain't no Vietnam. I wish it were; it would be easier." Colombia, a nation of 40 million at the northeastern tip of South America, had been at war with itself for thirty-eight years. The conflict attracted little concern in the United States until the late 1980s, by which time 90 percent of the cocaine coming into the U.S. market was Colombian. In fact, Colombia by then had become a mere shell of a nation, a haven for drug cartels, including Pablo Escobar's infamous Medellín cartel, that routinely bribed judges, journalists, police, and politicians. Their most notable ally was President Ernesto Samper, whose corruption blocked the United States from an a more aggressive counterdrug offensive until the end of his presidency, in the summer of 1998.[*]

When Andrés Pastrana succeeded Samper, U.S. officials cheered. Finally, there was a leader Washington trusted and liked. But the tasks facing the new president proved daunting. By late 1998, the main rebel groups—the FARC and the ELN[†]—were well financed and equipped by hundreds of small cartels that had sprung up in 1993 after Escobar was killed. In addition, a growing right-wing paramilitary group, the United Self-Defense Forces, received significant money from drug traffickers and collaboration from some elements of the Colombian military.

In 1998, President Pastrana, seeking a peaceful solution to the civil war and hoping to calm the nation, ceded a swath of southern Colombia the size of Switzerland to FARC as a "demilitarized zone" designed to induce FARC leaders to participate in negotiations with the government. But far from bringing peace to that bit of southern Colombia, the territory became an untouchable training and recruiting ground for FARC guerrillas. The guerrillas used the demilitarized zone to launch strikes into surrounding provinces. Their successes flowed, in part, from the government's spiritless 140,000-strong military and from simple geography. Coca grows well and is processed under thick jungle, impenetrable by standard aerial spy cameras. The country's hundreds of river arteries provide protected, canopied transportation routes for guerrillas and drugs within the area and into bordering states or the Caribbean.

The guerrillas and paramilitaries, in turn, mimicked the ruthlessness of the drug traffickers they protected. And the Colombian military routinely committed human-rights atrocities.[4] Some 40,000 civilians had died in this conflict over ten years. Another 2.1 million had fled their homes seeking safety or been expelled by one of the factions.

---

[*] Interestingly, Samper had also presided over efforts to smash the Cali cartel and a dramatic expansion of efforts to destroy coca crops. During his tenure, though, the United States "de-certified" Colombia twice, meaning it was ineligible for counterdrug aid because Washington deemed its government had not made a sincere effort to stop drug trafficking.

[†] Spanish acronyms for the Revolutionary Armed Forces of Colombia and the National Liberation Army.

Washington was pouring millions of defense dollars into the problem, but by most accounts, it was losing the drug war. The CIA's high-resolution spy satellites indicated that cocaine production rose steadily. Sprayers destroyed nearly 200,000 acres of coca plants, but replanting persisted. Although the U.S. Army and the Colombian government claimed a decline in the tonnage produced, the CIA believed Colombia's coca crop increased in 2001 for the seventh year in a row, enough to make 800 tons of cocaine.

In July 2000, the U.S. Congress agreed to fund Pastrana's "Plan Colombia," a wide attempt, also supported by European countries, to strengthen governance, promote regional development, and curtail drug production. Some $519 million of the $1.3 billion U.S. aid package went mainly to train three Colombian antinarcotics battalions and purchase sixty-one Black Hawk helicopters. The choppers would be used by the military and police to raid drug labs and spray coca crops with herbicides.[5]

Wilhelm had written the military section of Plan Colombia and he tried hard to make it militarily sound. He had thwarted a State Department plan to create fifteen small, counterdrug Colombian units with limited capabilities. Instead, he insisted on training three larger battalions based on an American model, with scouts, mortarmen, forward support, an intelligence cell, and a psychological operations staff.[*] With all those functions integrated into one unit, he believed, the Colombians would have a better chance of defeating the enemy. Green Berets, limited to 400 in the country at a time, would train these battalions.

Wilhelm also designed a Colombian "Joint Intelligence Center," modeled after his own intelligence-collection center back at headquarters in Miami. He put the multimillion-dollar facility in a watertight tent surrounded by sandbags. Staffed jointly by American and Colombian analysts, it processes information collected by both countries on the movements of and communications among drug producers and traffickers.

---

[*] Despite its ominous name, psychological operations, or "psyops" troops in Colombia mainly run a DARE-style counterdrug program in schools and hand out balloons to kids.

Plan Colombia, however, had two fatal design flaws. Although the Colombian military could win territory from the guerrillas and drug traffickers, it lacked the men to secure and hold it. The guerrillas usually just waited the army out, until its soldiers returned to their camps, then went back to business as usual.

A second flaw originated in the Washington policymaking process. In an effort to avoid the type of ghastly human-rights abuses waged by paramilitary forces fighting rebels in El Salvador, Congress drew a distinction between the fight against drugs and the fight against insurgents. Such a decision could only have sprung from the Washington bureaucracy: barely a soul in Colombia had ever seen the two scourges as anything but thoroughly intertwined. Separating the guerrillas from the narcotraffickers "won't work here," offered Ken Ellis, the straight-shooting director of the programs of the U.S. Agency for International Development (USAID) in Bogotá in November 2001. His credentials included two decades of field experience in El Salvador and the Caribbean. "You must either negotiate the issue away or one side has to be strong enough to win."

Plan Colombia was meant to buy time for the political and economic solutions to work. But the United States never threw its full diplomatic weight behind the Colombian peace process. It refused, for instance, to meet with the rebels or even to allow third parties to hold back-channel discussions. Of the $1.3 billion in U.S. funds spent on Plan Colombia, only $3 million went "to support the peace process."

More thoughtful political solutions were hampered by vacancies in the George W. Bush administration's top civilian policymaking positions dealing with Latin America. After Bush's election, it took his administration more than a year to fill the top Latin America jobs at the State Department and USAID. By May 2002, no successor had been named to replace Gen. Peter Pace, the CinC who had become the vice chairman of the Joint Chiefs of Staff eight months earlier. Nor had the administration appointed a permanent director of its office of Special Operations and Low Intensity Conflict, which managed counter-narcotics efforts at the Pentagon.

What's more, the economic centerpiece of Plan Colombia, "alternative development assistance"—i.e., replacing coca plants with other marketable crops and wildlife—went nowhere in the plan's first two critical years, 2000–2002. By the beginning of 2002, not one coca plant had been pulled from the ground. USAID's Ellis worked out of a sterile, marble-and-chrome high-rise in Bogotá's small, industrial business section. No one from his staff, no managers of the drug-substitution program, were allowed to go into Colombia's coca-growing region because their security could not be assured.

Yet Ellis had $30 million to spend for the crop-substitution program. "It's been very, very slow," Ellis said in his office, patrolled by armed guards. "The security situation makes it impossible." Beginning in May 2000, the Colombian government had signed "pacts" with 35,000 families who farmed medium-to-large plots of land totaling 37,500 acres. Each family pledged to stop growing coca by July 2002; after signing the pledge, each was entitled to emergency assistance—usually a number of chickens and a three-month supply of chicken feed valued at $900. By March 2002, however, Ellis and others at the U.S. embassy had judged the effort a failure.[*] Some other model would be required. Meanwhile, the violence in Colombia claimed another 3,000 lives that year. "It's not a matter of money," Ellis complained. "What you need is the absence of armed groups." But the rebels were not on the U.S. agenda. Neither was "Dragon 4."

"Dragon 4" was the code name for a tough Colombian officer, Colonel Castilloblanco, who oversaw the training battalion at the Larandia base. He had no patience for crop substitution. "The part that is very slow is the economic part, the social part. It should be better calibrated," Castilloblanco said, standing on a grassy hill watching the mock destruction of a drug lab by one of his anti-narcotics battalions. He was not going to wait around for crop substitution to begin.

Castilloblanco's troops repeated the drug-lab exercise the next day for visiting Colombian lawmakers who held the purse strings of his military budget. Chest out, hands clasped behind his back, he stood surrounded by aides as six Black Hawk helicopters materialized from the horizon, flew in formation, and landed in the splaying grass.

Castilloblanco's troops, like the rest of Colombia's armed forces,

---

* As of February 15, 2002, only 7,300 people had received any assistance.

had much to overcome. Between 1996 and 1998, FARC's aggressive offensives had killed at least 200 people, mostly soldiers and police, and captured another 220. Colombia's military was losing badly. A Defense Intelligence Agency study warned that if nothing changed, FARC could take over the country in five years.

Beginning in 1998, military leaders had begun a painful restructuring. They nearly doubled the number of helicopters, created a 4,000-strong rapid reaction force, and retrofitted five old turboprop planes with heavy machine guns and infrared radar for night operations. They also gave soldiers a pay hike, hoping to reduce their dependence on young draftees and giving experienced soldiers a reason to stay longer.

FARC, meanwhile, had become the richest insurgency in Latin American history. Its wealth and incredible worldwide distribution system were often compared to the Al Qaeda financial web that supported terrorism. An estimated $200 million a year in protection money from drug traffickers and lucrative kidnapping ransoms poured into FARC's treasury. FARC bought new uniforms, new weapons, and new recruits. From a force of 10,000 in 1995, FARC had grown to 15,000 by 2002. FARC was the only self-sustaining insurgency around, which made it all the more dangerous. Cutting off its supply of outside money and weapons would not be enough; the Colombians—or someone else— would have to tackle FARC head-on.

On the verge of total war, Colombia still spent only $3 billion a year on defense, just 3.4 percent of its total gross domestic product. The military remained too small to station troops in areas it recaptured from the guerrillas, and not mobile enough to mount quick attacks. "They use the helicopters like a taxi service," one special forces trainer scoffed. The Colombian military, not known for its grit, was turning increasingly to paramilitaries to do the dirty work.

Colombia expected the Americans to turn that attitude around. Green Berets had designed the drug-lab exercise at Larandia to push local soldiers into more aggressive action. These exercises had all the elements they needed to overcome lethargy: a surprise landing from out of nowhere, covering other soldiers with gunfire as they neared the mock drug lab, throwing grenades to distract attention. One soldier carried a bullhorn; He was to yell out an ultimatum to those inside the drug lab. The ultimatum was something the special forces had insisted on, knowing that that was how things would be done in the United States. Congress would want Colombia's military to give suspected drug dealers a chance to surrender peacefully, just as they wanted to think of the rebels and narco-traffickers as separate entities. But it didn't work that way in real life.

The same went for human rights. The Americans knew the entire training program would be killed by Congress if the Colombian army did not improve its terrible record of abuse. The trainers had built a Potemkin village in which to practice the proper handling of civilians and prisoners of war. They named it "Pista Derechos Humanos"— human rights obstacle course. Some Green Berets thought of human rights as exactly that—an obstacle to military victory. "These guys have been human righted to death," said one U.S. staff sergeant.

★ ★ ★ ★

SSGT. PEREZ GATHERED his men around him before the exercise began. They each crouched on one knee like a football team receiving final instructions before the big game. "Remember, don't exit to the rear of the helicopter. It will cut your head off," he said in Spanish, smirking. Off they went to the helicopters.

Half an hour later the exercise began with the thumping of helicopter blades echoing off the hills. When the choppers landed, out poured the men, advancing slowly, tentatively, across the grass. A wooden hut, the mock drug lab, sat in the center of the field. They approached it without suspicion, as if walking into their own peaceful neighborhood.

Boom! Boom! Boom! The grenades exploded. Machine-gun fire spewed from the hills where soldiers were hiding to provide cover for the assault troops. The officer with the megaphone called out, "Come out. Come out with your hands up. This is the military! Come out!" The whole scene looked like a slow-motion B movie.

"They need to be more aggressive!" Castilloblanco yelled at his aides. "They're acting like they're asleep." He clicked his fingers. "It doesn't look real enough. Move out as fast as you can. Don't waste time. Have them fire before they give the ultimatum . . ."

"Oh no, they can't do that," the American trainer butted in. "They shouldn't fire until after they give the ultimatum." Castilloblanco ignored him.

An hour later, when the troops had returned to base, Perez passed on the colonel's orders: "You need to be more dynamic. Make it real. The colonel says there are too many people walking slowly. Act more aggressive. After you hear the ultimatum, blow the lab." A Colombian first sergeant who was part of the raiding party raised his hand: "The assaulting team couldn't hear the ultimatum. If we can't hear it, the people in the lab can't hear it."

Good point—one more Washington caveat that does not hold up in the field.

Sfc. Joseph Back instructs Colombian soldiers in mortar tactics and maintenance at the Larandia Army Base near the jungle region once held by the rebels. SFC. JOSEPH BACK

In this exercise, as in Colombia generally, U.S. forces stood at arms length from actual combat. But an alluring smell of battle waffled through the air. The Green Berets circled like wolves. In an old, drafty cement warehouse, converted into a barracks, a wall map marked "secret" hung in the corner, covered with a poncho when not in use.

The map detailed a corner of wartorn Putamayo province bordering the Larandia base. FARC command posts and front lines were marked in red, for the enemy. Colombian troops appeared as green lines—the good guys. Tacked up on the map were grainy photographs of FARC commanders. The U.S. soldiers memorized the guerrillas' order of battle—its composition and hierarchy—just in case.

"Hopefully, we will one day accompany them" into the field, said a special forces major, standing in front of the map. "At least these guys drink beer and are Christians."

By February 2002, his day seemed closer. The Pentagon had recommended that President Bush issue a new, secret directive overturning Clinton-era restrictions. The directive would wipe out any distinction between counternarcotics and counterinsurgency and allow Colombia to employ equipment and training from the United States to fight the rebels head-on. No more word games.

Colombia's two guerrilla groups were already on the State Department's terrorist list. The paramilitaries were added on September 10, 2001, on the eve of Secretary of State Colin Powell's visit to Bogotá, called off because of the terrorist attack a day later. Pentagon leaders had next begun devising plans to elevate the conflict from a counternarcotics operation to a counterterrorism one. Green Berets in Colombia had seen it that way all along.

"Let's just call them narco-terrorists and go get 'em," said Felix, a staff sergeant at the U.S. embassy in Bogotá. FARC's actions certainly back up his interpretation. In late January 2002, FARC had dramatically stepped up its attacks. Guerrillas hijacked a commercial airliner, kidnapped a minor presidential candidate, and tortured and killed a senator, the seventh legislator killed in four years. On February 20, Pastrana, his patience worn thin, called an end to the peace talks he had supported without U.S. assistance for three years. He sent A-37 jet fighters, AC-47 gunships, and armed helicopters on the attack. They launched 200 sorties against eighty guerrilla installations in the "demilitarized zone," the first time in three years that Colombian forces had entered that territory. Some 10,000 troops invaded the zone a day later; they were well armed, but—more important—they carried expanded authority from Pastrana to control the movement of civilians.

In New York City, UN Secretary-General Kofi Annan "deplored" the turn of events. He appealed to all sides to respect international humanitarian law and to safeguard the 100,000 civilian noncombatants who lived in the zone. Civilians had suffered much more than combatants had in this cauldron of military and paramilitary violence, of guerrilla and drug-dealer chaos.

As President Bush and his war cabinet began readying the next front in the ever-expanding war on terrorism, Colombia moved closer to the top of the to-do list. Each month, it seemed, special forces were being dispatched somewhere far off, usually to countries suffering under incompetent, unprofessional, or abusive militaries: the Philippines, Georgia, Yemen, Somalia. U.S. troops were poised to return to Indonesia, too, where Congress had expressly forbidden them to go.

Chapter Ten

THE INDONESIAN
HANDSHAKE

* * * *

FROM 1965 TO THE END OF THE COLD WAR, THOUGH officially nonaligned, Indonesia was one of the staunchest supporters of the U.S.-led anti-communist coalition and a steadfast American friend in Asian political forums. Washington, in turn, rewarded Jakarta with unwavering support. For thirty years the United States supported Indonesian leader Suharto's authoritarian rule and a corrupt form of crony capitalism that bled the country of roughly $35 billion.

Suharto could not have ruled so long without sharing power with the military and allowing it a *dwi fungsi,* or dual function in society to protect the nation and engage in economic development. The military completely dominated all aspects of social and political life. Officers held key government posts and decisive voting blocks in the rubber-stamp parliament. Military structure in Indonesia's far-flung islands mirrored the civilian government down to the village level. National and local military commanders ran their own economies, which they partly used to pay and house their troops. They accumulated vast holdings in the most lucrative markets: timber, gold, and oil. An estimated 75 percent of Indonesia's defense budget was off the books.[1]

This decentralized system of semi-autonomous local military commands also kept the world's largest archipelago—comprising 17,000 islands and 300 ethnic and linguistic groups—from disintegrating into

INDONESIA

factional warfare. Indonesia, with 210 million Muslims, is the world's most populous Muslim nation, although largely secular. The military kept the country's significant minorities—Christians, Hindus, and Buddhists—in line too, often at a huge human cost.

Indonesia's military leaders had a habit of cutting off provinces from the outside world so as to move in secret and without restraint against their targets: small rebel groups, indigenous tribal peoples, and Suharto's political opponents. For a country so integrated into the global economy, when it came to the territories, Indonesia behaved more like Myanmar (Burma), whose brutal regime closed its borders to all foreigners, or like China, which isolated Tibet from the outside world.

With remarkable brutality, documented in gruesome photographs sold on the black market, the armed forces and their militia, crushed or sought to crush rebellions in the provinces of Aceh and Irian Jaya. Many of these conflicts continue. In their East Timor campaign, the army and militias killed or pushed into starvation through forced resettlement some 200,000 people over a twenty-five-year period. (Indonesia had forcibly occupied the former Portuguese colony in 1975, apparently with the blessing of President Gerald Ford and Secretary of State Henry Kissinger.)[2]

The UN and human-rights groups routinely criticized the slaughter in East Timor. But, for the first fifteen years of Indonesian occupation, Washington did not join the chorus of condemnation as Indonesian security forces routinely jailed, tortured, raped, and executed opposition activists. On the contrary, successive administrations and Congress funded a generous program to train and equip the Indonesian armed forces which was critical to giving Indonesia the capacity to subdue Timorese resistance.

In 1991, however, Indonesian troops gunned down more than 270 civilians in Dili, the East Timor capital, garnering headlines around the world. In retaliation, Congress banned Indonesia from receiving American training under the International Military Education and Training (IMET) program. This cutoff greatly upset the Pacific Command CinC, special operations leaders, and other Pentagon officials who believed continued access to Indonesian military officials would guarantee that the Americans "could pick up the phone in a crisis and get through." That access, they believed, was more important than making a point about human rights. Sanctions would do little more than antagonize the Indonesian military and leave the United States with no contacts in a critical Pacific theater country.[*]

The power of the American military example, U.S. military officials argued, would convince foreign militaries to stop kidnapping, torturing, and abusing their citizens. In truth, there was little or no evidence that this approach had ever worked in Indonesia. But a succession of CinCs and special operations commanders had become so dogged in pursuing their mission to engage the Indonesian armed forces that they often ignored or minimized the terrible acts of violence committed by the Indonesian military against its own people.

Indonesia became a case study in how persistent CinCs in the Pacific, and their supporters at the Pentagon, worked around congres-

---

[*] In response to the cutting of military ties, Indonesia suspended bilateral programs they knew the U.S. military favored, such as a long-term joint sea-lane-mapping project.

sional and State Department roadblocks to maintain military ties. When a fiesty U.S. ambassador tried in 2000 to hold the Indonesian armed forces accountable for their crimes in East Timor, Adm. Dennis Blair, the CinC, went to battle. Blair's partial victory in the skirmish was a testimony to the diplomatic heft that the CinCs had accrued over the preceding ten years.

Indonesia had always been a distant, but favorite stop for the American military brass. Exotic and friendly, the Indonesians flattered American generals and admirals with elaborate dinners and ceremonies. During the four and a half years in the 1990s that Col. Charles Don McFetridge was defense attaché at the U.S. embassy in Jakarta, he counted 150 visits by American generals and admirals. Some came to see and learn. Some came to arrange exchanges. Some came just to relax and enjoy themselves.

The TNI (the Indonesian acronym for its armed forces) impressed Americans who knew something about the militaries in Asia. Its leadership, many of them IMET graduates, appeared professional and disciplined. Some Americans especially cottoned to Kopassus, their high-quality special operations unit. Kopassus entertained visiting American officers with spectacular displays of discipline and uncanny, almost superhuman skill. Its "flash-bang" shows, as McFetridge called them, featured soldiers jumping through fire, troops covered by poisonous tarantulas, soldiers breaking bricks with their hands and riding motorcycles blindfolded. The show impressed and baffled everyone who saw it.

Kopassus had its own secret weapon: a cosmopolitan, English-speaking young commander, Subianto Prabowo, who just happened to be married to one of Suharto's daughters. His military lineage included two uncles, a lieutenant and a sergeant, who died fighting the Dutch for Indonesia's independence. His father was a prominent economics professor whose political popularity earned him the reputation as the John F. Kennedy of his day.

As a child Prabowo lived predominantly overseas and was conversant in six languages. On his return to Indonesia, he entered the military and quickly became the darling of the American military, from whom he collected both experience and honors. In 1980, Prabowo became a distinguished allied graduate of the U.S. Army Special Forces Officer Course at Fort Bragg. In 1995 he became the first foreign officer to earn the Special Forces' coveted parachute insignia for mastering a risky high-altitude, low-opening jump. He trained with the U.S. Army's 25th Infantry Division in Hawaii and attended the elite Command and General Staff College at Fort Leavenworth, Kans.

At the age of 43, Prabowo became the youngest general in Indonesian history. By then, he had already been deputy commander of Detachment 81, a special counterterrorism unit, and had received training from Germany's crack Grenzschutz Grugge 9. Twice he commanded all Kopassus troops in East Timor. For years a certain phrase had been repeated in the secret dossier that the U.S. intelligence community kept on Prabowo: "He is self-confident, innovative, aggressive, and well-trained." Someday, they noted, he might be president.

With his access to both Indonesian and American military leaders, Prabowo became the best-known flag officer in his country, renowned for his social skills. In 1998, Defense Secretary William Cohen toured Prabowo's special forces base outside Jakarta. A well-kept facility, it sported drawings of screaming skulls as road signs. Just around the block stood a bright pink, three-story shopping mall owned by Kopassus. For Cohen's visit, Prabowo's troops performed karate, raced through burning buildings, and slithered down ropes from black helicopters. Prabowo ended another show for the regional CinC at the time, Adm. Joseph Prueher, with his troops standing shoulder to shoulder singing the Indonesian version of the 82nd Airborne Division's song. The adrenaline on the reviewing stand was palpable, said one observer. Prueher was pleased and excited.[3]

Much of the fireworks and the spit and polish of his troops were produced by Prabowo money (or his wife's actually—her personal wealth was estimated to be between $150 and $300 million). He pumped money into the organization to pay for better housing and equipment, and even for tuition at private U.S. military colleges for some cadets.

The brass from the U.S. Special Operations Command was especially enamored of Prabowo's troops. Gen. Wayne Downing, its commander from 1993–96, parachuted with Kopassus. Brig. Gen. Charles Holland, head of U.S. Special Operations forces in the Pacific from

June 1995 to June 1997, who later replaced Downing as head of all special operations units, was so impressed he pioneered an expansive Air Force special operations program that included instruction on base protection, anti-aircraft defenses, and forward air-control missions.

Prabowo, who became known among the diplomatic corps in Jakarta as "Washington's man in Indonesia," also had a very dark side. Defense Intelligence Agency (DIA) reports dating back to the mid-1990s describe a split personality and a number of allegations against him. Page-long sections of the reports, those titled "Human Rights Issues and Indonesia's Elite Army Forces" and "Allegations of Human Rights Abuse against LTG Prabowo" were entirely blacked out by DIA officials from copies of the file released under a Freedom of Information Act request.

American officers witnessed Prabowo publicly berate lower-ranking officers with abandon. "He has a ferocious temper, is ruthlessly ambitious, and can be exceptionally petty," a defense intelligence profiler wrote in one DIA report. "He is easily depressed and becomes withdrawn when he senses he is losing. He is a ruthless opponent, capable of doing the unorthodox and ready to use any means to achieve his objectives." McFetridge, whose job as defense attaché was to get to know Indonesian military leaders, found Prabowo to be one of the most fascinating people he had ever met. Friendly. Generous. Urbane. Brutal. Vindictive. Cruel. Nurturing. "Ambitious beyond a Greek tragedy."

Prabowo introduced human-rights training to some of his troops, but he also admitted to U.S. officials that he had formed controversial Timorese militia groups designed to break rebel ties within their community and intimidate pro-independence advocates.[4] Questionable Kopassus strongarm tactics filled diplomatic and intelligence cables from the U.S. and Australian embassies in Jakarta during the late 1990s. The Australian embassy's military mission maintained deeper contacts with Indonesian armed forces than did any other country. They knew Kopassus lay behind the killings and torture in East Timor and Irian Jaya.[5] Behind the vaulted doors of Australia's defense intelligence section in Jakarta were maps and diagrams outlining chains of command, local commanders' names, and their secret channel for communicating with the Kopassus leadership in Jakarta. The Australians shared most of this information with the Americans, with whom they had an almost seamless intelligence relationship. Australian and American analysts sat side by side in the largest Australian listening posts in Asia.

Even so, U.S. Pacific Command officers downplayed the human-rights allegations against Kopassus. They attributed misconduct to poor pay and training, not to a premeditated campaign against the Indonesian people. They also dismissed the argument, made often on Capitol Hill and in some parts of the State Department, that American military support might legitimize the wrong people and relieve the pressure for democratic reform. The message that American actions did send was clear: ignore what the U.S. government says in public, for in reality it condones the status quo.

In 1991, shortly after the first restrictions were imposed as a sanction for the Dili massacre, U.S. military officials found a way around the congressional roadblock: the Joint Combined Exchange Training (JCET) program, whose particulars remained classified until 1998. On paper, the JCET program was peddled to Congress as a way to train U.S. Special Operations Forces overseas. In reality, it allowed the military to train foreign troops from countries such as Indonesia, Colombia, and Pakistan whom Congress had likewise blacklisted. Between 1991 and 1998, U.S. special operations forces conducted forty-one training exercises with Indonesian troops, at least twenty-six of which were with Kopassus.[*]

McFetridge loved the program. He had attended the Indonesian war college as a major in the early 1980s and had great respect for the

[*] The training involved counterterrorism, mission planning, sniper skills, close-quarters urban warfare, crowd control, and rapid infiltration of troops. It also included discussions of international human-rights standards. The JCET provision, Title 10, Section 2011 of the U.S. Code, requires that the Defense Department submit an annual report to Congress detailing country-by-country training. Following a series of articles by the author in the *Washington Post* in July 1998, Congress rewrote the provision to require more detailed accounting. The Defense Department complied but also made parts of the report classified. In 2002, the department proposed to Congress that it be relieved of its reporting requirement altogether: "It is overly burdensome," the department told Congress in a proposal to amend the 2003 Defense Authorization Bill. "The Department has received no queries from the Congress concerning the contents of the reports submitted to date."

Indonesian military. "It's one of only a few formerly colonized countries in the world that has gained independence through revolution," he liked to say. "There's us, Vietnam, and Indonesia."

McFetridge traveled to East Timor a dozen times to look into allegations of human-rights abuses. Of course, he always traveled with an Indonesian military escort. McFetridge had talked to international humanitarian groups, but found "no smoking gun" on Prabowo, he said. He also believed the number of dead in East Timor had been greatly exaggerated. Closer to 40,000 people, he thought, had been killed since 1975, not the 200,000 commonly cited by the UN and nongovernmental organizations. "Where are the killing fields?" he asked. The best weapon pro-independence activists had, McFetridge asserted, was propaganda.

When McFetridge, instructed by Washington, began to push the issue of civilian control over the military, the Indonesians became incredulous. "They would look at me and say, 'We're not training civilians to be generals. . . . They thought I was on a completely different frequency."

McFetridge was on a different frequency than one of his embassy colleagues, too. Ed McWilliams, a feisty State Department political counselor, met frequently as part of his job with human-rights activists and representatives of nongovernmental organizations. He roamed the Indonesian streets with a camera during anti-Suharto demonstrations. He gathered evidence about Indonesia's military involvement in East Timor and in the disappearance of a growing number of political opponents to Suharto's rule.

By 1996, the Pentagon was pushing aggressively to restore the IMET program. In December of that year, McWilliams sent Washington a classified "dissent channel" cable against the idea.[*] "Those who promote IMET as a basis for improving ABRI[†] performance in the area of human rights are pointedly unable to demonstrate any positive IMET impact," he wrote. The 1970s and 1980s, during which

---

[*] The "dissent channel" is a means by which State Department officials can express their opposition to a U.S. government policy without going public.

[†] Armee Bayan Republik Indonesia, the name of the Indonesian army in Bahesa Indonesia, the country's official language.

military-to-military training and contacts were vast, he pointed out "were years of broad-scale ABRI human-rights abuse and unaccountability before the laws." Nor was it likely that maintaining the sanctions would cause Indonesia to abandon "its 30-year course of generally constructive engagement in the region. . . . However, tying the United States to an unpopular, corrupt, militaristic regime through continuation/expansion of military-to-military relations will undermine long-term U.S. interests in Indonesia," he concluded. The U.S. military was entirely unswayed. That same year, Prabowo had been the star of the Pacific Command's Special Operations Conference in Hawaii.

In October 1997, even as the Indonesian economy tumbled and wage and price protests bled into the streets, American special forces were giving lessons to their Indonesian counterparts. At a housing construction site owned by the Lippo Group conglomerate eighteen miles outside Jakarta, twelve U.S. soldiers diagrammed a straightforward mission: find the enemy somewhere in a warren of plywood rooms, blow a hole in the wall, and kill or capture as many as possible while trying not to shoot each other. The participants in the staged drama were sixty soldiers from Kopassus and the Jakarta-area military command, Kodam Jaya. Using the U.S. Army's "laser tag" equipment with a couple of Puma and Super Puma helicopters for heightened atmospherics, U.S. commanders taught the Indonesians how to plan and conduct close-quarters combat and other fine points of urban warfare. "We would say to Kopassus, 'What do you need?'" said McFetridge. "They would say, 'What do you have?'"

Several months later, popular discontent with Suharto's regime burst into the streets. By February 1998, a number of influential political activists had disappeared. Rumors among the diplomatic community suggested Prabowo was involved. McFetridge and the U.S. ambassador in Jakarta, J. Stapleton Roy, urged Prabowo to obtain the activists' release, but Prabowo denied any involvement. Separately, McWilliams was submitting detailed accounts suggesting Kopassus was behind the disappearances and alleged torture.

Despite mounting concerns, during the next three months special forces troops held three more training exercises with Kopassus. Finally, in May, McFetridge learned that McWilliams had been right all along. An Indonesian he considered to be highly reliable, with firsthand information, told him that Kopassus's Group 4 intelligence unit had engineered the political kidnappings. Here was the smoking gun that McFetridge had insisted did not exist. McFetridge informed Ambassador Roy immediately, but neither confronted Prabowo.

Under so much heat, the Pentagon finally suspended the JCET training in May 1998, just as Indonesia erupted in anti-Suharto demonstrations. Indonesia's military leaders closeted themselves at their headquarters in Cilankap and completely shut down contact, albeit temporarily, with the U.S. military. Suharto was soon forced to step down. The country's road to democracy was again open, after thirty-one years, this time apparently with the Indonesian military's support.

Admiral Prueher, Ambassador Roy, and Vice Chairman of the Joint Chiefs of Staff Joseph Ralston—the three U.S. officials most active on the matter—instantly transferred their faith to the new armed forces chief, General Wiranto. A tall, movie-star handsome officer, he uttered all the right words in Bahasa Indonesia: Military reform. Civilian control. No complicity in East Timor. Wiranto also accused Prabowo of ordering the disappearances and alleged that Prabowo's troops may have shot students at Trisakti University that spring. After a council of military officers found Prabowo guilty of exceeding orders in the kidnapping of activists in 1998, Wiranto publicly yanked Prabowo's stars from his epaulets and forced him to retire. Prabowo has always denied any personal involvement in the wrongdoing.

Preuher liked what he saw. He met with Wiranto several times, including in one eight-hour-long session, to talk about bilateral relations. The admiral was impressed with what he heard, too, and so were his subordinates. Ralston and the Pacific Command's Special Operations commander, a brigadier general, accompanied Defense Secretary Cohen to Jakarta, where they mapped out with Wiranto a renewed military-engagement plan that included ship visits, humanitarian relief, and construction projects. Cohen raised the issue of continuing violence in East Timor and expressed his desire to see the military brought under civilian control. They left impressed by Wiranto. "There is solid evidence they are listening," the brigadier said

Adm. Dennis Blair, CinC of the U.S. Pacific Command.
U.S. PACIFIC COMMAND

after the trip. "I have total faith in Wiranto. . . . They are pushing ahead and they have a plan. Something that concerns me is their pace. You just can't click this thing off overnight."

The violence was over. The Clinton administration was optimistic about a new day for Indonesia when Adm. Dennis Blair, an intellectual with a deep commitment to shaping the post–Cold War world, took over as CinC in the Pacific in February 1999. A sixth-generation naval officer, Blair's family tree includes two other admirals, but none as high-ranking as he. His great-great-grandfather, Tom Williamson, had been chief engineer for the Confederate Navy while, at the same time, his son worked as an engineer for Union admiral David Farragut on the USS *Hartford* during the Battle of Mobile Bay.

Blair's reserved Maine demeanor obscured a lifelong penchant for pranks. He was twice president of his 1968 Naval Academy class but he ranked second, not first, in the class because he partied so much with his pals. His classmates remember in particular "a cold windy night spent trying to bridge the gap between the laundry rooftop and the smokestack ladder," according to his yearbook. Blair's father was a submariner. So when service selection night at the academy came around, the confident upperclassman told Navy officials that he, too, wanted to join submarine warfare, but that he would accept only the attack class, "not the ballistic-missile or nuclear subs that sat around waiting for World War III." They sent him to surface warfare. The first time he walked onto his ship as an ensign and took a deep breath, he knew he was where he belonged. "I remember how my dad smelled when he got home, the diesel oil, sweat, paint," he said. "That was what the Navy was about." Although he still carries his weathered "shell-back" card, traditionally received after crossing the Equator for the first time, Blair distinguished himself more at the helm of military power in Washington than at sea.

In fact, Blair was part of a small, offbeat intellectual clique that the Navy has always tolerated. A Rhodes scholar who studied at Oxford University alongside Bill Clinton, he later won a prestigious White House fellowship, then served as a member of the National Security Council (NSC) staff, the Navy's prestigious Strategic Studies Group, and as the Pentagon's chief liaison to the CIA.*

In the spring of 2000, at the age of fifty-three, tanned and taut from tennis and jogging in Hawaii, Blair still seemed a tightly wound Mainer at heart. At Annapolis, his classmates reported that his favorite possession was his formal "Blue Service" uniform, a reference to a car he and his friends illegally owned and would drive into town on weekends. As a CinC, over staff protests, he made his travel team change into service dress uniform even for a five-minute drive from an airport arrival to the hotel. He often spoke so softly and in such a monotone that he was hard to hear. His averted gaze left the impression of shyness, when really he was more like a submarine, showing only the tip of the periscope as he steadily plowed ahead.

Blair's command includes forty-three countries and 60 percent of

---

* Blair was also Chairman John Shalikashvili's Joint Staff director and in that position shepherded through the first mammoth Quadrennial Defense Review, a once-every-four-years look at how the U.S. armed services would be used and the type of equipment and force structure it would take to accomplish combat missions in the post–Cold War era.

the earth's population. It keeps an eye on four of the world's largest armies, those of China, India, and North and South Korea.

From the late 1950s to the mid-1970s, the Pacific CinC's job had been to wage the war in Vietnam and to manage the Pacific bases that supported it. The CinC also closely monitored the Korean Peninsula and supported the commander of U.S. troops in South Korea. The CinC's Pacific forces also supported a series of counterinsurgency operations in Malaysia, Thailand, Cambodia, and Laos. In the 1980s the command's focus shifted to what the Pentagon saw as an offensive military threat to Taiwan from China, and to weapons proliferation, particularly by communist North Korea.

In the 1990s, military relationships were redefined across the Pacific. The Philippines pressured the U.S. military to leave its islands. The November 1991 closing of the gigantic Subic Bay Naval Base and Clark Air Field in Luzon symbolized a new independence and a hostility toward traditional U.S. ties. Protests against the U.S. military presence surfaced in Japan, as well, swirling mainly around Okinawa, where thousands of U.S. servicemen were stationed. The Pacific Command responded with a new strategic vision, dubbed "cooperative engagement" by Adm. C. R. "Chuck" Larson, then the CinC.

Larson re-established military-to-military relations with Vietnam and China in the post–Tiananmen Square era and each succeeding CinC—admirals R. C. Macke, Prueher, and Blair—improved on his efforts. Their strategy was premised on the belief that the United States had no significant threats left in the Pacific region—not really even from China, which signed a historic "constructive strategic partnership" agreement with the United States in 1997.

North Korea remained worrisome, given its collapsing economy and continuing missile-development program. And Taiwan was a perpetual blister, but the CinCs believed China and the United States had achieved an unspoken truce there, too: if Taiwan stopped demanding independence, it would, de facto, have it. Blair had expressed impatience with Taiwan in 1999 when he told a closed-door congressional panel that Taiwan "threw a turd in the punch bowl" of the delicate China-Taiwan-U.S. relations with its pro-independence rhetoric.[6] Hard-line Republican members of Congress who criticized China's

Taiwan policy were too belligerent in their approach, Blair scoffed later to colleagues.*

By 1999, when Blair took over the Pacific Command, Indonesia was well into the economic tailspin that had swept Asia two years earlier. Vice President B. J. Habibie was appointed to replace his mentor, Suharto. The U.N.-sanctioned referendum on independence for East Timor, which had been Habibie's idea, was just months away.

Blair was optimistic about General Wiranto and how he would handle the emotional vote on East Timorese independence. He credited Wiranto with trying to reform the armed forces. Blair believed Wiranto when the general said he wanted to get the military out of politics. He also said he saw no convincing evidence that Wiranto was directing the militia violence in East Timor, as many Indonesians were alleging. Privately, he criticized members of Congress and the administration who lumped Wiranto in with what Blair believed to be a group of ill-trained rogue forces doing the killings.

Blair was willing to fight for his position, as well. When the Clinton administration, at Congress' urging, threatened to expel seven Indonesian officers studying in the United States as punishment for the TNI's role in violence against political opposition figures in Jakarta, Blair and the Pentagon resisted and forced the issue all the way to the top of the National Security Council. The NSC held half a dozen meetings to resolve the matter. Blair also won Chairman of the Joint Chiefs of Staff Hugh Shelton's approval to pay for the remainder of their stay with CinC Initiative Funds, a $25 million annual pot of money that the chairman controls.

The U.S. concern about East Timor didn't resonate with the Indonesian leadership, however, noticed Richard Holbrooke, U.S. ambassador to the United Nations, who pressed Washington's case in Jakarta, Dili, and New York. The Indonesians were determined

---

* Blair would later express surprise at the lack of Asia expertise in President George W. Bush's Defense Department. Given the administration's initial focus on China and North Korea, the team seemed shallow on substance, context, and history, Blair told associates. Blair had never viewed China as quite the belligerent that Defense Secretary Donald Rumsfeld's staff was making it out to be. Blair's closest colleagues believe that view cost him the chairmanship of the Joint Chiefs of Staff.

not to let an insignificant island define their standing with the rest of the world.

Meanwhile, since January 1998, seven intelligence analysts at the "Joint Intelligence Center, Pacific" (JIC), the world's largest military-intelligence center, in a windowless concrete building near Blair's headquarters in Hawaii, had tracked the movements of Indonesian military and militia forces in East Timor and Indonesia. The Indonesia desk in the JIC had grown from one to nine persons and maintained a round-the-clock "crisis action" mode. Over the preceding year, the analysts had received a tenfold increase in imagery and a fivefold increase in electronic collection. It was actually too much to process.

In April 1999, the intelligence analysts watched and read reports of Indonesian security forces terrorizing Timorese civilians and forcing refugees out of their homes and villages. The militia's intentions seemed clear: they meant to intimidate and control the citizenry and activists who were organizing a plebiscite for independence, a vote encouraged and sanctioned by the United Nations and Washington. The violence was bubbling into a wholesale rampage. Blair's hypothesis was being disproved; Indonesia's military was still wholly in control. The perpetrators of repression weren't "rogues" outside the chain of command, they were part of a predetermined campaign.*

The NSC directed Blair to meet with Wiranto. Together with Ambassador Roy, Blair worked out his talking points. The admiral would warn his counterpart that he should take action to stop the

---

* Among the most stunning evidence arrived only in April 2002 with reports in the *Sydney (Australia) Morning Herald*. The articles detailed telephone intercepts made by the Australian Signals Directorate's Shoal Bay listening post in the Northern Territory and an EP-3 Orion surveillance plane. The intercepts showed regular phone calls between militia leader Eurico Guterres and former military intelligence chief Maj. Gen. Zacky Anwar, keeping Anwar informed about the militia's operations. In other intercepts, a Kopassus ground commander is heard issuing instructions to Guterres. In all, the intercepts appear to show Wiranto and other top officials engaged in a covert intelligence operation set up to win the referendum. The top-secret intercepts were published in the newspaper the same day that an Indonesian ad hoc court began a series of trials of eighteen mid-level officers, civilian officials, and militia members accused of crimes against humanity in East Timor. No senior officers were likely to stand trial, however.

violence or meet American and international ostracism. Shelton and Ralston had been on the phone with Wiranto, too, threatening to withdraw U.S. support for billions in International Monetary Fund loans Indonesia needed. But Blair and other top Pentagon military leaders were inclined to cut Indonesia some slack. They believed the military's poor human-rights record reflected its financial straits and lack of discipline. The human-rights organizations dug in, citing years of abuse at the hands of the military.[7]

On April 8, 1999, Blair's armored car worked its way through the tangle of Jakarta's bumper-to-bumper traffic, rusted taxis, and food carts to a quiet oasis of palm-lined driveways, manicured lawns, and a pristine officers' golf course. An honor cordon of soldiers and sailors positioned along the route at Cilankap, Indonesia's Pentagon, saluted as he passed. Blair decided it was "generally not a good tactic in a first meeting to do nothing but shake your finger in your interlocutor's face." He would mix hope for the future with a reminder that the United States expected Wiranto to stop the violence in East Timor and allow the referendum to proceed without bloodshed. In Wiranto's office, the meeting was cordial. Blair stressed the positive. "I look forward to the time Indonesia will resume its proper role as a leader in the region," he told his host, according a cable of his conversation.

Blair invited Wiranto to a military seminar in Honolulu and promised to train troops in crowd control. He could provide the seminar venue through his $25 million a year Asia-Pacific Center for Security Studies. He also said he would work to reinstate the U.S.-sponsored IMET program. Neither the tone nor the substance of what Blair said seemed to reflect the weighty message that some in the State Department had hoped Blair would convey. State Department officials who read a rendition of the meeting in an embassy cable to Washington were disappointed he had not been more forceful.

Wiranto told Blair that the Army was being "unfairly blamed" for supporting anti-independence militias operating in East Timor. Wiranto "was emphatic," the cable read, that as long as East Timor was a part of Indonesia, it would be the army's job "to maintain peace and stability" and to disarm both the militias and the pro-independence groups. Blair was inclined to believe him. "Fairly or unfairly," Blair told him, "the international community looks at East Timor as a barometer of progress for Indonesian reform. More importantly, the process of change in East Timor should proceed peacefully."

Blair left the meeting hopeful. But over the next week he learned of a massacre in Liquica, East Timor, that had taken place just two days before his April meeting with Wiranto. Militias had stormed the town, and many of Liquica's people, including women and children, had taken refuge in a Catholic church. The soldiers fired tear gas into the church, forcing those inside to flee, then slaughtered them with machetes and machine guns. When it was over, fifty-seven people lay dead.

Blair telephoned Wiranto to express his concern. "You have told me you understand your responsibility for law-and-order in East Timor, but it is clear from my reports and from news reports that your soldiers are not carrying out their responsibilities. We expect you to do better." Wiranto pleaded ignorance and "admitted he was shocked" by the militia violence in Liquica and Dili according to another cable. Don't worry, he assured Blair, disarming the militia "will be easy."

In fact, UN officials and a senior Indonesian intelligence officer on the ground at the time told the *Washington Post*'s Keith Richburg that Maj. Gen. Zacky Anwar, who was working behind the scenes as the army's top commander in East Timor, had secretly organized thirteen militia groups, one for each province. Their members were drawn from pro-Indonesian partisans. (Anwar was a former Kopassus member known as one of "Prabowo's boys.") Anwar's militias nicknamed themselves "Red and White Iron" and "Thorn." Over time, they killed sixteen UN election monitors. In April, tens of thousands of pro-independence supporters were herded from villages into the city center of Liquica and kept as prisoners with little food and water. Armed militia and the Indonesian army made sure they did not escape.

UN officials on the island told visiting U.S. senator Tom Harkin (D-Iowa) to expect widespread violence. Even the new U.S. defense attaché who replaced Don McFetridge privately voiced speculation that Wiranto knew and was coordinating the violence. White House and State Department officials furiously worked the phones, warning, threatening, and cajoling the Indonesian authorities not to let the violence spread. Shelton got into the act too. But, astonishingly, at no point did Blair ask the special operations officials who worked most closely with Indonesia to reach out to the contacts they had developed through the IMET or JCET programs to try to arrest the violence. Such contact was precisely the military's rationale for continuing those programs in the face of congressional opposition. For years Pentagon officials had argued that interaction, even with tainted militaries like Indonesia's, would pay off in a crisis: "You could pick up the phone when you needed to and someone would answer." But as 10,000 armed militia members flooded into East Timor in advance of the plebiscite and President Clinton admonished the Indonesians to use restraint, no one at the U.S. Pacific Command below Blair picked up the phone.

Lower-level special forces officers and soldiers who trained over the years in Indonesia said that in such a politically sensitive situation, they would not have called their counterparts without a direct request from above. And there was no such request. "It is fairly rare that personal relations made through an IMET course can come into play in resolving a future crisis," Blair would later explain. For him, the value of training with the Americans was its potential long-term benefit. "Militaries that are doing something bad at times go into their shell," he said. "It's them against the world." A better strategy, he insisted, was to make them feel a kinship with, not isolated from, the norms of more professional militaries.

After the East Timorese voted overwhelmingly for independence on August 30, 1999, Blair, back at his Hawaii headquarters, thought, "Touchdown!" Indonesia's problems would abate. Expectations at the Pentagon were that the worst was over, that East Timor had won its independence and the Indonesian military would honor the vote. His entourage headed west to congratulate Wiranto on a smooth referendum. But actually, nothing was going smoothly in East Timor. Angry militias reacted to the vote by unleashing what the Vatican called "a systematic campaign of political assassination." Militias murdered the head of the Vatican-sponsored Caritas charity and the eighty-two-year-old father of East Timorese independence leader Xanana Gusmao. While Clinton and other world leaders pondered their next move, the militias killed women and children and drove 240,000 East Timorese over the border to West Timor. Some 1,000 people would die and 75 percent of East Timor's infrastructure was ruined.

Blair and other top U.S. military officials took a forgiving view of the violence surrounding the referendum. Given the Indonesian military's record of brutality, they argued, it could have been worse. "What the military did was absolutely remarkable," said Ralston, who thought their performance was great, compared to what it could have been.

Blair had hoped to congratulate Wiranto. But as his plane began the long flight from Hawaii to Jakarta on September 8, the secure phone line rang. The NSC insisted that Blair take a different message to Wiranto, one the admiral had hoped to avoid but that he ultimately supported: the United States was severing all military ties with Indonesia.

Upon reaching Jakarta, Blair and his cherubic-looking aide-de-camp, Air Force Maj. Joe Diana, rode alone in a Volvo limousine to Wiranto's headquarters. There they found a table set with sixteen tea cups to welcome the expected U.S. entourage. "So," one of Wiranto's aides asked. "Where is everyone else?" Blair asked to see Wiranto privately, then informed him dryly that American patience had run out. His troops had acted dishonorably. He told him he must allow UN peacekeeping troops onto the island and that the United States was severing military relations. U.S. support for international loans was also at stake.

The next day, during a stop in Hawaii en route to Auckland, President Clinton publicly accused the Indonesian military of direct involvement. "The Indonesian military is aiding and abetting the militia violence," he said. "This is simply unacceptable." He suspended what little U.S. arms sales remained in the pipeline and cancelled scheduled training and conference invitations. He did, however, leave the door open to one form of military contact: sending American ground forces into East Timor to quell the violence and restore stability.

Pentagon officials opposed U.S. military intervention. They had just ended the Kosovo air war and thousands of U.S. troops were now occupying that province. Speaking before a panel of senators on the same day, General Shelton made the Pentagon's position clear. "I cannot see any national interest there that would be overwhelming, that would call for us to deploy or place U.S. forces on the ground in that area," he said.

Even Senator John Warner (R-Va.), chairman of the Senate Armed Services Committee and no fan of Clinton's foreign interventions, was skeptical, given the level of violence. "We are now seeing another chapter of virtual genocide taking place, of these hopeless, helpless people. But there is a distinction" between East Timor and Kosovo, Warner insisted. In East Timor, "we took a very active role as a member of the United Nations in inducing [the East Timorese] to take the actions which precipitated this problem of recrimination. . . . And it's an issue that this particular senator finds most troublesome as relating to whether we do or do not join other nations in offering some military assistance. Personally, I haven't arrived at my own conclusion."

Meanwhile, international pressure was increasing to send U.S. troops to East Timor to prevent more carnage. Blair had proposed sending in a small ground force but that was rejected at the Pentagon and White House. As Blair landed back home in Hawaii, Clinton was only hours away from a refueling stop at Hawaii's Hickam Air Force Base on his way home from New Zealand. The president touched down at 1:30 A.M. Blair rushed out to greet him.

Secret Service agents drew the curtains in the Hickam "Distinguished Visitors" lounge and National Security Adviser Samuel "Sandy" Berger noshed on snacks set out on the coffee table. Blair presented the president with an alternative he knew the Pentagon supported: let the Australians take the lead and send in only a few U.S. intelligence, communications, and logistics personnel. They discussed how to get the Australians in without violence. Berger and Blair argued over cutting off military programs altogether. Capitol Hill wouldn't allow it to continue, Berger argued. Blair tried to save military education courses for senior officers.[*]

---

[*] Blair's position on military training and education merits attention. He believes the United States should maintain open military channels with all countries with whom it is not at war, including senior officer visits, military education, and invitations to attend international conferences, all aimed at exposing closed and problematic militaries to professional officers and their thinking, especially in the area of civilian control. Beyond that, military contacts should be modulated to serve mutual interests: counterterrorism, counterdrug, counterpiracy, and search and rescue cooperation are among the most obvious. In-depth professional exchanges, training, combined exercises, and arms sales must be more acutely tailored to the country and U.S. interests, broadly defined.

But the East Timor violence, which did not altogether end when the Australian-led peacekeeping force finally entered and the Indonesian forces backed down, had caught Capitol Hill's imagination, and it sparked indignation. Senator Patrick Leahy (D-Vt.) won easy passage of an amendment demanding concrete reform by the Indonesian armed forces before military ties could be restored. The legislation called on Indonesians to prosecute army and militia wrongdoers and to cooperate with the UN. Further, it stipulated that the Indonesian army-controlled militias allow refugees to return home and live in safety.

Leahy thought Blair was either insincere or extremely naïve to believe the Indonesian army had changed. "As long as I have been in the Senate, the Pentagon has said that U.S. engagement would professionalize the Indonesian military," scoffed the avuncular, white-haired Leahy. "That has been disproved time and time again, and the final straw was the debacle in East Timor." Blair heard all this from Leahy but quickly began a campaign he hoped would one day bring the two militaries back in contact. He brought ten Indonesian officers into a large multinational exercise in May 2000 as observers. He also planned a trip to Indonesia as a sign that he was not giving up on Wiranto or his armed forces.

By then, though, a new U.S. ambassador had taken up his post in Jakarta. Ironically, Robert Gelbard, a gruff-talking, tough-minded New Yorker, had a familiarity with, and respect for, the military that was rare in the Foreign Service. A career diplomat, Gelbard proudly carried a well-worn 7th Special Forces Group commemorative coin in his pocket, a memento given to him for years of work on secretive counter-drug operations as ambassador to Bolivia in the late 1980s. He liked the brave special forces soldiers he had gotten to know in the jungles of Latin America.

The special forces community liked Gelbard, too. As head of the State Department's counternarcotics office, Gelbard had worked closely with Army Special Forces soldiers all over Latin America. They had even invited him to speak at their annual ball, one of the few occasions Green Berets can be found in formal uniforms. When Gelbard gave up the Latin America portfolio, he plunged into the Balkans mess, helping to implement the Dayton Peace Accords and efforts to capture war criminals. During the Kosovo air war, Gelbard headed Operation Matrix, a clandestine effort to intimidate cronies around Yugoslav president Slobodan Milosevic.

Gelbard appreciated the value of what he called "the secret handshake" between foreign militaries. The American officers he knew had credibility with their Indonesian counterparts that no civilian could match. He also understood and admired the professionalism with which the American military approached problems around the world. For all those reasons, it amazed him how naïve the U.S. military leadership had been in its dealings with Indonesia.

He summed up the Indonesian military's attitude toward its unacceptable behavior as "unconditional entitlement." Indonesia didn't need to pay its international loans on time. Nor did it feel pressure to reorganize its economy to meet obligations to international financial institutions. Indonesian leaders lied to their own people. They felt no need to account for past atrocities. They made promises to their American counterparts, then excuses, then promises again. "The Indonesians feel they are so important they will be forgiven their trespasses," Gelbard said. "We've been engaging with these guys for decades and they've repeatedly jilted us. . . . Unfortunately a lot of people in the Pentagon and Honolulu [i.e., Pacific Command headquarters] have made themselves such eager suitors it convinced the Indonesian military that the longer they waited, it would all be just fine."

Gelbard found convincing evidence of Indonesian military misdeeds. His list was long: military atrocities in the Moluccas, Aceh, and East Timor; Kopassus's complicity in the mass rapes of ethincally Chinese women during the May 1998 protests; Prabowo's link to, and Kopassus's involvement in, the continuing violence in East Timor. "My strategic concept was not to ignore the [Indonesian] military, but I wanted them to pay a price of admission" for U.S. engagement, he said. "I wasn't going to hold them to the same standards as Sweden, but you had to ask something of them." Gelbard wanted accountability, and unlike the ambassadors who preceded him—Paul Wolfowitz, then Roy—he told the Indonesians so, in public.

Wiranto was soon dismissed by the civilian government for his failure to control the military. Blair wanted to go to Indonesia to meet his successor, reopen relations, begin a push for deeper ties, and encourage the Indonesians to adopt reforms along the way. He let Gelbard know he planned to visit soon. But Gelbard wasn't buying it. None of Leahy's conditions had been met for renewed relations. In fact, evidence grew that Indonesia's army was resisting political reform and was deeply implicated in the intimidation of political dissidents in East Timor and elsewhere in the archipelago.

Gelbard cabled his objections to Blair's trip to the State Department. He cited a dramatic increase in militia violence and an increasingly hostile attitude by the Indonesian armed forces toward him. The armed forces had refused him permission to fly in his U.S. C-12 airplane around the islands as a means of examining the troubled provinces. Indonesia's civilian defense minister had publicly denounced U.S. meddling and had refused to meet with him. Gelbard believed Blair's visit would undermine President Clinton's decision to cut off military ties and the message it sent regarding the army's involvement in the East Timor violence.

An American ambassador's opinion is supposed to trump that of other U.S. officials abroad, and it usually does. The ambassador grants permission to every U.S. government employee—military, law enforcement, CIA, other diplomats—who wants to set foot in his or her assigned country. This is the red card an ambassador holds, one used judiciously, and rarely.

Tough calls about foreign policy are supposed to be made in Washington. Gelbard needed his State Department colleagues to carry his case forward. They were quickly overwhelmed, however, as they had been to an increasing degree, by the CinCs' well-organized, familiar Washington front, which included Vice Chairman Ralston and Chairman Shelton. Blair had other heavy-hitters on his side, including Defense Secretary Cohen and Deputy National Security Adviser James Steinberg. After several meetings of the NSC deputies—the second-ranking officials at the NSC, the State and Defense Departments, and the CIA—Blair's position prevailed.

Officials in Washington saw the decision as a military triumph that underscored the growing foreign-policy clout of the regional CinCs. Blair's regular visits to Washington, his aircraft, his permanent Washington liaison office, the Joint Staff colonels working on his behalf at the Pentagon, and his 1,000-person Pacific Command simply swamped Gelbard and his comparatively smaller staff, who operated from 6,000 miles away. Gelbard had an armored car, a small plane to fly him around Indonesia, and secure telephone lines. He had an overworked embassy staff—most of whom were assigned to other government departments—and an ineffective State Department bureaucracy in Washington. That was about it.

Prior to Blair's arrival in Jakarta, the admiral and Gelbard had a series of long phone calls to work out the ground rules. Gelbard had exacted a promise that there would be no U.S. commitment of military engagement and that Blair would have to stress the need for Indonesian accountability for the East Timor massacres.

The day before Blair's scheduled departure, the view from his conference room window at the Pacific Command was postcard-perfect: an American flag waved in a light breeze. The sky was deep blue above the swaying palms. Colonels huddled in Blair's office to review a report from the U.S. defense attaché in Indonesia, the chief U.S. military analyst on the ground there. The dispatch recapped some negative remarks President Wahid had made about military cooperation with the United States. The attaché "thinks that, in the long run, things are going to improve," said a colonel, reading from an embassy cable. But the attaché also recommended that Blair's trip be postponed.

Blair was unfazed. "I don't think an ambiguous speech by President [Abdurrahman] Wahid should stop this. . . . Barring some huge cataclysmic event, we'll press forward," he said. Blair's staff cautioned that the trip could still be nixed by Jakarta or Washington by the time Blair reached Singapore, his first overnight stop. But the admiral was more concerned about the ambiguities of the U.S. position. How were the Indonesians to be judged? "Where's the finish line?" he asked his staff.

They looked at each other. No one really knew. The staff would query the Joint Staff in Washington. A vague answer awaited Blair when he arrived in Singapore—so vague that after analyzing the Joint Staff's cable from the twenty-fifth floor of the Shangri-La Hotel over-

Adm. Dennis Blair, commander of the U.S. Pacific Command, center, leaving a meeting with top Indonesian naval officers during his first trip to Indonesia after military relations had been severed because of the military's complicity in the violence in East Timor. Behind Blair, to the left, is Ambassador Robert Gelbard, who initially opposed Blair's visit to Jakarta. DANA PRIEST

looking the city-state's skyscrapers, Blair shrugged and said, "We'll know it when we see it."

The tug-of-war with Gelbard was fully joined. The ambassador had revised Blair's Jakarta schedule, which the admiral's staff suspiciously regarded as an effort to rein him in. Gelbard planned to join Blair in his meetings with Indonesian military officials, but he had ruled out a CinC visit with the civilian minister of defense, who had riled Gelbard. "This is going to be a strange visit," said Blair, shaking his head.

The tension between Blair and Gelbard was as thick as Jakarta's steamy humidity as the CinC's sparkling white jet touched down on April 2, 2000. A hot wind joined Gelbard in greeting Blair on the tarmac with a stilted handshake. Gelbard's rumpled dark polo shirt clashed with the crispness of Blair's bright white uniform. They walked at arm's length to the VIP lounge without speaking a word, then sat in near silence as Indonesian officials processed the admiral's fifteen-person entourage.

Gelbard had invited Blair to stay at his residence. Time without their staffs might give them an opportunity to iron out differences, both hoped. Gelbard could tell him about his trips to see the camps of destitute refugees in western Timor. "There's a real bitterness against the rest of the world over East Timor," said Gelbard. "The Indonesians are unwilling to stop the militia violence. I've been in the camps; they play an intimidating role. Seven thousand people, mostly children, died in those camps in the rainy season. I feel it is very immoral to let them stay in those circumstances."

Even at dawn, Jakarta's downtown streets teem with traffic. Siren blaring and dodging street-sweepers, Blair and Gelbard's car arrived at Cilankap. They marched together into meetings with the deputy of the Indonesian armed forces, the air force chief of staff, and the head of the navy. Blair was solicitous, asking about plans for military reform, but getting nothing concrete—no white paper, no general goals, and no specific plans. Change takes time, they said. As for East Timor, "That is behind us," one general told Blair dismissively.

Blair was quick to disagree. He pressed the U.S. case. "General, the army has behaved very unprofessionally and committed reprehensible acts. . . . You have to have accountability trials," Blair insisted.

By the end of the first day, Gelbard had impressed Blair with his grasp of the situation and knowledge of Indonesia. Gelbard, on the other hand, found Blair more realistic about the Indonesian military than he had expected, given the Pentagon's aggressiveness in pushing the trip. "They were furious at what he said," Gelbard later recounted proudly of Blair's statements. "They aren't used to a government speaking in one voice. Now, all of a sudden here was Admiral Blair. He was terrific. The Indonesians have been hearing all this from me. They needed to hear it from Blair; he knows the secret handshake."

Blair had the same message for three high-ranking Indonesian officers at a dinner in Gelbard's residence. The admiral pushed. The generals warned. The U.S. attitude "is good in a sense that we need wake-up calls," said Lt. Gen. Agus Widjoyo, a reformer and the army's chief of territorial affairs. "But don't push too hard because it could backfire."

Before Blair left Jakarta, he and Gelbard vowed to speak directly more often. They prepared a joint cable to Washington outlining the step-by-step approach they had agreed to take: small exchanges with the Indonesian navy and marines. Nothing with the army, which had shown no sincere effort to change. Such convergence of views was little more than tactical, though. Neither had really changed the way the other viewed the Indonesia military.

Over the ensuing two years, military-to-military contacts went forward in fits and starts, mirroring the declining state of affairs in Indonesia and its military's continued involvement in economic and political life. But Blair remained optimistic. "The pace of reform . . . is slower than we would like. But I am constantly reminded what a long distance [the army] has come." Gelbard, on the contrary, believed progress toward reform had been "virtually zero. . . . In fact, they've gone backwards."

Meanwhile, the Bush administration appointed a more conciliatory U.S. ambassador to replace Gelbard. With the exception of a few carefully selected scapegoats, the Indonesian military escaped punishment in the East Timor accountability tribunals. The U.S. embassy suspected a number of retired and active military of funding Al Qaeda–affiliated groups. The TNI, in fact, had fostered the training and arming of the terrorist group Lashkar Jihad in the Moluccas. Gelbard and other longtime Indonesia watchers suspected that, with an eye on national elections in 2004, the military had begun fomenting ethnic instability in the hope that Indonesians would vote an end to their experiment with civilian-led government and return to what they knew best, a military regime.

★ ★ ★ ★

IN THE FALL OF 2001, Prabowo, by then a businessman, applied at the U.S. embassy in Jakarta for a routine visa. American officials who had once embraced him as a potential president spent several months considering his request before giving him some bad news: he would not be going to the United States. To be polite, they referred him to Section 212A3 of the U.S. Immigration and Naturalization Act, which denies entry to criminals, including individuals suspected of kidnapping, rape, and torture of compatriots.

In April 2002, East Timor elected its first president, the former guerrilla leader Xanana Gusmao. That month, before an audience of foreign businessmen meeting in Jakarta, Prabowo hugged Gusmao, whom the general's Kopassus had tried to kill. "I think I was chasing Mr. Xanana Gusmao for many, many years and he eluded us, and so as warriors, we salute and we respect a worthy and strong warrior," Prabowo declared. "There have been excesses, violations. There have been breakdowns in discipline, breakdowns in correct rules of engagement. . . . One tradition or school of thought is those that say, 'We don't care about the feelings of people. . . . We have to go in and if there are civilian casualties so be it, collateral damage.'"[8]

"The word 'amok,'" Prabowo concluded, "comes from the lingua franca of this archipelago."

As the war on terrorism spread across the globe, Blair and the U.S. intelligence community found terrorist links in Indonesia they had not known about before. Even the State Department became more hospitable to training the old Indonesian military in the new post–September 11 environment. Up until Blair retired in mid-2002, he worked to win support from Congress to train an Indonesian anti-terrorist unit. In early August, the Bush administration announced a resumption of military relations with Indonesia. U.S. special forces would be sent to train a counterterrorism unit.

In Indonesia, the anti-terrorism mission has always been the job of Kopassus.

THE
CinC and
His Soldiers
in Kosovo

Chapter Eleven

FORCE TRUMPS DIPLOMACY
IN THE BALKANS

* * * *

O N OPENING NIGHT, MARCH 24, 1999, GEN. WESLEY Clark fidgeted in the study of his nineteenth-century Chateau Gendebien in Mons, Belgium. Surrounded by special assistants, he followed the "Night 1 Attack Time line" spread out before him. Several hours earlier he had given the command to commence NATO's first war; now he waited for the chain reaction to ripple throughout Europe and land back on his desk.

That afternoon, Brig. Gen. Dan Leaf, the blue-eyed commander of the Air Force's 31st Air Expeditionary Wing, had gotten the call. He had leaped into his dark blue Mercedes staff car and driven to the south end of the runway on Italy's Aviano Air Base. For two and a half hours, he watched as sixty-nine aircraft—strike fighters, electronic jammers, attack planes—loaded up, taxied out, and took off.

"It's like having 120 daughters and sending them off on their first date at the same time," Leaf thought. Waves of American B-52 bombers from England, stealth B-2 bombers from Missouri, and F-117 fighter jets flying from Italy streaked toward Yugoslavia. That country's president, Slobodan Milosevic, had refused NATO demands to stop the vicious purge of ethnic Albanians from the 4,200-square-mile southern Serbian province of Kosovo and to pull back his troops. His refusal had pushed the alliance over the edge. Together with warships in the Adriatic Sea, the planes aimed a barrage of cruise missiles and gray precision-guided bombs at formidable Serb air-defense nodes, command, control, and communications installations, aircraft and missile factories, weapons-storage sites, and two small Yugoslav army headquarters.

When the belly of the first B-52 opened up, a 3,000-pound, self-guided conventional air-launched cruise missile dropped out of its bomb bay. Instantly, the missile's engine ignited in a tiny puff of smoke and its fins folded out. The pre-programmed global positioning system took over, navigating its course with the help of satellites. An internal computerized map and timer ticked down the minutes until impact.

It was early afternoon in Washington when the missile crashed into target no. 10. The missile's hull of specially shaped metal fragments split apart and pierced the tin-and-concrete walls of a fuel depot and SA-6 surface-to-air missile factory outside Pristina, the capital of Kosovo. One ton of PBXN-111 explosives sent swordlike shards of glass flying into the air. The building's corrugated-metal walls and rafters were torn into large strips. Secondary blasts from the fuel tanks on the ground consumed the building in a spectacle of orange flames.

Dozens of other missiles and winged bombs streamed in close behind and the first stealth B-2s entered the "vulnerability window," where they were in the range of Serb anti-aircraft weapons. This first wave would last an hour and ten minutes; forty-five of fifty-two targets were struck, acres of land scorched, three daring Soviet-made MiG-29 aircraft shot down, three Serb pilots wounded in action.

The next morning, Capt. Steve Warren, a fresh-eyed infantryman from New Jersey, arrived in the carpeted offices of Clark's headquarters in his stiff baggy combat fatigues. He had recently been transferred to Clark's staff from the Korean Demilitarized Zone, where the Army's idea of a real war loomed large. The exhausted colonels in their smart office uniforms laughed and asked him why he was wearing BDUs, his camouflage fatigues. "Man, this is war!" he shouted back.

This wasn't a war, the colonels responded, rolling their eyes. It was "coercive diplomacy," they said, mocking Washington's new standoff parlance. "Coercive diplomacy" was an Orwellian term for bombing Milosevic into submission—kind of B-52 behavior modification. On the scale of war aims, political leaders thought, getting Milosevic to call off his forces wasn't worth American or European blood.

Some NATO political and military leaders had expected Milosevic to back down after just two or three days of bombing. When that didn't happen, the Clinton administration left Clark nearly alone in the critical opening days of the air war to persuade the alliance's nineteen nations that the short fight they—and he—had planned now required a rapid, major overhaul. On the scale of just how much responsibility had devolved to the CinCs over the preceding decade, nothing could match the improvised Kosovo operation.

Clark had doubts about the initial plan's meager size—only fifty-two targets were struck the first night—but after a year of coaxing the allies, he and the White House felt this was the biggest and best operation he could get NATO to approve. And as early as the second night, he began adding targets and aircraft to the war against Milosevic. Clark began another battle on a separate front, as well, this one against his own Pentagon.

Clark's conflict with Defense Secretary William Cohen and the service chiefs had begun before the war. He had wanted the Balkans declared a "major theater of war," which would have required the Defense Department to guarantee proper resources. But most of his contemporaries opposed getting involved there at all. They hadn't fully grasped the compromises required to work in a demanding coalition such as NATO. They rejected Clark's notion that a war could be incremental and still succeed. And some of the Joint Chiefs considered Wes Clark too independent, too camera-friendly, and too close to the civilians on the other side of the Potomac. Some suspected he had gotten his fourth star because President Clinton had called him "my friend." They were acquaintances and both had grown up in Arkansas. Both had been raised by stepfathers from a young age after their biological fathers had died. But as grown men, they rarely spoke on the phone or hobnobbed socially. Never mind: the Pentagon elite assumed they did.

Behind the personality clash, though, was a bigger issue: Most of the Pentagon leadership still outright opposed using military power as an instrument in a human-rights-driven crisis that did not clearly affect vital U.S. interests. Clark, on the other hand, had accepted the administration's rationale for intervening in Kosovo. More than simply carrying out the president's orders, Clark believed the United States and NATO had an obligation to stop the ethnic cleansing of Kosovar Albanians. He had dealt personally with Milosevic during the five preceding years of harsh brutality in Bosnia. He wanted to stop him once and for all.

Equally important, Clark believed Washington had an obligation to save NATO's standing as a relevant alliance. If, after fifty years, the political-military coalition could not meet its first post–Cold War challenge, why should it even continue to exist?

* * * *

CLARK HAD GROWN UP in Little Rock, Ark. His father, a lawyer and city politician in Chicago, died when Wes was not quite four years old. His mother moved back to Little Rock and remarried a banker whose last name was Clark. Only when Wes Clark was in his early twenties did the dark-haired Southern Baptist[*] discover that his biological father, Benjamin Kanne, had been Jewish. His grandfather, Jacob Nemerovsky, had fled Minsk, Russia, in the late 1890s during a pogrom.

A competitive swimmer, Clark pushed himself consistently, putting in long hours at the office and training field and getting by with little sleep. He ranked first in his class at West Point, and despite earning seven demerits for keeping an illegal gerbil in a shoeshine box, he went on to be a Rhodes scholar and White House fellow. That was just the beginning for the kinetic figure with darting, charcoal eyes. At forty-three, he became one of the youngest brigadier generals.

But even Clark started out like many young Army officers, eager to make his mark in the big war, Vietnam. Had the U.S. military killed or captured more Viet Cong early on, their supporters would have lost heart and given up, he believed. The insurgency would have been defeated. Instead, it felled him first, during broad daylight on February 19, 1970.

On that day, he was commanding an infantry company[†] on recon-

---

[*] During the Vietnam War Clark converted to Catholicism.
[†] Alpha Company, 1st Battalion, 16th Infantry (Mechanized).

naissance patrol near Long Thanh, thirty miles east of Saigon, looking for the enemy along a hard-packed trail with no footprints. The path had just petered out near a small stream with a footbridge. The young captain pulled out his map, looked at his compass, and took a couple of steps forward. As he was turning to the left to speak to his point man, he dropped his rifle. He had never dropped his rifle before, not at West Point, not at Ranger school. Puzzled, he looked down at his hand. Something white was poking out of it. A dark liquid stained his right pant leg below the knee.

"My God, I've been shot!" he yelled. "Get down!"

Clark jumped down. With a leg, hand, and arm that wouldn't respond he scrambled behind a hill. "Get that machine gun up here! Watch the flanks! F.O., get the artillery going! . . . Am engaging. Acknowledge."

He was hit by four rounds, but no major bone, artery, or organ was struck. Clark left the area on a helicopter, with stretchers hooked to straps on the ceiling. Months later, he received a Purple Heart, Silver Star, and command of a company[*] that maintained training tanks for officers in the Armor Officers Basic Course. The company was full of men wounded in Vietnam. Clark immersed himself in the details of tank parts and inventory, and in the lives of the men he saw struggling to recover.

Years later, he and the Pentagon's elite struggled with the nuts and bolts of a new, chaotic world. As director of the Joint Staff's J-5 office of strategic plans and policy, the Pentagon's foreign-policy brain trust, Clark had scurried to figure out the difference between Tutsis and Hutus when Rwanda imploded. He had witnessed NATO's 1994 air patrols over Bosnia grow into strikes against Bosnian Serb forces, then endured the terrible impotence of the UN troops on the ground as the Muslim "safe havens" they were supposed to protect—Srebrenica, Zepa, Gorzade, and Bihac—were encircled and fell in 1995 to Serb forces. Crimes against humanity had followed.

Gen. John Shalikashvili, then chairman of the Joint Chiefs of Staff, had sent him to the Dayton Peace Accords as military adviser to the negotiating team headed by the president's special envoy, Ambassador Richard Holbrooke. But he really went as Shali's eyes and ears, to

[*] Charlie Company, 6th Battalion, 32nd Armor, 194th Armored Brigade.

make sure Holbrooke didn't make too many promises on behalf of the Pentagon. Some 250,000 people had been killed in Bosnia before the United States and NATO intervened to stop the bloodshed—three times as many in one-third the time as had died in El Salvador's civil war.[*]

After scores of trips to Bosnia and European capitals, Clark grew to respect the tall, bellowing diplomat's determination to end the war in Bosnia. They even amused one another. Once, on a dare from Holbrooke, Clark had jumped into the Adriatic Sea off the third-floor balcony of the Kastile Hotel near Split, Croatia. "Not bad for fifty!" he joked to Joe Kruzel, who jumped with him that night. Days later Kruzel, deputy assistant secretary of defense for Europe, was killed on a mountain pass in Bosnia when his vehicle skidded off the muddy, dangerous Mount Igman route.[†]

For his work at Dayton, Clark earned a fourth star and his first CinC posting, to the U.S. Southern Command. He stayed there only twelve months before being tapped to take over the SACEUR job, the CinC among CinCs, from retiring Army Gen. George Joulwan.

The European CinC is a unique post. Clark, like all men in the post before him, ran both the U.S. European Command and NATO's military structure. He was, in name and fact, the Supreme Allied Commander, Europe. Subordinates called him simply SACEUR, dropping the "the," and making it sound like "master." These two jobs have always been held by one person, who inevitably finds himself tugged between his allegiance to the United States and his multinational NATO responsibilities. Washington expects him to carry the U.S. portfolio, but NATO requires the SACEUR to represent all its member states, although within that alliance the United States ranks first among equals. The SACEUR is the glue that holds squabbling neighbors together and the shock absorber who can neutralize criticism of one European nation by another.

---

[*] Although 250,000 dead is the commonly cited figure, it is much disputed. Unofficial UN figures circulating among Bosnia experts put the death toll closer to 120,000.

[†] Also killed with Kruzel were Ambassador Robert Frasure, the president's special envoy to Bosnia and Holbrooke's deputy, and Col. Nelson Drew, director of European affairs on the National Security Council Staff.

Gen. Wesley Clark, NATO's Supreme Allied Commander and CinC
of the U.S. European Command, holds a press conference during
the Kosovo war. DEPARTMENT OF DEFENSE

This juggling act demanded that Clark keep nineteen rolling marbles on the table at once, which was his natural pace anyway. He had help too: eleven special assistants, four schedulers, four protocol officers, a dozen security agents, five drivers, and helicopters all over Europe. His penchant for control reminded some on his staff of the indomitable Gen. Alexander Haig, for whom Clark had served as a special assistant when Haig was SACEUR. Clark considered Haig, who would go on to become President Reagan's secretary of state, a mentor.

The SACEUR oversaw the U.S. nuclear arsenal in Europe and, until 1989, monitored the movements of the 600,000 Soviet troops who remained in Eastern Europe after World War II. As head of the U.S. European Command, he controlled the 109,000 American troops based in Europe and could lay claim to another million back in the United States. (In day-to-day reality, the European Command job fell to the deputy CinC.) He would lead NATO's combined force of 7 million if it became necessary. There was no military job like it anywhere.

Each SACEUR since the first, Gen. Dwight Eisenhower in 1950, has exercised the kind of overt political power that Western democracies do not normally hand their generals. After the Cold War ended in the late 1980s, it was not NATO's civilian secretary, Manfred Woerner, but its military commander, Gen. John Galvin, who pushed hardest to reshape the alliance. NATO had for so long focused on the Soviet military threat that it had become frozen in place. Galvin transformed the alliance from a purely defensive entity, waiting to detect and respond to a Soviet attack, into an offensive tool that would reach out to the newly freed nations of Eastern European and beyond. He recrafted the alliance's strategic concept, recalibrating its focus on a forward defense and a nuclear response in Central Europe. Galvin forced NATO to look to its flanks: the Mediterranean, the Balkans, and, eventually, toward the newly independent states in Central Asia.[1]

Shalikashvili, the SACEUR from 1992 to 1993, and Joulwan, who succeeded him, continued Galvin's focus on Eastern Europe and NATO's periphery. They encouraged new relationships with formerly nonaligned or Soviet-leaning African states. They pitched its Partnership for Peace (PFP) program as a kind of "Q-course"(qualifying course) for the growing list of NATO wanna-bes. That list included twenty-seven nations by 2002. The PFP formed the basis for NATO's peacekeeping corps in Bosnia, Kosovo, and even East Timor. In March 1999, NATO expanded from sixteen to nineteen members.

The SACEUR was also the first to feel the absence of civilian organizations prepared to handle postwar reconstruction in new eras, both after World War II and after the Cold War. When NATO finally sent troops into Bosnia in December 1995, Joulwan repeatedly prodded the disjointed civilian agencies, such as the UN, that were charged with running things, to get organized. He worried about being handed their jobs—school integration, road reconstruction, economic revitalization, policing—if they were not successful. But his authority over them was negligible and his persuasive efforts were reduced to lectures. He could prod and push in a hundred meetings, as he did, but unless the civilian agencies received the same push from their political capitals, nothing ever changed. In frustration, he once drew the UN administrator in Bosnia a wall-sized timeline covered with hundreds of tiny boxes representing dozens of civilian agencies that were supposed to implement the UN reconstruction plan for Bosnia. Of course, he was unsuccessful. The civilian mountain was too big to move, and it fell woefully behind on the job.

The Dayton Peace Accords had ended the three-year war in Bosnia, but as a long-term political framework, it had major flaws. The accords set up two national entities, based on ethnicity and geography, that would be joined together by a weak central government. Each of these entities—the Bosnia-Croatia federation and the Republika Srpska—maintained fiefdoms for black-market racketeers and survived on ethnic hard-liners who financed their respective intelligence agencies, armies, and political parties.

In an annex to the accords was a set of duties for the military that Holbrooke believed was originally too narrow and would greatly hamper the mission if not changed. Seeking to broaden the military mission, Holbrooke had held a contentious set of talks between the State Department and the Defense Department.[2] The two departments disagreed substantially over the tasks that NATO's Implementation Force (IFOR) should perform on the ground to secure peace and stability in post-Dayton Bosnia.* These internal negotiations received little attention, but they help explain why the military remains in Bosnia today. In the beginning, the Pentagon wanted to take on only the easiest, clearest jobs, to avoid the plague of "mission creep," the tendency to extend the military's job beyond its original parameters. The Army, in particular, worked to avoid an expanded mandate, even at the cost of the mission's long-term success. Holbrooke, representing the State Department, had no one else but the military to turn to. Eventually, the Army did agree to patrol demilitarized zones separating the ethnic factions. Initially, the military balked at even simple jobs like keeping roads open or voting areas cleared, although it later took them on with much success. The

---

* IFOR, which stands for Implementation Force, was the peacekeeping force in Bosnia. IFOR included troops from NATO member countries, plus some countries that were not then members, including Russia, Poland, and Hungary. In 1997, IFOR became SFOR, or Stablization Force. The parallel peacekeepers in Kosovo are called KFOR, for Kosovo Force. KFOR includes troops from nineteen NATO and eighteen non-NATO countries, including the United Arab Emirates, Ukraine, Morocco, Jordan, and other countries that wanted to show goodwill or prove they were worthy of NATO membership.

zones of separation turned out to be no big deal. Shalikashvili nixed any effort to round up the war criminals who made a public farce out of IFOR's presence as they roamed about freely.

Shali, who had become chairman by the time the Dayton Accords were signed in December 1995, had been adamant about prohibiting troops from trying to snatch war criminals. He joked that he would extract a promise from every new SACEUR to adhere to that policy. The military, he argued, was no good at such narrow, pinpoint abductions. To administration officials who prodded him, he would say, "You're nuts! You just told me Mogadishu was the stupidest thing we'd ever done."

Nor did the Pentagon want to deploy into the Serb part of Bosnia, the Republika Srpska. As Holbrooke tells it in his memoir, *To End a War*, Army leaders argued against disarming the sides within the demilitarized "zone of separation," wary of the troubles Army troops might run into trying to enforce it.[3] They didn't want to be saddled with rescuing civilian aid workers either—even U.S. citizens, who might get into trouble in Bosnia. In the end, the American leadership refused to take on any policing duties whatsoever, and even opposed giving the International Police Task Force a mandate to arrest troublemakers, fearing it might incite local groups to take revenge against IFOR.

The military's apprehension about Bosnia amounted to a kind of agoraphobia: only if the troops were kept isolated behind barbed wire would the military agree to a peacekeeping mission. At first they even insisted that IFOR's headquarters be in Hungary or Italy, not in Sarajevo, the capital of Bosnia.

Holbrooke believed such restrictions would impede implementation of the Dayton Accords, since U.S. troops were the only real enforcer available on the ground. As a compromise, Clark worked out language that was acceptable to Shali and his generals. It stated that IFOR had the "authority" to do more, but not the "responsibility." This left the decision in military hands. He and Holbrooke also added a "silver bullet" clause that would give future military commanders the flexibility to take bolder actions. The clause also gave those commanders the freedom to use force when they deemed it necessary, without prior civilian approval.

By the time Clark became SACEUR in July 1997, NATO peacekeepers had been on the ground eighteen months. An alphabet soup of government agencies—the EU, the Organization for Security and Cooperation in Europe (OSCE), USAID, the UN—and humanitarian agencies were there too, but in woefully small numbers. Still poorly organized, they weren't getting much done.

But the mission, as Army commanders defined it, was a success: few people were illegally crossing the demilitarized zones of separation. Violence had leveled off. But civilian authorities throughout NATO and back in Washington believed the effort to rebuild Bosnia was failing. Chief among them was NATO's secretary-general, the Spanish diplomat Javier Solana, and he told Clark as much at their first meeting: "Wes, you must make the NATO mission in Bosnia successful. It is the only operation NATO has and it must succeed. . . . NATO cannot succeed with its mission if the international mission as a whole is not successful. This is not a matter of simply protecting your forces. You must actively help the civilians succeed. . . . You are going to have to do more to help the overall Dayton implementation succeed."[4]

"It was a heavy charge," Clark wrote in his memoirs. "It struck at the heart of what some of the military leaders had been attempting to do, namely, to restrict their involvement in assisting the civilian aspects of implementing the Dayton agreement. Solana was asking me to push the NATO military into a more active role. . . . It raised all the flags of mission creep and of involving the military in police work, which we had labored at Dayton to avoid."[5]

But if you can lose a war through timidity and miscalculated maneuvers, can't you lose a peace in the same way? Why weren't the competitive, hard-driving officers living in mud-caked camps around Bosnia grumbling about not winning the peace? That was their mission too. Wasn't the Army judging them on how well they carried it out?

Eventually Clark came to agree with Solana. He gave his soldiers in Bosnia a mandate for improving conditions there that was as comprehensive as any since World War II, when U.S. soldiers had helped stabilize and rebuild Western Europe and Japan. Clark and his immediate subordinates acknowledged that, in Bosnia, much of what they were trying to do was off the books—not illegal, but just the broadest interpretation of the military annex signed at Dayton.

Most of their actions were aimed at Bosnian Serb hard-liners, the fiercest opponents of the peace accords. These hard-liners were tools of Milosevic, who wanted to control the Serb half of Bosnia. Clark tried shutting down offices of the Serb MUP, the special police who were used to intimidate political moderates. He wanted the troops to support the controversial Bosnian Serb president of Republika Srpska, Biljana Plavsic. He also wanted British troops to close down a police station in Banja Luka, which was in their sector, where a coup plot against her was being hatched.

Solana approved of the new activism; it was just what he was looking for. But Defense Secretary Cohen, reflecting the Pentagon's concern about creating more problems for itself in Bosnia, seemed perturbed. "Sir, I am within your intent, aren't I?" Clark asked Cohen at a meeting called to discuss his use of forces to pressure Dayton's naysayers in Bosnia. "Just barely," Cohen replied, without elaboration.[6] Without an explicit order to stop, Clark plugged away.

At the U.S. government's urging, Clark agreed to use IFOR troops to shut down the nationalist, propaganda-spewing Serb radio stations. They seized four radio towers and blocked the electronic transmission of television broadcasts from Serbia proper. Not everyone favored such aggressive action; Clark had to issue written orders to compel his reluctant field commander, Gen. Eric Shinseki, to carry out the operation.*

Still, progress was slight. Clark knew the Muslim, Serb, and Croat fiefdoms were fueled by corruption and blackmarketeering. He wanted to call in an anti-corruption hit squad that could dismantle their Mafia-like organizations. The Joint Chiefs of Staff initially opposed this notion, and the FBI declined to help. The State Department declared that police investigation was its province, but then didn't follow through. Clark persisted. He persuaded the State Department to pay for a gumshoe—a U.S. customs agent and former Cobra gunship pilot who had worked for Joulwan and Clark in Latin America. His army of one was a start. But his

---

* Shinseki became Army chief of staff in June 1999. Many observers believe he brought to that job, too, the same level of extreme caution that he had exercised in Bosnia.

investigations were considered controversial back at the Pentagon, which saw little benefit in leaning so far forward.

By 1998, with his aggressive IFOR commander, Gen. Montgomery Meigs, Clark had rewritten the military's operational plan for Bosnia and sold it to the Pentagon and the State Department, who got the White House to approve it, as well. The new plan recognized soldiers as instruments of political reform, said Meigs and Clark, not just guardians of public safety. Commanders were encouraged to banish troublemakers and to funnel international aid to reform-minded local leaders.

Cohen, in particular, was wary of Clark's efforts. In 1999, on the eve of a raid in Mostar that was six months in the making and aimed at disrupting illegal funding for radical Croat politicians, Cohen overrode a plan to dispatch a clandestine Navy SEAL team to help. Clark could not guarantee that no American would get hurt, so Cohen yanked U.S. troops out of the operation. French troops went ahead with the raid anyway. They walked in the door without a problem and walked away with eight cubic feet of computerized files that helped demonstrate the Croatian government's complicity. The U.S. pullback highlighted the tension between the activist CinC and his more cautious colleagues in Washington.

But the U.S. military created other problems related to the Mostar treasure. IFOR headquarters was run by an American four-star general. The computer files were turned over to him. Unaccustomed to sharing intelligence with other countries, the general and his subordinates treated the files as a private collection. For two years, IFOR headquarters refused to share them with international police investigators trying to indict Croatian individuals on corruption charges and war crimes. U.S. intelligence officers, interested chiefly in force protection, spent those years analyzing the documents for threats to IFOR personnel. Over the next two years, the anti-corruption team grew to include Pentagon officers, Justice Department crime analysts, and two battalions of Italian carabinieri police with experience in mafia-busting.

Periodically, Clark went to Bosnia himself to shake things up. In the spring of 2000, clandestine Delta Force commandos, their index fingers a half-inch off the triggers of assault rifles, bumped through rough weather in three Black Hawk helicopters to bring Clark and his entourage across the mountainous path from Sarajevo to Banja Luka, in northeastern Bosnia. Bulbous extra fuel tanks were bolted to the chopper rails to allow them to fly extra distance in the event an assassination attempt forced them off course. A three-layered security perimeter surrounded Clark as he darted under the whirl of rotary blades and into the SFOR peacekeeping base in northeastern Bosnia and headquarters of the British-led sector.

Having come for a sensitive exchange with field commanders, the peripatetic commander plopped into his chair. He had something on his mind that had nothing to do with military doctrine, tactics, or strategy. Use your martial law–like authority, he told the officers, American and European. "You can impose any law." Have your soldiers detain and chase out nationalist hard-liners. Don't be afraid of disorder and isolated incidents of violence against NATO troops. Funnel foreign aid to economic projects tied to the moderate political opposition, he continued. Create a pretext to search the offices of suspected mafia-like criminal networks and put the suspected ringleaders in jail for seventy-two hours, the agreed-upon limit for detentions without cause. And don't ask Washington, Paris, London, Berlin, Rome, or Ottawa for leadership or direction, nor wait for them to provide it. "What you have to do is try to see the larger problem and see where you can modify your instructions" from civilians back home. "You have to push the envelope. If you put this strategy down [on paper] and circulate it, it's dead."

The assembled commanders seemed charged up by the tough talk, but even so, they listed the reasons why their home offices might object. It was the same story Clark had been hearing for years. He felt as if he were "pushing on a pillow." "Orders didn't get carried out. They got thrown back to capitals" by reluctant commanders, he complained. Too many of them just wanted to end their peacekeeping rotations without incident—i.e., without casualties. No one judged them on whether they actually accomplished the job they were asked to perform. Did anyone ever ask how many political extortionists had been run out of town? What moderate political alternative groups had SFOR helped with security and humanitarian relief? How many special police organizations had been closed down? What evidence had been gathered about illegal intelligence networks? What truly uncensored radio programs did IFOR's civil-affairs soldiers get up and running? Clark knew the answer to all these questions: not nearly enough.

Leaving Banja Luka, Clark headed straight for Srebrenica, site of the worst mass murder in Europe since World War II and a symbol of the powerlessness of the UN and international organizations. On July 11, 1995, during the war in Bosnia, Serb forces had overrun this isolated Muslim enclave and overwhelmed Dutch peacekeepers. Then, over several days, Serb forces had murdered 7,000 men and boys as the Dutch battalion retreated to a UN compound.

Clark went to Srebrenica for his final trip before retiring as SACEUR in April 2000. The town was occupied by another group of Serbs, who had been kicked out of their homes in Sarajevo during the war. More than five years had passed since the Dayton Accords had been signed, but only one Muslim had returned. The man, an eighty-six-year-old, "could care less if he lived or died," as long as he did it at home, Tom Miller, the U.S. ambassador to Bosnia, told Clark when he arrived on a bright, sunny day to greet the press and a couple dozen townspeople.

Clark had come to hold a press conference with Miller announcing a new initiative to build homes for ten Serbs and fifteen Muslims who would relocate to Srebrenica. "It's a very hopeful day," Clark told a crowd of townsfolk and reporters gathered in the bright sunshine near the new homes. "When I see the blossoms in this apple tree, it reminds me how this is a time of rebirth and hope." But it was all for show, a fact that became clear when Clark and Miller were alone with the mayor in his new house. "Will you really live here?" Clark asked the Muslim mayor. Not really, he explained. His safety was in jeopardy. His real home was near the Yugoslav border and the Serbs would exact revenge if he challenged the status quo in Srebrenica. "We are still frightened about what happened in 1995."

"Move three families here, two over there," urged Clark. "Take some risk, we'll support you. We're proud of you. . . . Here's my coin." He handed the Muslim mayor a half-dollar-sized Army memento inscribed with Clark's signature and command logo. "Be a leader."

"Mr. Mayor, this is the time to move," pleaded the ambassador. "Don't let people forget about Srebrenica."

Symbolic gestures would be no substitute, however, for the U.S.

Army's reluctance to reorder the Bosnian jigsaw puzzle. This became clear again when Clark and Miller hopped back into the van to drive to the general's helicopter. The Army, Miller informed Clark, had refused to set up a substation in Srebrenica to give Muslims a real sense of security. Too big a drain on manpower, they said. It would take as many soldiers to guard it as to staff it. No wonder the Muslim mayor wouldn't move back. If peacekeepers with guns and tanks weren't committed, how could they expect him to be? This was one of a thousand small examples that cemented the status quo and prevented real change in Bosnia.

Getting Muslims to move back to Srebrenica required a game of musical chairs. Serb families from Sarajevo had moved into Muslim homes in Srebrenica because other Muslims had taken over Serb homes in Sarajevo. To get Serbs back into their homes in Sarajevo would require Muslim leader Alija Izetbegovic's help. His forces controlled Sarajevo, and they could get the Muslims to vacate Serb homes if he so ordered. But none of this seemed likely to happen.

Clark's helicopter was taking him to Sarajevo, the Bosnian capital, where he would make a final plea to Izetbegovic the next day. In fact, he was scheduled to meet with all three members of Bosnia's tri-presidency—one Bosnian Muslim, one Bosnian Serb, and one Croat. But at 10:30 P.M. the night before, the Serb president had cancelled. He would be sending a second-tier deputy in his place.

The snub further darkened Clark's mood. The weight of six years of slogging through Bosnia dominated his hotel suite, where the staff gathered to work through the affront. Clark slouched well down into his chair; only his tilted head kept him from being entirely prone. He looked like he should be asleep, but out of his mouth came a string of combative directives. "I think we should say to the deputy, 'You're not welcome!' This is personal! I'm not talking to any f—— deputy. Let's make an unannounced visit to the Serb president's office. I want to rip him in the press. Why shouldn't I go to him straight out?"

The staff perked up at what they considered a strange, off-the-cuff idea—probably just the boss thinking out loud. Nonetheless, half a dozen arguments against it flew at him. "I'm just casting about for a way to create a wedge between [the Bosnian Serb president] and Milosevic," Clark responded. Shun the deputy by leaving the Serb chair empty at a news conference, an aide suggested. Heads nodded in approval. The meeting broke up without a decision.

The next day, there was no empty chair. The three men sat stone-faced across a small library table from the SACEUR and his interpreter. On one wall hung a dreadful, dark painting, all black sky and muddy moon in thick oil paints. It captured the ambiance perfectly.

Unemployment in Bosnia stood at 60 percent. War criminals remained at large. Milosevic still held power in Belgrade. Serbs desperately wanted to return to Muslim-controlled Sarajevo and Clark needed to get Izetbegovic to break the deadlock. But he had little leverage. Surely Izetbegovic understood that. Go to Srebrenica, Clark urged, and welcome the Serbs back to their homes in Sarajevo. "I'm not sure," the frail Muslim president responded. "General Clark, this is Bosnia. It's a very complicated country." Five years of peace had brought only slight political advances and negligible economic ones. The entrenched power structure in Bosnia would survive long after Clark had moved on. In fact, Bosnia never benefited from a coordinated organization that brought the civilian, nongovernmental, and military resources of the United States and Europe together. All those elements were necessary to force a change in the order of things, but each branch merely picked at a part of the problem. The participants often admitted as much themselves.

This doleful pattern would repeat itself in all other peacekeeping missions in the 1990s and into the twenty-first century, when the U.S. occupation of Afghanistan and Iraq loomed large. By the end of Clark's tenure as SACEUR, the U.S. government writ large was barely paying attention to the Balkans. Hard-line factions in Bosnia understood this perfectly.

Clark glanced at his watch. It was time to leave. "Give my best to [the Bosnian Serb president]," he told the Serb deputy. A chance to hold the Serbs accountable would be lost, this time by Clark himself. Or was it, as Clark insisted, just not the right moment to stir things up?

He snapped his head back toward his aide-de-camp, seated against the wall. Maj. Stephen Twitty jumped up and handed him three gift-wrapped navigational clocks, which Clark passed out. There were smiles and hand-shakes as the general inched toward the door. But halfway to it, he stopped and grabbed Izetbegovic by the elbow. "You've got to do something now!"

he whispered urgently. "You've got to do something now!" In the corner, Twitty shook his head and sputtered, "A fifty-dollar navigational clock for war criminals!" Or at least they should have been considered criminals for having stalled their country's progress and healing.

At dinner that evening, Clark made one more forceful pitch to senior UN and American officials in Sarajevo, who were complaining that Europe and Washington had forgotten about Bosnia. They were depressed; someone mentioned the *Titanic*.

"You have to be able to accept some disorder and incidents," Clark urged guests around the table—generals, ambassadors, UN officials. "Use incidents as excuses to do more information-gathering and intimidation. There's no Fourth Amendment here. We aren't under the U.S. Constitution. Put them in jail for seventy-two hours. Break some china, get the Serbs to react to you. Call a spade a spade. . . . If you want to keep SFOR here, you have to use SFOR. . . . It's like the Chinese Cultural Revolution. You have to keep the conflict going. You have to engage the imagination."

Some in his audience nodded in agreement, but most sat long-faced over plates of steak and glasses of red wine.

"The legacy of this is yet to be written," Clark told them, trying to conclude on an optimistic tone. "We improvised the whole war in Kosovo. You're improvising the whole Bosnia strategy. You have the authority to make this happen."

But did they really? As long as a serious disconnect existed between the U.S. and European capitals and their emissaries in places like Bosnia, Kosovo, and postwar Afghanistan not enough would get done. Billions of dollars and thousands of hours of soldiers' time would go to waste. Clark knew better than anyone how painful transcontinental disconnects could become.

★ ★ ★ ★

CLARK HAD BEEN dealing with Milosevic for five years before he got his first clear shot at him. By late 1998, Clark was squarely on the side of Madeleine Albright's State Department, pushing the president's national security team to stop Milosevic once and for all. The Kosovo war launched in the spring of 1999, Clark would say later, violated

THE BALKANS

©2002, THE *WASHINGTON POST*.
REPRINTED WITH PERMISSION.

almost every principle of war he had learned as a cadet, including the need for a clear objective. For starters, President Clinton, in his address to the nation announcing the war, had showed Milosevic his limits: "I do not intend to put our troops in Kosovo to fight a war," Clinton had pledged from the Oval Office.

Another problem was the issue of casualties: The U.S. Congress was unwilling to accept many. Unfortunately, Milosevic, like the rest of the world, knew this. As for NATO's commitment, most of its nineteen members were willing to endorse only an incremental military action, one that began small, the antithesis of Colin Powell's insistence on overwhelming force. For this and other reasons, the Joint Chiefs of Staff, opposed going to war against Milosevic.

Several weeks before the war began, the Joint Chiefs had held a secret "tank" session to discuss Kosovo. They questioned whether U.S. national interests there were strong enough to warrant a military confrontation. They doubted the ability of air strikes alone to force Milosevic back to the negotiating table.[7]

Clark had not been informed the meeting was taking place, a breach of protocol and an indication of the rough waters ahead.

It would not be the last time the chiefs voiced their dissent. Their doubts also found their way into a highly unusual barrage of public critiques by recently retired generals shortly after the war began. Some of the criticism was even coordinated by the Air Force public affairs staff, who briefed retirees on details of the air war before they appeared on television talk shows. The retired generals complained that NATO couldn't fight this war in the most effective way: knock-out blows to Belgrade and Milosevic from the get-go, or nothing at all. Incrementalism was bound to fail. Clark, they insinuated, faced a choice: were he a real Army "warrior," he would fall on his sword and resign because the president had taken ground forces off the table. The restraints on tactics and targeting that Clinton, British Prime Minister Tony Blair, and French President Jacques Chirac put on the air campaign were mostly unacceptable to the generals, too. From the start, however, Clark chose the other route: he furiously pushed his own government, and those of the eighteen other NATO nations, to expand the war beyond the meager parameters that he, Solana, and the White House had sold them on originally.

Clark would later say he'd seen a 40 percent chance that the war would end within three days. But he remained certain it would never have begun had the alliance members been asked to approve strategic strikes on Belgrade from the start or to contemplate the worst-case scenario—the introduction of ground troops. He convinced himself, and eventually even some skeptics, that "if you line up international law, good diplomacy, and modern military power, you can achieve strategically decisive results without decisive force."

Kosovo would be the first true alliance war since World War II.

By the opening night of the Kosovo air war, Clark's staff had produced forty separate plans of an air war, recounted Gen. John Jumper, then commander of the U.S. Air Force in Europe.[*] Some deeply criticized using air power alone, without troops on the ground to help flush out the enemy. NATO ultimately settled on a three-phase campaign that would become more intense the longer it lasted.

As early as the second day, Clark began prodding NATO diplomats

* Jumper became Air Force chief of staff in September 2001.

and Washington officials to reassess their initial prognosis, and he began talking privately about the need to plan for the worst case, a ground war. He asked the Pentagon for two dozen low-flying Apache attack helicopters that he believed would be more effective than high-altitude jets and long-range bombers at hitting the dispersed Serb forces who were doing the damage in Kosovo.

A Tomahawk cruise missile launches from the bow of the USS Philippine Sea *headed for a target in Kosovo on March 24, 1999, the first night of the NATO air war against Serb forces. The U.S. Navy cruiser was operating in the Adriatic Sea.*   PETTY OFFICER 3RD CLASS RENSO AMARIZ

Over the coming weeks, he enlarged the air war into a much larger, more lethal operation. He tripled the number of aircraft, quadrupled the number of approved targets, and sent aircraft to strike downtown Belgrade. He pushed the Air Force to go after individual tanks and small groups of soldiers with their million-dollar bombs.

A target-approval process developed that required political leaders in Washington, Paris, and London to okay any targets that posed the possibility of twenty civilian casualties or more. Clark pressed U.S. and European leaders to give him authority to approve these targets and more. Eventually much of Serbia's civilian infrastructure—the bridges, broadcasting stations, electrical supply facilities, political party offices—was damaged or destroyed by NATO aircraft.* But by then, the NATO alliance was in with both feet. Political risks abounded, but over the weeks, individual member governments grew proud of the way they had stuck together.

Some mistakes were made. After a B-2 bomber struck the Chinese embassy in Belgrade, Clark and Solana geared up for a round of complaints and admonition when they met with the NATO ambassadors on May 26. Clark showed them aerial photos of a building in Belgrade that he next intended to strike, and pointed out how close it was to the embassies of Belgium and the Czech Republic.

"So I guess I should tell my people not to sleep in the embassy tonight?" Belgium's ambassador asked.

"That's exactly right," Clark responded. "And board up the windows."

"Can we use tape? Or should we use plywood?" asked the Czech ambassador.

"Plywood," Clark said.

His strategy, he would later explain, "was to press the envelope. . . . I would talk to people on the telephone each day and meet with them to expand the envelope of thinking. All of this was in the context of intensifying the air campaign." But, he added, "no single target was more

---

* The report of the UN Independent International Commission on Kosovo is extremely thoughtful on the subject of attacking civilian or so-called dual-use targets. Under "targets" in its section on international law and humanitarian intervention, it concludes, "Such targeting is questionable under the Geneva Conventions and Protocol I [of the conventions], but it must be acknowledged that state practice in wartime since World War II has consistently selected targets on the basis of an open-ended approach to 'military necessity,' rather than by observing the customary and conventional norm that disallows the deliberate attacks on non-military targets. . . . The NATO campaign was more careful, in relation to its targeting, than was any previous occasion of major warfare conducted from the air. . . . There is no evidence of deliberate civilian targeting of civilians. There is, nevertheless, reason to question the selection of targets relating to the civilian infrastructure of the [Federal Republic of Yugoslavia, the federal union of Serbia and Montenegro] in which the probability of civilians being present and killed was quite high."

important . . . than the principle of alliance consensus and cohesion," especially since no one could be sure when, or if, Milosevic would concede. Clark's real challenge would be to sustain NATO's political stamina as the war grew more intense. The choice, as he saw it, was not between a larger versus a smaller war, but between an incremental war versus none at all.

"I don't want to get into something like the Rolling Thunder campaign, pecking away indefinitely," he told U.S. commanders in a secret videoconference during the war.* "We've got to steadily ratchet up the pressure. . . . We also need to become increasingly relevant to the situation on the ground. Otherwise we are at risk of being paused indefinitely. We'll lose public support." He had to keep the military momentum going, even if the political and diplomatic process moved in fits and starts. One midnight in early April, after a spell of bad weather had grounded NATO's bombers, Clark, standing in the study of the chateau, whipped open his blue pocket notebook containing the target numbers. "I want to hit this, this, and this," he told his special assistant, Navy Capt. Marc Ferguson. Hours later five Navy ships in the Adriatic launched thirty-nine weatherproof cruise missiles.

At times Clark ordered planes onto the tarmac in anticipation of getting political leaders in Brussels, Washington, London, or Paris to approve targets for them to hit by take-off time. Such improvisation challenged, indeed exasperated, some of his subordinate military commanders.

---

* Operation Rolling Thunder, the campaign to bomb North Vietnam, which lasted from March 2, 1965, to October 31, 1968, has become military shorthand for undue civilian meddling in war. As Scott Cooper argues eloquently in "The Politics of Airstrikes" (Hoover Institution *Policy Review,* June–July 2001), this is a wrongheaded analysis of why the Vietnam air campaign—and the war itself—was lost. Until March 1972, North Vietnam "waged a guerrilla war against the South, a war that was not vulnerable to air attack and that required few external supplies, thus negating efforts at air interdiction." In other words, it was the strategy itself, not the civilian hand in it, that failed. "The simplistic slogan 'let the warfighters fight' is useless nostalgia for an era that never existed," writes Cooper, a Marine Corps pilot who flew missions in Kosovo. The Kosovo air campaign "featured lots of scrutiny, lots of argument about which targets should be hit in what order, and the political ramifications of each strike," he noted. "That is the way it should be."

At dusk on April 2, Vice Adm. Daniel Murphy Jr., commander of all NATO's naval forces during the war, was directed to bring sixteen Tomahawk cruise missiles to "mode 7," their highest state of readiness, but not to launch them. NATO's diplomats were still deciding whether to allow strikes on the first Belgrade targets Clark proposed—the Serbian Federal Ministry and Serbian Interior Ministry buildings, which sat opposite each other at the southern end of Kneza Milosa Street, several hundred yards from a medical complex holding 4,000 of Belgrade's 5,000 hospital beds. When the satellite phone rang in Murphy's cabin on the USS *LaSalle*, afloat off the coast of Israel, he turned the black-plastic encoded key and a fifteen-second warble signaled the line was secure. "You're authorized," a voice on the other end told the commander.

Previous Tomahawk operations, beginning with the 1991 Gulf War, had been painstakingly deliberate and time-consuming. Strike crews had been given days to prepare cruise-missile launches, to program the turbofan engines, the digital maps, and the navigational sensors—and to triple-check their work. Now, the ministers had deliberated so long that Murphy's staff had only thirty minutes to retrace those steps. They had to make sure the right flight path and the right aim point had been electronically transferred to the right missile.

"Okay, let's everyone take a deep breath," Murphy told the eight men on watch from his battle staff. "We're going to double-check everything." The Tomahawk strike officer then typed a "code Indigo" tasking message—the command to launch—to two ships and a submarine in the Adriatic. Within minutes, sirens blared and brilliant strobe lights lit up the decks on faraway ships. Hydraulic hatch doors on the missiles' coffins rolled open. The first of the twenty-foot-long tubes lifted upward, away from a wall of gas and fire, at 11:41 P.M. Within seconds of each other, seven missiles headed east-northeast, toward nos. 92 and 101 Kneza Milosa Street at an average speed of 400 nautical miles per hour.

The Serbian Federal Ministry is a block-long, white-stone, seven-story, pre–World War II building. Across from it sat the even larger Serbian Interior Ministry headquarters, built of steel and dark-brown glass, home of the special Serbian police responsible for most of the ethnic cleansing in Kosovo. In the target book, target no. 58, the v-shaped Interior Ministry, had three aim points. One was the easternmost structural beam; the second, the baseboard on the eastern wing—both chosen to collapse the building onto itself. The third aim point was the office of the commander of the special police. The first two were chosen to avoid damaging the hospital and medical complex one block to the rear when the building collapsed. The third was intended to make a point, a symbolic point since the building had been emptied of furniture, computers and personnel. Days before the bombing began, someone had leaked word that the structure was on NATO's to-do list.

Murphy and his crew had to wait an hour and four minutes until impact. Murphy knew that a successful strike could embolden NATO, but that a mishap would send it off course completely and nix the growing momentum.

At 12:45 P.M., three 1,000-pound Tomahawk cruise missiles from the Adriatic ended their exacting 380-nautical-mile journey and pierced their targets, triggering a roaring explosion and avalanche of flying glass, concrete, and stone. Murphy knew U.S. targeteers had calculated how far shattered glass would fly. The choice of warhead and angle of impact determined whether concrete would be blown one block away, or three, or whether the shards of glass would simply graze or would imbed in a person's skin.

Aboard the *LaSalle*, Murphy and his officers were watching Serb television, via CNN. As thick flames leaped skyward and smoke billowed, the crew marveled at the scene. One block away, windows in the hospital's maternity ward, from where the camera crew was filming, weren't even cracked. "We are in uncharted waters here," Murphy thought.

★ ★ ★ ★

THE AIR FORCE, which planned the air campaign on a daily basis, resisted its improvisation. Clark's chief detractor had been the commander of the air operation, Lt. Gen. Michael Short, a bulldog of a man with a wide, strident gait. Before the war, Holbrooke, sent to convince Milosevic to pull his troops from Kosovo, had asked Clark to "find me an Air Force version of you" to make the American threat to go to war sound credible. Clark assigned Short, who delivered an ultimatum that was blunt and foul-mouthed, just what everyone wanted: "I have B-52s in one hand and U-2s (surveillance planes) in the other," Short told Milosevic. "It's up to you which I'm going to use." In their talks, Milosevic had suggested he might just turn off Belgrade's air defense missiles, but not remove them from Kosovo, as a last-ditch attempt to avoid NATO bombing. "Mr. President!" Short had exploded, "You're pounding sand up my ass!"

Short had flown 276 combat missions in Vietnam and led F-15E air strikes in the Persian Gulf. From the start, he had pushed Clark for permission to hit large, strategic targets like government offices, military headquarters, and power stations in Belgrade. Such strikes had worked to demoralize the enemy troops in Iraq; this strategy formed the foundation of air-power doctrine—heavy blows to targets with high military, economic, or psychological value as a way to collapse the enemy's will.

But Clark and Solana knew NATO members opposed hitting such high-impact, politically sensitive targets right away. And there was no stomach in Washington to go it alone. Clark wanted Short to focus on striking the tiny clusters of Yugoslav army units and tanks that were well hidden throughout the country. Clark believed the Yugoslav army was "the center of gravity," even for the air campaign. Milosevic, he judged, would fold without his military's support. Although Clark wanted to hit the higher-value targets in Belgrade, too, NATO approval for those targets did not come until later.

Short had never wanted to fight in a coalition, for they were too constraining. Short also believed, contrary to Clark, that Milosevic cared little about his military. He complained about the inefficiency of using expensive missiles and bombs to hit the kind of small targets Clark was intent on destroying. In protest, Short dragged his feet at striking some targets Clark had ordered, forcing Clark to either fire him or put up with his resistance.

As NATO commanders at thirteen bases across Europe watched with discomfort, the disagreement between Clark and Short surfaced in the classified videoconferences conducted every day during the war. Expressing his satisfaction weeks into the war that, at last, he might get to strike the Serbian special-police headquarters in downtown Belgrade, Short verbally jousted with Clark: "This is the jewel in the crown," he said.

"To me, the jewel in the crown is when those B-52s rumble across Kosovo," replied Clark.

"You and I have known for weeks that we have different jewelers," returned Short, hunched down in his chair, his arms folded in disgust, as they often were during those tense days.

"My jeweler outranks yours," Clark shot back with a laugh.

After seventy-eight days—and 6,300 tons of munitions; 26,600 bombs and missiles in all—Milosevic capitulated. NATO had survived, but the damage to Yugoslavia was extensive.

An estimated 10,000 Kosovar Albanians had been killed by Serb forces at the war's beginning.[8] Some 863,000 civilian had fled as the war went on. Another 590,000 fled their homes and villages to hide in the hills and valleys of Kosovo.[9] Most have since returned. At least 500 civilians were accidentally killed by errant NATO bombs and missiles. Another 580 Serb soldiers and police perished. Thousands in Yugoslavia were injured. Serbia's major rivers were severely polluted; nine major highways, seven airports, and fifty-nine bridges were destroyed. Telecommunications lines were damaged, and two-thirds of the main industrial plants nearly destroyed.[10] Seventy percent of the country's electrical production capacity and 80 percent of its oil-refining capability had been knocked out. Milosevic-controlled news media outlets lay in ruins, as did the Belgrade Socialist Party headquarters. But not a single U.S. or allied military service member had died in hostile action.

A UN commission headed by former South African president Nelson Mandela declared the war "illegal but legitimate." Illegal because it had not received prior approval from the UN Security Council; legitimate because, in the commission's words, "all diplomatic avenues had been exhausted and because the intervention had the effect of liberating the majority population of Kosovo from a long period of oppression under Serbian rule."[11] The war, Mandela's commission declared, "was neither a success nor a failure; it was in fact both."* On the one hand, it had forced Milosevic to withdraw his army and stop the repression

---

* The commission also explored the allegation that NATO's actions had provoked a fiercer ethnic cleansing than would have otherwise taken place—the chief charge by critics of the air war. To this, the commission answered: "The NATO air campaign did not provoke the attacks on the civilian Kosovar population, but the bombing created an environment that made such an operation feasible."

of ethnic Albanians. Because of the war, Albanians now had basic interim rights until a final political settlement could be worked out. But on the other hand, the intervention failed to prevent ethnic cleansing. Milosevic remained in power for sixteen more months.* The Serbian people lost their way of life. In a startling reversal of ethnic cleansing, hundreds of Serbs were killed by Albanians shortly after the war ended. Some 99 percent of Kosovar Serbs would flee Kosovo for their own safety over the coming year.

Shortly after the war ended, Defense Secretary Cohen ungraciously forced Clark to retire a couple of months early, with no option to extend his tour another year, a customary courtesy. Still, the general watched the retreat of Serb forces with great satisfaction and presided over the movement of nearly 42,000 NATO troops, 7,000 of them American, into Kosovo in June 1999.

The Pentagon, which refused to take the lead in the Kosovo peace-keeping operation, as it had done in Bosnia, put a one-star Army general in command of the U.S. troops. A new commander and a new set of troops would rotate every six months into the 900-square-mile American sector in southern Kosovo, a place no bigger than Los Angeles County. Inappropriately, the Army's peacekeeping plans were based largely on commanders' experiences in Bosnia, where conditions were entirely different.

To a remarkable degree, U.S. soldiers entering Kosovo would be left on their own to figure out the mission. Most would do the best they could. But it did not always work out well.

---

* Milosevic conceded power on October 5, 2000.

Chapter Twelve

WAGING PEACE IN KOSOVO

* * * *

"Go in bold and cocky," lt. col. george bilafer told his eight AH-64A Apache helicopter crews before they lifted off in the 4 A.M. darkness. "They need to know NATO's in town. If anyone so much as flinches, make sure you take them out." The men of the 6th Squadron of the 6th U.S. Cavalry switched their 30 mm Chain guns to "flex" mode so that the elephant-trunk barrel under each Apache's chin could swing from side to side, trolling for prey. That should scare any troublemakers on the ground, Bilafer, a former Delta Force pilot, thought. He had seen people freeze in fear and confusion when they heard the Apache's deafening rumble and saw its big gun pointing down at them.

With all weapon switches "hot," Bilafer flew through the morning grayness washing over the rugged Kacanik defile from Macedonia into Kosovo. A little white square, the "constraint box," danced around the lower half of his cockpit monitor, waiting for him to "lock on" to the slightest twitch of an artillery gun below. "Pgundir Norm" the monitor read: pilot in control of the gun, and in position to direct fire. Hand on the grip, finger on the red button, just press down and out would fly a Hellfire missile whose kinetic energy can melt a tank from the inside out. "Go ahead, somebody squeeze the trigger off on me," Bilafer said to himself, "we're close enough to engage."

In fact, Bilafer knew his pilots weren't allowed to do a thing unless the fleeing Serb thugs shot at them. He sat helplessly inside his Apache, watching with night-vision scopes and heat-seeking detection

KOSOVO

©2002, THE *WASHINGTON POST.*
REPRINTED WITH PERMISSION.

equipment as Serbs torched farmhouses and apartments, sheds and stores by the dozen. He could see the smoke billowing from windows and flames leaping upward. But his "rules of engagement" said he couldn't do a thing to stop it.

"How dare they do this to somebody?" thought the forty-year-old Bilafer, who had flown attack helicopters for nineteen years and was now an Apache squadron commander.

As daylight broke, his combat air patrol hovered just feet above the treetops, providing cover and reconnaissance for British troops being airlifted onto the bridges and tunnels they would de-mine and secure along the one road from Macedonia into Kosovo. Albanians looked up at him, smiling and waving as they swarmed out of the woods. Where did these thousands of people come from? The welcome reminded some crews of the pictures they'd seen of French cities liberated after World War II, and of battered Kuwait City after the Gulf War. Having been raised on a cattle farm in Stow, Mass., Bilafer noticed that the corn was about three feet high. Doesn't look like there's been a war here, he thought. Then he saw the bloated cows, dozens of them, lying slaughtered in the fields. How bizarre.

He pushed down on the "up-down stick" at his left hip and the Apache's hard wasp-like body swooped lower, just above the telephone wires, for a better look. Puffs of smoke popped up from the tree lines like tiny cotton balls. Serb mortars, no doubt. He inspected village after village, peering into the rubble. The place was covered in it; dirty clothes and broken furniture and piles of debris and tree branches concealing tanks and military trucks. Small knots of men milled around vehicles. Soon he saw long convoys of tanks, trucks, and stolen buses and cars loaded with Serb troops.

Behind Bilafer on that gray Saturday morning was a massive allied convoy, 50,000 American and European troops and hundreds of tons of war equipment. As they had divided Berlin fifty-five years before, the great nations of North America and Europe would slice up Kosovo.[*]

By 8 A.M. the Apaches were escorting a Mardi Gras parade of multinational units marching in immediately behind the retreating Serb army to take up their assigned positions throughout the 4,200-square-mile province. First came the British 5th Airborne Brigade and the legendary warriors of the Royal Gurkha Rifles. British Chinook helicopters ferried in armored personnel carriers dangling beneath their bellies. Tanks, cannons, and collapsible extension bridges piggybacked on oversized flatbed trucks, mixed in with ambulances, and British Challenge battle tanks. Next came Italians sporting the black-rooster-feathered cockades of the Bersaglieri Division, then the French Framework Brigade, and the Germans, returning to occupy the Balkans once again, but this time as peacemakers.

The Kosovar Albanians were exuberant, waving red-and-black Albanian flags and covering tanks and soldiers with kisses and red poppies from the fields. Even if NATO nations weren't going to celebrate the war as a victory, the ragged ethnic Albanians would. NATO had saved them.

"NAH-TOE! NAH-TOE! NAH-TOE!" Albanian children and toothless old men cheered from the sides of the roads until dusk turned to

---

[*] The sectors in Kosovo include those run by the Americans, British, French, Italians, and Germans. Each of these nations worked within their sector with units from other countries. Most notably, the Russians worked in the northeastern part of the U.S. sector. The first U.S. troops to enter Kosovo were 2,100 marines from the 26th Marine Expeditionary Unit at Camp Lejeune, N.C., who had come ashore in Litochoro, Greece.

darkness. The cheers made Bilafer feel great. For the last two months he had sat on a muddy airfield in Albania, practicing every day in the sweltering heat, hoping to be called into the war against Slobodan Milosevic's Yugoslavia. Instead, on June 12, 1999, they called him in for the peace.

The SACEUR, Gen. Wesley Clark, had wanted to use the all-weather, best-at-night Apaches to chew up Serb forces at close range. But Pentagon and White House officials, worried about casualties, had nixed the idea. Gen. Joseph Ralston, vice chairman of the Joint Chiefs of Staff, had told White House officials that casualties could be "50 percent within days," one White House official recalled. The figure was much higher than any commander in the theater had calculated.

The Defense Department had spent $15 billion over two decades to make the Apaches the least vulnerable attack helicopters in the world. It spent another half-billion dollars to send 6,200 troops and 26,000 tons of equipment to transform a muddy airport in Tirana, Albania, into an Apache launching pad. But instead, the vaunted helicopters came to symbolize everything wrong with the Army as it entered the twenty-first century: its inability to move quickly, its resistance to change, its obsession with casualties, its post–Cold War identity crisis.

Although it was not evident to Bilafer at the time, the same forces that thwarted his participation in the war would sabotage the mission of the U.S. ground troops sent in to bring peace. Their mission was to create the conditions under which a new, democratic, multiethnic political system could survive. That would be much harder than taking out tanks and troops at night.

The murders and overt violence of noncombatants certainly decreased after the troops arrived, but 99 percent of Kosovo's Serbs had been either killed or driven out. A more enduring, invisible battle-field emerged quickly. The peacekeepers of the NATO Kosovo Force (KFOR) didn't even pretend to mobilize on it. It was a battlefield on which the struggle for ultimate power and control was waged by underground political structures and outlawed security apparatuses. Without a significant challenge from KFOR, these "parallel structures," as commanders called them, actually grew stronger under NATO peace-keepers. These hard-line groups were controlled mainly by Albanian separatists—many of whom had been NATO's allies during the war—and their Mafia-like organizations.

Most commanding generals, mid-level intelligence officers, and young soldiers who walked the streets identified these new power bases as the real obstacle to peace and stability. But political leaders back in Washington never expressly ordered the soldiers to do something about them. In fact, Washington's attention quickly shifted away from Kosovo once the war ended, leaving the U.S. Army responsible for an impossible mission's success. The same inattention would plague the U.S. mission in Afghanistan three years later.

★ ★ ★ ★

THE MORNING AFTER Bilafer's first day in the air, the bulk of the U.S. ground forces rolled in. Camp Able Sentry, the huge staging area and logistics base outside the Skopje airport in Macedonia, rumbled awake early. Like cattle rearranging themselves in a crowded pen, ten-ton trucks, Abrams tanks, and Bradley Fighting Vehicles pitched and revved, back and forth, on the crushed-rock gravel. One steel bull at a time, they lined up amid dozens of smaller soft-shelled Humvees for the drive in.

From his drab-green-tented headquarters, the commander of the U.S. peacekeeping contingent, Brig. Gen. John Craddock, a calm, deliberate armor officer, monitored the procession.[*] "It's like a barrel going over the falls," Maj. Erik Gunhus, a close aide, heard Craddock say, as 800 paratroopers from the 82nd Airborne Division[†] set up to cross the border with the marines and plunge into the chasm the world now calls "peacekeeping."

Most American soldiers think of peacekeeping as but a step away

---

[*] In Bosnia, NATO, at U.S. insistence, had put an American four-star general in charge. He had the authority to draw people and equipment from the Army's V Corps in Europe, the largest military unit anywhere, if he wanted to tweak the mission. In Kosovo, where the Americans wanted the Europeans to take charge, the head of the U.S. force was only a one-star brigadier general. If he needed to make changes, he had only the personnel and equipment someone else above him, usually his commander in the division to which he was assigned, would agree to give him.

[†] From the 2nd Battalion of the 505th Parachute Infantry Regiment.

from utter chaos, and two steps from combat. The Army packed accordingly. It hauled in half a division's worth of the basic combat backbone—115 tanks and Bradleys; 45 scout, attack, and utility helicopters; and 2,427 pieces of heavy equipment. It installed giant data pipes to pull classified, high-speed Internet information from satellites. It shipped in unmanned surveillance aircraft, bomb-sniffing dogs, global positioning systems, a targeting cell, and offensive combat planning units.

Engineers built the largest temporary military base since Vietnam. They leveled the rolling wheat fields of central Kosovo to anchor barracks for 5,000 troops, two gymnasiums, two dining halls, a library, a chapel, three recreation centers, and a pizza parlor.* But initially they gave Craddock only one counterintelligence officer and only two Criminal Investigative Division officers. Both worked only on cases involving suspected criminality by American soldiers, despite the prior experience of Bosnia, where organized crime blossomed after the bombing stopped.

As for the troops, their commanders passed out laminated "Rules of Engagement," the "Soldier's Card," which told them how to react in case of trouble: "Use the minimum force necessary to accomplish your mission. . . . If you have to open fire, you must: Fire only aimed shots, and fire no more rounds than necessary, and stop firing as soon as the situation permits." But there was no rules-of-engagement card for making a war-torn territory into a viable country, for soothing hatred and turning criminals into law-abiding citizens.

In his first days as commander of Task Force Falcon, the U.S. peacekeeping force, Craddock, an assistant division commander from the 1st Infantry Division, spent sixteen hours a day in videoconferences trying to convince his superiors in Europe that Kosovo "is not Bosnia!" "Look, this is going to be an absolute, unmitigated disaster if we don't figure

---

* As the retired chairman of the Joint Chiefs of Staff, Gen. John Shalikashvili, watched the bulky Army move into Kosovo, it reminded him again of another important reason the Army had to make major changes in its gargantuan structure. "They are running themselves ragged." The Army's reorganization under Chief of Staff Gen. Eric Shinseki had centered on making several brigades more mobile with wheeled rather than tracked vehicles. It wasn't enough. "How can you have an army of 1.5 million, and 50,000 deployed, and it's nearly broke?" Shalikashvili quipped in an interview. "There's something that's crazy."

out how to fix some things," he told his superiors in Europe. "We've got no law and order, no civil works."

Many Army commanders who went into Kosovo had already served a tour in Bosnia. They figured they understood "the Balkans" now. But they did not. In fact, their secret operational orders[1] for Kosovo completely ignored both the flood of angry ethnic Albanians returning home and the reverse Serb exodus. Even the "Intelligence Preparation of the Battlefield," the intelligence information on which the deployment was built, assumed that the Serb leadership would stay.[2]

The Bosnia peacekeeping mission began in December 1995 and continues today. It was framed by the Dayton Peace Accords, which had sliced Bosnia into two parts along ethnic lines. NATO troops were there to keep the sides apart and to encourage the building of moderate political forces and civil administrations.

In Kosovo, however, there was no buffer zone; Serbs and Albanians shared neighborhoods and streets. Serbs in government positions before the Kosovo air war fled Albanian revenge. Those who remained were under constant threat from the ethnic Albanians, NATO's unofficial ally during the war.

With his glasses and helmet on, Craddock looked like Elmer Fudd. But he was unflappable. As a lieutenant colonel in the Gulf War, he had commanded the 4th Battalion of the 64th Armored known as the "Tuskers." As part of the 24th Infantry Division, he had led his unit on the famed "left hook," a two-hundred-mile push into Iraq to block the retreat of the Iraqi forces that had invaded Kuwait. His battalion had wreaked a five-mile-long path of carnage on the fleeing Hammurabi Division in the controversial Battle of Rumaila, two days after the cease-fire.

The Gulf War was clarity itself compared to Craddock's duties in Kosovo. Here there were no banks, no property records, no birth or marriage registrars, not even a place to register the dead in the mass graves at Ljubenic, Djakovic, Cara Luka. No one fought fires, drove trash trucks, or chlorinated the water, either. When Craddock's officers went into villages seeking community leaders with whom to work, they found self-appointed cliques of suspicious-looking men who drove fancy cars—former Kosovo Liberation Army (KLA) rebels and their friends. "It's the Wild West," he told his staff.

Craddock bore another albatross: the Pentagon's obsession with casualties. Partisanship was strangling Washington politics in the summer of 1999, as the Monica Lewinsky scandal continued to rock the capital. One soldier's death would become not the stuff of heroic legend, but mud for the fight between Democrats and Republicans. With this in mind, Craddock's original orders had been to station his troops at two large, well-protected bases. This made no sense to him. The troops had to be in the villages, among the people, not hunkered down. Be seen. Get to know people. Stop the exodus. Get Serbs and Albanians talking again.

U.S. Army soldiers from the 82nd Airborne Division based in Vrbovac, near Vitina, Kosovo, keep an eye on the village from a hill overlooking it.   LUCIAN PERKINS–©2002, THE *WASHINGTON POST.* REPRINTED WITH PERMISSION.

Soon after he arrived, Craddock realized their battles would be fought street to street. He ordered his troops to pull their tanks and Bradleys up next to factories, churches, farmhouses, and police stations. They sent tank squads to guard Serb churches twenty-four hours a day and tried to talk Serb families, and especially Serb notables, into staying. A sound plan, but it didn't stop the exodus. Week after week, bedraggled columns of cars, trucks, carts, and tractors headed north and east into Serbia and Montenegro. Some 100,000 Serbs had left by the end of the summer.

Before the war, 154,000 Serbs and 2 million ethnic Albanians lived in Kosovo. Milosevic's ethnic-cleansing campaign and the NATO bombing had changed the population mix considerably. About 90 percent of the Albanians had been displaced from their homes, and nearly 950,000 of them had fled abroad. By June 24, not even two weeks after the war ended, nearly 150,000 of those Albanians had returned and a reverse exodus of Serbs had begun. "In areas where Serbs had committed atrocities against Albanian families, the Albanians struck back hard and without mercy," said a military intelligence officer who was filing daily reports. In areas around Urosevac, headquarters for one of the two American battalions in the U.S. sector, the Serb population dwindled from 5,000 to less than 25 in three months.

★ ★ ★ ★

WHEN LT. COL. TIMOTHY REESE's armored battalion* got the order to go to Kosovo, his first reaction was simple: "What are we doing?" Reese had just come off a combat-training exercise at the huge maneuver-training center at Hohenfels, Germany. There, his tanks had fought an enemy that used Soviet tactics. That wouldn't really help him in Kosovo, though. "What is it that we'll do each day?" he asked his deputy task force commander once he got to Camp Bondsteel.

In truth, he never got a useful answer. "We were making it up as we went along," said Reese.† To help himself figure it out, Reese carried a copy of UN Security Council Resolution 1244, the overarching mandate for NATO's Kosovo mission. It stated, "Establish and maintain a secure environment, including public safety and order; Monitor, verify and, when necessary enforce compliance with the conditions of the Military Technical Agreement. . . . Provide assistance to the UN Mission in Kosovo, including core civil functions until transferred."

To stop the violence, the Army used Bilafer's helicopters and other

---

* The 1st Battalion of the 77th Armor Task Force.

† When he first arrived on June 23, Reese was assigned the problematic western portion of the U.S. sector. It included "Dodge City," as Bilafer and other officers called Vitina, an ethnically mixed town near the border with Macedonia. Shortly after Brig. Gen. Craig Peterson replaced Craddock and the 3rd Battalion of the 504th Parachute Infantry Regiment, 82nd Airborne Division, arrived to replace the 2nd Battalion. Peterson moved Reese's heavier battalion to the quieter eastern portion of the American sector. Peterson did this because he believed the 82nd's troops had more experience walking around troubled villages than a heavy tank battalion did, and he thought Reese's heavy armor would deter Serb army probes.

conventional equipment. The Apache pilots would turn on their thermal and infrared imaging for a night's manhunt. Only minutes away from anywhere in Kosovo, they would fly in, spotlights sweeping the ground. The gunfire would stop. The bugs would scatter. Sometimes Bilafer's pilots might follow a column of smoke or a report of a looter on a particular street. Skeletal x-ray images floated across their goggle lens. Above Urosevac or Vitina or Gnjilane, these choppers created a sense of omnipotence: everything was a potential target. Bilafer's "Sixshooters" had a sense of righteousness. They named themselves "Task Force Big Duke," after John Wayne. Like the Duke, the Apaches provided theatrics for ground troops. But their capabilities did not always fit the target, which was often a lone grenade-thrower in a city stuffed with three-story apartment buildings and alleyways.

Infantrymen brought their field equipment onto busy streets. Armored vehicles mounted with machine guns lumbered along narrow, cramped roads. Soldiers on foot carried standard Army radios with five-foot-long antennas that flopped with each step like long whirly-bird hats. Many soldiers bought simpler walkie-talkies at Wal-Mart before they deployed. Troops carried $3,000 night-vision goggles that could spot a sniper at midnight, but they didn't always have flashlights to search the trunks of cars.

American soldiers all over the U.S. sector were finding themselves saddled with other unfamiliar responsibilities. One lieutenant set up a phone company board of directors in Vitina. Another, only eighteen months out of law school, wrote the procedures for, and then conducted the first postwar preliminary criminal hearing in Kosovo. It took place during a downpour, in a small tent lit by a chem-light stick. Young officers led political meetings—in their own ways. To limit arguments between Serbs and Albanians, sometimes they timed each side with stopwatches.

To develop a "campaign plan," Reese held a twice-weekly "battle update briefing" (BUB) at his headquarters at Camp Monteith, the smaller of the two U.S. bases. Around a rectangular table, officers struggled to thwart what they saw as the real enemies to peace: the decrepit state of basic services and the ubiquitous Albanian underground, which was committing most of the crimes. He encouraged his subordinates to act like cops.

At the BUB one night, a captain, "Warlord 6," reported that his soldiers had visited a suspected member of the local Albanian mafia. They had pocketed two notebooks filled with names from the man's desk. They hoped these notebooks would amount to the organization's "Who's Who." Did anyone notice the theft? asked Reese. "No witnesses," Warlord 6 responded. Good.

In another city, teenage Albanian thugs were harassing elderly Serbs and children. "Question them—a scared-straight kind of program," Reese suggested. "Put them in a security checkpoint. Let them freeze a little."

"What if the parents overreact?" asked Command Sgt. Maj. Willie Day, the battalion's top NCO.

"Do everything right by the book, no blindfolding or anything," Reese answered. "You can very well lock up the parents if they can't control their kids."

Zitinje, twenty miles south of Pristina, was Reese's greatest challenge. Former KLA rebels had been assaulting and harassing the city's 350 remaining Serbs without much concern about how KFOR might react. Capt. Torry Brennan, a dashing, dark-haired, thirty-year-old Virginia Military Institute graduate wanted to put his entire company there to stop the violence.[*] But the village was too isolated and tanks were too clumsy to maneuver easily through its narrow dirt streets. So he moved in a platoon from the experienced 82nd Airborne Division, thirty-six soldiers in all. Brennan knew it wasn't enough.

By mid-July, after a Serb farmer was killed in his own field, Brennan felt a need to pressure the town's self-appointed political leadership. For that, he called on Reese. "There's a new sheriff in town," Reese told the town's Serb mayor and his Albanian counterpart. "We either work this out or we'll take people in." They nodded politely.

Days later a Serb farmer and his wife were coming down from their fields, crossing the main bridge, when a sniper killed them both. Two weeks later the Serb mayor's son and daughter were ambushed and killed by gunmen as they drove home from a party.

---

[*] Brennan commanded the Alpha Company, 1st Battalion, 26th Infantry Regiment, which was attached to Reese's 77th Armor Task Force.

Reese ordered Brennan's troops to search every structure in Zitinje, nearly 300 in all, including barns, stores, offices, and woodsheds, looking for weapons and clues to the murder. On July 26, three platoons began knocking on doors at 2 A.M. Helicopters buzzed overhead. The search yielded little—two automatic rifles, five AK-47s, some pistols, and a couple of uniforms from the Serbian special police—but by the standards of what such searches produced in Kosovo, they thought theirs had been a success.

Less than a week later, a Serb farmer was shot dead while picking plums in an orchard. He was the fourth man killed in ten days. "There aren't enough troops," farmer Ilija Savic told a journalist who had come to town.[3] Brennan felt his impartiality give way. He was no longer just protecting the peace, he was protecting the Serbs. "I was measuring my success as a commander in that area and I couldn't protect them," he said.

Brennan was not surprised when the Serbs came to his headquarters to tell him they were leaving town, en masse, for the provincial border. They wanted KFOR's protection. He told them to be lined up and ready to go early in the morning. But the conversation greatly depressed Brennan. Knowing his men could not protect the Serbs' homes, he arranged for the Serb villagers to bring their valuables and farm animals—horses, cows, goats, pigs, ducks, and chickens—to a farmhouse the Americans could guard.

On the morning of August 1, a scene from *The Grapes of Wrath* unfolded. With two Black Hawk helicopters floating above, a line of 150 beaten-up tractors and ox-drawn wagons overloaded with people, pots, and furniture set out under the steaming sun on a thirty-five mile trek to the border. A tank platoon guarded key intersections and soldiers stood along the way out of town, their Humvees mounted with machine guns, warily watching the gathering Albanian crowds.

The U.S. soldiers had confined local Albanians to their homes to avoid a confrontation. But Albanians in Radivojce, several miles away, had gotten word of what they considered a triumph. They lined the side of the road to taunt the Serbs as they passed through. "U.S.A.! U.S.A.!" "NAH-TOE!" "NAH-TOE!" Then "UCK! UCK!"* "Yeah! Go to Serbia

* UCK is the Albanian acronym for the KLA.

now. It's where you belong."[4] The Serbs, mostly old men and women dressed from head to toe in shapeless black shifts, stared straight ahead. Brennan was horrified. Children in the convoy kept looking at him. Wasn't he supposed to protect them? They cried out, "Why are we leaving? Why?"

Lt. Jason Green, redheaded, round-faced, and fresh out of West Point, was manning an intersection in Klokat, a Serb village several miles away, with his tank platoon. He had joined the Army to become a tough, ramrod-straight soldier like the ones he had imitated every Halloween as a child. Now he found himself embroiled in something he never signed up for. Plastic army soldiers and war movies never looked like this.

Rumor spread among the Klokat Serbs that KFOR was forcing the Serbs out of Zitinje. They quickly massed, 200 strong, to block the road, and converged on the caravan of tractors, which came to a cold stop amid the angry yelling. Serbs pushed in toward Green's platoon.[*] The motion alarmed the soldiers and they got fired up as well. No one was going to push them around. They glanced frantically at each other, looking for instruction.

Serb women pushed forward, spitting, yelling in the soldiers' faces as the soldiers stood with their backs toward the tractors and cars they were ushering through. "Sir! I'm going to shoot them. I'm locking and loading," one of Green's privates yelled out. "No, man!" Green shouted back. "You can't do that. Just hang out. I'm working with the translator." Truth was, Green wanted to do the same. The translator told the crowd the soldiers had not evicted the Serbs, they were trying to protect them. But they would not listen.

When Brennan arrived several minutes later, two sergeants had their rifles loaded, locked, and pointed upward. The tank-mounted machine guns were loaded too, and the gunners were pointing them at the crowd. "They're ready to shoot," Brennan thought.

"Keep them at bay," Brennan instructed Green. "Pull out the troublemakers from the crowd if you can." Just contain it. Keep it under control. Don't endanger anyone, defend yourself at all costs. It was,

[*] 2nd Platoon of Alpha Company, 77th Armor Task Force.

after all, just a vocal demonstration by a crowd of mostly old men and women and a few teenagers and children. Brennan pushed through the crowd to find the Klokat Serb leader and get him linked up with the Serb leader from Zitinje so the latter could tell the former that KFOR was protecting them, not forcing them out. Green ran from sergeant to sergeant sternly issuing an order for calm. As he turned around, though, he glimpsed a Russian troop-transport vehicle making its way toward the demonstration. "Oh, man," he said to himself.

The Serbs, who considered the Russian's their allies and hoped the Russian soldiers would buffer them from NATO's demands, broke the soldiers' line and ran toward the vehicle. "*Russki! Russki! Russki!* Americans go home!" they shouted, becoming even more agitated. They thought the Russians were coming to stop the exodus.

Green got on his radio to Brennan, who was somewhere in the crowd. "Sir, I have a Russian convoy! There are six vehicles. I don't have the soldiers to stop them." Brennan found the Russian commander and his translator. Couldn't he just bypass the route? But the Russian commander refused—too much trouble. Besides, the convoy just wanted to pass through, he told Brennan. Indeed, the Russians merely rolled on by, slowly, leaning off their armored personnel carriers swinging their AK-47s triumphantly, flaunting the fact that they would not be compelled to follow U.S. direction.

The scene mesmerized Green. The Russians looked just like he would have drawn them. Chiseled features. Pale skin. Bright blue eyes. Striped blue-and-white undershirts. Cold warriors were passing right in front of him. It seemed unreal. He could not quite fathom the two armies' working together, given the suspicions that remained on both sides.

Some 2,000 Russians were part of the NATO peacekeeping mission. They patrolled with the Americans in Kamenica in the northeastern part of Kosovo, along the Serbian border. Their duties paralleled those of other countries who made up KFOR, but U.S. soldiers instinctively distrusted them. Two Special Forces "liaison teams" kept an eye on the Russians. The NATO and U.S. leadership, all the way up to General Clark, believed the Russians had wanted to create their own sector, where they could harbor hard-line Serbs and play by their own rules. In small ways they were constantly challenging NATO.

★ ★ ★ ★

ONE FALL DAY, Lieutenant Green and his platoon were on patrol in the easternmost part of the U.S. sector bordering Serbia, where they had received reports of unauthorized visits by Russian troops. The Russians had claimed to be escorting Serbian children to school. Just after lunchtime, Green pulled his three armored vehicles into the quiet schoolyard in Jasenovik to ask the teachers if they needed any more supplies.

Suddenly, the doors of the school burst open and out rushed four Russian soldiers trailed by seven hard-faced Serb men.

"Okay, we got 'em," Green muttered as he pushed open the door of his Humvee with his shoulder and charged toward the soldiers, stopping within two feet of the tallest and biggest, their lieutenant.

"Okay," he said to his interpreter, swinging his shoulders as if he were about to begin a schoolyard brawl. "Ask them what are they doing here."

Escorting children to school, the Russian officer replied, chin up, eyes unwavering.

"Ask him if he's tasked to stay all day."

Yes.

"Ask him how many days a week."

Six.

"Six! They go to school on Saturday?" he said, believing he had caught the Russian in a lie. He could feel the tension mount. He took a deep breath.

"Okay, stop," Green said abruptly to himself, using his hands to pat down the air and his temper. "Let's start over."

Deep breath. His voice softened. His body posture relaxed. "My name is Lieutenant Green. . . . Are there enough desks in the school? Do the students have enough paper?"

Seeing the incredulous gaze of his cynical thirty-year-old platoon sergeant, Green explained to Sgt. Eric Ebert, "I don't want to sound like I'm prying information out of him. . . . I'm just trying to make it easy for him right now."

"Is there a problem that we came here?" the Russian asked, with a hint of confrontation.

"It's not a problem, we just need to know when you're in the American sector."

Within five minutes, Green had the Russian commander's name and unit number, which he would pass to his own commanders. The matter would be resolved many grades above his single lieutenant's bar. But his troubles were not over as he walked back to his Humvee and headed out of the schoolyard. His reputation was now on the line.

"Hey Lieutenant Green, you're a pretty diplomatic guy," taunted Ebert, looking down from the gunner seat. "I wouldn't feel that way. I'd just not let them into the sector."

Green changed the subject. "Ever since I was a little kid I wanted to pick armor," he told a passenger. "There's something about a big powerful piece of machinery rolling over and killing everything. Why carry a gun when you can ride it? What I'm trained to do is command a platoon and kill other tanks."

Higher headquarters never told Green how the situation turned out, but as far as he could tell, nothing really changed. The Russians continued to be seen here and there in the U.S. sector. Mostly, Green felt relieved there was no coming-to-blows incident that could have sparked a serious diplomatic row.

In Zitinje, Reese still thought he could prevent further arson if he allowed Albanians to reclaim property with proof of ownership. His troops surrounded the empty Serb homes with concertina wire. But three days after the Serb exodus, the burning began anyway and continued for forty-eight hours. Seven U.S. soldiers moved into Zitinje. They shot like pinballs from blaze to blaze, trying to carry television sets, couches, animals into a courtyard where they could guard them. With no fire equipment, they took up shovels and tried to douse the flames with dirt. It wasn't enough.

"It was like a swarm of ants," said Reese. The soldiers just couldn't keep up. They began zip-stripping people (putting them in plastic zip-strip handcuffs) and throwing them in the "asshole pit," a little open-air barbed-wire enclosure they had built. Let the sleet and snow torture them a little.

"We were zip-stripping kids younger than my own," said Reese, speaking about the adolescents they detained. "Once we started doing that, I knew this game was up." He gave it one more try, pleading with the Albanian mayor to make it stop. "Look, we can't stop this without your cooperation, because you know we can't arrest the whole town," Reese told him. "But if you don't cooperate, we're leaving."

On Friday, August 6th, KFOR retreated. The Albanians moved in with gasoline and torches. Over the weekend forty more Serb houses burned.

Green watched the village smolder from the commander's hatch of his tank, parked at the crest of a nearby hill. His big bulls couldn't get there if they had wanted to; the charred frames of houses had fallen and blocked the road. The flaming drama demoralized his tank platoon. "Why am I down here?" Green asked himself, and then his company commander. "Why are we here?"

He felt he never got a good answer. The NATO nations behind this mission wouldn't, or couldn't, decide if Kosovo should be independent from Yugoslavia or forced to be a part of it. The Serbs, whom Green and the other soldiers believed would be the enemy as they had been during the war, turned into victims right before the troops' eyes. The former Albanian rebels, whom NATO had worked with during the war, became the new enemies. But troops weren't authorized to kill or capture this enemy, or to even arrest him. There were no jails big enough to hold them all. There was no criminal justice system to convict them. Sometimes, in frustration, the soldiers turned their anger elsewhere, closer to home.

Chapter Thirteen

DRITA'S KOSOVO

★ ★ ★ ★

*D*RITA PEREZIC, A BRASSY, FIVE-FOOT-TEN, "NEW YAWKER,"
rode into Kosovo with the American troops. But she entered a very different world than they did.

Drita had been born and raised in an Albanian American household on Staten Island. Hired as a translator during the Kosovo war, she had spent two months camping out in the hills of northeastern Albania with Army counterintelligence and civil affairs units working as liaisons to KLA fighters. She learned she could go without a bath and a toilet. She could live with her thick brown hair matted to her head until it got so grungy she took a knife to everything below the rubber band on her ponytail. Truth be told, she had lost her comb. "My mother would faint if she saw me," she thought. Drita cried when she saw her reflection in the Humvee's mirror. She was so dirty. "Everyone is dirty, but I don't look like a woman anymore."

Drita survived the throat-tightening fear of mortars lobbed through the pitch-black night. She endured the panic that gripped her every time an intruder approached her tent and tripped the security wire, sending red, white, or green bolts of light into the air. Usually it was a stray sheep from a nearby flock. The soldiers told her they were within artillery range of Serb forces. It took a minute before she figured out what they were saying. If we can hit them, they can hit us too. "I am so afraid of dying here," she wrote to calm herself.

The soldiers were as ignorant about Kosovo and the KLA as Drita

*Drita Perezic, an Albanian American from New York
who became the cultural "911" for nearly every
commanding general at Camp Bondsteel.*

ROBIN QUANDER

was about the Army. It drove her nuts. The soldiers made fun of the
KLA rebels because they were not "a real Army, like us." They saw
the world as weak versus strong: they were strong, everyone else was
weak. "Why does it have to be about who is stronger or weaker, like
just because the KLA is weaker than the Yugoslav army, somehow [the
Albanians] deserve to be burned out of their homes, raped, murdered,
and God knows what else?" The American soldiers were angry that the
Albanians couldn't beat the Serbs by themselves, that the U.S. Army
had to be there to help. They didn't want to be there.

At the same time, Drita quickly became fond of her newly adopted
family. They were like brothers to her. "You get so close to these people,
the soldiers, because you never know if you will see each other again.
These kids could die, they would die for me. They would die to protect
me. It is amazing."

She watched warplanes roar across the border on bombing missions.
She did not digest it like the soldiers around her, though—she worried
about the people on the other side. "They must be scared and alone. I

worry about my father's people. Many of their fighters will be killed. I worry about the enemy, the Serbs, many of them will be killed too. They are people too. I refuse to believe that things are either black or white, that there is a right and a wrong side. I pray for the innocent."

In refugee camps that sprang up in the hills of northeastern Albania, Drita absorbed the depth of hatred she heard in stories of Serb atrocities. She translated these tales for the counterintelligence units gathering clues about Kosovo from grandmothers, old farmers, doctors, teachers: ". . . and then my neighbor pointed to my house. . . . It was my former co-worker who broke the door down. . . . It was my former classmate who was standing there watching as I was beaten up in front of my wife and kids."

Stories about the babies kept her up at night. She could recall the terrible words coming from her own mouth as she switched from Albanian to English, interpreting for American officers. They became her stories, too.

"*Me thuan per 5 minuta me l'shua shtpine, shkoni ka keni ardhe,*" one woman told her. "They said I had me five minutes to get out of the house, go back to where I came from," Drita heard herself saying out loud. The withered mother ran around the house, frantically looking for the baby's bottle. But her time ran out.

"*Ma morren djalin prej dorres, nuk disha ku e kish shishen, deshta shishen me ja gjete djalit. Ma kethyen djalin i dekte, e m'than tash a je gati.*" "They took my baby from my arms," Drita repeated, her throat tightening. "I didn't know where his bottle was, all I wanted was to find my son's bottle. They handed him back to me dead and said, 'Are you ready now?'" They were both sobbing, Drita and the grieving mother.

The twenty-hour days and the raw ugliness of the gigantic war machine surrounded her—mud-caked trucks, boxes of explosives, heavy guns, and the race-car roar of the Apaches always coming out of nowhere, without warning. They frayed her. "What the hell am I doing here?" she asked herself.

At twenty-eight, Drita had already worked as a record promoter, done a stint as a banker on Wall Street, and set up a small advertising firm. But she was restless and looking for much more than a new business opportunity when she signed up for the Kosovo gig. She had not exactly bargained for what she got. Although she dressed in Army fatigues, flak jacket, and helmet, she didn't know how to shoot a gun. She hadn't ever seen a land mine, didn't know a thing about rank or chain of command before she left New York City in April. She smoked incessantly and cursed as much as anyone around her. But in a short time, she yearned to be accepted, to feel like one of *them*. She had sacrificed as much as they had on this mission. It hurt her deeply when they turned against her, when they turned their impatience and xenophobia on her.

"Hey, where did you learn to speak English so well?" the soldiers asked her.

"The Lower East Side, asshole!" she yelled back.

"Who the hell gave you the right to speak English?" the mean, stupid ones would yell at her when they felt like it.

When the war ended and her unit prepared to go into Kosovo, it first drove south through Albania to reach the staging base in Macedonia. The soldiers let Drita ride up in the turret of the Humvee. She took off her helmet and let her hair blow in the breeze. Albanians on the road threw flowers and chocolates to her. She felt like a prom queen riding on the school float. "My wave was perfect," she noted.

In the morning darkness on June 14, 1999, the day she first rode into Kosovo, Drita had bolted up from sleep on her cot in the huge, open maintenance bay at Camp Able Sentry. She was exhausted. Visions of minefields and of the dead had kept her awake. She was afraid they might look like her grandmother. The Army had allotted her two MREs (meals ready to eat) shrink-wrapped in heavy brown plastic, for the road march to Urosevac. What lay ahead? What if she got stuck on the route for days? At the mess hall, she filled a plastic bag with little square tubs of peanut butter and jelly, hot chocolate mix, cheese packages, and a handful of juice boxes.

Then she walked across the gravel to her assigned armored personnel carrier and climbed onto the cold metal seat behind the senior officer, a major in her Army Special Forces civil affairs unit. The tanks scared her, they were so big. There was so much stuff. "I have never seen anything like this before. God save us should we ever go to war, and God save the other side because this is a lot of stuff."

The troops riding with her were quiet and nervous, even the most senior among them. To calm herself down, she pretended to be in a music video. The moment was surreal enough to be one, she thought. This line of machines bumping along, like so many huge, green cattle. The knots of rag-covered kids rushing too close to the tanks were sometimes knocked to the ground by their weight. Black smoke from burning homes. Filth. Hunger. Sadness. Fresh graves. The camouflaged pant legs of a machine gunner standing in the turret in front of her.

She slipped Black Sabbath into her portable CD player, put on her headphones, then her helmet. She pushed the "Forward" button until the disc stopped at *War Pigs*:

Generals gathered in their masses
Just like witches at black masses.
Evil minds that plot destruction.
Sorcerers of death's construction.
In the fields the bodies burning,
As the war machine keeps turning.
Death and hatred to mankind,
Poisoning their brainwashed minds.
Oh lord, yeah!

After the first few miles, tears soaked Drita's face. She had been in Kosovo several years ago, but this Kosovo was a tattered body, torn and bludgeoned. Back then she had watched Albanian children, not allowed to attend public school, sneak home from basement classes. She saw Serbian shopkeepers ignore Albanian patrons, and doctors and nurses stand mute when their Albanian colleagues were removed from their jobs. She had been stopped and grilled every few blocks by Serbian police and ticketed if her answers didn't come fast enough, or if she drove too slowly or too fast. Kosovo spoke to her now as she headed in under the U.S. flag. "Look what has happened to me, look at what has become of me," she wrote in her journal. Kosovo's face was disfigured.

Blackened cars littered the streets. Like cheap bandages, masking tape was stuck on windows and doors to absorb the vibrations of grenades, mortars, and NATO's bombs. Miles of land-mine signs marked the roads. As her Humvee bounced along the dirt road, spray-painted graffiti flashed by her from the side of a blown-out building. "UCK + NATO." The UCK was the ethnic Albanian rebel force that Americans knew as the KLA. "UCK + NATO"—this was a minefield more treacherous than the ones along the side of the roads, she thought. The American soldiers had no idea what they were in the middle of.

"I know what will happen now," she wrote to herself one night. "The revenge will come and the Albanians will be fierce and they will hide behind us. The Albanians think we are allies. They love us Americans the most and expect the most from us. What will they do when they find out the soldier boy does not want to be here, does not care, and frankly, does not like them?"

She could easily translate Albanian into English. The Army, well, she was still working on that translation. At the big Camp Bondsteel base, the uniforms all had ranks, and ranks mattered there, but they were Greek to her. "The railroad tracks are captains," she told herself. "The gold flower is a major. I know a star means general, and the colonel has a bird on his shoulder." But everyone kept calling the one with a black flower colonel. It threw her off. He was introduced as a lieutenant colonel.

"Ask him when he will become a full bird?" one of her soldiers egged her on. She had no idea what he was talking about, but played along. "When will you become a full bird?" she asked the lieutenant colonel.

"Who are you and where are you from, soldier?" the lieutenant colonel yelled at her.

"I am Drita! From New York! And I sure as hell ain't no soldier, sir!" she yelled back.

Much more than a linguist, Drita became the cultural "911" for the first three American brigadier generals to command American forces in Kosovo.* They took her into top-secret meetings with KLA leaders and to strategy sessions with top aides, always depending on her to

---

* In 2001, the Army rehired Drita Perezic to train troops before they deployed for Kosovo. She later became a special adviser to the generals sent in to lead the U.S. KFOR mission.

explain what they were seeing around them. From behind the dark-framed eyeglasses Drita wore when her eyes tired, she watched a peculiar clash of supercultures: one the rigid demeanor of an Army soldier craving to go home, the other a centuries-old hatred between Serbs and Albanians, both vowing vengeance.

She wove lessons into stories and tried to make strange people understandable to the senior officers who asked for her help. In her spare time, late at night, she wrote papers on "The Canons of Leke Dukagjini," the moral and ethical principles of the Albanian people, on the "The Relevance of Kosovo Polje to Kosovar Serbs and Albanians."

"Serbs view Kosovo as the cradle of their civilization," she began one paper. *"On June 28, 1389 (St. Vitus day–June 15 according to the old calendar), Serbian Prince Lazar lost a battle against the advancing Ottoman Turks, the infamous Battle of Kosovo. It is following that defeat that the Serbian Kingdom's medieval power begins to deteriorate as the Ottomans take control of the area for over 500 years. . . .*

"The Albanians argue that they were present in Kosovo way before the Slavs migrated to the region in the 7th century. The consensus among Albanian Historians is that the Albanians are the modern-day ancestors of the Illyrians. The Illyrians being the oldest tribe of peoples to inhabit the Balkans; pre-Roman. . . .

"On June 28, 1989, an estimated one million Serbs from throughout Yugoslavia went to Kosovo Polje to commemorate the 600-year anniversary of the Battle of Kosovo. Milosevic took center stage . . . .using the myth of Prince Lazar and the Battle of Kosovo to gain political support from the Serb population as then president of Serbia. "Never again will they defeat you," said Milosevic. . . . Within the same year Kosovo's Autonomy is stripped. . . ."

Drita translated a second language and culture too, the one that divides American civilians from American soldiers, the growing civilian-military gap that is one reason missions like Kosovo fall from public view so fast. She rolled her eyes at the force-protection measures that seemed to have too many soldiers on edge. They were safer at Camp Bondsteel than she had been in New York City, she told them to their faces. "The soldier," as she called the young troops she traveled with, "is a fighter, a trained killer. He must have an enemy in order to justify his existence and make use of all his training. But he needs to be able to discern between a real threat and a created one."

She fumed that some soldiers would not go into the streets, walk around, get to know the people and stop treating the Albanians like thieves who had no reason to fear and hate the Serbs. The Americans knew little about that history. For all the Army unit lineages they studied, and all the ceremonial Army traditions they upheld, the soldiers took a naïvely ahistoric view of the territory they occupied. They seemed to have no context in which to put the violence unfolding before them. They hadn't been there when the Serbs were murdering her distant relatives, or taking young girls away to rape them. Moreover, they showed little interest in these things. Instead, many of them were drawn to, and trusted, things that seemed familiar: faces that reminded them of relatives, high-fives they knew from sports fields, anyone who could speak a little English.

When she went into the streets with her soldiers or generals, she absorbed more violence than they ever understood. Drita had been the first to tell the Albanian rebels to hand the Americans their rifles. The KLA fighters had looked straight at her and said, "I'm going to kill you if you come any closer."

Another time she had watched an Albanian soldier cry when the soldiers insisted he hand over his weapon so it could be registered at an arms site. She knew he would not be able to face his KLA commander without his weapon. "He was not crying because he was a baby, or scared, or even because his command would have his ass when he got back," she wrote that night in her diary. "He was crying because he had been dishonored in front of his own people, forced to hand over his weapons, forced to take his clothes off to reveal anything concealed. He was searched, he was neutered in front of his people, by us, by the Americans that he thought supported him."

When she accompanied soldiers to Serb towns, the villagers spat at her and tried to kick her. Young Serb children recoiled in horror when she came near, believing she would kill them. In Klokat, a predominantly Serb village, she finally broke down. "I did not want to let them see me cry but I could not help it. I kept asking if any one of them spoke any English and they kept on cursing me. They cursed the Americans, the Albanians, and they spat on me for being both."

Secretly, she befriended some Serbs too. The artist in Strpce. A little girl named Jovanka. She gave Jovanka's grandfather five dollars to buy the girl a present. He thanked her with tears in his eyes. "I am not the evil Albanian, I am human," she wrote in her diary. "I am not the destructive, plotting American, I am human. I want him to know that I do not hate him for what he is. I want little Jovanka to remember me so when she grows up, before she is taught to hate, she will remember to love."

Drita did the most grisly work, too. She collected evidence on war crimes. She interviewed distraught Albanian family members, like those in the village of Sojevo. They were looking for Zylfi Kastrati, born 1920. Body found in a well. Gunshot to the back of the head. The Serbs had dumped animals and humans in the wells to pollute the drinking water. "The stench is disgusting. The images sort of burn in your memory, so every time you blink, you see the dead person whether you want to or not. The skin gets so white and you just know that mass in front of you was once a person but no longer is. I hate it—every time I blink I see it—the frozen white face distorted and swollen. Dead."

Three bodies found by villagers on June 9, 1999: they were piled on top of each other, all shot at close range. Another find: eleven dead, including two women. One man was ordered to pour gasoline on his friends and lie on top of them. Other graves began to collapse when the bodies decomposed. "We are the first Americans the villagers have seen. The kids bring me bundles of flowers. I put them on the graves. I am so sorry I could not come sooner, before you were killed. I am so sorry."

On other days, she watched with disgust as American soldiers judged the Albanians by the fact that they threw their garbage around. "Garbage collection is what defines these people," she scoffed. Never mind that nothing works. The schools are a mess. The hospitals damaged. Land mines everywhere. Still, the soldier sees the garbage, and that's what he judges them by. If only they would clean up the garbage. "Sometimes I just want to scream at people for being so stupid."

She and the other Army linguists understood where the Army's naïveté could lead its soldiers. "The expectations are so high," Drita told every general and colonel she worked for. The Albanians, she explained, viewed Americans as not only liberators who would free them from the Serbs, but also as liberators who would help them break free of Yugoslavia altogether.[*] They called the troops of other NATO nations "occupiers." They called the Americans "*mik*"—friend, ally. "You need to go into the villages and tell them, tell them we are not on their side," she pleaded with U.S. officers.

Of the two competing groups, the Albanians were least like the Americans. Poorer and less educated, they were also Muslim, although many were secular. Some Kosovar Albanian women wore head scarves. Others put on makeup and tight-fitting clothes and flirted with soldiers. The culture confused some soldiers, but the Army had hired too few qualified Albanian-speaking translators to help them decipher it.

Distrust of the Muslim population had been imported from the U.S. peacekeeping experience in Bosnia, where thousands of radical Muslims from Afghanistan and Iran had come in the mid-1990s to volunteer in the civil war. The United States had forced Bosnian Muslim leaders to expel the mujahideen fighters before they would agree to implement the Dayton Peace Accords. But they hadn't gotten them all. A fear of terrorism and "blowback" lay behind Washington's refusal to arm the outgunned Bosnian Muslim army during the civil war.[†]

Many soldiers simplified these intertwined issues. The Serbs became the good guys; the Albanians, the bad guys. The Americans distrusted and ridiculed everything Albanian. Some lashed out at Drita, *their* Albanian—a convenient, safe target. "Your inbred cousins can't seem

---

[*] An independent Kosovo was not NATO or U.S. policy. Both endorsed a limbo state for Kosovo. They didn't support independence, as the Kosovar Albanians wanted. Nor did NATO outline how, when, or whether Kosovo was to be specifically reintegrated into what remained of Yugoslavia.

[†] NATO commanders knew of a web linking Bosnian Muslims with Islamic extremists. The Bosnian deputy defense minister, Hasan Cengic, had been in charge of smuggling weapons into Bosnia from Iran, Western intelligience and diplomatic officials told the *Washington Post*'s John Pomfret, who wrote a series in September 1996 about the involvement of radical Islamic states in supplying arms to Bosnia's Muslims. More than a dozen Islamic charities operated in Bosnia and Kosovo, some of them outlawed in their countries of origin. A few were on the FBI's list of financial fronts for terrorist groups. Intelligence officers in Camp Bondsteel believed members of one Saudi-funded charity had been monitoring KFOR's headquarters in Pristina.

to think straight, and if it were not for us, they would all be dead," one soldier scolded her. Other cruel words echoed in her mind years later: "The Serbs are so much nicer. They offer us alcohol and treat us like kings. The Albanians are stupid motherfuckers . . . You and your Albanian hillbillies have no idea about what democracy is. . . . You are not one of us. You are one of them."

Still, Drita had come to feel a part of the Army family. She had toughed it out with them, made it through the initial days of uncertainty and fear. She was their link to their new world, and many soldiers cherished her irreverence and foul-mouthed sense of humor. For some soldiers, however, the more contact they had with Kosovar Albanians, the more some of them turned against Drita. She found herself feeling as if her olive skin, dark hair, and ability to speak another language set her too far apart from the American Army universe.

Several times a day she had walked inside the tented top-secret intelligence cell on Camp Bondsteel, admitted by guards posted outside the "U.S. only" operations center. One day, as she chatted with the commanding general's political adviser, a tall, tight-haired captain began yelling at the adviser.

"Tell her it's U.S. only! U.S. only!"

Drita and the diplomat froze. She wore an American flag on the shoulder of her uniform, just like the captain did. She sat next to the general in his meetings. This guy must be kidding. She was ashamed of her harasser and, oddly, of herself. She bolted out, followed by the adviser, who was offering profuse apologies. "I don't fucking understand this!" she yelled. "I walk the minefields just like they do. I see the mass graves just like they do. I'm a fucking American!"

Chapter Fourteen

ELLERBE'S 82ND AIRBORNE DIVISION

★ ★ ★ ★

THE IDENTITY CRISIS AFFLICTING THE ARMY SKIPPED Lt. Col. Michael Ellerbe. While the Army's suffocating bureaucracy and clunky infrastructure paralyzed many young officers, Ellerbe, by contrast, was light, quick, and confident. He roamed Kosovo with his 9 mm pistol tucked into the chest plate of his Ranger body armor instead of latched in a shoulder holster like most soldiers.

Commander of the 3rd Battalion, 504th Parachute Infantry Regiment, Ellerbe was one of the Army's most experienced rising stars. The son of a Green Beret, he was pure patriot, broad shouldered, lean, and relentlessly optimistic, with the widest smile in the division. "He's a great American," was a favored Ellerbe expression, obligatory when he spoke of anyone he'd consider a friend or confidant. His deep, reassuring voice insisted that all disagreements could be resolved, that everything would work out fine. Young lieutenants and captains sought him out as a mentor and became devoted to him as they would a big, protective brother. "The Army will do the right thing," he often told his men when it seemed to them it might not. "The system will work."

Ellerbe grew up in the tough-edged Southern culture that still whiffs through the air around Fort Bragg, the enormous 200-square-mile Army post near Fayetteville, N.C., home to the 82nd Airborne Division. The town used to call its seedy side "Fayette-nam" before most of the strip joints, liquor stores, and discount gun merchants gave way to shopping malls and fast-food chains.

A West Point graduate, Ellerbe was commissioned in the infantry, qualified for Army Special Forces, and became a 7th SFG team leader. He taught close-quarters combat and counternarcotics tactics to officers from Latin America. He jumped into Honduras in the mid-1980s to show support for the contras in Nicaragua. He worked in the 3rd Army's operations cell in Riyadh, Saudi Arabia, during the Gulf War. One month after joining the 10th Mountain Division, he found himself as the operations officer for the infantry task force in Somalia. The next year, he was off to Haiti as the chief of operations. These deployments taught him to be comfortable in the chaos of angry, jeering crowds. He discovered the difference between frustrated, hungry people venting loudly and a real threat of violence from organized armies operating in the shadows.

Reading reports from the 82nd Airborne unit that preceded his into Kosovo, Ellerbe knew it would be nothing like the Gulf War. He figured it would be more like Haiti. God forbid it might be like Somalia, where he had nearly died in an ambush.*

---

* On October 3, 1993, Major Ellerbe, the S3, or operations officer, was at the Army's Somalia task force's university compound when word came that two Black Hawk helicopters, piloted by CWO Clifton Wolcott and CWO Mike Durant, had been shot down by Somali gunmen under the command of Mohamed Farah Aidid. Over an hour later, Lt. Col. Bill David, commander of the Quick Reaction Force of the 10th Mountain Division, took his Charlie Company, including Ellerbe, and a convoy of 100 vehicles to Durant's crash site. They were ambushed along the way, taking fire in front and from both sides. At one point Ellerbe's unit left its vehicles and ran to the sides of the road to shoot back. Bullets from second- and third-story windows flew at them, Ellerbe recalled. After regrouping at the airfield and picking up another company and some heavier armor from the Malaysians and the Pakistanis, they tried again. This time they came under attack from 82 mm mortars. Ellerbe was riding with David as he watched mortars explode around him. "It was like the Fourth of July," he recalled. One round landed beside a Humvee, throwing soldiers out the back and to the ground. He had only a 9 mm pistol, no doors on his Humvee, and only a tarp roof. Both companies eventually made it to the two crash sites at nearly 2 A.M. For three and a half hours they worked with the Rangers and Delta Force operators to stave off Somali militias and free Wolcott's remains (Durant had survived his crash and was taken hostage by the Somalis). They left when the sun came up. On the way back, they were again besieged. This time,

The main lesson he took from Somalia was "don't get any troops killed because they're untrained or unprepared. Prepare them for the worst. If you don't do that, you've failed as a commander." He had two missions in Kosovo: "Protect the force and create a safe and secure environment. If you don't create a safe and secure environment, nobody's going to kill you for that," he knew. "But if you lose large numbers of Americans, then you have a problem." But he had taken another, competing lesson from Somalia: "You can't send American soldiers somewhere and think they will do nothing. Other nations might just soak up UN dollars, but that's not how we raise American soldiers. We make them goal-oriented guys, so when you put them in a place, you've got to give them some focus."

In Kosovo, it would be up to Ellerbe and his six company captains to provide that focus. He might have talked tough about protecting troops, but every cell in his body trusted his commanders to take some risks if they thought it best for the larger mission. He would not second-guess them. He would stand by them and stand up for them and they knew that. That was certainly part of the 82nd's tradition—it was like a family that thought of itself as better than anyone else on the block.

An unofficial set of rules passed around the Fort Bragg barracks said it all: "After the demise of the best Airborne plan, a most terrifying effect occurs on the battlefield. This effect is known as the Rule of the LGOPs (little groups of paratroopers). This is, in its purest form, small groups of pissed-off nineteen-year-old American paratroopers. They are well-trained, armed to the teeth, and lack serious adult supervision. They collectively remember the commander's intent as, "March to the sound of the guns and kill anyone who is not dressed like you."

In the Army's pecking order, the paratroopers of the 82nd Airborne put themselves right near the top, just below the tiny covert Delta Force clan and the special operations commando Rangers—all small, elite units, highly motivated and as gutsy and independent-minded as it is smart to be. "Airborne!" "All the Way!" they call out to one another as

---

a dozen shards of hot shrapnel hit Ellerbe's left inner thigh. When he returned home, Ellerbe, who was awarded a Purple Heart, told his wife, "I thought I was never coming home."

they walk around Fort Bragg, home to the 82nd, one of three divisions that make up the XVIII Airborne Corps. The soldiers train to jump out of airplanes at night with eighty pounds of weaponry and survival gear around their waists. They perfect long marches, live by the unrelenting rules of hardened NCOs, and prepare all year to corner and cower an enemy. The 82nd had parachuted into World War II, kept the peace in Berlin, and invaded Vietnam, the Dominican Republic, Grenada, Honduras, Panama, and Iraq.* Not even God, soldiers repeated at Fort Bragg, could kill an 82nd paratrooper.

New recruits to the division don't start out thinking that way. Command Sgt. Maj. Gary Kalinofski, the 1st Brigade's gravelly voiced senior NCO, made them believe it. In his sparse office one day, he began the indoctrination of half a dozen recruits by putting away his normal bellowing and sounding like he might if he were courting his wife. Out of his pockmarked face came sweet, corny words, designed to give the young men, some of them mere teenagers, the impression that he would be there when they needed him.

"We're grateful and glad you're coming here, alright?" Kalinofski said, with soft, flirtatious eyes. "We've got to break you of all the bad habits, alright? I know what's in your head. You never knew where you'd end up. Well, you are at home now—with your family." The young men focused on the words coming from this father figure. "Never again will you be closer to anybody than you'll be with these people," Kalinofski

---

* After Vietnam, the 82nd deployed to quell civil unrest between a U.S.-installed military junta and leftist rebels in the Dominican Republic in April 1965. They participated in the sloppy 1983 invasion of Grenada, launched to restore order and protect American medical students. In 1988 President Reagan sent two of the 82nd's battalions to Honduras for Golden Pheasant, an operation, posing as an exercise, to scare off the Nicaraguan Sandinista army's advance against a critical supply depot for the U.S.-supported counter-revolutionary rebels who were trying to overthrow the Nicaraguan government. Nine months later, the division jumped into combat for the first time since World War II, for the U.S. invasion of Panama, launched to oust and capture Manuel Noriega, a former U.S. ally and CIA asset. A short seven months later, in August 1990, the 82nd was the first Army unit to deploy to Operation Desert Shield, the massive buildup of force in the Middle East that preceded the 1991 Gulf War. In the subsequent war, it drove north toward the Iraqi town of As Salman as part of the far-right flank of Gen. Norman Schwarz-kopf's "Hail Mary" operation.

told them. "The good news is you're home. The bad news is you'll have a lot more independence than you had before. . . . I don't ever lose a soldier in the woods with me. I don't lose them, alright? I lose them at night, when they're on their own. You go out and drink or do some other things. I don't lose them with me, but in the *environment.*"

The *environment*, the messy civilian world, was a place that would grow more distant and alien as these young men became soldiers. They would grow more conservative and narrow-minded than the people on the streets outside Fort Bragg. Every major study of civilian-military relations in America indicated so. Joining the Army had been voluntary since 1973. These days only 1 percent of Americans signed up. Kalinofski's job demanded that he make recruits feel wanted enough to stay and to re-enlist.

In his office, looking out onto a muddy training field, Kalinofski asked them to sit as close to him as they could. Some sat on the couch. Some knelt on the floor. They all leaned slightly forward, sweating just a little to be in the presence of the big man, daddy-rabbit.

"When you were living with mom and dad," Kalinofski said, leaning forward on his elbows from behind his large desk, "They made choices for you. You're going to have some freedom now. You have to think about that. Maybe you'll meet a girl, we don't do bed checks here. One of the biggest things you have to do is make the right choices. Don't drink and drive."

"Where are you from, son?" he said looking straight at each one. "Where are you from?"

Montana, sergeant major.

Buffalo, sergeant major.

Germany, sergeant major.

Los Angeles, sergeant major.

"Okay, good."

"Respecting others," he continued. "We expect you to act just like you would with one of your relatives at home. Remember that.[*] People

---

[*] Fort Bragg had had some high-profile problems with that. In December 1995, three white soldiers from the 82nd shot and killed two African Americans, Jackie Burden and Michael James, who were out for a walk in Fayetteville. One of the killers kept pamphlets on bomb-making and Hitler in his room. Months of Army

out there know what brigade you're in. As your surrogate father and mother, I'm not going to be real happy if you make the wrong choice."

Kalinofski would push them to run fast, fall hard, and shoot their M-4s with accuracy. His NCOs tried to ensure their uniforms were clean and pressed, that they didn't drink too much too often, and that they never thought about killing themselves or their wives. Before a long weekend, Kalinofski's NCOs would even make certain the turn signals, brakes, and registration tags on their cars were up-to-date and working. He wanted them back Monday morning, ready to go to war.

"It will take you two to three months before you feel like you're part of this team, alright? Here's the bottom line: I would never ask you to do anything I wouldn't do. My sergeants will lead out front."

His eyes stopped on a private in the corner, neck stiff, face pale and pimply and covered with nervous, adolescent stickiness.

"It will be okay, alright?" he whispered.

"Yes, Sergeant Major."

"This is a great brigade. This is a great division. The president of the great United States has our phone number right near his bed. The people of the United States, they know they're safe because of people like you."

Some fifty-five years after they had conducted peacekeeping operations in Berlin, President Clinton was sending the division back to Europe.

* * * *

WHEN HIS BATTALION was assigned to join the 1st Infantry Division's heavy armored tank brigade in Kosovo,[*] Ellerbe had just gotten 400 of his infantry troops ready for a biannual trip to the Army's premier joint training center at Fort Polk, La. His platoons had spent the spring practicing how to find and kill enemy troops in the wooded "St. Mère

---

investigations followed and uncovered efforts by right-wing militias, racist skinheads, and the Ku Klux Klan to recruit from among Fort Bragg's special operations units. Seven percent of the 17,000 soldiers surveyed on post said they knew someone who was probably a member of an extremist group.

* A task force of the 2nd Battalion, 505th Parachute Infantry Regiment, which guarded the Apache helicopters in Tirana, Albania, had come into Kosovo with the Marine Corps in June. The bulk of the 82nd's airborne force, however, did not arrive until mid-September, when Ellerbe deployed with his 3rd Battalion of the 504th PIR.

Eglise" drop zone on Fort Bragg's southern end. (The zone was named after the French town where 82nd paratroopers were massacred by German machine-gun fire as they floated to the ground in the early hours of June 6, 1944.) Each platoon was to defeat a dug-in "enemy," two squads strong, then call in mortars and howitzers, then fight its way out of a series of ambushes and mines.

To prepare his troops for peacekeeping duties, Ellerbe added three and a half weeks of training in close-quarters combat in an urban setting, something he had urged the Army to adopt after his experience in Somalia. Ellerbe's troops had learned to secure a street, enter a building, clear rooms, and detect snipers. They knew how to identify land mines and to load and fight from vehicle convoys.

Getting to Kosovo was not the kind of out-of-the cannon rapid deployment the 82nd Airborne Division advertises. Mechanical problems grounded their contract airliner at Seymour Johnson Air Force Base in Goldsboro, N.C., the first night. The flight was entirely scrapped the second day and the contract cancelled. On the third, a flat tire at the Boston stopover delayed takeoff for Paris, where, at Charles De Gaulle airport, the 800 "All Americans" sat on the tarmac in their Boeing 747 for four hours while flight attendants gamely replayed the cult film *The Matrix* for a second time.

Ellerbe's soldiers were undaunted, though, and ready for combat. For most of the young officers, it was their first mission in the "real world" as they called it, "my Panama."[1]

Soon after he arrived in Kosovo, Ellerbe learned not to count on military "intelligence" to interpret the world around him. Camp Bondsteel bristled with the National Security Agency's listening equipment, which poked up from the off-limits tents draped in camouflage netting. The Army monitored Belgrade and Pristina and was connected in real time to Washington, the CIA, and the European Command's intelligence center in Molesworth, U.K. But the Army couldn't see what was happening down the block. In fact, early on, only one "open source" analyst, a contractor, was assigned to read international newspapers. The Army invested in only a handful of qualified linguists to translate the vibrant local Albanian press.

To keep up on things, Ellerbe walked the muddy, garbage-strewn streets of his half of the American sector nearly every day, talking to Serbs and Albanians. He led town-hall meetings and negotiated the tricky subject of school integration. He quickly abandoned the invisible fence that most troops put around their personal space. If a bunch of Serbs got together to complain on the street and moved close in, that's just the way they do business, he would tell troops and UN police officers who felt threatened in crowds. Ellerbe pushed his captains and lieutenants to be out among the people, too, where he was clearly comfortable and at his best.

Above all, Ellerbe was a relentless optimist who approached problems in a quintessentially American way: if we can be rational, respect the historical grievances of both sides, surely we can move ahead. He offered examples from American history. He talked to Albanians and Serbs about the U.S. civil rights movement, explaining the years of courage, patience, and persistence it took African Americans and whites before they could live together. "Do you know about American history?" he asked at one town meeting, his voice resonating across the town hall in Vitina and slicing into the hours-long list of Serb complaints. "Do you have any idea what people like me had to go through to become part of American society?"[2] He told them about oppression and survival, and about being African American. "Should I hate all white people for what happened?" he asked. "Are you going to hate all Albanians and not move forward? When are you going to reach out to them?"

"See, because he's black, he understands," one elderly Serb whispered into a friend's ear.

To others watching him silently, Ellerbe's empathy toward the Serb minority tipped him into their camp. "I'm a minority, you're a minority, we have a likeness here. He was taking sides," said one of his commanders. Even some observers who agreed with his analysis of Kosovo thought he was too free with his views in front of his soldiers.

"Nobody is going to screw around with my Serbs," one of his lieutenants had been overheard telling visiting VIPs. Ellerbe shared his protectiveness.

"Listen, you'd better be impartial here," one of Ellerbe's commanding generals, Brig. Gen. Ricardo Sanchez, had warned him. "You can't go around saying, 'Nobody's going to screw around with my Serbs.' That's not your mission. Our mission is to be evenhanded. You need to make sure you don't fall into that trap."

* * * *

AFTER THE KOSOVO WAR, Yugoslav president Slobodan Milosevic and his military chiefs had forbade Serbs still living as minorities in Albanian communities to work with Albanians or to mingle with them in governing bodies. As for Albanians, many former KLA rebels joined the Albanian underground, which morphed into organized groups, including the UN-sanctioned TMK (the Kosovo Protection Corps), a so-called disaster relief group, and the outlawed MRP (Ministry of Public Order), a shadow police organization. The MRP fought its competitors with violence. At stake was governing power and a huge black-market economy.

By the summer of 1999, military leaders, the UN, and political leaders who sent American troops into Kosovo had had five years to understand some essentials: the hatred dividing ethnic groups in the Balkans was financed and organized by Mafia-like networks. These malefactors believed a multiethnic state threatened their grip on power. But Ellerbe and his soldiers would realize this only slowly, by connecting the dots. Ellerbe's baptism of fire, as those around him described it, came two weeks after he arrived on September 28.

On that day, violence lurked throughout Kosovo. Two rifle grenades fired into the Serb village market of Bresja killed two middle-aged men and a fifty-four-year-old woman, and injured forty-seven others. Miles away a young Albanian girl was killed after she picked up a land mine. Serb teachers Marko Stojanovic and Paun Zivkovic were only a sentence at the bottom of the news stories filed that day.

The two men and a woman colleague had returned to their Technical School in Albanian-dominated Urosevac to retrieve paperwork needed by Serb students to continue their education in nearby Strpce, a Serb enclave. The educators asked the Polish KFOR troops in charge of Strpce to escort them back to their high school and to a nearby cemetery, where one of the teachers' sons was buried.

Half a dozen Polish troops drove the teachers to Urosevac, where the Albanian principal of the school, a man they had worked with and trusted, let them in. Stojanovic and Zivkovic thought it would take a while to locate the proper records. They told the troops to leave them for an hour or so. Moments after the soldiers left, the principal made a telephone call; soon a black BMW appeared. From evidence pieced together later, it seemed to be the same BMW that Ellerbe's soldiers had often seen at MRP headquarters in Urosevac.

The teachers were gone when the Polish troops returned.

The kidnapping enraged Ellerbe, who saw it as a direct affront to KFOR. His headquarters sat a mere 300 meters away. "They were thumbing their noses at us, saying, 'We run this place, you don't.'" The next day, he ordered troops to search the MRP's Urosevac headquarters. In three hours they came up with only a couple of weapons and some old KLA uniforms. Ellerbe also paid a visit to Bendri Zqriri, the Albanian operations officer for the Urosevac area, to ask for help. "You know who did this," he told Zqriri, whom he respected as a straight shooter. "This is your chance to show us. . . ." Zqriri promised to cooperate and Ellerbe left hopeful.

He then drove to Strpce, fifteen miles south, to talk to the two kidnapped teachers' families. Abutting the magnificent Sar Planina Mountains, Strpce's lush green pastures swept up to purple and blue peaks. Haystacks out of a Van Gogh painting dotted the valley in the fall. But the landscape had proven a prison for the Serbs of Strpce, who were trapped by Albanians at the mouth of the valley. The families were deeply depressed and blamed KFOR for the teachers' disappearance. "You're the United States of America. You own this town," one of their wives told Ellerbe. "How could this happen? Why can't you protect our fathers?"

It was a question Ellerbe was already asking himself. He vowed to find those responsible. But first he and his small entourage—two interpreters, a security detail, an intelligence officer, and an officer from the Army Criminal Investigations Division—had to get through the crude roadblock of logs, tractors, and people. A crowd had gathered outside, along the main road, while Ellerbe was talking to the families. "The people of Strpce are tired of being ignored," a red-headed Serb schoolteacher told him. Zivkovic's daughters were more insistent. It was inexcusable that KFOR could not protect their father.

"But if you don't let me out, we can't do this investigation," Ellerbe insisted, as he was surrounded by the crowd. He was shocked to see so many Serbs. In fact, the Serb population of Strpce had more than doubled, to 14,000, since the war ended. Most were displaced from other villages. "We're here to help you," he explained to them. "We'll try to resolve this crime." But they continued to shout and push.

"It's not my job to fight you," he yelled over the noise. "I don't want to have to bust through the barricade." But the din continued.

He and his team sat down by the side of the road, leaning up against a house wall as two military police officers (MPs) stood guard. They would just wait the crowd out. But when one of the investigative agents snapped a photograph of the crowd, a Serb man jumped on top of the Army vehicle to stop him. Then the man grabbed the gunner's radio antenna and started to hit the gunner with it. Ellerbe bolted up, drew his Beretta pistol from his flak jacket, and thought to himself, "I'm going to fire two shots in the air and the next shot, I'm shooting whoever's on the vehicle."

He fired.

All hell broke loose.

"Shots fired!" Capt. T. J. Sheehan's radio crackled as he patrolled Urosevac. "Unruly crowd. RTO not with colonel," meaning the radio operator had gotten separated from Ellerbe and didn't know exactly what was happening.

"Why is he firing?" someone in the crowd asked. "Why is he firing?" They seemed surprised, even offended.

"I'm not here to kill you, but if you put your hands on one of my soldiers, I *will* kill you," Ellerbe insisted in a calm, but loud voice. "*Nisam dashao da vas ubijem,*" shouted Mia, his tiny Serbian-language translator, whose face was barely visible under the smallest Army helmet. She did her best to bark out Ellerbe's words in his commanding cadence as she stood by his side.

"Well, you don't have to shoot!" one of the protest leaders admonished. "Why are you taking pictures?" They assumed the U.S. military, like the Yugoslav army occupying Kosovo before them, wanted pictures to identify and arrest people. The Albanians hated the people of

Strpce, a place where Serb paramilitary units had lived during the war. Some sixty Serbs from Strpce already had been kidnapped since KFOR arrived. "Give us the film!" one shouted. "Give us the film!"

"No problem, I'll give you the film," Ellerbe replied.

"Give it to us—now!" one demanded.

"I can't give it to you now, there are other pictures on it that we need."

Finally, one of the murdered teachers' wives came down the hill to calm the crowd, which gradually dispersed. The roadblock was removed and Ellerbe and his team left. Hardly a victory, but it could have been worse.

Finding the kidnapped teachers and taking care of their families became Ellerbe's personal crusade. He returned the next day, with the developed pictures for the Serbs, and almost every day after that for several months. He ordered U.S. troops to escort the Strpce Serbs to Urosevac for shopping and to visit family. His soldiers helped them gather information about their Urosevac homes, many of which had

Lt. Col. Michael Ellerbe stopped by to chat with Lubica Stankovic, center, and her
Serb neighbor. They were among the twenty-four Serbs left
in Urosevac after ethnic Albanians returned to Kosovo when the 1999
air war ended.   LUCIAN PERKINS–©2002, THE WASHINGTON POST.

REPRINTED WITH PERMISSION.

been illegally occupied by Albanians. It was Ellerbe's way of showing the Albanians that he would not be cowed, that he was in charge. They had kidnapped three Serbs who dared enter their town; he would make sure a lot more Serbs came to Urosevac.

Ellerbe also set up an information center with the Polish military and hired two of the children of the kidnap victims to work there as translators. He talked the staff at Camp Bondsteel into holding nightly strategy sessions on the kidnapping. They assessed the validity of snitches and other intelligence their soldiers were gathering. "I've got to act on this thing," Ellerbe often said.

The officers stuck at Camp Bondsteel, who watched Ellerbe at these meetings and at their daily Tactical Operations Center briefings, were impressed with his zeal. "A lot of times, we tend to get overcome by inertia, not knowing what the law was going to be in Kosovo," said Maj. David Pierson, a military intelligence officer who had spirited debates with Ellerbe over strategy. "We become more concerned with keeping the immediate peace in the area than with solving any long-term issues. He was more focused on looking further down the road and getting things done."

But finding the teachers and their kidnappers went nowhere. The deputy commander at Bondsteel, Col. Steven Hicks, asked Ellerbe to back off a bit, and he did. He was upsetting the Poles, who "owned" Strpce because it fell in their tiny sector. But Hicks, like everyone else, knew "if anything was going to get done, it was done by the military." The UN police force was a mere 135 people scattered throughout the entire province; only a handful worked in Urosevac. "There was really no help from them."

Brig. Gen. Craig Peterson, the U.S. commander who succeeded Craddock, believed Ellerbe to be a great battalion commander—smart, articulate, and aggressive. Peterson appreciated Ellerbe's desire for action.

Peterson had been deployed three times on Bosnia peacekeeping trips.[*] He had designed a "mug book" of Bosnia's crooks that he carried around in his dark-green Army footlocker. He used the Army's own

---

[*] An infantry officer, Peterson had served as the 1st Armored Division's chief of staff when it had gone to Bosnia for the third time.

template: in secure vaults at the U.S. European Command headquarters at Patch Barracks in Germany, Army military intelligence officers had catalogued every bit of the Yugoslavs' Soviet-built equipment and the behavior of Yugoslav units. When electronic surveillance spotted a certain number of tanks and troop carriers, the model could predict that fifteen miles down the road there would be a column of troops. In the same way, Peterson tried to model the organized political crime networks that the UN, Interpol, the CIA, and military intelligence knew existed in Kosovo.

Peterson's intelligence staff put together a mug book for each village in the American sector. It looked like a police blotter, with page after page of names and pictures of political leaders, factory owners, former KLA members, police chiefs, and even, occasionally, someone simply listed as "murderer." Every day at 8 A.M., Peterson's staff would grade each crime incident that had occurred in the American sector—bombings, grenade attacks, property extortion, assaults, murders—and fit them into what Peterson called a "connect-the-dots matrix." It was good, old-fashioned detective work—not exactly the Army's specialty, but at least someone was trying to see the larger picture.

Ellerbe was doing the same thing from Devils' Den, his battalion command post in Urosevac. The soldiers had gotten lucky with two batches of documents they had seized. Under the floorboard of a Mercedes Benz driven by Beqir Krasniqi,* they found documents listing the names of over eighty members of the Policia Ushtarake (PU), the military police for the KLA guerrillas. The now-outlawed KLA had merely continued operations by moving into the TMK building in Urosevac, Ellerbe believed. Krasniqi was no ordinary document smuggler though, KFOR knew him as the intelligence chief for former KLA leader Hashim Thaci. This connection linked the outlawed PU to the KLA leadership, which had agreed to disband when the UN moved into Kosovo.

Another raid on the Urosevac municipal building's finance office

---

* Krasniqi at the time was deputy commander of the ZKZ, the MRP's intelligence arm, according to KFOR intelligence officers.

turned up boxes of records tying the MRP to a self-appointed "commission" in charge of evictions, illegal taxation, and other operations illegal under the UN rules governing Kosovo.[*] Ellerbe had been right: part of the outlawed KLA had simply morphed into the MRP and its intelligence apparatus, the ZKZ. Many of the same individuals had appointed themselves to seats of power in the *obstinas* (counties) and intimidated, threatened, assaulted—and sometimes allegedly killed—anyone who questioned their rule.

Ellerbe was connecting the dots, as Peterson had hoped. Ellerbe's intelligence shop drew up a "blood chart" to help the soldiers keep track of all the local players. It began not with enemy tanks and artillery pieces, as their Army model did, but with the troublemakers. It listed them by name and association and included links to other known "enemies." This became known at Devil's Den as the "asshole list." One by one, as the "assholes" were arrested or sent out of town, someone would slash a big red "X" through his silhouette.

Ellerbe also posted an "incident map" similar to the city street maps used at police headquarters to plot the locations of various crimes. To measure their success, "you have to have a marker on the wall," a comparison point, Ellerbe told his soldiers. They chose something thoroughly familiar and American: crime statistics from an American town with black-versus-white gang violence. They picked Gastonia, a North Carolina mega-retail center of 66,000 people. It did not occur to them that crime in their wedge of Kosovo and crime in Gastonia were totally incomparable.

Gastonia's police force came from the community and included black and white officers who could infiltrate gangs and recruit snitches. Ellerbe's unit couldn't infiltrate anything; no one spoke Albanian. The Gastonia police could draw on the FBI's decades-old gang task force for information, but in Kosovo, Ellerbe's lieutenants were on their own. The UN, which ran the interim Kosovo government, had not yet written new criminal statutes. There was no independent court system to try wrongdoers, no penal system to hold anybody for long.

---

[*] Ellerbe's briefing chart, under "Threat Organizations: Albanians," listed one "Commission for Evidence of Social and Private Property," among others.

Still, Ellerbe's S2 (his intelligence officer) worked up a "linkage chart" for the underground hierarchy. Now that they were beginning to connect the dots, Ellerbe needed to reorient his soldiers, to sharpen their mission, and a top priority was to shake up the corrupt structures, especially the shadowy MRP. How else to give the moderates a chance?

He drew up a "Specified Task List," a road map each of his company commanders could use to organize the daily activities of their squads and platoons. Specific Task 1 was "Force protection"—a defense plan for Ellerbe's headquarters. It would include four-troop foot patrols, two-vehicle convoys, and a plan to "transition to war" and station quick-reaction forces in case of hostage-taking.

Specific Task 2 was broader: "Establish a safe and secure environment." Under "methods," it called for observation posts at churches, ethnically segregated schools, foot patrols, house searches, curfews, KFOR security on weekly market days, and a series of traffic checkpoints. Under "end state," it noted that the task would be achieved when there was "no ethnic violence," a "crime level comparable to Gastonia, N.C.," and "gangs broken; leaders incarcerated."

Ellerbe's "favorite task," he told a colonel he worked with, was Specified Task 7A.[3] "This was the task that got us closer to a safe and secure environment." He defined it like this:

The task: Identify and neutralize UCK/TMK splinter groups.

The method: Strikes on UCK splinter groups, removing individuals from positions of authority who associated with splinter groups, discrediting those not promoting the legitimacy of the United Nations civil authority and KFOR.

The end state: UCK splinter groups combat ineffective; leaders incarcerated and unable to influence the populace or removed from positions of authority.

General Wesley Clark, five layers of command above, had been delivering this sort of tough talk in Bosnia for years, and in Kosovo for months. Ellerbe's chain of command seemed impressed too. They put his unit on every VIP tour. Senior civilian and military officials trooped through, as did members of Congress. Most of them heard about his plans for the MRP and other splinter groups.* They nodded approvingly.

Specific Task 7A got Ellerbe's lieutenants stirred up as well. Finally, something they could bite into, a call to arms, in the peacekeeping context at least. Ellerbe made it clear to them that he would not need to know every little step they took. He had given them a mission. They understood that KFOR's rules of engagement would serve as their limits. He would support their judgment calls. He trusted that when they had questions, they would ask him for guidance.

At headquarters, Brigadier General Peterson directed his battalions to survey "suspected MRP stationed in the sector" for the purpose of cracking down on the MRP.[4] But the crackdown never happened in his short, six-month stay. On December 15, 1999, Brig. Gen. Ricardo Sanchez took over from Peterson. A rough-looking but even-tempered straight-shooter, Sanchez had spent nearly five years in the 82nd.

When Ellerbe briefed Sanchez on his task list at his Urosevac operations center, Sanchez looked pleased. It was just what he had in mind. He turned to Ellerbe, leaned forward a bit, and offered one caveat: "I think you should classify that one," he said. Don't give away the game plan. Ellerbe thought that was a good idea too. He would move forward, encouraged by Sanchez's enthusiasm.

---

*As did XVIII Airborne Corps commander Gen. Dan McNeill, whose visit would become crucial later, when Ellerbe's actions came under question.

Chapter Fifteen

VITINA AND THE NEW MAFIA

★ ★ ★ ★

B Y THE FALL, THE ETHNICALLY MIXED TOWN OF VITINA in the southern part of the American sector had become the battleground for the future control of Kosovo: would KFOR and the UN civil administration govern, or would the violent, separatist, Albanian underground rule from below?

Brig. Gen. John Craddock, the first U.S. commander on the ground, had sent an early warning about Vitina to his bosses. Four Albanians "wearing similar pendants" around their necks had robbed an Albanian family. The pendants "may indicate the introduction of an organized crime element in Vitina. We must quickly identify and stop activity of this nature."[1]

Lying south of the Kosovo capital of Pristina, along Macedonia's border, Vitina hugged the Black Mountains of Skopje along a centuries-old smuggling route used by the KLA during the 1999 war to bring in supplies and reinforcements. Vitina was the first village on the Kosovo side of the border and the starting point of a paved road leading to Pristina and branching out to other parts of the province. After the war, KFOR commanders believed some large-scale violence and arson in Vitina was a feint planned by smuggling groups to divert KFOR's attention from convoys moving contraband through town.

Nearly three-quarters of the 50,000 people who had lived in the Vitina *obstina*, or county, in the 1980s were Albanians. Eight percent were Croats. During the 1990s, however, Serbs had become a 70 percent majority in the city, and they alone held political power.

Unlike most of the province of Kosovo, after the war seven villages in the Vitina *obstina* remained ethnically mixed, as did the drab city of Vitina itself. By the time the NATO bombing ended, the Serb majority in the city had been reversed: the population was now 80 percent Albanian. Right after the war, Albanians in the PPDK (Party for Democratic Progress in Kosovo), the political party created by former KLA leader Hashim Thaci, took control of most public works in Vitina, as they did throughout Kosovo. The UN Mission in Kosovo (UNMIK), which was supposed to run things, finally sent one representative to Vitina in August 1999, two months after the war ended.

Vitina's economic depression was profound and wretched. Horse-drawn wagons, scraggly chickens, barefoot children, and black-clothed old ladies clogged its dirt roads. Only about 10 percent of the workforce in Vitina had jobs. Most small businesses were owned and operated by Kosovar Albanians. Despite the preoccupations of poverty, the Albanians still found time to burn as many Serb homes after the war as the Serbs had torched during the war.[2]

To douse Vitina's flames, Ellerbe put Capt. Kevin Lambert and his Alpha Gators in charge of the city and surrounding towns. Ellerbe considered Lambert the most dynamic of all his company commanders. Physical, domineering, cocky, and a terrific soldier, Lambert looked like a close-cropped Tom Cruise and had a movie-star codename, "Mad Dog 6." Lambert had been to Haiti with the 10th Mountain Division and had caught Ellerbe's eye then. After Lambert's stint with the 3rd Ranger Battalion, Ellerbe had worked the phones hard to get Lambert back to the 82nd and assigned as one of his company commanders.

Like Ellerbe, whom he idolized, Lambert strutted around his slice of Kosovo with his Beretta close to his heart in a black-leather pistol holster secured across his back with duct tape. And, like Ellerbe, Lambert saw the MRP as behind the arson, kidnapping, bombing, extortion, and murder in Vitina.

By the time Lambert arrived in Kosovo in mid-September 1999, the MRP, unknown to KFOR, had established its own shadow police department in Vitina. MRP members patrolled the streets in pairs, wearing black pants and blue shirts. They followed American soldiers surreptitiously, watching where they went, whom they spoke to, what they said at public meetings. They carried MRP identity cards and had legitimacy within their community. They kept detailed property ownership lists and an incident log, just like the soldiers kept. They collected taxes and protection money.

The Alpha Company operations center, nicknamed "Gator Base," had been the headquarters of the brutal Serb special police, the MUP, who specialized in torturing Albanians and their Serb sympathizers. Lambert bunked in the former MUP interrogation room off the main entrance. There he installed a chin-up bar and stomach-crunching machine facing a large black flag with a familiar Ranger slogan: "Run with the best, die like the rest."

In the spring and summer, the soldiers liked to put detainees in the garages at the side of the building, what they called the "dog pound." They fed prisoners Army-issued rations and gave them blankets to sleep on. In the cold, snowy winter months, they kept prisoners in unheated basement rooms.

In no time Lambert had identified the rival Albanian power base and its enforcers and developed a general suspicion of other Albanians. He also quickly charmed Vitina's Serbs. He breezed through town each day on his daily patrols, shaking hands with Serb leaders, promising help to Serb church officials, chatting with Serb shopkeepers dressed in checked and flowered prints. He was mayor, police chief, judge, and jury. The Serbs welcomed him into their homes, shared feasts and holidays.

The clash between his military bearing and his peacekeeping duty manifested itself as nervous energy when Lambert had to sit through town-hall meetings with disgruntled Albanians and Serbs. At these meetings he could safely take off his flak jacket and helmet and try to look relaxed, but there was nothing relaxed about him. His knees bounced as the minutes ticked by, and he chomped hard and loud on his gum and clicked his pen or tapped it on his wedding ring. These meetings were tedious, nothing like the exercises he had excelled at: seizing a fictitious Central American airstrip, close quarters, urban combat, target practice with an M-4 carbine aimed at the face of a terrorist.

Capt. Kevin Lambert, commander of the Alpha Company, 3rd Battalion, 504th PIR, based in Vitina, listens to Serbs at a town-hall meeting in Vitina. LUCIAN PERKINS–©2002, THE *WASHINGTON POST.* REPRINTED WITH PERMISSION.

Meeting with Albanian leaders in an elementary school in Pozaranje, just outside Vitina, Lambert read from a list on three-by-five cards. Hunting season is cancelled. Downtown traffic has improved since KFOR banned unlicensed street vendors. "I want receipts showing how the new market taxes are being spent. Bring them next time. I need tips on the suicides last week of two teenage girls found hanging from trees."

Halfway through the list, the single light bulb overhead flickered out. They continued by candlelight, six Albanians, all dressed in black jackets and complaining about how Lambert's soldiers had jostled Albanian teachers who had stood in line the week before to collect UN stipends. They were just trying to bring order to the unruly line, Lambert explained. "This was the first time, and the first time is always painful," he said, cracking his knuckles. "We will try to do better next time. I am sorry."

But it was not the first time, or the last, that Lambert's soldiers had been rough with Vitina's residents. Some troops were demanding and abrupt at traffic checkpoints. They frisked people roughly and momentarily blinded them with the bright lights mounted atop their M-4 assault rifles. They made people lie down on the ground, even when the ground was frozen.[3] They forcibly evicted Albanian families from Serb homes, sometimes abandoning young children and their parents to the cold streets. Some soldiers roamed freely into stores and homes following rumors of illegal caches of weapons and ammunition.[4]

The soldiers saw themselves as an equalizing force, trying to restore rights to the remaining Serb minority while fighting a new, unarmed, civilian "enemy." They tried to stop the unofficial Albanian "authorities" from cutting power to milling plants when Serbs brought grain in. They convinced UNMIK not to force schools to desegregate, because they believed the Albanians would intimidate Serb children into leaving school altogether. They sent informers into the market-place to see if merchants were charging inflated prices to Serb custom-ers. They shut down stores that refused Serb business. Every day they escorted Serb children to school, and every week they took families to Serbia proper or to Macedonia to shop or visit relatives.

The troops often could not distinguish real threats from symbolic gestures of pride. On Albanian Flag Day, for instance, the soldiers detained a group of people who had been carrying Albanian flags banned because the flag symbolized support for KLA rebels who wanted an independent Kosovo. The soldiers made the women and children in one group lie down on the ground for half an hour, accord-ing to a KFOR interpreter at the scene. "Tell them to let us go home with our children," a woman pleaded.

Some KFOR soldiers who were not part of Lambert's company thought his men "were out for a fight,"[5] as one civil affairs team chief, a major, put it. Others thought they were just more proactive. "Their attitude and mannerism reminds me of the Marine Corps, which is noticeably different from the typical Army support units that I work with on Camp Bondsteel," said a Marine Corps captain who was part of the national intelligence unit at Bondsteel. Sometimes it was simply a matter of training and discipline. Stuck in a traffic jam once, a group of soldiers grew tired of waiting and a private first class yelled out, "Traffic control! Go Red!"—then fired a warning shot into the air.[6]

Lambert acted as if he owned Vitina and was suspicious of all "outsiders," even members of other Army units.[7] His soldiers were to question whomever they saw in town, even other American soldiers not in his company. NATO had asked the Italian carabinieri to form a province-wide detective force called the MSU (Multinational Specialized Unit) to track organized crime. The carabinieri made a particular splash in Kosovo with their swashbuckling ways, dark glasses, and movie-like SWAT uniforms. Lambert considered them a nuisance: "Hey, what are these knuckleheads doing in Vitina?" he complained to headquarters. "I don't know what they're doing."

Organized crime might have seemed like just a local problem to the lieutenants in Lambert's company, but its shipping routes and supply networks spread throughout the Balkans, into Europe, and across Russia. At a heavily guarded military compound in Pristina, a dozen carabinieri tracked its transnational links from inside a secret wood-floored tent, the intelligence cell for the MSU.

Col. Leonardo Leso headed the first group of MSU detectives to move into Kosovo. A veteran of the crime wars in Bosnia, the debonair Leso had exhibited remarkable patience as he watched the flow of drugs, money, weapons, and black-market cigarettes grow beneath his feet. "We can't strike," he said. "We have to convince the population to cut the links. The military deterrence is just not large enough."

Flow charts of extended ethnic Albanian families and their holdings covered the walls of Leso's intelligence cell. Some of these families operated in Italy. That the distribution and financial channels for terrorism and organized crime were the same was already apparent to Leso. A black market for diamonds and gems. International money laundering structures. Opium and cocaine. Illegal guns, explosives, even nuclear material—it all flowed through the same, untraceable, transnational spider webs.

The carabinieri knew the Americans disdained their flamboyant ways. The Italians sported dark glasses even on cloudy days. Most grew goatees or slick mustaches. They drank, flirted, and carried lots of weapons. Most of them didn't speak much English, which really ticked off the Americans—who, of course, didn't speak Italian. Not even crime, corruption, and terrorism could trump the ingrained tendency to act alone, as one nation, with narrowly defined national interests.

Neither group would tell the other what it was doing. But bouncing around the narrow, unpaved back streets of Vitina with the carabinieri, it wasn't hard to figure out. "There are new mosques all over," said one senior carabinieri officer along on the ride. "We want to know where they are collecting the money. . . . did you see the new minaret in Vitina?" Indeed there was a new, shiny gold one. "The Albanians are bringing cells of mujahideen here from various countries. I am investigating four or five groups. They are totally independent of one another."

American military intelligence had picked this up too, but at the time they didn't seem as convinced about its meaning, or as urgent about stopping it, as the Italians. Why wasn't the Army sharing intelligence? Why didn't the carabinieri work closer with KFOR soldiers? Trying to answer these questions, the Italian began to sputter and swing his arms. "The Americans are little boys with big weapons and they absolutely don't share information. We don't either," he said angrily, turning up his nose. "The big bullshit is, in ten years, this place will be full of terrorists. And they will put bombs in the New York subway."

When it came to sharing information, even U.S. Army units worked at cross-purposes in Kosovo. Lambert and Army intelligence butted heads often. The "field humint [human intelligence] teams" were Army Special Forces soldiers charged with gathering information on possible threats to U.S. soldiers. They cultivated members of the MRP, drank coffee at local cafés with them, and eventually recruited them to spy on another UN-condoned organization, the TMK.

But the MRP was also behind most of the crime in Vitina. "The humint teams had become so closely tied to the MRP that they could no longer see the forest for the trees," Ellerbe told his commander. "We have targeted the MRP, and they are cultivating the MRP and legitimizing the MRP."[8]

Lambert's company held its ground. He had once put a man named Gyner Kamberi, aka "Rambo," in jail. A skilled sniper with KLA credentials, Kamberi had approached Lambert early on: "After the war, the Albanians appointed me chief of police for Vitina."

"Well, guess what," Lambert shot back. "You're not the chief of police. And if I see you doing any law enforcement, I'm going to arrest you."

Several weeks later, Lambert's soldiers learned that Kamberi had weapons at home. Lambert's men conducted a search and found a sniper rifle, then brought Kamberi to Gator Base for arrest.

"I need to see my CI buddies," Kamberi insisted. When the U.S. counterintelligence officers showed up, they urged Lambert to release him.

"He's going to Bondsteel. Period," Lambert responded. "He has illegal weapons. If he has a problem, he can take it up with higher headquarters."

Not a week later, Brig. Gen. Ricardo Sanchez visited Vitina. When he saw Lambert, he scolded him. "Did you know you arrested a guy we were developing a relationship with?"

"Yes sir, I did."

"And you arrested him anyway? Why did you do that?"

"I called my battalion commander and he approved it," Lambert responded.

"You have to understand," Sanchez warned, "these things are very sensitive. . . . We're sending mixed signals."

"Roger, sir."

In fact, in the winter of 1999 there were fierce debates within KFOR over whether to legitimize the MRP. French, German, Italian, and British officials, with the support of some intelligence officers at Camp Bondsteel, believed legitimizing the organization was the best way to co-opt its members into the new interim government. "Federalize them," the thought went, just like the U.S. government had federalized the Alabama National Guard in 1963.

Ellerbe argued forcefully against MRP recognition, and he prevailed.

Lambert's best gumshoes were two platoon leaders, Lt. Sam Donnelly and Lt. John Serafini. They created "thug books" on their laptop computers, which they slung over their shoulders like weapons. They snapped digital photos of suspected troublemakers and described each crime scene. In addition to supervising foot patrols, Donnelly and Serafini often spent eighteen hours a day piecing together a crime puzzle they knew was right in front of them.

At the age of twenty-four, "Sammy" Donnelly was a Virginian who idolized Robert E. Lee. "Just below God," he would say. Since the age of five, he had wanted to follow in Lee's footsteps. With dreamy blue eyes and a broad smile, Donnelly, a 1997 West Point graduate, had turned his drive to excel as an airborne infantry officer into an obsession with taking down "the bad guys" in his new town, Vitina.

Behind him by one year at West Point was John Serafini, recipient of a Superintendent's Award for Excellence. The product of a liberal prep-school education and Boston upbringing, he boxed on the academy's team. One week after he landed at Fort Bragg, the newly minted second lieutenant was shipped to Kosovo. In Vitina, he replaced an older, iron-fisted platoon leader, a former NCO who had gone home. Filling those boots was not easy. Some soldiers thought Serafini was a bit of a bully who was trying too hard to prove he was in charge. "I want to show who the main guy in the town is," Serafini told an interpreter who had questioned his habit of knocking snowballs out of kids' hands.[9] But Ellerbe and Lambert had a lot of confidence in Serafini. "John Serafini is an officer who does not know how not to succeed," was how Ellerbe described him.

The lieutenants' determination jived with Sanchez's own aspirations for his Kosovo mission. Getting rid of the MRP in the American sector had become his top priority by the winter of 2000.[10] Sanchez sent 50 percent of his command's humint to Vitina because he believed it to be the center of gravity for former KLA rebels clinging to power.

Sanchez had plans of a higher magnitude, though. He had established a "future operations shop," modeled after the Army cell that works on war plans. In a newly constructed, top-secret "tin building" on Bondsteel's securest ground, planners put together schemes against the MRP and other splinter groups that were much more aggressive than any of Lambert's soldiers could imagine. One, code named Gold Star, called for the sequential arrest of half a dozen major figures in Vitina—those with gold stars next to their names. The goal was to make it appear as if KFOR had a high-level snitch.

But Sanchez was judicious. Before he put a plan in place, he required officers to have evidence that would stand up in an American court—a legal standard higher than the one set by the UN. He wanted the soldiers to identify alleged wrongdoers. Then Sanchez would dispatch agents from the understaffed Criminal Investigation Division for formal investigations. The "targeting" of individuals, and their arrest, would be done with his approval, he told his battalion commanders and staff. The soldiers weren't cops. They weren't trained to interrogate suspects. To his proactive airborne division, he counseled "tactical patience." In fact, Sanchez was so patient that few of his plans were ever executed.

But the forty-eight-year-old general had twenty-somethings on the ground who picked up the wounded every week and who watched people cry over relatives shot on the street in broad daylight. They were not patient and Vitina was their battle, their war. Donnelly and Serafini believed they were making progress.

They had clues and patterns. On November 30, a store purchased by an Albanian from a Serb was destroyed by two anti-tank mines taped back to back and attached to a detonation device rigged with a time fuse. Three days later, four adjoining businesses recently purchased from a Serb by Albanians blew up. The blasts hurled brick, glass, and pieces of a metal gate 150 feet. The explosive was two taped-up anti-tank mines.

That afternoon, Donnelly ordered his platoon to canvas businesses and homes in the area. He wanted a list of owners and the names of the people they had bought the property from. His troops also searched the MRP headquarters and confiscated a log of significant activities in town, just like the one he was keeping. "This was the first time that we made an open gesture to the UCK* regarding their involvement," Serafini typed on his computer that night.

Informants had told the two lieutenants what was really happening: the MRP was hitting Albanians who had bought homes or businesses from Serbs without paying a commission to the MRP. The MRP wanted to control all real estate transactions in Vitina, not only to make money, but to control Vitina's ethnic and political makeup.

More double anti-tank mines exploded over the next few days. The buildings fit the pattern too. They were formerly Serb owned, recently purchased by Albanians. On December 20, Mejdi Sidriu, a

---

* Lieutenants and others used the initials MRP and UCK (the Albanian acronym for the KLA) interchangeably.

frail fifty-year-old whom the UN had asked to sit as a judge on the new court, was gunned down in the middle of a busy street during the day. Donnelly raced to the scene, but, as usual, no one came forward with information. The next morning, Donnelly went to Sidriu's son's tiny one-room store to discuss suspects. Scores of men wearing white Muslim caps sat on mats along the walls, mourning. Some had been crying. The elder shook Donnelly's hand and motioned for him to speak.

"This is a terrible thing," Donnelly began. "This is what it's like when we don't live in peace. This kind of stuff is what we're here to stop, and we're going to have more of it unless someone talks to me and let's me know what's going on." The Albanians folded their hands in their laps and nodded. But all they gave him was silence, then tea.

As Donnelly was leaving, one of Sidriu's relatives whispered for him to come back to his house later. "I have some things to tell you," he said. Donnelly returned to Gator Base, picked up his team, went to the chow hall, then headed back out onto "Main Street" to patrol. It was cold and snowing lightly. As they turned the first corner, a man stumbled into the troops and fell to the ground.

"What's wrong?" Donnelly asked. He bent down and felt the man's clothes, which were wet with blood. "My father is down the street. He's shot. He's worse."

"We have a casualty! Gunshot wound!" Donnelly called on his radio. "Main Street. About 150 yards down from South Gate. Call for medevac!"

Donnelly left the wounded man with the MPs and bolted down the street as fast as he could. As he ran, forty pounds of equipment rattled and his helmet scooted back and forth on his head. "Gator Base! Gator Base!" he yelled into his radio. "Correction. Make that two victims, both gunshot wounds."

As he ran down the block, he heard the familiar sirens of two red UN Toyota 4-runners. They had parked hastily in the street. Good, he thought. But the eight UN police officers were just standing around, looking at the man, whose name was Jahja Azemi, as he lay on the ground, holding his left leg and babbling.

Donnelly was furious. Why weren't the UN police doing anything? He knelt down next to Azemi, who looked pale and was obviously sinking into shock. "Give me a coat!" he shouted to the police officers. "Come on! Give up your coat!" He put the coat under Azemi and ran his hands over the leg to find a wound. But Donnelly could not find the entry point so he took out his pocket knife and began cutting Azemi's pants leg from the cuff, carefully working his way up. He'd never done anything like this before. He could feel his own heart throbbing.

So much blood. It's his femoral artery, a UN cop declared. The femoral artery runs up. . . . He reached behind the man's testicles, gripped what he thought was the artery, and squeezed as hard as he could. "Hold on," he told Azemi. "Come on, hold on! Tell me something." Azemi mumbled unintelligibly. "Squeeze my hand. Squeeze my hand. You'll be alright."

Blood soaked through to Donnelly's own leg and tinted his body armor. Azemi blurted out a word in a panicked voice. A gulp of a word. Then another gulp. And then he went limp.

Twenty long minutes later, Donnelly helped lift Azemi's body into an Army ambulance, then ran him on a stretcher to a waiting Black Hawk medevac helicopter. Donnelly wasn't sure when, exactly, Azemi had died, but he knew he had. He threw down his helmet in anger. He was angry at Vitina. Angry at the assassins and at the witnesses who wouldn't help him. He was angry at the ghosts he kept chasing, night after night.

"You'd better be careful," his platoon sergeant warned him when he got back to Gator Base. "You're going to start to take it personally. You'll starting driving real hard. Just remember, don't take it personally."

As he roared back to the crime scene, Donnelly thought, someone's got to know something. By the time he returned, a name was buzzing through the crowd. Donnelly's interpreter recognized it as that of a man who had been seen earlier with a teenager now sitting in Gator Base's jail for an unrelated crime. At the jail, Donnelly burst into the cell and began yelling at the boy. "Who was the man you were with?"

He said he didn't know his name. "You've got to be kidding. You hang out with him and you don't know his name?" Donnelly was in no mood to play games, so he slapped the teenager, Donnelly recalled. "Who was it?" Still no answer. He slapped him again. "Tell me who that was."

He finally extracted the name of a man who lived in nearby Kabas. Donnelly took his squad and went there immediately. The troops recognized the house; they had taken down an Albanian flag flying outside of it. A KLA war hero's face had been painted on the side wall. Now his soldiers burst through the front door, rifles drawn, and spread out into the room.

To their surprise, the living room was packed with men seated along the walls. It was the Muslim month of Ramadan, when the devout fast from sunrise to sunset, and it was nearly time to end the day's fast. Women worked at the sink; a couple of kids played at their feet. The Albanians froze. Donnelly motioned to get the women and children out. He was still furious; his ready stance showed it.

"Look at my uniform! You can see it's soaked with blood. It's the blood of one of your countrymen! One of your own Albanians! And that's a bunch of crap! Someone in this room shot him. I know it and you know it. Tell me now because I'm in no mood to be fooled with!"

"I did it." The oldest man in the room raised his hand.

"Where's the weapon?"

The old man walked over to the counter and pulled open a drawer. A pistol lay inside. Donnelly raised it to his nose, smelling freshly burned gunpowder. His interpreter moved toward him and whispered, "This is the father. He's going to take the fall."

Right. Let's arrest all fourteen of them, Donnelly said. "You are all under arrest," he said and hauled them off to Gator Base. After questioning by UN police, five of the fourteen remained in custody. Azemi's shooter had confessed.

"L.T., good job," the head UN cop told Donnelly.

Gator Base had no running water, so Donnelly changed his uniform and washed his hands with cleansing foam. It was nearly 2 A.M., so he headed over to the murdered judge's relative's house. There the man sat for hours looking at photos Donnelly had on his computer, telling Donnelly who was an MRP member, who was just a KLA fighter.

"How do I stop this?" Donnelly asked him. He gave Donnelly the name of another Albanian who had been a high-ranking police official in Vitina under Serb rule. "He's next. If you don't watch him, he'll be dead in a couple of days." Donnelly was not sure how the judge's relative knew all of these things, but he trusted the man to tell the truth. Donnelly left at 5 A.M.

The next day he visited the former Albanian police official, who reminded Donnelly of his own father-in-law. The man was fat, with silvery gray hair and dancing, almost merry, crystal-blue eyes. He looked like Santa Claus and sat on a huge red fur couch that filled one entire room of his two-room house.

Donnelly or Serafini visited Santa Claus often over the next weeks, each time prying out a little more information.

Ellerbe was about to "shake things up," as he often described his goal to the soldiers. He had heard the story of Zitinje, of how the Albanians had chased the Serbs away, despite KFOR's warnings. Many of Zitinje's Serbs had relocated in Vitina. Ellerbe would not let that be the final word. Two days after Christmas the Zitinje Serbs decided to return home for a look. Ellerbe, thinking there would be a "massacre" if they were to return alone, sent his soldiers as escorts. They drew up a plan, isolated Zitinje, and led them into the village.

Zitinje was a graveyard of blackened bricks, once the walls of homes. Clothes and furniture were scattered about. There were no animals. As Serb families walked quietly up the hill, their shoes crunched on window glass and broken dishes. They whispered to themselves and shook their heads, and cried softly. Then they returned to their tractors and cars and bumped back to Vitina in the company of their burly protectors. A dozen men, burdened by the fresh memory of their destroyed village, gathered at a popular Serb café in the center of Vitina. Outside, it was raining and drab.

As the Serbs sat and drank, a young man in light-blue jeans, a black hat, and a short jacket came to the café door and threw in a concussion grenade. It rolled on the floor a few feet, then exploded. Ten Serbs were injured. The Americans would not have the last say. The Zitinje sojourn would not go unanswered.

Serafini ran to the scene with Sgt. Adam Gitlin. Someone in the crowd at the café sent Serafini to Sam's Pizzeria, an MRP hangout. Find Lulzim Ukshini, they told Serafini. He's the mastermind. Ukshini was one of the men in Serafini's computer file.

As usual, the tables at Sam's were filled with young men in dark clothes talking under a haze of cigarette smoke. On the walls hung huge, colorful portraits of ethnic Albanian war heroes posing in the grassy mountains where they had survived years of ruthless Serbian repression. Alpha Company felt sure plots were hatched here, messages passed, debts paid. Serafini cleared the restaurant of everyone except Ukshini.

Gitlin pushed Ukshini up against the wall and punched him. He buckled over into the fetal position on his knees. Then Gitlin dragged him to a back corner and held him against a wall. Serafini's translator said he watched as Gitlin choked him until he passed out. The translator poured water on Ukshini's face to revive him.

Serafini drew his knife, a Gerber with a six-inch, diamond-cut blade, black handle, and silver butt. He sat Ukshini at a table and threw the blade into the tabletop, the translator recalled. But Ukshini refused to confess and soon Serafini released him.[11] Another dead end.

That night, Serafini typed his notes: "Appears most likely to be a retaliatory strike against the Serbs directly for their return to Zitinje," he wrote. "This is certainly the most brash attack yet, as there was a great deal of KFOR presence within 100 meters of the site when it was attacked."

Finding murderers and arsonists was not Serafini's only problem. Some of his own soldiers were spinning out of control. As a platoon leader, he was responsible for four squads. Serafini's platoon sergeant, the NCO who would be expected to ride herd on the troops, was also new to the unit. Trying to shake off the stigma of being a new shavetail, Serafini found himself deferring to his weapons squad leader, a charismatic, physically imposing staff sergeant named Frank Ronghi.

Older and divorced, Ronghi seemed worldly to the young soldiers. He was as powerfully built as anyone in the squad. He boxed. He could do 400-pound squats and lift 300 pounds. He liked to look at himself in the mirror. He liked the Army, which he had joined in 1988, serving in the elite Berlin Brigade with follow-on deployments to the Persian Gulf and to Haiti.

The Army liked Ronghi too. By 1999, the thirty-five-year-old from a "good Catholic family" in Niles, Ohio, had made staff sergeant. As weapons squad leader in Alpha Company, he led about a dozen soldiers. In reality, he held sway over many more. He was usually in a good mood, singing as he patrolled. Ronghi's officers found him obsequious. He cut their hair, ran errands for them. They trusted him with money. He was their yes-man.

But within his squad, he played the tough. Ronghi regaled his soldiers with stories of his Mafia connections and how he had raped two young sisters in Haiti. He called himself "Nymphoman."[12] The girls of Kosovo "were getting to him," he told another soldier. It would be easy to get away with murder here, he said; he could just blame it on the Serbs.[13]

Ronghi and some members of his weapons squad became the neighborhood bullies. They sparred with local toughs but also pushed around people who just happened to step in their path, especially on market day. U.S. soldiers patrolled market day every week. Their commanders thought their presence would give the Serbs courage to venture out into a sea of Albanians, but it rarely did.

January 6 was a typical market day. Truckloads of purplish-greenish cabbage sat at the curbs next to buckets of potatoes and rows of sadly stacked tin cups and plastic bowls. Ronghi's squad was assigned to patrol that day. With a light snow covering the ground and occasional frozen patches, the street was slippery. Like a band of rough adolescent dogs, Ronghi's troops shoved themselves into boys and young men, knocking them to the ground and punching them in the shoulders, ribs, and groin.

An NCO head-butted men in the nose with his helmet. The jostling revved up the soldiers. They walked down the street shoulder-to-shoulder, blowing whistles as loudly as they could and knocking over anyone in their way. The soldiers grabbed teenage girls, pulling them to their chests and tugging at their jackets and shirts. "Give me a kiss," one specialist would say, and cursed them when they tugged away.[14]

"What are you people doing?" some of the Albanian men grumbled. The soldiers punched and handcuffed men who complained. One father who attempted to intervene was slapped in the face and punched in the ribs. "You're KFOR! You should be protecting us," another man spat out after he watched Ronghi grab women's rear ends.

"Hey, we're not as bad as the Serbs," Ronghi replied, then instructed a soldier to flexicuff the complainer and threaten jail.

An old deaf mute selling matches in the street was walloped on the head with a baton Ronghi carried with him. "I'm sick of Albanians," Ronghi said. "They are stupid, stubborn people. I'm tired of dealing with them."[15] But the deaf mute was outraged and gave Ronghi the finger. He was handcuffed and searched before being released on the street. He immediately went to Gator Base's front gate to complain. A crowd gathered, growing bigger and more agitated by the minute. Ronghi and his squad got worried, cleared their weapons, and retreated to the command post.

When Ronghi's superiors heard complaints, sometimes taken from newspaper accounts, they did not take them seriously. Instead, they believed the criticism was meant to make them back off their investigations. Other soldiers thought the hitting and harassing just wasn't a big deal: "I don't think there was anything wrong with the way we acted," Sgt. Brian Gaines later told Army officers. "It's too tense of a situation over in Vitina. I think our actions made us feel more relaxed. We were doing these things as a laughter thing, it wasn't psychopathic. The times that we grabbed these females, it was not like we were physically grabbing them, it was like we were just touching them by their clothes." As for the deaf mute, he explained, "We weren't, like, breaking-bones rough, but . . . I wasn't trying to make it easy on him."[16]

Ronghi warned his squad members to be tight-lipped about their actions. "What happens in this squad stays in this squad," was his favorite line, "or your body will never be found."

Two days after market day, on January 8, Serafini and Donnelly had the names of two suspects, brothers, in the grenade attack on the Zitinje Serbs at the café. At 11 P.M. one night Serafini and Ronghi drove the two brothers to an abandoned warehouse in nearby Klokat—a building the Serb paramilitary forces had used to torture and kill Albanians before the war.[17]

When Serafini, Ronghi, and Serafini's platoon sergeant, SSgt. William Langham, entered the building, they took off their heavy flak jackets, helmets, and webbing belts and laid them in a pile against the wall. Ronghi stripped from his waist up. "Hey Frank, what are you doing? You'll get cold." Serafini said.

"This is how we do it back home," he responded.

The soldiers cut off the brothers' flexicuffs with a Gerber knife, separated the men by fifteen feet and ordered each to stand about two inches from the wall, facing it. Then Serafini moved from man to man, questioning them. So did Ronghi. Who blew up the bar? "I don't know," the first brother insisted. "I am only trying to make money to feed my family. I have documents saying I am mentally sick. I don't do these kind of things."

Ronghi swung his muscular arm toward the man, punching him twice in the stomach. He doubled over and dropped to the cold, concrete floor. When the second brother turned his head to watch, Langham slapped him in the back. Serafini ordered Langham to punch him in the stomach. "Don't hit him," the first man pleaded. "He was shot. He has only one kidney."

Langham, a blond, athletically built paratrooper, ordered the man to take off his shirt so they could see the wound. And there it was, a large scar, ten inches long across his right side. A dense mound of flesh sat where the bullet had entered.

"I am studying in Pristina," the second brother said. "I come to Vitina only to visit my family once a month. I am not the guy you are looking for."

Hit him, Serafini ordered. Langham punched him in the stomach. Then Langham took him into an adjoining room and made him lean over a desk. "I don't know anything. Don't beat me anymore. I am a sick man," he pleaded. Serafini lost it. He grabbed his M-4 from the other room, took out the magazine, and cleared the weapon. Then he hustled back, put the barrel of the gun to the back of the second brother's head and said angrily, "Do you want to die?"

"You can kill me, but I don't know anything," the man said. "I'm only trying to make a life for myself."

Serafini turned to his interpreter. "I'm beginning to hate these people and I will find out who is doing these bombings and shootings even if I am the last person to stay here."

Meanwhile, Ronghi worked over the first brother. "Is it worth it not seeing your brother again? Just give us the truth." That didn't work, so he tried a different tack: "We know you are poor and we can give you firewood and food, just tell us who is doing all of this."

"We'll try to find out the information you want, tomorrow," he said.

"We can deal with that," Ronghi said, then he walked into the other room.

"Please, don't beat me anymore," the second brother pleaded.

"I'll let you go," Ronghi replied, "but you'd better find out some information in twenty-four hours or I will pick you up tomorrow and it will be worse." Ronghi put his clothes back on. "See how easy this can be for you," he said. The troops drove the brothers to a bus stop.[18]

The next day, January 9, Donnelly visited his silver-haired informant. He thought the Albanian underground must be feeling the heat. Some had started to complain about rough treatment by American soldiers. He and his commander, Captain Lambert, brushed that off as an indication that Donnelly was making progress, that the troops were making the thugs feel uncomfortable and unwanted. Now he pushed the old man for more information.

"You know, the real decisions are not made in the MRP headquarters," the old man told Donnelly. "They are made in the Drenica Café. Did you know the café is owned by Xhavit Hasani, a war hero?" Hasani was part of the "Macedonia mafia," a financier of the KLA during the war, the man said. He traffics in weapons and is wanted by Macedonian authorities for the attempted murder of three policemen.

Donnelly could not believe his luck. "He's a hero, huh? The big daddy? If I get rid of him, do I get rid of some of the problems?" he asked the old man. "Here's our big break. After all these witness-less investigations, you're telling me we got a guy wanted for the murder of three Macedonian policemen who's on the loose. If I go after this guy, I can shake things up a little bit."

Donnelly radioed for his squad and Serafini to meet him at the café. He found two of Vitina's well-known Albanian strongmen there. One was Daut Xhemajl, president of the hard-line ethnic Albanian PDK (previously the PPDK). KFOR intelligence believed the party had strong links to organized crime. Sitting with Xhemajl was Skender Habibi, vice president of the PDK, the "most outspoken radical leader in Vitina" and "considered to be involved in most if not all criminal activity in the sector," according to an Army intelligence rap sheet.[19]

Serafini knew the café well. Formerly a gathering place for Serb politicians—a "White House" in Serafini's word—the café had been given by the KLA to Hasani as a war trophy. The Albanians had renamed it, too, although U.S. soldiers still did not understand that "Drenica" was the turning point that had led the international community to support a war to liberate Kosovo.*

★ ★ ★ ★

AMERICAN PARATROOPERS, in fact, had no sense of how hellish life had been for Kosovar Albanians during Serbian rule. They didn't understand that in Vitina, Serb police checkpoints had sprouted up. Serb paramilitary units, police, and army troops raped, tortured, and murdered the townspeople. No one was allowed to sell food to an Albanian. Bread bakeries shut down when an Albanian walked in the door. Some twenty Vitina civilians and another twenty-three members of the KLA had been killed in the months preceding the war.[20] For every Kosovar Albanian brutalized in Vitina a hundred others in the province were tormented by Serb paramilitary thugs and their informants. Some of those informants were Kosovar Albanians, just like Donnelly's merry-eyed, silver-haired friend.

"Where's Hasani?" Donnelly demanded, speaking to Hasani's son behind the bar.

"I don't know," he shrugged.

---

* On February 27, 1998, Serbian special police forces and the Yugoslav army, desperate to stop the spreading rebellion among Kosovar Albanians, descended on the Drenica region of Kosovo with armored units and helicopter gunships, killing villagers and rebels alike. On March 5, they closed in on the infamous Jashari clan, leaders in the local KLA unit. Artillery pounded the walls of the Albanians' homes, and when they fled, snipers picked them off. In all, Serb forces massacred fifty-eight people, including dozens of women and children, some while they were trying to surrender. Human Rights Watch, which investigated the Drenica massacre, concluded that it was "a turning point in the Kosovo crisis," sparking greater internal support for the KLA and heightened international involvement. Self-defense militias sprung up in villages. The United States withdrew diplomatic concessions and leaked warnings about the KLA's larger plans. The war crimes court at the Hague—the International Criminal Tribunal for the Former Yugoslavia—subsequently declared jurisdiction over violations of humanitarian law in Kosovo.

"You don't know where your father is?"

"I haven't seen him in three days."

"You haven't seen your own father in three days? Right," he smirked. "Let me see the paperwork that says you own this café."

The son pretended to look around. "I can't find it."

"Then I'm going to close you down until you can show me the paperwork. Everyone out."

"Sam, what are you doing?" his interpreter whispered.

"You too Habibi. Move."

"No, I'm not getting up."

"Then I'll arrest you." Donnelly called his two biggest soldiers in. They lifted up Habibi. He wrestled himself away from their grip and walked out with them.

"I'll open you back up when you find the paperwork or if your father shows up at Gator Base. Right now, you're closed until further notice."

A small crowd had gathered outside the Drenica Café by the time Donnelly locked its front door. At Gator Base a few blocks away, several dozen people milled around near the front steps. The crowd quickly grew to several hundred.

"Sam, what the heck are we doing?" Lambert asked Donnelly when he got back.

"I closed Drenica."

"What? This is not a good idea," Lambert shot back. "We've got to get this crowd to disperse. This could be a potential risk to the soldiers. This is why you run things by the chain of command. Go reopen it."

"Sir, that's not a real good idea. It will show them I'm not in charge. Sir, that's going to make me look weak. Sir, we've got a big criminal here." He told him about Hasani's connections, his big break. "I guarantee you, he will show up. Let's just wait a bit."

"Nope. Go reopen the café. Now."

"Yes, sir."

Donnelly marched out, shouldering his way passed the crowds coming to join the protesters. As he got to the café, his radio crackled. "Hasani's at the front gate," Serafini reported from Gator Base. "And hey Sammy, Baftjari's here too." Heset Baftjari was known to the troops as a chief troublemaker and an associate of Hasani's.

"Well, scoop him up," Donnelly said as he unlocked the café door then headed immediately back to base.

This time Donnelly brought a Serb-speaking translator to question Baftjari, a little "psychological harassment" he thought would undo him. When Donnelly and Serafini didn't get any useful answers, Donnelly stuck a chem-light, a glowing plastic tube the size of a toothbrush, in Baftjari's ears and nose. Donnelly tapped Baftjari's knees with a hammer. Baftjari laughed. Donnelly felt ridiculous.

Hey, my friend Serafini, he's a good fighter, Donnelly said. Serafini gave the air a couple of karate chops. He grabbed Baftjari by the throat and held him against the wall. Still nothing.

By now, hundreds of Albanians were outside Gator Base. They weren't making much noise, just sort of milling around. But it unnerved the soldiers, who were unraveling a bundle of concertina wire and using it to sweep the crowd back from headquarters.

"Get the fuck out of here!" a soldier yelled as they plowed through the crowd. "Shut the fuck up!" screamed another. Troops began pulling out young men and searching them roughly. Soldiers atop an Army vehicle leveled their M-4s.

"Drenica! Drenica!" the protesters sang out. It was a tentative chant, typical of people who hadn't been allowed to protest for years.

The UN police, also headquartered at Gator Base, were supposed to be in charge of arrests and protests, but they never really were. Hasani was arrested and transferred to Camp Bondsteel's jail. "You got a big fish," a UN police officer told Lambert. The "catch" was much bigger than he could have imagined.

A Macedonian Albanian, Hasani was a founding member of the KLA and had achieved the status of a war hero in a land where war legends are the currency of kings. Before the war, he had turned his native village of Tanusevci, near the Kosovo border, into a logistics base and refuge for Albanian fighters. In 1999, he became a major source of the KLA financing and arms and was appointed a local KLA commander in Vitina. (In the winter of 2000, he would help finance the incursion by rebels into Serbia's Presevo Valley. By 2001 he would become a major figure in the ethnic Albanian insurgency in Macedonia. The United States was trying desperately to stop that insurgency without having to send American troops into yet another Balkans hot spot.)

Two days later, the local Albanian newspaper alleged that some soldiers were beating up Albanians and favoring local Serbs. The Klokat incident was cited, as were the incidents on market day. Ellerbe and Lambert thought the claims were part of an orchestrated campaign to pressure KFOR to release Hasani and to stop the company's investigations. "The Albanians see Hasani as one of their war heroes, one of their leaders," Lambert would later tell investigators, "and when we arrested him, we took away some of their power. . . . I chalk most of it up to propaganda."

Ellerbe asked Lambert to question his men. Lambert's troops told him Ronghi had hit someone on market day, but only in response to the man's pushing one of the soldiers. Lambert also got a watered-down version of the Klokat incident. One of the soldiers said Langham had grabbed a guy by his shirt, but that was it. Within a day, though, Serafini had come clean.

Lambert took pride in his company's actions. So did Ellerbe. What the soldiers had done "maybe was a little rash, a little quick," Ellerbe would muse later, but "didn't they get the right guy? Is he wanted in Macedonia? Yes. That's the balance. Maybe we should have done it in a different way, but you've got the guy off the street. This is a good day."

KFOR troops had sent a message all right. But at the time, they had no clue what it really was.

Chapter Sixteen

DISHONORING MERITA

* * * *

I N THE WINTER OF 2000, THE SHABIU FAMILY SAW VITINA as a refuge. Made homeless by the Serbs and by NATO bombs, the Shabius had fled their meager village of Debelde, near the Macedonian border. Ethnic Albanians, they had come to Vitina looking for an abandoned Serb home to occupy. They found one across the street from a five-story, ethnically mixed, yellow-cement apartment building, which happened to be the epicenter of violence in the city.

On January 13, two weeks after the family settled in Vitina—and just four days after the Hasani protests at Gator Base—Hamid Shabiu's daughter, Merita, went to meet friends who lived across the street in the cold yellow-cement apartments. At 9:30 A.M. she left her house wearing a dirty beige parka, red long-sleeved sweater, and blue jeans that bagged at the knees. On her wrist was a small, green cloth bracelet in the shape of a frog, a zippered pouch that held money for trips to the market.

As she walked up the apartment house's grimy concrete stairs, she ran into the inflated figure of SSgt. Frank Ronghi, with all his camouflage, armor, webbing, and weaponry. Ronghi had told his squad that he was going to check on a couple of families in the building who were mixed up in the unending confrontations there. He had been up on the third floor, working his way down, knocking on doors, looking for something. He went alone, contrary to the Army's standard operating procedures. Pfc. Michael Stegemoller, manning a nearby traffic post outside, had seen him walk into the building.

Merita liked and trusted the American soldiers. She knew they had saved the Kosovar Albanians. She was happy they had come to Kosovo to protect her now.¹ With a short, pixie haircut parted in the middle and kept off her round face with four plastic barrettes, she looked like a typical American girl. She tried to learn a little English.

As Ronghi walked down the staircase, three young boys ran past him, bolting out the glass doors leading to the parking lot. Ronghi's radio crackled. It was about 10:00 A.M., and Gator Base was calling: "Wolverine 4! Wolverine 4!" He turned the radio off without responding to his code name.

Merita was about eight feet from the door leading to the parking lot when Ronghi stopped her. He pulled her inside one of the storage rooms in the basement, behind metal doors and broken glass panes. The cement walls and floor were painted white but smudged dirty brown. He undid his belt and his camouflage pants fell down. He tore off Merita's clothes and he forced himself on her. As they struggled, she was scraped and bloodied by the rough floor and by Ronghi's tough hands.

When she continued to try to escape, Ronghi grabbed her, put his hand over her mouth, and told her to be quiet. But she kept talking, so he put her small neck in a tight brace, so tight in fact that he lifted her off the ground. When he released his grip, Merita crumpled to the floor, falling forward. "Her chin hit straight down on the ground, making a noise similar to the sound of a bone breaking," he would recall later. Her jaw was broken and her face bleeding. But still she made little gurgling noises. "So I put my left foot on the back of her neck," he recalled. He balanced himself with an arm against the back wall and the other on an overhead water pipe. "I pushed down with all my weight—and stood there."

Merita, only eleven-years old, died under his black combat boot. A sole-shaped bruise appeared on her back.

Ronghi rushed around the basement, looking for something to put her in. He found a couple of white sandbags in a room down the hall, stuffed Merita into them, and put her underneath the stairwell. He tried to soak up a blood spot in the room with some lime powder he had found and to cover it up with a couple of jars of red peppers stored there for the winter. He must not have noticed that her black tennis

Eleven-year-old Merita Shabiu stands with a U.S. Army soldier and two friends
near the apartment building where SSgt. Frank Ronghi murdered her.   U.S. ARMY

shoes had fallen off and so had her barrettes, or that a thirteen-year-old boy was looking down through the stairwell, wondering what in the world a big soldier was doing spreading white powder all around.

Ronghi hurried up the half-flight of stairs, made a left turn, walked out the door, and "returned to his normal patrolling," as he called it.

It was about 10:30 A.M. and Gen. Hugh Shelton, the chairman of the Joint Chiefs of Staff, had come all the way from Washington to Vitina for a troop-morale visit. The rest of Ronghi's company was on alert, securing roads for their VIP and gathering at Gator Base to meet with him.

At around 12:30 P.M., Ronghi, walking alone, ran into Pfc. Stegemoller and a translator, Mo, both sitting in a Humvee. Ronghi got into the front seat, put his hands on the steering wheel, and stared straight ahead.

"What's up?" one of the men asked him.

"Hey, don't start no rumor," Ronghi snapped back.

Gator Base called Ronghi on the radio. Be prepared to help block streets for Shelton's visit. This was his chance to hide the body, Ronghi thought.[2]

"I heard you were missing, were you getting your mack on?" Stegemoller asked Ronghi, using his unit's slang for having sex with women. Ronghi regularly sneaked away from his squad to have sex with a Bosnian-Croat woman with dark eyes and reddish hair whom he had nicknamed "Yugoslavia."[3]

Ronghi told the soldiers he had to take the vehicle to help with Shelton's security. He told Stegemoller to come with him, and they drove back to the yellow apartment building's parking lot. When they neared the parking lot, Ronghi ordered Stegemoller to duck. "Black ops," Ronghi explained. Bringing firewood to a Serb. "Cool," answered Stegemoller.

Ronghi got out of the vehicle, went into the apartment building, and came out carrying the bundle with Merita's body. Stegemoller felt it clunk in the back of the vehicle.

A little girl and boy walked by. Another young girl standing on a balcony above waved down to the soldiers. Stegemoller waved back from the turret. "Hel-lo!" she called out.

Ronghi raced the Humvee out of the parking lot and down the street. Mud and snowy slush splashed up into Stegemoller's face. People and cars moved to the side of the road to avoid being hit. Gator Base called on the radio and ordered Ronghi to an intersection to stop traffic for Shelton.

"Roger," Ronghi replied. But instead, he drove out of town, up a wooded road toward a little hill leading to an old monastery. There, he jumped out of the Humvee's cab and started looking around frantically.

"You got a body in there or what?" Stegemoller joked. "If I was going to hide something, I would put it up where people would not be inclined to walk, rather than down, where people do walk."

"Yeah, you're right, good point," replied Ronghi.

He walked around the side of the Humvee and up the snow-covered embankment, pushing aside the thick scrub brush. A few seconds later, he walked back out of the bushes, toward the vehicle.

"Hey, there's a thorn sticking out of your left cheek," Stegemoller told him.

"Yeah, good," he said, oblivious to the prick, which he plucked out.

"I killed somebody and it was an accident," Ronghi blurted out.

"Cool," Stegemoller replied. What a jokester, he thought.

Stegemoller untangled his legs from the turret seat and hopped down. They walked to the back of the Humvee and Ronghi opened the back hatch. The shape was unmistakable and there was a spot of blood on the bag.

Stegemoller recoiled. "Come on, hurry up," Ronghi pressed.

Together they pulled the bunch of white woven plastic sacks from the back. Stegemoller could feel Merita's head. They carried her up the embankment just below the brush line. It was an awkward climb and at one point they dragged her by the legs. Blood rushed out of the bundle, turning the snow a yellowish-red.

The sight of so much blood weakened Stegemoller. He kicked snow over the spots as they dragged her up further, deeper into the woods and then into a ditch. Stegemoller kicked snow over her head.

"Good work," Ronghi told him. "You've done this before." Stegemoller didn't answer. They walked quickly back down to the Humvee and sped back to town.

"We make a good team," said Ronghi, chatty as they drove back to Vitina.

"Yeah," Stegemoller responded obligatorily.

"You are the brains, and I am the brawn."

Ronghi gabbed on about having Mafia connections and about having committed other crimes elsewhere. "It's easy to get away with things in the Third World. . . . I was living out a fantasy. . . . All I need is a good snow."

About an hour had passed since they had last had radio contact with other soldiers.

"Where've you been?" asked the first soldier they saw from their unit.

"Stuck," said Stegemoller.[4]

Ellerbe's paratroopers looked forward to a shot of support from Shelton, whose salty mouth and Southern drawl reminded them of home. Shelton was not a fan of these inconclusive peacekeeping missions. He told the soldiers that the Pentagon was working on a plan to bring them home. One senior NCO asked Shelton if the Army would write a training manual to help soldiers figure out peacekeeping. "Our forces are fully prepared for peacekeeping operations," Shelton replied. If you are trained and ready to fight a war, the transition to peacekeeping just isn't that hard.[5] Some of the soldiers listening knew Shelton didn't understand their challenges in Kosovo. If only he could walk Vitina's streets with them, maybe then he would understand.

Lambert and Donnelly thought Shelton's visit significant. The Pentagon, thousands of miles away, must have been impressed with what the soldiers were doing in Vitina. Isn't that why Shelton, Gen. Wesley Clark, and members of Congress came to Vitina? The troops took it as a compliment.

Ronghi and Stegemoller, driving back to Vitina, heard Shelton's chopper lift off.

By bedtime, Stegemoller could no longer keep the secret. He found his squad leader, Sgt. Christopher Rice. "Can I talk to you in private?" he whispered. They went outside.

"Can I trust you?" Stegemoller asked. "Can I really trust you?"

"Yes, but will it cost someone's life?" Rice queried.

"It already has," he answered, then told Rice what had happened.

Rice found his platoon sergeant, Staff Sergeant Langham, who told Stegemoller to take them to the spot where they had put the body. They wanted to make sure this wasn't a prank. Walking through the snow at night, the soldiers saw a mound of snow. Langham began rubbing the snow away and found a can. Good, he thought, maybe this is a joke after all and there's just trash under here. But then his hand touched Merita's foot and he saw what looked like a dark blue sock. "Oh my God, please don't let that be a sock," Langham said.[6] They moved closer. "Oh, my God, it's a foot."

Merita lay in a fetal position. He could see her skin through the bag. They left the body, rushed down the hill, and drove back to Gator Base. Ronghi was asleep on his cot. "Frank, we need to talk," he said, shaking his foot.

Ronghi gave them a story about seeing two men take the girl into the apartment building. He found her dead and he panicked. Worried that he would become a suspect, he hid her body in the woods.

"You don't think *I* did it?" he asked Rice.

Lambert was at Gator Base, discussing Albanian claims of abuse by U.S. soldiers, when Langham arrived. "We're getting so close to breaking this thing wide open," Lambert was saying. "Look at this propaganda they're printing about interrogations at the Warlord Base in Klokat." He held up an Albanian-language newspaper. "If we're going to break this thing open like we want to, you've got to be above reproach. They are going to try anything to keep us from making progress . . ."

"Sirs, I need to talk to you," Langham told Serafini and Lambert, who cleared the room.

"There's a little girl . . ." Langham was sobbing like a baby by the time he finished the story. Lambert was dizzy and trembling. He called Ellerbe.

"What do you want me to do? I can put him in my jail cell."

"Do it," Ellerbe replied.

Soldiers guarded Merita's body until the Criminal Investigation Division's forensic experts could arrive. At Camp Bondsteel, it was around 2:30 A.M. when Maj. Brian Heslin, an Army lawyer, was summoned to see the Brig. Gen. Ricardo Sanchez. "What's going on?" asked his tent-mate.

"There's been a murder. I've got to go to the TOC [tactical operations center]."

Drita Perezic was in the TOC when Heslin arrived. "It's a little girl," a member of Sanchez's staff told Drita. "We found the body. We don't know what to do."

Gathered around the table were the chief of staff, a medical officer, the general's political adviser, the lawyer, and Sanchez. "What now, Drita?" Sanchez asked. He was crying. How could one of Merita's saviors become her murderer? It was unfathomable.

Engineers set up a makeshift morgue in a tent. After Merita's body was brought in and laid on the table in preparation for the autopsy, Sanchez visited the tent alone. Walking in, he couldn't help but see his own son lying on the table; he had been only nine months old when he was killed in a traffic accident. The pain had been unbearable then and now he felt it again. He prayed for both of them.

"God bless you," he whispered to Merita.

The next day, Drita and a military police investigator went to the Shabiu house. Drita put her arms around Merita's mother when she told her that her youngest daughter had been found in the forest, dead.

Merita's mother collapsed.

Donnelly was disgusted by the news, then outraged. The unit's reputation will be ruined, he thought. His opponents in Vitina will link the murder to the Klokat and Baftjari beatings. They will use it to stop his investigations. He wanted to get back out on the streets right away.

Over the next several days Ronghi confessed to the murder and was sent to Germany to stand trial.

On January 16, after an Army autopsy, Merita's body was returned to her family. The imam was unable to perform a preburial ritual required by Islam because the body had been disturbed by doctors. The holy man ordered her buried immediately. The family asked several KFOR soldiers to be pallbearers.

After the funeral, the soldiers returned to the Shabiu home for an official mourning ceremony. MRP leaders came to the house, too. One of them was the first to speak, even before the imam. The hierarchy of power was unmistakable to Drita.

"Who did it? Which one did it?" he asked the Americans present. "We believe Lambert had something to do with the crime. If they beat us, they can also kill us."[7] Other MRP members in the room nodded in agreement. They offered stories about Lambert and his unit. They talked about Klokat, about beatings during house searches. The local Albanian newspapers were filled with accusations and denunciations against KFOR.

Sanchez called a meeting of Albanian leaders the following week. He wanted to tell them about Ronghi's arrest and confession, and to express his condolences. Five men came to Gator Base to meet with Sanchez. Among them was Skender Habibi, a former KLA commander and now leader of the PDK in Vitina. Army intelligence had dubbed Habibi "the most outspoken radical leader in Vitina" who "should be considered the primary target for intelligence-gathering." Habibi, one intelligence summary concluded, "is considered to be involved in most if not all the criminal activity in [the] sector"—meaning not just Vitina, but the entire American sector.

Sanchez began the meeting with words of empathy and condolence. "Being a father, I understand the pain of this tragic incident," he said. "We are absolutely committed to treating everyone with dignity and respect."

Habibi spoke up first. "This is God's will," he began. "We can make this all go away for you if you release our compatriot, Mr. Xhavit Hasani."

Ellerbe and Sanchez sat up, recoiling from his words.

"Releasing him," Habibi continued, "would return Vitina to a more stable environment and absolutely nothing will come out of this incident. The family will not blame KFOR."

Sanchez couldn't believe what he was hearing. "Absolutely not," he said. "I will not even contemplate that offer." He ended the meeting.

The demonstrations in support of Hasani intensified. The MRP threatened Hamid Shabiu if he did not denounce the Americans. The UN and "KFOR will leave here one day, [but] we will always be here," one MRP member told him.

The MRP wanted to prove that no other organization, including KFOR, could protect the Kosovar Albanians. Many soldiers had drawn nearly the same conclusion. Certainly Ellerbe and many other soldiers at Bondsteel were feeling the same way. "We created an environment for the Albanians to cleanse the Serbs, and then we said, 'Hey wait a minute, we can't save them,'" said Major Heslin, the lawyer at Bondsteel. "That was the helplessness and frustration that permeated everything."

Meanwhile, the Army launched several investigations. The criminal one focused on Ronghi, who was court-martialed in Wüerzburg, Germany, and sentenced to life in prison without parole. The other inquiry focused, at first, on the platoons in Captain Lambert's company. As the investigation began, Lieutenant Colonel Ellerbe relieved Lieutenants Donnelly and Serafini of their regular duties. No more patrols, no investigations, not even any checkpoint inspections. They were quarantined behind the wire until the investigation ended or they shipped home, whichever came first. "Keep your head up," Ellerbe told Donnelly and Serafini. "The soldiers' morale is going to hinge on your morale. Their opinion is going to hinge on your opinion. You need to stay upbeat and positive." Lambert's Alpha Company was moved to Urosevac. Another company from another division replaced it in Vitina.

Hasani's arrest created a significant crisis for the United States and the UNMIK. Both feared that Hasani's detention would provoke a violent retaliation by Albanian rebels against KFOR troops throughout the province. After several weeks, Brigadier General Sanchez wanted to release Hasani because he could find no legal reason to hold him. The Macedonians could not produce a document showing that Hasani was a suspect in any crime. Neither Kosovo, nor the UN, which was its government, had extradition treaties with Macedonia anyway.

UNMIK officials begged Sanchez to keep Hasani until they could transport him to Macedonia. The officials believed the symbolism of releasing him, of such an obvious KFOR retreat, would show the rebels and other Albanian splinter groups the shallowness of NATO's sway over Kosovo.

* * * *

THE UN'S FEEBLE CONTROL of Kosovo's political dynamics and KFOR's paper-thin understanding of what was really going on were being revealed all across Kosovo. In the rusting mining city of Mitrovica, where the 82nd Airborne Division was about to suffer its last stand, KFOR's mandate and authority had almost entirely vanished.

Mitrovica, eighteen miles south of the Serbian border, was in fact the real border between Serbia and Kosovo. Before Slobodan Milosevic's ethnic-cleansing campaign, Mitrovica had been dominated by ethnic Albanians, except for a Serb enclave in the southern part of the city. Kosovo's oldest Albanian mosque had stood in Mitrovica until Serb forces blew it up and bulldozed the rubble.

After the war, a tidal wave of Serb refugees from other parts of the province had pushed nearly 10,000 ethnic Albanians out of their Mitrovica homes. Those Albanians that the Serbs could not run off, they tried to kill or scare to the southern side of Mitrovica's muddy Ibar River, which divides the city.

As the NATO nations divided up Kosovo for peacekeeping duty, Mitrovica fell to the French. This was lucky for the Serbs, who had deep historical affinities with the French dating back to World War I. French troops had disregarded the UN mandate to create a multiethnic province. The French minister of defense, Hubert Vedrine, told U.S. officials he would not support multiethnicity in Kosovo. Instead, France was content to rule over a bifurcated city in a bifurcated province, just as it had in Beirut in the early 1980s when it enforced the Green Line dividing Christians and Muslims. It was just easier—and maybe more realistic—to do it that way.

Mitrovica's new Serbs took this as a sign of French sympathy, and emboldened by it, they used the peacekeepers' first winter to intensify efforts at ridding the area of Albanians. On February 3, 2000, five ethnic Albanians died at the hands of a Serb mob. Shortly afterward, Serb hard-liners went house to house, smashing in Albanian doors, throwing grenades, and shooting. At least ten people died. When the French did little in response, nearly 1,500 Albanians fled the northern part of the city. Not long after, the French police officer in charge at the time was sacked under NATO pressure.

The more militant Albanians who stayed behind in the remaining southern pocket were outraged at both the Serbs and their KFOR protectors. They launched a rocket against a UN bus under KFOR escort, killing two Serbs, and bombed a Serb café. On February 13, Albanian snipers wounded two French soldiers. The next day KFOR arrested forty ethnic Albanians.

Gen. Klaus Reinhardt, a determined German officer and commander of all NATO forces in Kosovo, turned to the United States for help in disarming both sides. Brigadier General Sanchez in Camp Bondsteel stepped up, ordering Ellerbe to Mitrovica, along with Ellerbe's Bravo Company, commanded by Capt. Michael Pratt. A West Point 1993 graduate, Pratt was as serious as they come at the young age of twenty-eight.

The mission, as briefed by the French, included cordons and searches in both the Albanian and Serb quarters, a standard operation for American peacekeepers, but only really a cover. The real mission was to re-establish KFOR's pre-eminence. For that, no Army doctrine exists, nor any specific guidance. But it was what General Wesley Clark had often advocated when he talked about "using forces not force."

Bulked-up, amply armed troops, with their in-your-face potential for lethality, could force behavioral change, the thought went. Clark urged Reinhardt to break the Serb resistance using "pressure, intimidation, and embarrassment." Reinhardt agreed. Although twelve other nations had come to town to support the French, Reinhardt looked to Bravo Company to break the deadlock of violence, to cow the Serbs, and to integrate the Serb-dominated north side of the river.

Ellerbe, having established good relationships with the Serbs in the American sector, figured he could treat the Serbs in Mitrovica the same way. He expected them to respond in kind, despite daily news reports about the tensions in that city. Ellerbe moved in with some 350 troops, bolstered by extra medevac helicopters and military police. Within hours of their arrival, the Americans had converted a cold, drafty warehouse in the Albanian southern half of the city into an operations center, although Ellerbe, even then, had misgivings about the lack of planning on the part of the French, who would lead the operation.

Operation Ibar was to be the largest weapons sweep in Mitrovica since KFOR's arrival, but it was hardly a surprise show of force. The UNMIK administrator, French diplomat Bernard Kouchner, had announced it on Saturday, February 19, 2000, the day before it began. "We are planning to intensify searches of homes, premises, vehicles, and persons to find and confiscate weapons." The UN would restrict demonstrations, limit the number of cars and people on the Ibar River bridge, and impose a daily curfew from 6 P.M. to 6 A.M. The number of KFOR police officers in Mitrovica would double to 600. "We are determined not to allow Kosovo to descend again into inter-ethnic violence."

Even so, Mitrovica's people seemed shocked when 2,300 troops from a dozen countries began pounding on their doors at 7 A.M., demanding that the occupants open up. Bravo Company was assigned the heart of the problem, just north of the bridge. The few doors that didn't open, the Americans kicked in. They confiscated AK-47s, grenades, rifles, and pistols.

Captain Pratt had also assigned squads to search a university apartment complex on the main thoroughfare. To control traffic in and out of the complex, his soldiers manned two checkpoints on either side of the apartments, unrolling concertina wire to limit the routes in. Two French companies assigned to seal the area from trouble hadn't shown up by the time the search began.

As Pratt's soldiers swept into the building and up the stairs, Ellerbe and his security detail went looking for Oliver Ivanovic, the leader of Mitrovica's Serbs and an official of the Serbian National Congress, which opposed KFOR's presence in Kosovo. Ellerbe figured it was senseless to do this without giving Ivanovic a chance to cooperate. Besides, U.S. soldiers had great relations with the Serbs in the American sector. Ellerbe figured that Ivanovic probably knew this.

At the coffee shop below Ivanovic's office, Ellerbe started up a conversation with a small knot of Mitrovica Serbs. He talked about basketball; Yugoslavia has great basketball players, he flattered them. One Serb woman at the newsstand told him she had fled another part of Kosovo because Albanians had burned her house down. Here, with the Americans around, she felt safe. He bought a cup of coffee in a white Styrofoam cup.

When Ivanovic arrived, Ellerbe explained his mission. Then, as a gesture, he talked about his good relations with the Serb religious leader, Popa Dragon Kojic, and with the small, vulnerable Serb communities in his sector around Vitina. Ellerbe thought he had made a connection with Ivanovic and he began to walk casually down the street, coffee cup in hand. He reminded some in his presence of Dorothy from *The Wizard of Oz*, moving unknowingly in the land of angry Serbs, assuming he was back in Kansas—or at least Vitina.

Within minutes a little round man butted through Ellerbe's security detail and started raising hell about Ellerbe's Albanian interpreter, who was in the middle of their Serb-only turf. "Tell me what you're upset about," Ellerbe said in a calm, reassuring voice. "Tell me."

Remove the Albanian or we'll kill him, he threatened. "You have an hour."

No problem, said Ellerbe, we'll move him.

The crowd around the lieutenant colonel swelled. It included Ivanovic's men, provocateurs who were taking instructions from him by cell phone.[8] They shouted at Ellerbe and demanded that he remove the concertina wire.

"Okay, let's move the wire," agreed Ellerbe, who believed that a much stronger perimeter of French soldiers had been set up around the apartment complex. "We didn't come here to fight anyone," he told the crowd. "We came to do a search. Let's get it over with. We're here to confiscate weapons because it will make everyone safer."

By then, 200 Serbs crowded the streets around Ellerbe. The French general in charge of Mitrovica, Brig. Gen. Pierre de Saqui de Sannes, waded into the crowd and, in front of them all, told Ellerbe that the

U.S. troops would not just be asked to conduct the weapons search, but were there also to help resettle Albanian families into the northern half of the city. It seemed like a setup intended to bring hostility onto the American troops. People in the crowd shouted their disapproval and pressed in closer around the general. Retired New York cops working as UN police got nervous and began pushing the crowd away.

"Relax," Ellerbe said to one of the police officers, "this is how we do business." The Serbs, he explained, always got close to the soldiers. It was no big deal.

Pratt's team had been in the college complex for some time by now. The search was routine, like most of them are in Kosovo—ten AK-47 assault rifles, four M48 rifles, seven blocks of plastic explosives, one pistol, one machine gun, one grenade, one arrest. "We're done," Pratt told his soldiers as he approached a courtyard in the middle of the apartment complex.

Pratt had borrowed a set of bolt cutters from French troops in a courtyard behind the building. When he sent four paratroopers to return them, they got their first look at the large crowd forming outside. They summoned Pratt, who ran into some angry young men, one of whom drew a knife. Pratt and his six soldiers charged their weapons and took aim. Just then, more Serb men rushed up. "Come on motherfucker, shoot me!" one yelled at Pratt in English, his chest out. He wasn't armed, so Pratt immediately lowered his rifle.

"Shoot me! Shoot me!" the man continued. "Come on. You won't shoot me, you coward!"

"I wasn't going to shoot him for trying to punch me," Pratt later said.

Within seconds, a couple of UN police joined the confrontation, sneaking up behind Pratt and blasting pepper spray into the face of the Serb with the knife and the other threatening to hit Pratt.

"Get your men out!" Pratt ordered the platoon leader with him, not wanting to get trapped by the arriving swarms, who were angered about the pepper spray, but had missed the opening scene.

Outside, a block away, as the concertina wire was dragged off the main road, the crowd rushed past. Chaos erupted on the street outside the apartment. Ivanovic's men ordered the crowd to move toward the Americans. The troops and their vehicles were blocked. Pratt, by then outside himself, ordered his men to stand shoulder-to-shoulder near their vehicles. With no guns drawn, they pushed back women and kids and jittery young men spitting in their faces and heaving trash.

Theirs was the only cordon there. The French, charged with establishing a tight line, were still nowhere in sight. "The French set them up," said ABC News correspondent John McWethy, who was in the middle of the riot with his camera crew. "They let them think there was an airtight cordon around the university. There wasn't shit."

The crowd was becoming even more unruly.

"Code Red!" Pratt yelled at his troops, who had their guns loaded and at the ready. "Hold your line! And hold your fire!" Pratt knew they were charged for a fight. "Just hold on," he said, grabbing one soldier by the shoulder. "Don't escalate it or it's going to get out of control. We'll get out of this OK. That's what they want you to do, shoot."

The first thing to fly were snowballs, then stones and bricks. The Serbs shouted anti-NATO slogans, denouncing NATO's bombing campaign. A well-groomed man wearing a bright yellow jacket jumped in front of Pratt and spat, in English, "You wouldn't listen to us when you were bombing us from the sky! Now you'll listen to us!"

Well, at least this isn't about us, Pratt thought. "We're just the ugly Americans."

At this point, Ellerbe, walking calmly down the street with a cup of coffee, came upon Pratt's troops. Oh no, Ellerbe thought, this is bad. It was the first time he had felt threatened in Kosovo. Somalia flashed before him: Mortars exploding. The ping-ping-ping of bullets. No cover. The crowd. Narrow streets. No easy exit. His bloodied leg. The bodies of dead Somalis. "This is going to be worse than Somalia," he thought to himself as the crowd swelled to 300. "I'm going to kill a hundred civilians today."

He scurried to find the French commander, Brigadier General de Sannes. "If your intention is to fight these guys, we can do that," Ellerbe said. "But there's nothing to be gained here, sir."

"Stand by," the general said, and he darted away to call his own commanders.

"We need to get out of here now," Pratt told Ellerbe. "The guys are taking all they can." They both knew that any soldier could start shooting and be justified under their rules of engagement, which permitted them to shoot in respond to the use of deadly force.

De Sannes rushed back and permitted the U.S. troops to leave.

"Put your weapons down, go back to your trucks," Ellerbe instructed. Soon French KFOR troops moved in between the paratroopers and the crowd and began firing tear gas. "Whatever you do, don't stop," Ellerbe told the troops as they climbed into their Humvees and troop carriers.

But the road out proved a gauntlet. The lead French armored personnel carrier stopped almost immediately after it started to roll. People three deep crammed both sides of the street. Bottles and bricks bounced off the vehicles. A man with a crowbar ran up to Pratt's vehicle and knocked off the mirror. Two wine bottles bounced off his windshield. The gunner in the turret was pummeled.

A brick struck machine-gunner Sgt. Michael Price in the face, breaking his nose and blackening his eyes. As a light snow fell and heavy objects jetted through the air, another gunner in a slow-moving armored personnel carrier jerked back on his fifty-caliber machine gun. His whole body tensed to fire as he leveled the barrel at the crowd. But he didn't fire, and the troops moved out slowly, under a hail of hatred. "Go back to where you came from!" people in the crowd shouted.

When they reached the warehouse headquarters, Ellerbe's soldiers were beside themselves. Why were they not allowed to defend themselves? It was the "typical bar-fight mentality," their officers thought.

"Why didn't we stay there?" one yelled at Pratt.

Ellerbe stepped in quickly. "You did the right thing," he told them in his low, monotone voice, which was in calm contrast to the piqued emotion in the room. "You demonstrated a significant amount of discipline. The average guy couldn't have done that. The crowd was demonstrating hostility and a hostile intent. You had the authority to shoot them. But what would you have gained? There were women, children, and old people in that crowd."

A while later, the French general informed Ellerbe he wanted him to take his troops out into the city again, right away. This time, he wanted the Americans to search a Serb hospital that refused to accept Albanian patients. Ellerbe protested and called Brigadier General Sanchez. "If you don't get more information about the operation I'm not going to do it," he told Sanchez. "Boss, this is bad."

They agreed to put off the hospital search. Sanchez ordered Camp Bondsteel to send them face masks, riot gear, pellet-filled bean-bag rounds, rubber bullets, and an extra MP company for the next day.

The next day, 75,000 ethnic Albanians, many from Kosovo's central Drenica region, the birthplace of the KLA, marched on Mitrovica. Waving Albanian, U.S., and UN flags, they climbed atop NATO tanks and armored vehicles and tried repeatedly to cross the barbed-wire barricades. A small group of boisterous Serbs on the northern end of the Ibar River bridge taunted them with nationalist Serb hymns blasted over amplifiers but ultimately left when they saw the renewed U.S. show of force.

Behind the scenes another sort of protest was taking place. General, Reinhardt called Ellerbe to his office. He was upset. You should have stayed at the university yesterday and fought the Serbs, he said. Only the Americans can show the Serbs that KFOR is in charge. Reinhardt wanted Ellerbe to send his men back to the same quarter to "establish a presence." Could you do that? Reinhardt asked.

No we could not, Ellerbe said firmly.

What Reinhardt wanted, in reality, was to use the troops as bait, Ellerbe figured. In Mogadishu UN commanders had wanted to use American "presence patrols" to show challenging local gangs the power of a violent a U.S. response. Demonstrating force was a way to earn respect. In Kosovo, the Mitrovica operation was supposed to demonstrate American strength and resolve, to prove that the Americans and KFOR could—and would—take on the Serbs. But neither NATO nor the Americans were ready or willing for that kind of enforcement this time in Mitrovica.

* * * *

THE PEOPLE IN Washington who sent Ellerbe's soldiers to Kosovo wanted them to take a risk that they themselves shunned. Clark, Reinhardt, Sanchez, Ellerbe, Lambert, and Pratt knew it would take resolve and strong actions to reverse the downward spiral of corruption in Kosovo. So did experts at the National Security Council and the State Department's envoys on the ground. But specifics were politically risky, so the mission would remain vaguely defined: create a "safe and secure environment."

The troops either pushed too hard, as in Vitina, or retreated too fast, as in Mitrovica. It was a no-win situation. Officers on the Pentagon's E-ring were already snickering about the snowballs in Mitrovica that had "forced them off the battlefield," one Pentagon colonel chuckled.

The civilian-run Defense Department, and the Army itself, had failed for ten years to come up with a clear and reasonable peace-keeping doctrine that could be taught to every officer and soldier and routinely practiced at its training centers, as traditional combat was. Ellerbe had thought about this lapse often. "They don't want to define it," he concluded. "It's too hard."

In June 2001, the Army's Training and Doctrine Command released a revised "operations" field manual, which included a new doctrine on peacekeeping. Dropping the controversial name, the doc-trine writers dubbed these missions "stability and support operations." That seemed a start.

Two days before Ellerbe's battalion left Kosovo, Captain Lambert participated in a traditional ceremony transfering authority from his battalion to the incoming one from the 101st Airborne Division. Serb and Albanian community leaders, about forty people, attended. After the ceremony, Lambert shared hugs and handshakes with people in the gym. The 101st officers scoffed at the show of affection and friendship between Lambert's soldiers and the locals. "We won't be close to them," one of new officers told Lambert. "Well don't be surprised," Lambert responded.

As he made to leave, Sanchez pulled Lambert aside. Sanchez said he was recommending that disciplinary action be taken against Lambert—a letter of reprimand. "I thought I should tell you personally before you heard it somewhere else."

Lambert was floored. "Sir, what brought you to that conclusion?"

"You're a seasoned commander and you could have and should have known what was going on in your unit and tried to prevent it." As the company's commanding officer, Lambert was being held responsible for

Ronghi's murder of Merita Shabiu, the boorish behavior of his enlisted soldiers, and perhaps even the investigations by his lieutenants.

"Yes, sir."

Lambert marched up to his room. His fellow company commanders followed. He tried to contain himself, but the more he talked, the angrier he got. When he saw Ellerbe a half an hour later, he broke down, sobbing.

A day later, Lambert hoisted himself into a CH-47 Chinook helicopter with the rest of the battalion officers for the ride out of Kosovo to Macedonia. "This is how it all started," he said to Pratt, who was sitting next to him. He was thinking about the ride in on the same bird, and all that had happened to his unit and to his life since then. And of how little had changed in Kosovo during his stay.

After a quick, easy ride into Camp Able Sentry over the Kacanik defile and back into Macedonia, Ellerbe headed straight for the command post to finish up some paperwork. At around 9 P.M., Col. John Morgan III, whom the Army had put in charge of the investigation of the unit, showed up. "I'm recommending you for a general officer . . . reprimand . . . unhealthy command climate . . . exceeding the scope of your military duties and assignments . . . not the commander's intent. . . ."

Ellerbe looked at him, stunned. "You've got to be kidding me," he said. "You have read this thing completely wrong. Over time, you'll find out you were wrong."

★ ★ ★ ★

IN MARCH 2000, the UN finally handed Xhavit Hasani over to authorities in Skopje, Macedonia. His imprisonment there shook the Macedonian government. Albanians in Kosovo threw up a series of roadblocks along the one road leading from Macedonia to Kosovo. On April 2, 2000, forty masked men armed with automatic weapons and bazookas captured four Macedonian soldiers near Tanusevci, Hasani's hometown on the Macedonian border. In a secret deal with Macedonian authorities, the masked men exchanged the soldiers for Hasani. Days later, Hasani, trailed by dozens of cars draped in red-and-black Albanian flags, returned triumphantly to Vitina.

This swap sparked another uproar. Macedonian opposition parties criticized the government for violating the law and negotiating with terrorists. Their protests threatened the teetering government coalition of President Kiro Gligorov.

Meanwhile, Hamid Shabiu yearned to honor his daughter with a proper grave, to protect her in death as he could not protect her in life. But he had no money. The Army would pay only for a coffin. For months, Merita's unsealed wooden coffin lay under a mound of mud in a barely recognizable graveyard in Vitina, marked by two wooden stakes. "It's being destroyed every moment," Shabiu told a visitor in the spring of 2000.[9] "It collapses inside. Then the animals, especially the dogs, want to get the body, so they dig to get the body."

Army lawyers, noting that Kosovo had not been designated a "foreign claims area"—meaning the U.S. government would not be financially responsible for damage its soldiers had caused—convinced Sanchez that paying for a grave would be a bad idea. Such a move would open the floodgates for thousands of claims by farmers whose fields or roads had been destroyed by KFOR equipment or confiscated for the Army's use.

In the end, the Army paid for a funeral and gave the family about $5,000 for other expenses. But that was it. No food and no medical care, although the family had been severely shocked by what had happened, so much so that their youngest son stopped going to school. When Sanchez left Kosovo in June, so did the Army's heartfelt obligation to do anything else for the Shabius. Drita Perezic and a few reservists still at Camp Bondsteel helped the family survive. They scavenged food from the mess halls and collected old clothes from soldiers. In December 2000, the last time Drita visited the Shabiu family, she found them with one day's worth of cooking oil. They had been kicked out of their house in Vitina and were living in the nearby hills, in a shack.

Ronghi, meanwhile, is living in a shack of his own making. He passes each day in the bleak, gray light that fills his six-by-ten-foot cell at the Army's U.S. disciplinary barracks at Fort Leavenworth, Kansas. He has a bed attached to the pale yellow concrete wall, a small desk the size of a tray table, and a stainless-steel sink that doubles as a toilet. From the heavy steel-mesh door and inner wall he can see only a concrete hallway and the indirect light coming from a window that is too high for him see outside. "He's just another Joe in here," said a guard.

In April 2001, a Skopje court tried, convicted, and sentenced Hasani in absentia to thirteen years in prison for attempted murder, illegal possession of arms, and three other offenses. Officials accused him of orchestrating the armed Albanian insurgency in Macedonia. Hasani's underground continued carving up Kosovo into fiefdoms roughly mirroring the former KLA's seven military zones during the war.

The Army's investigation into the 3rd Battalion grew to 657 pages. Soldiers gave testimony about the beatings at Klokat, Sam's Pizzeria, the closing of Drenica Café, market days, and the rest. Ellerbe's Specific Task 7A came under particular scrutiny. The chief investigator treated that instruction—to neutralize and incarcerate KLA leaders and splinter groups—as if it were the smoking gun, the explanation for the soldiers' inappropriate actions. He blamed Ellerbe for being too aggressive, for stepping over the line. But investigators never even asked Sanchez if he had been aware of 7A or whether he had signed off on it, which he verbally had. Nor did the investigation mention that many other VIPs had been briefed on that task, part of Ellerbe's mission as he had defined it.

On September 18, 2000, the U.S. Army's European Command released results of the Army Regulation 15-6 Report of Investigation titled "Unit Climate and State of Discipline within the 3rd Battalion, 504th Parachute Infantry Regiment, Task Force Falcon, Kosovo Force." The Army statement issued with the report concluded, "The report raised questions about the leadership, readiness, training, and discipline of this battalion." The investigator, Colonel Morgan, "found a situation in which some members of one unit were behaving in a manner inconsistent with the command's rules of engagement, the Uniform Code of Military Justice and the Army's core value. . . . The incidents detailed in this report of investigation are not in keeping with the Army's core values and should never have occurred.

"Unit members violated the limits and terms of their military assignments by intimidating, interrogating, abusing, and beating Albanians," Morgan found. As for Ellerbe, the investigator found that Specified Task 7A—the effort to "neutralize" Albanian troublemakers—" was outside [the commander's intent] and the Battalion Commander's emphasis on this task permeated the unit's climate and created a set of conditions that provided his subordinates the opportunity to step over the line of acceptable conduct (e.g., criminal misconduct, excessive use of force, and lack of dignity and respect for others.)" He recommended a range of administrative and judicial punishments for the soldiers involved. A subsequent, internal Army investigation, however, found that Specified Task 7A "was briefed to the entire chain of command and was known by all." Eventually, five enlisted soldiers, four of them from Ronghi's platoon, received administrative punishment under Article 15 of the Uniformed Code of Military Justice. Four officers—Ellerbe, Lambert, Serafini, and Donnelly—were also given various forms of administrative punishment. Subsequently, all received promotions or were selected into competitive Army schooling programs.

Army chief of staff Eric Shinseki asked another four-star general, U.S. Army Forces Commander John Hendrix, to review the appropriateness of the promotions. Hendrix suggested the promotions be reviewed by yet another command. They were, and none of the promotions were revoked. All four officers remain in the Army, in good standing.

Hendrix also recommended that all soldiers deploying to Kosovo first go through a "mission rehearsal exercise" that tries to simulate situations the troops are likely to encounter in Kosovo. The Army has since spent millions training troops about searches, civilian crowd control, traffic checkpoints, and "respect for others." As future deployments would show, however, the mission remains baffling to many soldiers.

The Army also abandoned its efforts to end the political-criminal axis that has come to control Kosovo, a dishonor to Merita's memory and to efforts to establish a truly safe and secure environment for her young survivors, her brothers and sisters—the future of Kosovo. By the summer of 2002, the Defense Department, looking to save money, was seriously considering closing the U.S. Army Peacekeeping Institute at the Army War College.

A framed and mounted photograph that Ellerbe gave his lieutenants defines peacemaking in a way the Army never would. The photograph—of his lieutenants in a line, Ellerbe in the middle, all in full "battle rattle"—hangs in Kevin Lambert's living room, right next to his wedding announcement. It hangs in Donnelly's small on-base apartment at Fort Stewart, Ga., in Pratt's dingy company headquarters at Fort Bragg, and in Sheehan's orderly headquarters company down the road. Below the photograph was Ellerbe's counsel to them: "The art of leadership, the art of command, whether the forces be large or small, is the art of dealing with humanity. Only the officer who dedicates his thought and energy to his men can convert into coherent military force their desire to be of service to the country."

Chapter Seventeen

VITINA, ONE YEAR LATER

* * * *

THE LAND BETWEEN MACEDONIA AND KOSOVO LOOKS a lot like Appalachia's coal country. Steep hills, narrow passes with streams cutting through cracks of earth below—and soiled plastic trash bags hanging like ornaments off leafless trees. By the end of 2000, Kosovo had changed: the window-replacement business was booming, and satellite dishes sprouted on apartment balconies. Piles of moist, brown dirt sat exposed in the small cemeteries along the roads.

The soldiers had changed, too. They seemed only to be impersonating soldiers. To hitch a ride in their white minivan, a flak vest and helmet were required—that was a first. "Ma'am, do you have your seat belt fastened?" the lieutenant colonel in the passenger seat asked before he would allow the driver to turn on the ignition.

Half a dozen liter bottles of Kopri purified water rolled around on the van's floor, in case anyone felt the onset of dehydration during the two-hour ride. Many soldiers wore small water bladders on their backs. A little plastic hose attached to the bag wrapped over a shoulder and up, conveniently, to the jaw line. Adolescent pacifiers. The Army was addicting its newest soldiers to them.

Protecting the force had gone that much further. Troops had always looked ridiculous in the placid streets with forty pounds of armor and webbing. Worse now, the mantra of safety had infected soldiers' self-perception. They acted nervous. They worried about little things.

"What the hell was that?" the command sergeant major yelled as a camera flash went off.[*]

These days in Kosovo, before starting his engine, a driver was expected to check off a "risk management worksheet."

There will be narrow points in the road. Check.

Intersections are chaotic. Check.

There are often children on the side of the streets. Check.

Be prepared for roads with no shoulders for emergency pull-offs. Check.

At the Macedonia-Kosovo border the contrast in mission and culture was as visible as the posters greeting travelers: "Don't Drink and Drive—KFOR" said one customs window. "PDK," read a political advertisement on the next one. That hard-line political party seeking an independent Kosovo was still using intimidation, violence, and KFOR complacency to get it.

"What's that red flag with the birds on it?" the driver asked a new Army major who had arrived to take charge of the public affairs office on Camp Bondsteel, where he would issue official pronouncements for the Army's peacekeeping mission.

"I don't know," replied the major. But he should have known. It was the national flag of Albania and stood for independence and self-determination for thousands of KLA fighters and ordinary Albanians. They had given their lives for that goal; Serb forces had

---

[*] This incident reminded me of another time, in East Timor, when Adm. Dennis Blair sat for a typical military briefing inside a room on a barge that the marines were sleeping on, a few feet away from the shore in Dili. The briefer began with the standard "threat assessment." On the list: mosquitoes. The admiral's physician had insisted everyone in Blair's entourage take malaria pills, even though our stay was only for twenty-four hours. Keep your sleeves rolled down and buttoned, too, he instructed, even though the temperature was above 100°F. Some of the marines wore long underwear, too. Only Blair's State Department–appointed political adviser, Ambassador Charles Twining, an old Asia hand, had dared snicker at these measures. He rolled his sleeves up. When the marine briefer finished, the next briefer was ushered in. She was a wisp of a woman, a Dane from a human-rights organization who had been there for months. She was wearing—gasp!—a sleeveless blouse!

"Did you notice her sleeves?" I taunted the admiral's aides.

"Yeah, better safe than sorry," they said without laughing.

killed and maimed thousands of ethnic Albanians for merely dreaming of freedom. "Oh yeah," the major said a few minutes later, "It's an in-your-face kind of thing for the Albanians."

Two troop units had rotated into Vitina in the year since the 82nd Airborne's troops had left. The soldiers patrolling Vitina had been moved into an old machine milling factory, behind barbed wire and sandbags off the main road into town. They weren't even aware that the UN police building in town used to be the former MUP headquarters, and after that, Gator Base.

"No spitting," the sign at the entrance of the post read. "Welcome to Task Force No Slack 2/327."* The 101st Airborne Division's "Screaming Eagles" were nesting inside.

The warehouse hosted a cappuccino bar, a wide-screen television, Internet access, and posters setting forth the unit's mission statement. Rule number one: "Respect and dignity . . ." The Army was nothing if not reactive to criticism.

Out on the street, sympathies for the Serb minority remained strong.

Milorad Danic was an old Serb man the soldiers had nicknamed "Mele." He smelled so bad he was hard even to look at, a noxious mixture of sour alcohol, stale cigarettes, and old dirt. His pants and shirt were covered with dust, and his boiled-wool jacket had become a sort of Velcro patch, attracting every piece of food, drink, and furniture fuzz he had encountered in the past year. His teeth, broken and mossy, hid under a long, unkempt gray mustache. Mele's fingers were stained with tobacco—not yellow, but a deep brown-orange, like petrified wood.

In another world, Mele would be the town drunk most straight-laced Army men avoided. But in Vitina, he befriended every American captain who came through, charming them with his courage in walking the Albanian-controlled streets unescorted. "Captain Lambert was wonderful," he said one day, reminiscing about the Army captains and lieutenants he had known. Kevin Lambert had assigned soldiers to escort Mele around town, he explained, after Mele's friend had been shot plowing his field. Mele had invited Lambert to a pig roast, for

* 2nd Battalion, 237th Infantry, 101st Airborne Division.

which they first needed to kill the pig. Lambert had wanted to shoot it with his pistol.

"No! No! Don't shoot it!" Mele had yelled. "We have to slit its throat." It was cleaner that way, and Mele did it himself. Lambert's only problem, Mele thought, was that he wouldn't accept a drink.

Mele had been born in Vitina and spent most of his life there. After working construction in Stuttgart, Germany, he had come home to a small plot of land and some honey-making bees. There he had helped his brother, a member of the Yugoslav army, build a modest, one-story house with a low, ornamental metal fence a few blocks from Mele's own home.

Mele's coat pockets were crammed with snapshots of his bee box in his brother's side yard, but his brother had fled to Belgrade at the end of the war and Mele had taken charge of the house in his absence. The snapshots were his evidence.

Several months before, Albanians had broken in and occupied the house. Mele complained to KFOR, which had been evicting squatters since they came to Kosovo. The commanders disliked their soldiers' having to kick people our of their homes. It was nasty work, mission creep and all. They had pressured the civilian UN administration into taking on a job that everyone agreed should be the UN's anyway. Complain to "UNMIK-P,"* the soldiers told Vitina residents; the police handle evictions. KFOR commanders had recently handed out guidance from Camp Bondsteel: soldiers should promote "police primacy" in all but life-threatening situations, it said. KFOR hoped to turn its entire mission over to the UN someday.

The problem was, the UN wouldn't handle evictions. The police weren't confident they could prove who owned what house with the paperwork most people provided. Moreover, they didn't like provoking hostilities. People get mad when you take their homes away. So, in reality, UNMIK still relied on KFOR to do the job.

For the past four months, Mele had visited the police station a dozen times, marching past the regal sky-blue UN flag and the flying-saucer-sized satellite dish, up concrete steps into the bare waiting room with two chairs. From there, he could peer into the watch sta-

* Stands for UN Mission in Kosovo-Police, the UN police force.

tion, where inevitably three or four policemen from Africa, Southeast Asia, Europe, and America were leaning back in their chairs in front of bright, new computer terminals. He watched as they filled out forms and played video games. "Video games are for kids," he barked as he spat on the ground in disgust one day.

Sometimes the police officers made him wait three or four hours to file a complaint. Sometimes they immediately turned him down. Five times he got them to take his statement. Albanians were occupying his brother's home, he told them. Here's proof of ownership. Here are pictures of my bee boxes. He yelled at them until they wrote it down.

On a frigid, drizzling day in December 2000, Mele met up with Lt. Benjamin Saine, a relaxed, earnest Army platoon leader, and pressed his case again. Saine, who had helped Mele change the locks on his brother's home, took his squad to check out the house. They walked up to the gate and were discussing the collection of empty plastic bottles on the front porch when a man wearing a black-leather jacket and dark whiskers came out the door. Saine motioned to his soldiers and led them out of the yard. It wasn't their job to get into it. He'd just wanted proof someone was around.

Saine reported the alleged squatters to his commander, Alpha Company's Capt. Darrell Driver. A few minutes later, Driver opened the weekly Serb town meeting at a local church in Vitina. At a wooden table in the front of the room, five burly Army soldiers sat shoulder-to-heavy-shoulder, hunched over to endure another round of long-winded complaints. The old Serbs, with canes and crutches but not many teeth, wore rubber slippers and thick woolen socks. They packed themselves together on benches inside the freezing-cold room and spoke up angrily as the sun set and the room grew dimmer and colder.

The session started with grumbling about the UN police. They sit in their cars. They won't patrol. They won't stop illegal woodcutting. They won't stop illegal squatting. No one but KFOR will do a damn thing, they shouted. It wasn't what Captain Driver wanted to hear. His message today, like last week's, was that people had to turn to the UN police, not KFOR, for help.

Driver knew privately, however, that even the UN bosses could not persuade the UN police to do their job. Contrary to what Driver thought

Capt. Darrell Driver, company commander in the 3rd Battalion, 237th Infantry,
101st Airborne Division, walks through the streets of Vitina with Milorad "Mele"
Danic. Mele's brother's home was taken over by ethnic Albanians.
Driver's soldiers evicted them.   DANA PRIEST

before he came to Kosovo, there really was no UN police force, per se. Rather, when the United Nations decided to take up a peacekeeping mission, it would ask its member states to pony up police. They were usually retired cops on contract. In Kosovo, the police force included people from fifty countries. The Americans on the force were mostly retired cops from the South, men looking to make a quick, big buck (their pay was over $75,000 a year in 2000, plus handsome per diems). African states, Pakistan, India, and other countries often sent people with political connections who wanted a good-paying job, although many didn't have policing skills. The British sent police from Northern Ireland—who are the best, since they usually honed their careers on the violent streets of Belfast.

This mishmash of "officers" had no common training or language. The last thing they wanted was to risk their lives in Kosovo. Creating a professional, standing police force has long been a goal of the UN leadership, but it remains only a goal, and a critical one in this age of peacekeeping, which more accurately should be dubbed "policekeeping."

The UN police, who lived not behind the protected walls of Bondsteel but in unprotected homes in the communities they patrolled, didn't want to trigger bad relations with the locals, either by enforcing the UN mandate, or by doing anything so bold as to investigate and arrest local mob leaders. "Vitina is seething with organized crime. I know it, our investigators know it," said one UN police officer. "The Albanians are into brass-knuckle extortion. They haven't touched us and we haven't touched them. If we did, that arrangement would tank. I'm not a coward, but I don't want to die here."

The UN administration lacked the leverage to get its police to perform. Gen. Joseph Ralston, Wesley Clark's successor as SACEUR and European Command CinC, gave up on them soon after he took the post. "I have written off UNMIK-P," said Ralston. "The solution is local police."

Eighteen months into the mission, American soldiers had reduced overt crime to nearly zero. But the underground criminal network that Lt. Col. Michael Ellerbe, Lambert, and others chased was still running Vitina in late 2000, and appeared ever more deeply embedded. The troops still talked about Skender Habibi, the hardline PDK leader. He was on their private "most wanted" list.

Melena Modica, UN representative for the Serb minority in Vitina, hated the passivity of the UNMIK-P. "It's a farce," she said. "There is an international presence, a civilian administration, but no one is in charge at the end. I'm not in control of phones, electricity. At this point there's a parallel government run by the pro-independence Albanians. KFOR is stepping down at the wrong moment."

Modica, a fashionable Italian with long brown hair and diamond earrings, had been fighting the UNMIK-P. The police were supposed to be evicting Albanian squatters illegally occupying Serb homes, but they refused to do it. "UNMIK-P is the only one who should react," she said at the town meeting, in her heavily accented and awkwardly structured English, which was translated into Serbian for the old men and women who had come to complain about getting their homes back. "If they don't react, come to me and Captain Driver and we will talk to them. UNMIK-P is in charge of all occupation of housing."

Mele, marinated by a morning at the pub, had heard all the UN's excuses before and would have no more of it. "When can I have back my brother's house? When will you turn out the Albanian terrorists who are illegally occupying it?"

Driver, the senior U.S. officer at the meeting, cut him off. "We will settle your case after the meeting, Mele."

"Captain Driver will do as much as he can, but the police are in charge," Melena reminded Mele.

"We'll take care of it after the meeting," Driver said again. "You and I." Man to man. They nodded to each other and winked. A pact.

The Serbs asked the American soldiers to kick the mafiosi out of town. Called the Black Eagles, Eagle Security, and Leopard Security, these upstart protection rackets hired thugs who carried guns and intimidated people, they said. Their enforcers were members of the banned MRP, according to Army intelligence. Rambo Kamberi and Habibi were among them.

"We know you are responsible for everything," an old man pointed to Driver, "that's why we're telling *you* these things."

Driver shrugged and smiled at Melena. "I'm trying. . . ."

When the meeting ended Driver told Mele that he and Lieutenant Saine would go to Mele's brother's house and make the Albanian squatters leave. But, said Driver curiously, "We don't do evictions."

Driver, square-faced, with extra-short hair and a stern, pinched brow, had joined the Army reserves in high school, won a scholarship to Notre Dame, and became an officer in 1994. He chose infantry because that's what the Army is all about. "If you weren't in the infantry, you were just supporting the infantry."

"I see our role as crisis management," he said on his way to Mele's brother's house. "It felt good" to help Kosovo, "but in the long term, it's difficult." Like Ellerbe, he often gave Kosovars references from American history. He told impatient Albanians stories about American patriots who fought eight years for their freedom from the British before gaining independence. It took even longer to write a constitution, he cautioned them. Sometimes he spoke of racial integration in the United States, of African Americans jailed trying to earn the right to vote. "What did they do," he asked rhetorically, "when they got out of jail? They went right back out on the streets to protest again."

Dusk had settled in by the time Driver and Saine reached Mele's brother's house.

A four-year-old in a purple sweatshirt answered the door and stared up as far as his head would take his eyes without falling backward. He marveled at the soldiers, as if he'd just opened a Christmas present, all these GI Joes standing in front of him. Wow! With clear brown eyes, big ears, and milky skin, he stepped closer to SSgt. Chris Dohl, a corn-fed twenty-six-year-old with no neck, a refrigerator of a man with a wad of tobacco in his cheek and a helmet that covered his eyebrows. The kid was smiling up at him, checking out his gear. Dohl was trying to scowl.

"Is your father here?" Driver asked the boy.

A thin man with week-old stubble, a family friend, appeared behind the child. Dohl tightened his grip on his M-4 carbine as he stood behind Driver.

"No," the man answered, slipping on his shoes, which were piled up on the front porch with five other pairs. Another man, who turned out to be the boy's uncle, came to the doorway. Behind him trailed two more children and his wife, a heavy-set woman with pretty peach lipstick and a soft hint of blush on her face, a face wrinkled with skepticism. Her strong, heavy arms were folded across her chest. She could have been a housewife from Driver's West Memphis, Ark., neighborhood greeting a bill collector.

The uncle began speaking, but Driver had absentmindedly brought only a Serb-language translator. Half an hour passed, the day slipped to darkness and the cold to freezing, before an Albanian speaker arrived from the base.

"Find out what their names are," Driver ordered the new translator, then asked the three adults, "Where are you from? Why have you moved into the house?"

They were Fehmi Hajdari, his wife Haxhire Hajdari, and their three children, ages four, five, and seven. Fehmi had grown up in Vitina, he said. He'd been away in Germany, working. The other man, Ekrem Rashiti, was from the Presevo Valley, where Albanian insurgents had just begun a campaign to seize Serbian territory.

"Why have you moved in here?" Driver asked.

"We have nowhere else to stay," answered Fehmi Hajdari.

"Here's the deal," Driver responded. "You can't just move into other people's houses. The UN is setting up a shelter. You need to move out of this house tonight. You have one hour. You have one hour to leave."

"But the owner is not here," pleaded Hajdari, shrugging his shoulders and throwing up his arms.

"You have one hour," Driver said sternly. "Gather up all your things."

"I have no place to go. I'll stay in the yard."

"No you won't," Driver shot back. "It's 16:50. By 17:50, you need to have all your things away."

"We didn't take anything by force," the man tried. His two boys stepped away from Dohl and hugged their father's legs. Still dazzled by the soldiers, they became confused by the tone of voices swirling around them.

"You took this by force," said Driver. "You can't take something that's not yours. You go to the UN and tell them what your problem is. Your time is ticking. You need to start packing."

"We're going to stay in the street," the man said.

"Okay," said Driver. "You have one hour."

There was silence. A standoff.

Dohl looked worried behind his imposing rifle and gear. "Nothing prepares you for this," he whispers from behind his soldier's mask. "All these kids around. . . ."

The soldiers walked into the house just to make a point: the house was no longer the Albanians'. A junk heap greeted them. Loose trash. Empty soda bottles. Food wrappers. No furniture in the living room.

SSgt. John Billings, a more experienced and tough-talking NCO, arrived. "In an hour, I'm going to escort you and your family out of the house with your stuff," he bellowed. "Start packing, we're not talking about it anymore."

"And if anything happens to this house," added Driver, "I'm going to hold you responsible."

"Keep an eye on them," Billings told Dohl. "Make sure they don't destroy anything."

Fehmi appealed to Dohl, wide-shouldered and bursting with weaponry, but slightly younger than the other growling soldiers.

"There's no real owner," he pleaded.

"Make a phone call, get some friends," Dohl replied. "You have one hour. Move your stuff out the way you moved it in."

A soldier began to help the frightened children into their coats. But as soon as the mother, Haxhire, spotted that, she pulled the two boys close to her, peeling off their coats. "I'm not leaving this house!" she yelled, her face even angrier than her tone. "I'm not going anywhere!"

Dohl chuckled to himself, an "oh yeah? just watch," kind of chuckle.

"It's cold!" she said. "The kids are cold! How would you feel? Where am I supposed to go with the kids?"

"Well, where would you go if you didn't move into this abandoned house?" Billings shouted back.

"We can't find a place tonight," her husband whined. "We're coming with you!"

"Well, you might end up in the warehouse [KFOR's jail], where it's really cold," Dohl warned with an irreverent laugh.

"Hey!" Dohl shouted to her, "you have forty-five minutes to get out of this house!"

A flood of hostility poured from the woman and her husband. The translator summed it up for Driver in a quiet monotone: "They are saying they aren't going to leave."

"So you're saying you're not going to leave in an hour?" Driver demanded. "Is that your contention? That even if we give you that time, you aren't going to take it."

They shook their heads no. There was not a trace of fear on the woman's face, just stone resolution.

Driver looked at his watch. It was 5:05 P.M. "Okay," he instructed his troops, "start moving their stuff." Four soldiers walked into the house and into the bedroom.

"Okay, what's yours in this room!?" one soldier demanded.

Fehmi opened the dresser. "Those are our clothes," he said softly, as if again trying to prove his family belonged in the house. "These are too," he pointed to other drawers.

"The heater goes," Billings said. "Start putting everything in bags."

"We don't have bags!" the woman shouted. "We're not going anywhere."

"Put the jackets on the kids. You can be detained," Billings said, looking at the woman.

"We're not going anywhere!" she repeated, looking him straight in the eye.

"Tell this guy to put his hands up," another sergeant in the room commanded the translator.

The husband complied, but his wife dug in, pulling the two kids closer to her.

"We'll take care of the kids," Lieutenant Saine told her gently. "We'll put shoes on them."

But she would hear nothing about shoes.

Her hands were folded across her chest as they had been since these four, now six, soldiers burst into her life. She wasn't budging, and she wasn't about to let them be friendly.

"Put your hands up!" Dohl yelled at her, "or else I'll force them up."

Billings and Dohl grabbed her forearms. She tried twisting herself away. The children screamed, "Mommy! Mommy! Mommy!"

The two soldiers pushed the woman against the wall. Her face was unchanged, blank, as the two men, heavy with flak jacket, helmets, and weapons, pinned her to the wall. She continued to struggle.

Saine tried to push the kids—who were now hysterical—out of the room.

Billing and Dohl forced the woman's arms down and behind her back. Her body collapsed onto the mattress on the floor. They knelt on top of her, their knees in her back, their shoulders against hers. They pulled her hands together and she grunted for air and dignity.

"Give me a double!" Billings shouted, as Dohl handed him a pair of zip-strip plastic handcuffs.

Then they lifted her by the elbows, forcing her to stand, and pushed her into the foyer. Dohl pointed to the ground: "Sit! Sit! Sit!" But she didn't budge. Billings pushed her shoulder and she dropped down, squatting on the floor, but not sitting.

A soldier picked up her black jacket and put it around her shoulders. Her kids were wailing. They still didn't have their shoes and jackets on. When the soldiers tried to help them now, they shrieked and ran away. Their mother yelled at them too.

Outside, in pitch darkness, behind the house, Driver had been talking to the two men, who both cooperated in their handcuffing. He had made a deal with them. They could stay in the house until tomorrow morning. "By 10:00 tomorrow morning, you will have gone to the UN and asked about the shelter because KFOR has thrown you out," he said. "That's the agreement."

He cut their handcuffs and they all walked back into the house. Having severed the plastic cuffs from the woman's wrists, the soldiers left the house.

"You guys are acting worse than the Serbs!" she growled as they descended the front steps and made their way into the street. They walked back to the base in silence.

The next morning, Driver went to the UN building in Vitina for a joint security meeting between KFOR and the dozen international organizations in town. As he walked into the building—which had been Lambert's Gator Base—Driver saw the two Albanian men from the night before. He immediately reached out his hand to shake theirs. Had they moved out yet? No.

"You know you must go to the community shelter," he told him.

"Where is that?" Fehmi replied.

Just then, Maj. Matt Fellinger, a civil affairs officer, walked up. He had already been briefed on the problem.

"We'll try to find you some shelter," Fellinger told Fehmi.

"I would really like to turn this over to the responsible agency," Driver said to Fellinger, gesturing into the meeting room, where a disjointed collection of people from the wealthy Western world's aid agencies sat: the United Nations High Commissioner for Refugees (UNHCR), the Italian carabinieri, a guy from the Organization for Security and Cooperation in Europe dressed from head to toe in bright white, a couple of nonprofit humanitarian organizations from Europe and the United States. When it came to the subject of evictions, all seemed confused, except Melena Modica from the UN. She would send notices to people illegally occupying houses, she told them. They would have three days to leave, after which UNMIK-P would evict them. And if the UN police don't do their job, Melena vowed to report them to the UN's higher headquarters.

"So," she turned to Mark Holmes, a seventeen-year veteran of the Sylacauga, Ala., police force, now on contract with UNMIK-P for a hefty sum, "please tell me what is your role?"

"I'm not up-to-date on this issue," he said from his chair in the corner, near the back wall. Everyone in the room rolled their eyes. Later Holmes explained that "the issue has gotten very technical. People have paperwork to support their claims and it's gotten too time-consuming for the police to verify the paperwork." In fact, UNMIK was supposed to have set up a property-dispute board months ago. But a year and a half into the mission, it still had not done so.

From the UNHCR, Kaoru Nemoto, a Japanese woman in black tights and a pink scarf, reported that her organization had reversed its decision to open a shelter in Vitina for refugees—IDPs, internally displaced persons, they called them. They had decided it wasn't necessary. The IDPs could find shelter in the larger city of Gnjilane, thirty miles away, she had concluded.

Driver had already told Hajdari and Rashiti they could stay in the shelter. "Well I've got some IDPs right here," Driver told her. "What can you do for them now?"

"Oh, okay, send them to Gnjilane," said Nemoto pleasantly, smiling, as if she were sending them to a shoe store instead of a clothing store.

"They can't get to Gnjilane," said Driver, exasperated.

"Well, they can use public transportation," Nemoto replied.

By 4 P.M. that day, Lieutenant Saine left Camp No Slack to see if Hajdari and Rashiti had moved from Mele's brother's house as they had agreed they would. Driver and Saine agreed that if they had not left, Saine was to head straight to the UN police station and get the police to go to the house and evict them.

Saine got as close to the house as the front gate, saw Hajdari fly out the door, and scurried away. "They're still here. Let's go get UNMIK-P," he told his soldiers.

But getting the UN police out at night would prove as hard as getting the Albanians to leave. When Saine stepped into the old Gator

Base, it looked like an emergency room without the blood. Small knots of people wandered in and out. Fifteen conversations went forward at once, only a few in fluent English.

"We're here to escort you to Mele's house, where the Albanians won't leave," Saine told the station commander. "They were told they had to leave their home by 10:00 this morning and they haven't left yet."

The station commander, an American from Colorado, couldn't help right away, he told them. "I've got two units on UXOs [unexploded bombs or land mines] and one on a collision. I have no one to send."

Holmes, the retired cop from Alabama, walked into the conversation. "Yeah, I hear the lady was using the kids as a buffer. We could lock up the kids, give them to social services," he suggested to his boss.

"I don't have a problem with that, but what kind of social services do they have here?" the station commander replied.

"You're not in Kansas anymore," the cop from Colorado remembered being told the day he arrived. His was a guerrilla war. The U.S. troops lived in bases heavily guarded twenty-four hours a day. He and the rest of the UN's scrawny international force lived in town, completely unprotected. He often went to bed listening to the sounds outside. What did I do today? Whom did I offend? Was that a footstep? Is someone out there planting a bomb under the house right now?

"It's like diving into a cold river," he said. "You know it's going to be cold, but you don't know how cold. Then it takes your breath away."

None of it was worth getting killed for, he said. The Albanian-Serb conflict wasn't his. That was one big reason there hadn't been a real effort to clamp down on the brass-knuckle extortion among Albanians. And if KFOR were to leave, "I would pull out with them. . . . Within two days every Serb in the area would be killed."

A lieutenant interrupted: the UN police bomb squad needed his help. "They have no map, no translator, they don't know where they are," he said to no one in particular. "I'll send a patrol over to help."

The station chief promised to dispatch police to Mele's house as soon as some became available. Saine's squad agreed to wait for them in the Green Park, a patch of painted green pebbles and benches KFOR had helped build near Mele's house. After 40 minutes, Hajdari showed up.

"We've been waiting for you," he told Lieutenant Saine. "I thought you would come to check the house. I'd like to buy the house, if they want to sell it. . . . It makes no sense for me to live in a refugee camp. I was born and raised in Vitina."

"But that is not your house," Saine replied

"I talked to the real owner, he said I could buy it."

"I don't want to talk about it anymore," said Saine. "We talked about it already."

"If we have to leave, we'll leave. But we shouldn't have to. The kids are scared. They didn't sleep well last night. It doesn't make sense, how you acted last night. What you did, and then you let us stay. KFOR is favoring the Serbs." Hajdari drifted back down the street to his illegal abode.

Fifteen minutes later a slow-moving red jeep rolled up next to the soldiers. "Excuse me! Excuse me!" called out the driver, a dark Ghanaian who spoke in quick bursts, every phrase uttered with an angry upturn at the end of it. "I'm looking for an officer in the green park. Do you know where that green park is?"

"That's me!" said Saine. "I'm the officer. You're looking for me! Follow me. I'll take you to the house."

The Ghanaian pressed his mouth up to the milk-carton-sized radio he clutched. "Warrior X-ray. Warrior X-ray. Negative. KFOR is here. They are saying we need to go with them. Over."

"Where is the complainant?" asked a second officer, a lanky Indian man with an accent so thick the troops had to ask him to repeat everything he said. "Where is the complainant? Where is the owner?"

"He lives in Serbia," Saine explained. "His brother is watching over the house. He lives around the corner. The Albanian man was working in Germany and moved here. His family moved in yesterday. But the family is gone now and they want us to inspect the house."

"They came from Germany yesterday?" asked the Indian. "I don't understand properly. Where is the complainant?"

"He lives in Belgrade. . . . Never mind. . . . Come with us. The house is just over here."

The Indian stepped out of the car. The Ghanaian stayed on the radio. Saine gently pushed the tall Indian toward the head of the line of soldiers approaching the front door. Police primacy. UN police in front.

But when the group reached the porch and Hajdari came out, the Indian police officer didn't have a clue what to say. Instead, he took a few steps backward, leaving Saine in the lead.

"Come in, look around. We didn't touch anything," said Hajdari. The troops entered. The Indian officer moved into the corner, watching while Saine and his men looked at the windows and walls, and went through the few drawers. In one of them they found a plastic grocery bag filled with legal-looking documents.

"These are the papers to the house," Hajdari exclaimed. "They are mine. You see. I own the house. The owner sold it to me. These papers prove it."

Saine stopped in disbelief. Wait a minute. You could almost hear his mind churning. "Hold on. You need to leave these documents here," he said to no one in particular. "There's no way to know whose they are. . . . Oh, God." Then Saine froze for what seemed like forever. Think this through. What should I do? Thirty seconds passed. The room full of soldiers and the Albanians stood frozen too, watching him think.

"Umm," Saine started off slowly, "I'm going to take these documents and give them to the UN, give them to the lady in charge of housing and they'll figure out who the owner is."

Then, having finished the inspection, everyone walked outside, ready to leave.

But the Ghanaian was now marching up the front porch steps, ready for action. Shouldn't he be making an arrest? After all, that's why KFOR dragged him out in the dead of night, right?

"Is he the complainant?" he yelled, pointing to Hajdari.

"No!" the troops responded in unison.

"Oh, he's the owner?"

"No, no, no!" said Saine shaking his head.

"Well then, who made the complaint? Where is he?"

"He lives around the corner."

"Who came to lodge here illegally?" demanded the Ghanaian.

"They did," Saine says, pointing to the two men.

"But they say they bought the house. Have they reported this to the police? Should we arrest them?"

The Indian stepped up. "Is there a case against someone?"

Pause.

The Ghanaian interrupted with a final decision: "We must take them to the police station."

"No," said Saine. "They are leaving the house now."

"Where is the complainant? We have to see him," the Ghanaian demanded. "We must take him to the police station too. They will make statements."

Saine had had enough. For months he and his soldiers had seen to it that no Albanian trespasser would know where Mele lived. They feared the Albanians would destroy Mele's house. Or worse. But Saine held no hope that the Ghanaian or the Indian would understand this. So Saine gave up and turned to the Indian in disgust. "Fine. They're yours," he said before gathering his squad and returning to the base.

Captain Driver, back at Camp No Slack in Vitina, was not happy the police had taken the Albanians and Mele to the station in the same car. "What? I can't believe it. Let's go down there," he said, pulling on his battle gear.

Down at the UN police station, Driver, exasperated, asked a British officer if two Albanians and an old Serb man were being detained. "No, they're gone," the Brit said rather vaguely. Driver moved on, seeking out the tall Indian officer.

"Oh yes," the Indian answered earnestly. "They are being detained downstairs. And the owner's brother is being questioned upstairs."

"Great," said Driver, bounding up the stairs and through the doorway of the office. The rattle of his canteen made all heads in the room turn in surprise. The Ghanaian was intently questioning Mele, but he straightened up when Driver walked in. "We are just taking statements," he explained, sitting across the table from Mele and a Serb translator. Then he yelled a command to a Jordanian policeman in the room: "We will release the two IDPs [Albanian squatters] right now, in front of this officer!" The Jordanian hurried out the door and down to the basement jail and soon the two Albanians were walking out of the station.

"These people are crazy," Hajdari whispered as he scooted by.

Mele's creaky legs carried him slowly to the bottom of the stairs.

He, too, shook his head in disbelief, but he smiled when he saw his friend, Captain Driver, who handed him the stack of papers from the house. "Anyway," said Driver. "Your house is free."

"Can I go tomorrow and look at it?" he asked.

"Sure, we'll give you the key."

The Mele house incident was over. It was one of a thousand examples of UN impotence and the sort of strained judgment calls KFOR soldiers made all the time. Driver and his men walked once more down the muddy streets of Vitina, moving aside for the horse-drawn carts and battered old small cars that zipped by, stuffed with young men, probably up to no good.

The next day, at a meeting, Serb mayors wanted to talk about Mele's house, and the Albanians from the Presevo Valley they believed were orchestrating a squatters' resettlement. But Modica cut them off: "Captain Driver did not do an eviction. He avoided people occupying a new house, because this is a crime. . . ."

They looked confused, with good reason.

Afterword

THE MISSION

* * * *

*L*T. COL. STEVE RUSSELL STEPPED OVER CLUNKY METAL cargo rollers lining the floor of the C-130 transport plane at Ali Al Salem Air Base in Kuwait. He plopped down on the canvas seat, squeezing in between other soldiers leaning up against the plane's walls. We first met when he was a major in Kosovo three years earlier. Russell had planned daily peacekeeping duties for U.S. armored soldiers there. Now gray at the temples, he was headed to Afghanistan to train rival warlord armies, hoping to turn them into a unified national force. Success was a long-shot, but the lieutenant colonel brimmed with enthusiasm and purpose.

"I have much more hope about this than Kosovo," he shouted over the plane's roaring engines. "These people just aren't as fractious and divided as they were in Kosovo."

Russell's analysis challenged history. Postwar Afghanistan was postwar Kosovo times ten. Warlords still reigned and "green on green" skirmishes between U.S.-armed factions occurred weekly. Tribal and ethnic divisions finely sliced each province. Poverty burrowed deeper, and the American presence and grasp of the surroundings were much shallower than they had been in Kosovo. Yet the stakes for the United States in Afghanistan were much greater, given Afghanistan's recent hospitality to Al Qaeda, the terrorist network headed by Osama bin Laden.

The lieutenant colonel's optimism echoed in my mind dozens of times during a visit to Afghanistan in the spring of 2002. His attitude reminded me of the pride in Gen. Charles Wilhelm's voice when he told of getting food to starving Somalis before the operation collapsed in tragedy; of Lt. Col. Tim Sherwood's conviction that Army Special Forces could make the Nigerian military more professional; of an MP platoon in Bosnia that sneaked Army rations to the blackballed Serbs of Srebrenica, home of heinous war crimes but also of increasingly desperate and depressed Serb children.

The same sense of purpose had captivated the Army civil affairs units flown into Afghanistan "to win hearts and minds," as the Army has called its good works since Vietnam. The 489th Civil Affairs Battalion, made up mostly of Army reservists from Kentucky, lived in one of the cramped, dust-filled tents at the end of a long line of tents at the Bagram Air Base, the U.S. military headquarters in Afghanistan. A collection of destroyed buildings and fields of twisted, blown-up vehicles surrounded the site, which was guarded by hundreds of land mines planted during Afghanistan's twenty-three years of war.

The Kentucky reservists included a park ranger, a college student, a cellular-phone salesman, and a computer distributor. They shared the base with infantry troops and Special Forces teams still conducting combat operations, and with pale CIA analysts and National Security Agency techno-nerds.

The base's most notable landmark was the mortar-pocked air-traffic-control tower, once used by Army Special Forces Team 555 to direct warplanes against Taliban soldiers during the first phase of the U.S. war against terrorism. It stood not far down the road from a makeshift prison, where suspected terrorists were held for interrogation. The tower had since been taken over by a Missouri Air National Guard air-traffic-control squadron.* They had laid 800 tons of stone and 1,000 yards of cement to make the runway in front of the tower usable. From inside the tower, three flights of steep, metal stairs above the runway, the new Air Force air-traffic-control team surveyed a fleet of Chinook and Black Hawk helicopters and A-10 Warthogs, the combat fleet for the unconventional war America was still waging in the country. Gigantic C-17s and C-130s—flying warehouses, really—continued to

---

* The 241st Air Traffic Control Squadron from St. Joseph, Mo.

ferry in vast quantities of men and machines. Afghanistan remained a combat zone, so planes descended in a corkscrew pattern or a deep dive to thwart anti-aircraft fire from below. Day and night, the planes roared in and out under the punishing sun or the dazzling twinkle of a million stars.

Whereas the air-traffic controllers and infantry troops were trapped on base, the tiny civil-affairs teams were supposed to venture "outside," beyond the perimeter, each day. With their own assigned vehicles, they traipsed through minefields to reach bullet-pitted mud-walled villages on the Shomali Plain. The cheerful band was led by Maj. Bryan Cole, who looked like a tanned ski instructor and was actually a park ranger in civilian life. Cole's men passed out boxes of palm dates, school supplies, and leftover Army rations. Weathered old Afghan women yelled angrily at them, wanting more. Dirty, rag-clad children chased their jeeps begging for ballpoint pens. Men from each family demanded an equal share of the charity.

Cole's reservists were a critical part of the minuscule American postwar reconstruction effort outside Kabul. Some 80 percent of Afghans lived outside the capital. The reservists, who believed in their mission, and called themselves the "vanguard," were part of a 300-strong, country-wide effort. With a $2 million stash from the Army, they were trying to help a crippled Afghanistan walk again.

In his civilian SUV, Cole careened down the broken asphalt road to Kabul, edging toward the land-mine markers on either side. Purple jasmine flowers and red poppies carpeted the vast plain, sharing the magnificent expanse with twisted T-55 Soviet tanks and bullet-ridden shipping containers that the Northern Alliance had used as airless prison cells. The whole place was like nothing the Kentuckians had ever seen. Strange things popped up every day. Women in wind-blown burkhas looked like bright blue ghosts sweeping across the horizon. Bright purple ointment covered the infected faces of children. Most men casually carried rifles over their shoulders. Afghans in motley uniforms demanded bribes for parking.

"Disneyland with a minefield," laughed Cole. Other soldiers felt the same. "If Somalia were an amusement park, Afghanistan would be its parking lot," they joked.

Cole and two engineers had climbed the crumbling walls of a roofless hospital in Charikar, north of Bagram, stepping over piles of human excrement to measure for repairs that were years away at best. In their hot, baggy fatigues, they had hiked into the gracious, snow-capped mountains, where, for the first time in five years, farmers were tilling the soil. There, the Americans tracked the elusive source of spring water for irrigation pipes they hoped to lay. The melodic music of Ahmed Zahir, long banned under the Taliban, sounded freely across

Maj. Bryan Cole, of the 489th Civil Affairs Battalion, led a group of reservists from Kentucky on a mission to help feed impoverished Afghans and rebuild their country. DANA PRIEST

the valley as Cole's engineers probed for the bottom of a concrete water-storage tank.

The Afghanistan war had two fronts now. The first one targeted tiny bands of Al Qaeda fighters burrowed into tunnels and hiding in villages in the southeastern mountains along the border with Pakistan. They were isolated, surrounded, and monitored from every conceivable angle, and it was only a matter of time before the United States and its allies killed or captured nearly every one of them. The U.S. military had learned much from its recent war in Kosovo. Its weapons were better, more precise, more lethal. Navy and Air Force flyers worked well with Army Special Forces. Covert operators were everywhere.

A second front, where the war's outcome would ultimately be determined, had opened in the late winter. This was Cole's battlefield, and victory was not at all certain. Creating a new civil order was more difficult and more perilous than any single military operation, as Machiavelli observed nearly five hundred years ago.[*] But to this battle, the United States carried surprisingly little from its past. Between Bosnia and Kosovo, U.S. and European leaders had taken one giant step forward in acknowledging that serious change requires long-term efforts. In Afghanistan they were taking two steps back.

Even a basic principle—security first—had been set aside by Donald Rumsfeld's Pentagon. Afghanistan's International Security Assistance Force (ISAF), made up of Afghans and allied forces, was confined to Kabul. No one saw this as the best way to ensure security in Afghanistan; it was just a matter of money and commitment. The allies didn't want to pay for or staff a nationwide force. Interim Prime Minister Hamid Karzai had flown around the world pleading for support to expand the security force nationwide. UN and U.S. military commanders on the ground agreed with him. Without security, aid workers would be reluctant to work outside the capital, green on green violence would spread. Karzai's tenuous hold on power would be gravely challenged.

The British had agreed to lead the ISAF operation. Now they wanted out, fast. The Turks, who had promised to take over from the British, were slow on the uptake, and they would soon abandon the job too. For postwar Kosovo, nineteen NATO nations and a dozen non-NATO ones had sent peacekeepers and police officers. The police in Kosovo weren't very effective, but at least they showed up. In Afghanistan, they weren't even showing up. "There's real concern in Europe that we don't walk out of here and leave the place," said squadron leader Tom Rounds of the Royal Air Force, describing Britain's attitude as he sat on a pile of wooden boxes at the Bagram base. As for positioning peacekeepers throughout the country, he moaned, "We just don't have the troops to do that. It would take thousands. Where are you going to get them?"

---

[*] "There is nothing more difficult to take in hand, more perilous to conduct, or more uncertain in success, than to take the lead in the introduction of a new order of things." Machiavelli, *The Prince* (1513).

The former CinCs of Europe, retired generals John Shalikashvili, George Joulwan, and Wesley Clark, all peacekeeping trailblazers, watched from the sidelines in astonishment. "Our level of resources doesn't match our level of national interest," quipped Clark.

"I sense no stomach for what it takes to do this right," Joulwan groused in disgust. "We're learning all the same things over again. We're better than this!" They were even more stunned—and deeply disappointed—when the White House turned its attention to the possibility of waging a new, "preemptive" war against Iraq before finishing its job in Afghanistan. After all, Osama bin Laden was still on the loose, Al Qaeda had dispersed across the globe; the United States faced its first Code Orange alert—credible intelligence of high risk of attack—on the one year anniversary of the September 11 attacks. The war on terrorism was far from over.

★ ★ ★ ★

TWELVE YEARS OF reluctant nation-building and the United States still hadn't spawned an effective civilian corps of aid workers, agronomists, teachers, engineers—a real peace corps—to take charge of postwar reconstruction in Afghanistan or anywhere else. Relations between the military and civilian sectors remained ad hoc. So was coordination between U.S. and international aid agencies.

Some progress was evident. The United Nations, leading the reconstruction effort, figured it would take $15 billion over the next decade to overcome the country's most basic problems. A collection of nations had pledged $4.5 billion over five years, but they had not actually paid up. The White House ponied up $400 million for 2002. USAID said it was moving faster than it had in forty years. The Afghan interim government had been installed and was getting paid. Reopened schools were immediately overcrowded, and $110 million in contracts crept along somewhere in the pipeline. Tents erected by the United Nations Children's Fund for tens of thousands of refugees returning from Pakistan sprouted like poppies across the country. Thousands of tons of seed wheat had been distributed. Tens of thousands of textbooks were on the way.

But the disparity between rhetoric and need was obvious. On the same day that Cole and his men measured hospital roofs and school walls in Charikar for repairs, President Bush compared the American commitment in Afghanistan to Gen. George Marshall's program to rebuild Europe after World War II. "We know that true peace will only be achieved when we give the Afghan people the means to achieve their own aspirations," the president said from a podium at the Virginia Military Institute. "Peace will be achieved by helping Afghanistan develop its own stable government. Peace will be achieved by helping Afghanistan train and develop its own national army. And peace will be achieved through an education system for boys and girls which works."[1]

The $13.3 billion Marshall Plan directed an unprecedented flow of U.S. capital into strengthening Europe's economic engines and expanding foreign trade. A wave of military civil-affairs units swept into Europe immediately following World War II to set the stage for the Marshall Plan, which sought to rebuild economic infrastructure and political traditions. The Army, under a U.S. military governor, quickly turned its few remaining infantry and cavalry units in Germany into a gendarmerie. Known as the U.S. Constabulary, the battalion-sized units worked closely with counterintelligence teams to stop the growth of clandestine groups.

Only two days after the German surrender, Gen. Dwight Eisenhower charged U.S. peacekeepers with a set of duties strikingly similar to those issued to Lt. Col. Michael Ellerbe's troops in Kosovo. Soldiers helped rebuild water systems and electrical plants; repaired sewage pipes, roads, and bridges; and dealt with massive numbers of concentration-camp survivors and former slave laborers. They guarded monuments and fine arts collections, and carried seed to farmers and coal to stoves. From the start, the American occupation of Germany, which lasted from 1945 to 1953, faced a problem similar to that encountered by the 82nd Airborne in Kosovo some fifty years later. Regional teams were tasked with re-establishing political life at the local level. Troops were to close down the Nazi legislative and judicial machine, seize leaders, and identify other Germans they could work with.[*] That part of the mission was controver-

---

[*] By mid-1946, Germans had assumed many political responsibilities. Denazification, writes military historian Forrest Pogue, had been successful at the top levels. In local communities, former Nazis ran towns and villages. The troops arrested war criminals and the party leadership but generally left everyone else alone. They restored full rights to most members of the Nazi Party after levying soft fines on some of them.

sial back home, "not a job for soldiers," scoffed Gen. Lucius Clay, who later became military governor of Germany.

In postwar Germany, battalions like Ellerbe's passed the jobs onto companies like Capt. Kevin Lambert's, and to platoon leaders like Lt. Sam Donnelly deployed far from headquarters. Just like themselves, Ellerbe's and Lambert's predecessors received little specific instruction from Washington as to how to proceed. Soldiers were left to figure out the mission themselves.* The toll on units was high, as they lost cohesiveness and discipline. Within two months, the military government concluded it should have formed a civilian police force.

"We are working in the best traditions of George Marshall," Bush declared on April 17, 2002. That was hardly true. Only hours after Bush's speech, the president's feisty defense secretary weighed in. The president, Rumsfeld clarified, had no intention of sending U.S. troops to Afghanistan as nation-builders. Rumsfeld might need troops elsewhere. He was pushing plans to send tens of thousands to invade Iraq. The White House was promising even more than a Marshall Plan for postwar Iraq. A military proconsul, the administration suggested, could turn Iraq into a democracy.

* * * *

MEANWHILE, A COUPLE of dusty miles down the road from the Bagram Air Base, General Babajan, the local warlord who had worked with Special Forces Team 555, met with the Kentuckian Major Cole in the general's courtyard. Surrounded by budding grapevines and eager assistants, the general warned U.S. officers about the political repercussions of delaying reconstruction. In sharply pressed combat fatigues and shiny black businessman's shoes, Babajan ruled the plains north of Kabul

---

* In *Americans as Proconsuls,* Earl F. Ziemke writes, "When the first military government detachments entered Germany in September they did so without any approved guidance on policy." All military government activities had political consequences for the shape and character of the future German nation, "but the guidance at the top was so meager that policy development—such as it was—was being left to the random actions of detachments in the field." (Earl F. Ziemke, "Improvising Stability and Change in Postwar Germany," in Robert Wolfe, ed., *Americans as Proconsuls* [Carbondale: Southern Illinois University Press, 1984], pp. 55, 58.)

alone. War had been vanquished, but Babajan, like the American CinCs, thought of this period of peace as an intermission between wars. The Americans and their allies had to move much more quickly, he insisted. Afghan commanders had believed the promises the allies had made at much-heralded international donor conferences in Bonn and Japan.

"There's no water in this valley. Please hurry up," Babajan told Cole. His people didn't understand the delay in beginning projects they had been promised. They accused the general of pocketing foreign relief money. Repair the wells first, Babajan told Cole. Then the roads. Put school construction off until next year.

"I know it's difficult but we have to follow the process," Cole answered politely. "We'll try to rush the projects out as fast as we can." Twenty-eight wells were already slated for improvement.

"The process," layered with U.S. bureaucrats in several countries, seemed to take forever. Cole's recommendations for rehabilitation projects first had to go to Kabul. Then to the U.S. army base in Kuwait. Sometimes elsewhere. Then back down to Afghanistan, and on down to a Bagram contracting office, which would hire local companies that hired local labor. So far, six of Cole's projects had been approved. Schools, a clinic, a bridge, and roads. Six weeks had gone by, though, and nothing had yet gone out for contract.

Cole had escaped "the process" only once when he noticed engineers at the allied base at Bagram tearing down latrines with hammers to make room for chemical toilets. He convinced a group of Polish soldiers to carry the smelly boxes to a refugee camp five miles away. He returned to check on the latrines often. They were the one project he had completed.

Cole kept smiling in the face of all this. He was just that kind of guy—a good-natured American. He took Afghanistan in stride. "You have to accept what you can control and what you can't control." Still, "the process" dragged him down a bit. He knew the projects could shore up support for the new local authorities. The political payoffs of visible improvements would be high. "What I'm looking for is quick impact while we wait for the big money to come in," he said. "I really think the donor countries will come through." But the big money would be slow, he knew.

Babajan wasn't so optimistic. With a bright white smile lurking behind his dark mustache, he tried to warn Cole: "If you don't help us, you know, we're all a little crazy and we may start fighting again," he said. "You promised many things for Afghanistan and we want you to keep your promise."

Postscript

The New Idealism

* * * *

F IFTEEN M-16 RIFLES STOOD UPRIGHT IN THE SAND.
A lonely helmet rested atop each silent gun. A field full of U.S. 3rd
Armored Cavalry Regiment soldiers listened as the soft, sad sound of
"Amazing Grace" floated over their patch of desert 200 miles northwest
of Baghdad. Within three weeks in the spring of 2003, U.S. forces had
captured the city and taken over Iraq. But the war had not ended with
the occupation of Baghdad and the disappearance of Iraq's army units
and Saddam Hussein. The U.S. Army was now fighting a war with an
enemy it could neither understand nor catch. The soldiers could feel
him all about, an invisible resistance against the great American military on its most ambitious mission ever.

The insurgents, a collection of former Baath Party loyalists, criminals,
foreign provocateurs, and religious jihadists, were in a race with
the hundreds of American and Iraqi engineers, water specialists,
construction workers, teachers, development experts, and local politicians working to create Iraq's new order. It was not yet clear which side
would win out.

November 2, 2003, had been a tactical defeat for the good guys. The
enemy had downed a 10-ton Chinook helicopter ferrying U.S. troops,
killing fifteen soldiers immediately. Fifteen helmets and rifles were
there as a reminder that this war had taken a turn that virtually neutral-
ized the U.S. military's overwhelming size, strength, and technology.

Defense Secretary Donald Rumsfeld dismissed the attacks as a sign of desperation. The enemy could not even fight fairly, he scoffed. Somehow that seemed to matter to him.

In fact, the ongoing war was beginning to look like a war of adaptive, unconventional tactics, the kind that had driven the United States into retreat before—in Vietnam, after the 1983 bombing of the Marine barracks in Lebanon, and after Somali clansmen had downed Black Hawk helicopters in 1993. U.S. intelligence had it that Saddam Hussein directed his men to read *Black Hawk Down*, an account of America's aversion to casualties in that less-than-vital conflict.

In Iraq, the insurgents had led U.S. forces onto *its* battlefield, a battlefield of car bombs and truck bombs and deadly donkey carts, of remotely detonated explosives. They struck U.S. allies, too. The Italians, Jordanians, Turks, United Nations employees, even the International Red Cross, had been attacked. Some had pulled out. Others, like the Japanese, never got in. Next, predictably, the insurgents' goal would be to provoke U.S. forces into cracking down on Iraq's civilians. Alienation from the occupier would certainly follow. Already children were refusing to pick up the candy thrown from American tanks, believing stories that it was poisonous.

The American military was good at many things, but guerrilla warfare in an alien culture, in a place where it lacks even the basics— enough translators, MPs, qualified intelligence specialists, and small assault teams—had never been one of them. Even so, U.S. troops were trying hard. That was no surprise.

What was surprising was the unprecedented breadth of the new mission Bush's administration had foisted on the U.S. military since the September 11, 2001, Al Qaeda attacks. No demands made on the military during the Clinton 1990s began to compare with the missions it gained after that—combat operations in Afghanistan, Iraq, and around the world, with the charge to dismantle terrorist networks and to find Saddam Hussein, Osama bin Laden, and Al Qaeda's reborn organization. These tasks stretched the military thin and poorly fit its traditional role as warfighter. Bush had also put the military in charge of rebuilding in Afghanistan and Iraq. These extended nation-building missions created a deep angst within the armed services not seen since Vietnam. Even Republican politicians worried about this reliance on the U.S. armed forces and Bush's continued insistence that the United States lead these efforts, a position that drove away longtime European allies whose peacekeepers had worked cooperatively with U.S. forces for a decade.

Rumsfeld remained the obstinate unilateralist, although he used the word "coalition" often. Since coming to the Pentagon, Rumsfeld had restored a much-needed civilian control over the military. But he did it in a style that was condescending and abrasive to officers with years of hard-knocks experience. Moreover, at Rumsfeld's urging, Bush had shortsightedly put U.S. forces at the center of his post–September 11 foreign policy under the doctrine of preemption. Iraq was seen by many as merely the first target. Bush put the occupation of Iraq under the control of Rumsfeld and under the intellectual direction of his deputy, Paul Wolfowitz.

Wolfowitz had detailed a small, mostly civilian Pentagon cabal to work in secrecy. All were like-minded policy wonks—derided by critics as "chickhawks" for their lack of military service—quick to reject the most basic ground-truths. Directed by undersecretary of defense for policy Douglas J. Feith and his newly created Office of Special Plans, they crafted a plan for re-creating Iraq that ignored the concerns expressed by the CIA, the Defense Intelligence Agency, and the State Department's Bureau of Intelligence and Research, as well as most Washington-based think tanks, all staffed with world-class Iraq and Middle East experts.

The Clinton administration had Haiti, Bosnia, Rwanda, and Kosovo to absorb the difficulties of refashioning countries with soldiers. By the 1999 Kosovo conflict, even some conservatives in Washington were willing to give the United Nations the lead in peacekeeping operations, if for no other reason than it would reduce the cost—in money and lives—to the United States. The Bush team ignored the lessons taught by these past interventions. They refused to swiftly deploy an adequately funded, staffed, and organized civilian team of reconstruction experts. They did not reach out to the vast, experienced networks of international aid organizations. They let huge, multimillion-dollar construction contracts go to their friends.

Moreover, they ignored the number-one lesson of all other peacekeeping missions: that security must precede nation-building. Without reasonable security, rebuilding and reordering were unlikely in Iraqis.

Instead, Feith's clan, schooled in the Reagan administration under the tutelage of then Defense Secretary Richard "Dick" Cheney, predicted the Iraqis would welcome the United States with open arms, as Europeans had done at the end of World War II. Their plans for reconstruction downplayed the dangerous competition for power between Iraqi Sunnis and Shiites and by Iranian religious militias that quickly seeped into the country. The decision to keep the U.S. force light and to disband the largely apolitical Iraqi army set back the nation-building timetable.

Disturbing results followed. Famished, lawless Iraqis made off with the antiquities of civilization once Baghdad fell. Residents looted Iraq's largest nuclear facility at Tuwaitha that remained unguarded by U.S. troops during the war. One million tons of unmonitored weapons and explosives in depots around the country became the cache for belligerents who used the materiel to attack U.S. troops.

Bush had declared an end to major combat operations in Iraq in May 2003. Since then, an average of four American soldiers had been killed each week. By the summer, attacks on U.S. forces began in earnest, with about a dozen ambushes a day. By late October, the number had tripled. A volatile power vacuum existed mainly in central Iraq, the so-called Sunni Triangle, a swath of land running west and north of Baghdad. Here Hussein's regime had provided jobs and had accorded special political status to the minority Sunni Muslim population. U.S. forces tried everything they could think of to tame the area.

In Fallujah, Army units conducted large-scale raids, search-and-seizure operations, and then handed out soccer balls and money as reparation for unintended civilian killings. Troops encircled Auja, Hussein's native village, with barbed wire and required all males over the age of fifteen to carry identity cards. Elsewhere there were massive helicopter and tank sweeps and house-to-house raids, more effective as a show of force than as a tactic for finding insurgents. In June of 2003, for example, soldiers hit Thuluiya with house-to-house raids seeking Hussein sympathizers. Of the more than 400 detainees netted, two remained in custody as of late October.

Such shows of force had the unintended consequence of alienating many Iraqis from U.S. troops, U.S. civilians, and UN workers there to rebuild the country. Several Iraqi mayors and police cooperating with U.S. authorities were assassinated. One father killed his son, an informant on behalf of the Americans, so that his anti-American neighbors would not assassinate his entire family as they had threatened. U.S. soldiers bulldozed a swath of date palms and fruit trees along a major roadway in retaliation for an attack against their unit. Vietnam came to mind; Israel might be closer to the truth.

In the fall and winter of 2003, the unanswerable question hovered over Iraq—would instability and resistance to the occupation, so clear in central Baghdad, spread throughout the country, emboldening the invisible enemy and demoralizing U.S. forces and their Iraqi supporters? The Americans weren't sure. They did not know for certain who was behind the violence. Rumsfeld blamed foreign terrorists streaming in from Syria and what he liked to diminish as "dead-enders," men with no future. Defense officials seemed eager to show—without proof—that Saddam Hussein was somehow in charge. Such a role for Saddam Hussein would certainly discredit critics who thought they were witnessing the emergence of a substantial and popularly supported guerrilla movement.

In fact, in confidential briefings in Baghdad, U.S. administrator Jerry Bremer, who led the Iraq occupation, estimated that 95 percent of the threat came from loosely organized former regime loyalists. Good intelligence, he conceded, remained a critical problem. U.S. forces had too few personnel fluent in Arabic or armed with a cultural knowledge of Iraq. Without such tools, he could never hope to understand who was organizing and funding the attacks, much less fathom the structure and capability of the enemy. Bremer doubted there was any national coordination. He readily admitted to having no evidence of links between the former regime loyalists and the foreign jihadists who were most likely sacrificing themselves as suicide bombers. So far, there was no evidence to support the assertion from Washington that Al Qaeda had moved fighters into Iraq in any significant way.

* * * *

IN SEPTEMBER 2003, gusty winds chased the Black Hawk and Chinook helicopters carrying Rumsfeld and a crew of reporters and cameras as they bounced across Iraq's vast plains. Machine gunners were alert for antiaircraft fire from below as they circled Baghdad, Mosul, Tikrit and prepared to land. Rumsfeld had flown 6,000 miles from his perch in Washington to tour Afghanistan and Iraq's major cities with a media entourage in tow. The feisty defense chief blamed the media for America's deepening worries about Iraq and Afghanistan, and especially about leaving U.S. troops in both countries for the foreseeable future. This trip was meant to tell the world that things were going just fine.

"It looks like Chicago," a gleeful Rumsfeld declared after flying over Baghdad at night in a Black Hawk. Progress in Iraq, "dwarfs any other experience I'm aware of," including Germany and Japan after World War II, and postwar Bosnia and Kosovo. (Not a single U.S. soldier had been killed by enemy attacks in Kosovo, but never mind.)

The media was ignoring "the story of success and accomplishment," he said from behind a table in the marble-walled palace adjacent to Baghdad International Airport, the protective bubble where his entourage stayed well away from the conflict. The violence in Iraq was like the violence "in every country in the world," he announced at dinner; Rumsfeld brought out crime statistics from American cities to compare to murder rates in Iraq. He smiled at his discovery. "My goodness," he beamed—how low the Iraqi numbers were.

"I'm not being Pollyannaish," he told reporters later when they challenged his optimism. "I'm telling the truth."

Standing awkwardly next to Rumsfeld at some of his briefings was Lt. Gen. Ricardo Sanchez, head of U.S. forces in Iraq and the same officer who had sent Capt. Kevin Lambert's 82nd Airborne company home early after they awkwardly tried to create a safe and secure environment in postwar Kosovo; the same man who had cried over eleven-year-old Merita Shabiu's dead body at the makeshift morgue at Camp Bondsteel. "It is disturbing to me when I watch the news, the focus on the bad," he told reporters, his holstered 9mm Beretta slung across his chest, 82nd airborne style. "We ought to make sure America knows that their sons' and daughters' sacrifices are for a good cause." Asked about a spate of car bombings and a blast at the UN headquarters that killed 24, Sanchez's answer stunned the group. "There is no tactical threat, no strategic threat to the coalition." One platoon of American soldiers—roughly 80 men—"can defeat the threat readily," he said. But later, after the cameras stopped rolling, he added: "it's definitely a combat zone."

Did Sanchez really mean to say there was no threat in Iraq? Or did he mean no conventional army-to-army threat? Or was he just saying things he knew Rumsfeld wanted to hear? The contradiction captured the quandary perfectly.

Rumsfeld dealt with serious questions about ongoing violence as he had with questions about weapons of mass destruction. He dismissed them. Earlier, he had been the Bush administration's pit bull, arguing that the existence of these weapons justified going to war. Now, Rumsfeld did not mention the subject during his thirty-minute meeting in Baghdad with David Kay, the CIA representative in Iraq who coordinates the WMD search.

"I have so many things to do at the Department of Defense," he explained. "I . . . have to compartment things, and that is, in my view, something the intelligence community is working on, and working on effectively."

Some soldiers thought they had been sent to Iraq precisely to thwart the WMD threat. They asked the secretary about WMD when he visited their base in the northern city of Mosul, and Rumsfeld said weakly, "I have a feeling they will, in fact, continue to work on the problem."

At a final Baghdad news conference, reporters asked the feisty defense secretary twice about the weapons search. "Can you please give us at least one example of what is the result today" of the search? one journalist asked.

"I'm inclined not to," the secretary replied. "I'll tell you what the situation is: the situation is that it's an important question."

Watching Rumsfeld's attack on the news media brought to mind President Richard Nixon's vice president, Spiro Agnew. In 1970, Agnew had lashed out at the press for its attacks on Nixon's flagging Vietnam policy, calling reporters "nattering nabobs of negativism." There are many differences between the U.S. wars in Vietnam and

Iraq, but one stunning similarity is the administrations' reliance on U.S. armed forces to bring radical social change to a country as alien to most soldiers as the planet Mars. That had nothing to do with the news media or its coverage.

Yet long before success in Iraq or Afghanistan was assured, President Bush expanded the military's mission again.

On November 6, 2003, as the 3rd ACR mourned and honored its fallen, Bush strode to a podium in Washington carrying a vision for the world more ambitious even than President Ronald Reagan's aspirations for a free Eastern Europe and Soviet Union. "We believe that liberty is the direction of history . . . and we believe that freedom, the freedom we prize, is not for us alone. It is the right and the capacity of all mankind."

Aiming his soaring rhetoric at the Middle East, he announced that "it should be clear to all that Islam, the faith of one-fifth of humanity, is consistent with democratic rule." Bush reproached past American policy for supporting dictators and despots, and he challenged U.S. allies, notably Saudi Arabia and Egypt, to "show the way toward democracy in the Middle East." Even Reagan had exempted the Islamic crescent of countries from his world vision.

The revolutionary, hope-filled speech reminded me of the recent, eloquent promise the president had made to Afghans in the spring of 2002. The U.S. commitment there, he said then, would be as grand and as sweeping as George Marshall's had been in Europe. Not long after, however, Bush approved a plan to withdraw U.S. forces from nearly everywhere but Kabul. No other country had come up with the forces necessary to staff the international security force, although NATO had begun that job recently. Eventually Bush backed the creation of a number of small outposts throughout the country, but they failed to squelch the reemergence of Afghanistan's crusty warlords. Afghan poppy crop production shot up too, and many humanitarian organizations that had operated even under the Taliban pulled out due to security concerns. The Taliban and Al Qaeda regrouped and began mounting serious attacks.

One of Rumsfeld's Pentagon cabal traveling on the trip to Kabul in September described the large Taliban infiltration, estimated to be about 1,000 men, as a positive development. "When they began to move from smaller units to larger units, they began to expose themselves," he said. "When they organize themselves, they provide us with an opportunity to defeat them." In the previous two weeks, U.S. forces had killed 200 Taliban.

Downplaying the troubles in Afghanistan and a growing insurgency in Iraq, Bush reached even higher in his Washington speech, to a new idealism. "We've reached another great turning point, and the resolve we show will shape the next stage of world democratic movement," he intoned. " . . . Securing democracy in Iraq is the work of many hands. . . . This is a massive and difficult undertaking. . . . It is worth our sacrifice, because we know the stakes: The failure of Iraqi democracy would embolden terrorists around the world and increase dangers to the American people and extinguish the hopes of millions in the region.

"Iraqi democracy will succeed, and that success will send forth the news from Damascus to Tehran that freedom can be the future of every nation. The establishment of a free Iraq at the heart of the Middle East will be a watershed event in the global democratic revolution. . . .

"Sixty years of Western nations excusing and accommodating the lack of freedom in the Middle East did nothing to make us safe, because in the long run stability cannot be purchased at the expense of liberty."

The idea that the U.S. military could force democracy to bloom anywhere was antithetical to the very notion of free will and liberty. Particularly in the Middle East, where religion and government institutions are virtually one, the symbol of American military power and its use by successive American presidents to prop up corrupt regimes had inspired the likes of Osama bin Laden to run the infidels out of his country. Indeed, in 2003, the U.S. military pulled out of Saudi bases it had used for more than a decade.

Moreover, Bush's rhetoric was not matched by his actions or policy initiatives. As president, Bush had never coupled this vision for a democratic Middle East with well-funded economic and social policies that could prod the region toward democracy. He showed little interest in weaning the United States off Persian Gulf oil in order to liberate U.S. foreign policy from its oil addiction. Nor had he adequately funded research into alternative energy sources.

Most critically, Bush had not acted as an honest broker between Israel and the Palestinians. He had never used the $2.6 billion aid package to Israel as leverage to compel its government to abandon illegal settlements and share Jerusalem. He seemed to ignore the negative impact his global war on terrorism was having on human rights in the Middle East and elsewhere. Sending suspected terrorists into the hands of foreign intelligence services to be imprisoned without trial and, in some cases, tortured, is surely not a way to win the hearts and minds of people contemplating a challenge to authoritarian rule.

Bush had not tied U.S. weapon sales or military training to efforts by Mideast countries to modernize and diversify their oil-dependent economies. He had yet to induce those governments to educate the next generation of leaders comfortable with the technology and language of the global economy. His administration had not created larger exchanges for Arab students like those of the Pentagon's military-to-military training programs whose goals were to win students over to the notion of civilian-led democracies and free markets. Bush had not taken the case for women's rights in the Middle East to the United Nations, as President Carter did in his campaign to defeat South Africa's racial system of apartheid.

If Bush were serious, he would have transferred Deputy Defense Secretary Paul Wolfowitz to the State Department, where the friendly, former academic could turn his unbounded zeal for a democratic revolution in the Middle East into political and diplomatic—not military—initiatives. Instead, Wolfowitz spent his days trying to figure out how to use military operations to achieve political reform.

Reagan had waged a different war against the Soviet Union, one not based on U.S. military confrontation, but on diplomatic feats employing a chessboard of alliances to outmaneuver the opponent. Missiles and bombs and a two-million-man army stood on the sidelines as a threat. Beleaguered and bankrupted by their own failed adventure in Afghanistan, the Soviets could listen to Reagan speak to them from a respectful distance. But the final decision to move against the old order was theirs, not his, as it should be.

Perhaps George Bush misread that recent history. He could not be dissuaded. Not by more Al Qaeda bombings, or another chopper full of soldiers downed in Iraq, or America's isolation from the world community. The president pushed on, using American troops to carry out his risky idealism. Their mission had become overwhelming, and success was not at all certain.

NOVEMBER 2003

List of Interviews

Sfc. Frank Antenori, William Arkin, Col. Dana Atkins, Lt. Col. Al Aycock, Brig. Gen. Charles Baumann, Lt. Col. George Bilafer, SSgt. John Billings, Adm. Dennis Blair, Maj. Donald Bolduc, Terry Boyd, SSgt. Val Braddock, Lt. Col. Seth Braverman, Capt. Torry Brennan, Lt. Col. Mark Browder, Maj. Gen. Doug Brown, Col. Keirn C. Brown (ret.), Ronald Brown, Lt. William Byrd, CSM Joseph Callahan, Tech. Sgt. Calvin, Col. Manny Chaves, Maj. Gen. Peter Chiarelli, Maj. David Christie, Gen. Wesley Clark, Victoria Clarke, Cpl. Jason Cleary, Maj. Bryan Cole, Maj. Tom Collins, Timothy Connolly, Steve Cortese, Brig. Gen. John Craddock, P. J. Crowley, Capt. Brian Cullen, Vesko Dajic, Milorad Danic, Col. William Darley, Capt. Mike Davis, Graham Day, David Desroches, Maj. Joe Diana, CWO David Diaz, Col. Dennis Dimengo, Capt. Loran Doane, SSgt. Chris Dohl, Capt. Darrell Driver, Maj. David Duffy, SSgt. Eric Ebert, Lt. Col. Michael Ellerbe, Kenneth Ellis, SSgt. Hamid Fathi, Maj. Matt Fellinger, Capt. Marc Ferguson, SSgt. Bruce Fitton, Amb. Wyche Fowler, Lt. Col. David Fox, Joseph Fuduli, Brig. Gen. Leslie Fuller, Amb. Robert Gelbard, Sfc. Ken George, Sfc. Steve Gernet, Capt. Matt Godfrey, Capt. Felix O. Gonzales Jr., Paul Gonzales, Lt. Jason Green, Maj. Erik Gunhus, Haxhire Hajdari, Morton Halperin, Brig. Gen. Dennis Hardy, Sen. Tom Harkin, Maj. Yusef Hasan, Lt. Col. Jeffrey Haynes, Maj. Brian Heslin, Col. Stephanie Hoehne, Lt. Col. Brian Hoey, Brig. Gen. Jack Holbein, Amb. Richard Holbrooke, John Hamre, Mark Holmes, Maj. Mike Hopkins, Herbert Howe, Lt. Col. Frank Hudson, Lawrence "Rob" Hughes, Charles Ikins, Lt. Col. Maryellen Jadick, Dale Jeffries, Amb. Jon Jeter, Gen. David Jones (ret.), Gen. James Jones, Gen. George Joulwan (ret.), Sgt. Maj. Gary Kalinofski, Gen. John Keane, Denny Klauer, Maj. Gary Kolb, Franklin Kramer, Maj. Joe LaMarca, Capt. Kevin Lambert, Maj. William Lambert, Maj. David Lathem, Brig. Gen. Dan Leaf, Sen. Patrick Leahy, Capt. Joe Leardi, Col. Leonardo Leso, Lt. Col. David Limb, Maj. Earnest Lloyd, James Locher III, Adm. T. J. Lopez (ret.), Maj. Mark Marchant, Bernd McConnell, Capt. T. McCreary, Lt. Col. Neil McElhannon, Col. Don McFetridge (ret.), Chris McMullen, John McWethy, Ed McWilliams, Gen. Montgomery Meigs, Col. Peter Miller, Amb. Tom Miller, Cliff Milloshi, Maj. Del Monroy, Vice Adm. Daniel Murphy, Col. Victor Nelson, Col. Nilgun Nesbett, Frank Norbury, Amb. Robert Oakley, Martha Brill Olcott, Sgt. Gilbert Pack, Amb. Anne Patterson, Drita Perezic, William Perry, Brig.

Gen. Craig Peterson, Maj. David Pierson, Rear Adm. Stephen Pietropaoli, Carolyn Piper, Amb. Laurence Pope, Sgt. Robert Powers, Capt. Michael Pratt, Amb. Joseph Presel, Vice Adm. Craig Quigley, Gen. Joseph Ralston, Lt. Col. Timothy Reese, Timothy Reiser, Keith Richburg, Alina Romanowski, Sfc. Tom Rosenbarger, Stanley Roth, Squadron Leader Tom Rounds, Amb. J. Stapleton Roy, Lt. Col. Steve Russell, Lt. Benjamin Saine, Capt. Joseph Salinas, Brig. Gen. Ricardo Sanchez, Isa Selimi, Lt. John Serafini, Gen. John Shalikashvili (ret.), Kris Sharp, Amb. Michael Sheehan, Capt. T. J. Sheehan, Gen. Henry Shelton, Lt. Col. Tim Sherwood, Maj. Michael Shillinger, Lt. Gen. Michael Short, Rear Adm. John Sigler, Capt. John Singley, Milar Slanojevic, Jovahovic Slavica, Walter Slocombe, Pfc. Ian Smith, R. Jeffrey Smith, Capt. Kelly Smith, Col. Al Sohlberg, Maj. David Spencer, Capt. James Spivey, Mitar Stanojevic, James Steinberg, Maj. Rick Steiner, Charles Stevenson, SSgt. Martin Stewart, Maj. Gary Tallman, Col. Richard Thomas, Sgt. Maj. Beau Todd, Maj. Gen. Frank Toney, Lt. Gen. Esen Topoyez, Lt. Gen. Bernard Trainor (ret.), MSgt. Rick Turcotte, Amb. Charles Twining, Maj. Stephen Twitty, Nancy Walker, Sen. John Warner, Col. Volney Warner, Maj. Steve Warren, Mark Whitting, Gen. Charles Wilhelm, James Williams, Vice Adm. Thomas Wilson, Col. Michael Worden, and Gen. Anthony Zinni; members of U.S. Army Special Forces: teams of the 3rd Battalion, 3rd Special Forces Group, and Operational Detachments Alpha 532, 534, 555, 574, 595, 761, 772, 785, 050, 051, 053, 054, and 055; and others who asked to remain unnamed.

Acknowledgments

I am deeply grateful to my *Washington Post* editors, especially Leonard Downie and Steve Coll, for giving me the time, resources, and peace of mind to finish this book. The John D. and Catherine T. MacArthur Foundation provided generous funding, and Joseph Klaits's wonderful Jennings Randolph fellowship program at the U.S. Institute of Peace gave me office space and sustaining fellowship.

Among those in the military, at the Defense Department, and in the diplomatic corps whose patience and time I consumed in great quantity, I wish to acknowledge Kenneth Bacon, Adm. Dennis Blair, Maj. Gen. Peter Chiarelli, Gen. Wesley Clark, Maj. Tom Collins, Lt. Col. Michael Ellerbe, Maj. Sean Gibson, Maj. Erik Gunhus, Lt. Col. Jeffrey Haynes, Col. Stephanie Hoehne, Lawrence "Rob" Hughes, Lt. Col. M. J. Jadick, Denny Klauer, Maj. Gary Kolb, Maj. Joe LaMarca, Maj. Mark Marchant, Col. Peter Miller, Capt. T. McCreary, Ambassador Anne Patterson and her C-12, Drita Perezic, Rear Adm. Stephen Pietropaoli, Carolyn Piper, Ambassador Laurence Pope, Ambassador Joseph Presel, Gen. Joseph Ralston, Brig. Gen. Ricardo Sanchez, Gen. Henry Shelton, Maj. Rick Steiner, Ambassador Charles Twining, Maj. Steve Warren, Gen. Charles Wilhelm, and Gen. Anthony Zinni.

Others who lent a critical eye to my writing include William Arkin, Tom Frail, Bill Goodfellow, Chris Holbrook, David Horowitz, Adam Isacson, Bruce McWilliams, Shirley Meyer, Joy Olson, and, especially, Marilyn Thompson.

For technical and graphics assistance, I thank the computer department at the *Washington Post*, Michael duCille, Nicholas Goodfellow, and Seth Hamblin.

For friendship and support, I am grateful to Delia Abucejo, Henry Champ and Karen DeYoung, Cissy de la Vallee and Tony Quay, Haley

Goodfellow, Kajal Guha, Mary Jo Hogan, Stephen and Ann Elizabeth Lovett, Anne and Jack Priest, and Howard and Susan Stewart.

I thank also my agent, Gail Ross, my tireless editor, Edwin Barber at W. W. Norton, and his friendly assistant, Deirdre O'Dwyer, Col. Keirn C. Brown (ret.), who lent his military expertise, and Traci Nagle, a thorough copyeditor.

And again, my family, Bill, Nick, and Haley, put ap with my absences and long hours and always welcomed me home—or downstairs from the study—with open arms.

Notes

Introduction

1   Gen. George Marshall, speech to *New York Herald Tribune* forum, Oct. 29, 1945. He expressed similar views in a Nov. 17, 1945, speech to the Salvation Army's national convention. Both speeches are excerpted at www.marshallfoundation.org.

Chapter One

1   Tom Ricks, interview with Rumsfeld, May 17, 2001, transcript on www.defenselink.mil.

2   Henry Kissinger, *Years of Renewal* (New York: Simon and Schuster, 2000), p. 175.

3   The panel's key insights: "Military doctrine and forces are created in the image of the economies that spawn them; Military forces, although multi-purpose by nature, are formed around a core set of threats that they are designed to defeat; Asymmetric confrontations have historically generated decision outcomes, whereas symmetric confrontations tend to be exhaustive." The panel's key findings: "Decisive military advantage begins as an asymmetric tactical advantage; Operational advantage is based on information and control resting on a bedrock of tactical advantage; Strategic advantage rests on superior resources and the ability to engage the enemies' center of gravity; Tactical advantage without strategic advantage tends to be temporary in nature." Panel chair Enders Wimbush said the group also concluded that "military power by itself is never enough to sustain your predominance. . . . The U.S. cannot avoid history. We aren't going to be an exception. All predominant states thought their predominance was eternal. All failed." From "Sustaining Military Dominance: Examples from Ancient History," Office of Net Assessment, Office of the Secretary of Defense, summer 2001. Slides provided to author.

4   Tom Ricks "Rumsfeld, Bush Agendas Overlap Little," *Washington Post*, Jan. 11, 2001.

5   Rumsfeld, in speech titled "Bureaucracy to Battlefield," Sept. 10, 2001, transcript available at www.defenselink.mil/speeches/2001.

6   Rumsfeld, press conference with president of Uzbekistan, Oct. 5, 2001, transcript available at www.defenselink.mil.

7   Ibid.

For more on national missile defense, the Shelton letter, and the Rumsfeld commission, see: Bradley Graham, *Hit to Kill* (New York: Public Affairs, 2001).

Chapter Two

1   In the 1960s, the diplomatic budget accounted for 4 percent of the total federal budget. By 2000 it was less than 1 percent, or about $20 billion. This budget funds 250 embassy and consular staffs and facilities, as well as U.S. contributions to international organizations, peacekeeping operations, and other foreign activities. The operations budget includes bilateral development and military aid, special projects, and U.S. contributions to voluntary United Nations programs and multilateral development banks. Richard N. Gardner, "The One Percent Solution," *Foreign Affairs*, July–August 2000, pp. 2–10. Gardner served on the secretary of state's Overseas Presence Advisory Panel, which studied and recommended changes in funding for U.S. diplomacy.

2   Colin Powell, with Joseph E. Persico, *My American Journey* (New York: Random House, 1995), p. 576.

For a more complete reading of Clinton, the issue of gays in the military, and the McCaffrey snub, see James Kitfield, *Prodigal Soldiers* (Washington, D.C.: Brassey's, 1997), p. 429.

Chapter Three

1   For a more complete history of the 5th Marine Division, see Ron Brown, *A Few Good Men: The Story of the Fighting Fifth Marines* (Novato, Ca.: Presidio Press, 2001).

2   Graham Cosmas, *U.S. Marines in Vietnam, Vietnamization and Redeployment, 1970–1971*, U.S. Marine Corps History and Museums Division (Washington D.C., 1986), p. 42.

3   Casualty figures come from Brown, op. cit., interviews with Zinni, and

interviews with Lt. Gen. Bernard Trainor (ret.), Zinni's battalion commander at the time.

4   Interview with Trainor.
5   Anthony Zinni, speech to the U.S. Naval Institute, March 2000, at
    www.usni.org/Proceedings/Articles00/prozinni.htm.
6   Ibid.
7   For the Unified Command Plan and links to each command, see
    www.defenselink.mil/specials/unified command.

Chapter Four

1   According to the classfied Central Command Theater Engagement
    Plan.
2   Briefing slides, Central Command, April 2000.
3   Seymour Hersh, "King's Ransom," *New Yorker*, Oct. 22, 2001.
4   *Frontline*, Oct. 9, 2001.
5   Senate Committee on Armed Services, "Report of the Joint Committee
    on the Investigation of the Pearl Harbor Attack, 1946," *Defense
    Organization: The Need for Change*, Senate Report 99-86, 99th
    Congress, 1st sess. (1985), p. 153.
6   Powell, op. cit.
7   Michael Duffy, "Grenada: Rampant Confusion," *Military Logistic Forum*,
    July–August 1985, p. 23.
8   Senate Committee on Armed Services, *Defense Organization: The Need
    for Change*, p. 620. Cited in James R. Locher III, "Taking Stock of
    Goldwater-Nichols," *Joint Forces Quarterly*, Autumn 1996, p. 10.

For more on service inoperability, see Bill Owens and Ed Offley, *Lifting
the Fog of War* (New York: Farrar, Straus, and Giroux, 2000). For service performance in Vietnam, see Bruce Palmer, Jr., *The 25-Year War:
America's Military Role in Vietnam* (Lexington: University of Kentucky
Press, 1984).

Chapter Five

1   See the State Department's 2000 and 2001 annual country reports
    on human rights in Uzbekistan, at www.state.gov/g/drl/rls/hrrpt/.
    Also see Matthew Brzezinski, "Whatever It Takes," *New York Times
    Magazine*, December 16, 2001, p. 72.
2   Bob Woodward and Dan Balz, "At Camp David, Advise and Dissent;

Bush Aides Grapple with War Plans," *Washington Post*, January 31, 2002.

3   For more on Dostum, see: Ahmed Rashid, *Taliban* (New Haven: Yale University Press, 2000).

4   State Department country reports 2000 and 2001.

5   Human Rights Watch reports on Uzbekistan, at www.hrw.org/europe/index.php.

6   Mark Bowden, *Black Hawk Down: The Story of Modern War* (New York: Penguin, 1999).

For further readings on Central Asia, begin with Martha Brill Olcott, *Central Asia's New States: Independence, Foreign Policy, and Regional Security* (Washington D.C.: U.S. Institute of Peace Press, 1996), and Martha Brill Olcott, Anders Aslund, and Sherman W. Garnett, *Getting It Wrong: Regional Cooperation and the Commonwealth of Independent States* (Washington D.C.: Carnegie Endowment for International Peace Press, 1999).

Chapter Six

1   Francis J. Kelley, *The Green Berets in Vietnam, 1961–71* (Washington, D.C.: Brassey's, 1991).

2   Shelby Stanton, *Green Berets at War* (New York: Ivy Books, 1985), p. 19. For a more complete description of Operation White Star, see pp. 20–37.

3   Shelby Stanton, *Vietnam Order of Battle* (Washington D.C.; U.S. News Books, 1981) as cited by U.S. Army Special Forces Command.

4   Stanton, *Green Berets*, pp. 37, 172.

5   Palmer, op. cit.

6   Stanton, *Green Berets*, p. 37.

7   John L. Plaster, *SOG: The Secret Wars of America's Commandos in Vietnam* (New York: Onyx Books, 1997), p. 24.

8   Bowden, op. cit., p. 355.

Chapter Seven

1   For a good summary of Northern Alliance factions, see the Federation of American Scientists Web page at www.fas.org/irp/world/para/northern_alliance.htm.

2   Human Rights Watch country report on Afghan warlords, at www.hrw.org/europe/index.php.

Chapter Eight

1   "Jews Should Be Blamed—Farouk," *News*, Oct. 29, 2001, p. 21.

2   "America Is the Terrorist," *News*, Oct. 29, 2001, p. 19.

3   Karl Maier, *The House Has Fallen: Midnight in Nigeria* (New York: Public Affairs, 2000), p. xxiii.

4   Defense Intelligence Agency records.

5   "United States and Africa: Report Challenges U.S. Military Role in Africa," *Africa News*, March 22, 2001. See also William Hartung, *And Weapons for All* (New York: HarperCollins, 1994).

6   Samantha Power, *A Problem from Hell: America and the Age of Genocide* (New York: Basic Books, 2002).

7   International Crisis Group, *Sierra Leone: Time for a New Military and Political Strategy*, April 11, 2001.

8   Refugees International Bulletin, Jan. 16, 2001, available at www.refintl. org.

For other reading on African militaries, see Herb Howe, *Ambiguous Order: Military Forces in African States* (Boulder, Colo.: Lynne Rienner, 2001).

Chapter Nine

1   This memo first appeared in Jonathan Stevenson, *Losing Mogadishu: Testing U.S. Policy in Somalia* (Annapolis, Md.: Naval Institute Press, 1995), pp. 65–66. It was confirmed to me by Wilhelm in interviews.

2   Walter LaFeber, *Inevitable Revolutions: The United States in Central America* (New York: W. W. Norton, 1984), p. 66.

3   Section 124, Title 10, U.S. Code.

4   State Department Country Reports on Human Rights. See also the annual reports published by Human Rights Watch.

5   For police numbers and other details about Colombian aid, see www.ciponline.org.

Chapter Ten

1   Defense Intelligence Agency official.

2   Documents obtained by the National Security Archive under the Freedom of Information Act, available at: www.nsarchive.org. See: East Timor revisited.

3   Defense Intelligence Agency documents about Prabowo declassified at

my request under the Freedom of Information Act.

4 Ibid.

5 Interviews with Austrilian defense officials in Jakarta, July 1998.

6 A version of this story first appeared in the *Washington Times* in a July 30, 1999, article by Bill Gertz. Blair's staff later corrected the *Times'* version slightly.

7 For reports on human-rights violations going back years in Indonesia, East Timor, Aceh, the Moluccas, Irian Jaya, and elsewhere in Indonesia, see the State Department's annual country reports on human rights (www.state.gov) and Human Rights Watch reports (www.hrw.org).

8 Reported by Agence France Press, April 20, 2002.

Chapter Eleven

1 See the London Declaration of 1990, where this strategy is first laid out. Available at www.nato.int.

2 Richard Holbrooke, *To End a War* (New York: Random House, 1998), pp. 215–27.

3 Ibid.

4 Wesley K. Clark, *Waging Modern War* (New York: Public Affairs, 2001), p. 80.

5 Ibid.

6 Ibid, pp. 99–102.

7 Bradley Graham, "Joint Chiefs Doubted Air Strategy," *Washington Post*, April 5, 1999.

8 This figure remains much in dispute but is used in the report of the UN's Independent International Commission on Kosovo, available at www.kosovocommission.org.

9 Ibid, p. 90.

10 Ibid, p. 93.

11 Ibid, p. 4.

Chapter Twelve

1 Operational Orders 99-01 and 99-15.

2 NATO Plan #60507, Draft 9.

3 "Serb Villagers Flee under Watchful Eye of US Troops," Reuters, Aug. 2, 1999.

4 Ibid.

Chapter Fourteen

1   U.S. Army Europe, "Unit Climate and State of Discipline Within the 3rd Battalion, 504th Parachute Infantry Regiment, Task Force Falcon, Kosovo Force," Army Regulation 15-6 Report of Investigation, Sept. 18, 2000, pages unnumbered. Hereafter cited as Army 15-6.

2   Lucian Perkins (*Washington Post* photographer), "In a Land Without Trust, Peace Is Elusive," www.pressroom.com/~lucian/usarmy1.html.

3   Army 15-6.

4   Ibid.

Chapter Fifteen

1   Copy of memo provided to author.

2   KFOR Civil Affairs says 230 Serb homes burned after the war, representing about 20 percent of all Serb homes; 255 Albanian homes were burned during the war. Cited in an internal OSCE report, made available to the author.

3   Army 15-6.

4   Ibid.

5   Ibid.

6   Ibid.

7   Ibid.

8   Ibid.

9   Ibid.

10   Ibid.

11   Ibid.

12   Ibid.

13   Ibid.

14   Ibid.

15   Ibid.

16   Ibid.

17   Ibid.

18   Ibid.

19   101st Airborne Division, intelligence officers' internal assessment of prominent Albanian individuals, "Rak Intel: Albanian Personality Book."

20   Vitina Council for the Defense of Human Rights and Freedom, pp. 2–3.

Chapter Sixteen

1   Statement of Hamid Shabiu at the court-martial of Ronghi in Germany.

2   Army 15-6.

3   Ibid.

4   Ibid.

5   According to soldiers at the meeting.

6   Army 15-6.

7   Army memo to Sanchez regarding meeting, Jan. 16, 2000, copy provided to author.

8   Interview with R. Jeffrey Smith, (*Washington Post* reporter on the scene that day).

9   Steven Erlander, "The Ugliest American," *New York Times Magazine*, April 2, 2000.

Afterword

1   Speech on April 17, 2002, (www.whitehouse.gov/news/releases/2002/04/20020417-1.html).

For further reading, see Forrest C. Pogue, *U.S. Army in World War II: The European Theater, The Supreme Command*, U.S. Army Military History Series (Washington D.C.: U.S. Government Printing Office, 1954), pp. 511–12; Robert Wolfe, ed., *Americans as Proconsuls: United States Military Government in Germany and Japan, 1944–1952* (Carbondale, Ill.: Southern Illinois University Press, 1984), pp. 55, 58; Harold Zink, *American Military Government in Germany* (New York: Macmillan, 1947); Earl F. Ziemke, *The U.S. Military in the Occupation of Germany, 1944–46* (Washington D.C.: U.S. Army Center for Military History, 1975); Ralph Willett, *The Americanization of the Germany, 1945–1949,* (New York: Routledge, 1989); and Julian Bach, Jr., *America's Germany: An Account of the Occupation* (New York: Random House, 1946).

Index

Page numbers in *italics* refer to illustrations.